PASTOR
CRAFT

PASTOR CRAFT

ESSAYS & SERMONS

JOHN T. PLESS

Pastor Craft: Essays and Sermons

Published by:
1517 Publishing
PO Box 54032
Irvine, CA 92619-4032

Publisher's Cataloging-In-Publication Data
(Prepared by The Donohue Group, Inc.)

Names: Pless, John T., 1953- author. | Corzine, Jacob, writer of supplementary textual content.
Title: Pastor craft : essays and sermons / by John T. Pless ; foreword by Jacob Corzine.
Description: Irvine, CA : 1517 Publishing, [2021] | Includes bibliographical references and index.
Identifiers: ISBN 9781948969604 (hardcover) | ISBN 9781948969611 (paperback) | ISBN 9781948969628 (ebook)
Subjects: LCSH: Pastoral theology. | Clergy. | LCGFT: Essays. | Sermons.
Classification: LCC BV4011.3 .P66 2021 (print) | LCC BV4011.3 (ebook) | DDC 253—dc23

Printed in the United States of America

Cover art by Brenton Clarke Little

In Memory of

Mr. Clifford Diseko of the Lutheran Church in Southern Africa

And

Bishop David Rakotonirina of the Malagasy Lutheran Church

Both of these men died while I was in the process of compiling the material for Pastor Craft. *Faithful confessors of the cross, their partnership in the Gospel was a great gift to me. Having them as students made me a better teacher.*

Contents

PART I: SERMONS

PREACHING FOR PREACHERS: ORDINATION, INSTALLATION, AND ANNIVERSARY OF ORDINATION SERMONS

PART II: THEOLOGY IS FOR PROCLAMATION:
ESSAYS FROM THE CRAFT OF PREACHING

Preface

Seminary faculties are typically arranged in four departments: Exegetical theology, dogmatic theology, historical theology, and practical theology. Exegetical theology might be described as the eyes and ears of the church, reading and listening to the Holy Scriptures. Dogmatic theology is the mind of the church, thinking through and laying hold of the message of the prophetic and apostolic Word, rightly distinguishing the Law from the Gospel. Historical theology is the church's memory, recalling God's faithfulness and learning from the Christian past. Practical theology is the mouth, hands, and feet of the church as the word of the cross is proclaimed and taken into the world where Christians must live and die.

For the past twenty years it has been my duty and delight to serve as a professor of practical theology, teaching courses in pastoral theology, liturgics, catechetics, and theological ethics at Concordia Theological Seminary in Fort Wayne, Indiana. The primary focus of my work these last two decades has been to equip future pastors to be the mouth, hands, and feet of the Gospel. It is largely out of this work that the present volume emerges. *Pastor Craft* is a sampling of sermons and essays coming out of my own calling as a pastor and teacher of the Church. A few of the essays were written while I was pastor at University Lutheran Chapel in Minneapolis, but the majority of the essays and all of the sermons come from my time on the faculty at Concordia Theological Seminary. But I would quickly add that my seventeen years of campus ministry in Minneapolis were foundational and formative for what I do as a professor.

The sermons are offered in the conviction that theology is worthless if it cannot be preached. Whether in the seminary chapel or a parish pulpit, theology is for proclamation to use the phrase of the sainted Gerhard Forde. A significant number of these sermons were preached at the ordinations of former students, sending them on their way with the confidence that the Word of the Lord is not bound but has free course. It is hoped that not only students and pastors might be encouraged and refreshed by the sermons but also lay people who read them devotionally. Two of the sermons were preached at the funerals of beloved mentors and fathers in Christ, Rev. Dr. Kenneth F. Korby and Rev. Dr. Lowell Green. Several of the sermons were preached in the daily chapel services held here at the seminary where I teach. Others were preached in congregations or at conferences.

The essays span the spectrum of topics that confront pastors in our age. All were written with the conviction that there can be no divorce between doctrine and practice. As Franz Pieper reminded an earlier generation of pastors, all doctrine reduces to practice.

In addition to the sermons, there are some essays on preaching first published on *Craft of Preaching*. I'm grateful to Pastor Bob Hiller, who curates this 1517 blog. These essays seek to provide theological commentary on the preaching task, especially in light of motifs in the church year.

Pastoral theology cannot afford to be abstract or theoretical. It must be responsive to the various circumstances and situations in which the church lives and breathes. A few of these are "period pieces" reflecting the so-called "worship wars" of the 1990s or my own church body's flirtation with American Evangelicalism. Those who know me know of my appreciation for the nineteenth-century Bavarian pastor, Wilhelm Löhe, and the twentieth-century German-Australian theologian, Hermann Sasse. Their imprint can be seen in these essays as well. I will be forever grateful for the privilege to serve with Dr. Norman E. Nagel at Valparaiso University's Chapel of the Resurrection (1979–1983). From him I learned that it is "the Gospel that Lutherans care about."

The pastor is not a soloist. He stands within the company of preachers. He is part of a brotherhood bound together by a common Lord and common confession. It is a fraternal office as Ulrich Asendorf once described it. We have received a robust legacy from our fathers in the faith: Luther, Chemnitz, Walther, Löhe, Sasse, and others. What we have received, we are to hand on to others. Gratefulness for the legacy we have been given obligates us to the responsibility of passing it on. This volume represents a small effort to do just that. For those who have studied with me in Fort Wayne, Pretoria, or in other classes and conferences across the globe, I hope these pages will bring to remembrance what they heard in the classroom. For others, it is my prayer that these sermons and essays will enliven their faith in Christ crucified and deepen their capacity to speak of Him with clarity and confidence.

I can't begin to enumerate all those who have influenced and shaped me as a pastor and teacher. It would be impossible to sufficiently recognize the host of students whose attentive engagement and probing questions have made me a better teacher. These students now serving as pastors throughout the world make St. Paul's thanksgiving in Philippians 1:3–6, my own: "I thank my God in all my remembrance of you, always in every prayer of mine for you all making my prayer with joy, because of your partnership in the gospel from the first day until now. And I am sure of this, that he who began a good work in you will bring it to completion at the day of Jesus Christ."

Likewise, it would be difficult to list by name all of the brothers in office and colleagues who have enriched not only my thinking but my life. However, three do standout: Rev. Dr. Matthew C. Harrison, Rev. Dr. Mark Mattes, and Rev. Dr. James Arne Nestingen.

Special thanks goes out to the Rev. Dr. Jacob Corzine, one of the most competent young theologians within confessional Lutheranism, for writing the Foreword to this volume and also to Mr. Stephen Byrnes of 1517 Publishing for the invitation to prepare this work.

John T. Pless. M.Div.; D. Litt.
Concordia Theological Seminary
Fort Wayne, Indiana
Tuesday in the Tenth Week after Trinity 2020

Foreword

I came to know John Pless as a student during my first year at the Fort Wayne Seminary in 2003. He had been teaching a few years already, and students were beginning to realize that they had someone remarkable in Professor Pless. That Spring, the more senior students banded together to exchange their currency, a mountain of beer, for an extra-curricular course on the Church Year. I was blessed as a new student to be invited to join. The course was a cornucopia of information about the church year and grounds everything I still draw on today. He accepted the beer, but, in return, his currency was never beer; it was always theology.

Besides being a phenomenal teacher, he is also very hospitable. His students ultimately got to know him at his house, where he would slowly sip, and generously share what he had to offer. In groups of 5 or 6, occasionally as a whole class, and once in an independent-study course, I visited Pless's on-campus home and learned to know his sense for Lutheran Theology and his pastoral heart.

I suspect that he is best known in the classroom for his literature lists. Every class includes a topical outline with a literature list at the top. Those lists are detailed, and they are lengthy. They include articles and specific sections of books, all of which he has read. Still today, Pless seems to have read everything. He reads widely, critically, charitably, and with comprehension. It is frustrating to run into things I used to know and have forgotten, but when that happens, I call Pless because he always still knows!

Since finishing at the seminary, I have gotten to know Pless differently. He is quick to make clear to former students that they have transitioned to being his colleagues. I now know him as a close friend and marvel as he travels the world, teaching Lutheran theology and Lutheran pastoral practice wherever he is invited—Germany, Singapore, South Africa (this is a small sampling). A friend once remarked that to ask Pless what he has coming up is to invite a tidal wave of international speaking and teaching engagements, continuing education courses around the country, and ordinations to be attended and preached. That friend was right. One might duly include in the list Pless's regular trips to North Carolina to visit his parents.

As he travels, Pless is universally well-received, at least by those who choose to invite someone so unashamedly Lutheran. I've seen him teaching beside Bavarian Lutherans with multiple degrees in Löhe's Neuendettelsau. He is equally in his element fielding questions from young African men hanging on his every word as they seek to understand the meaning of Lutheran pastoral practice for their churches back home. The respect he receives surely stems in part from the respect he shows. He arrives unassuming and grateful for the opportunity to teach the gospel because, again, that is his currency. No honest question goes unconsidered. Rarely, I think, is he caught unsure how to respond. Perhaps his patience for "gotcha" questions is a bit limited.

In his *Three Books About The Church*, Wilhelm Löhe wrote that the Lutheran church is the "unifying center of the confessions," suggesting that the Reformed and Roman Catholic churches live, theologically, on either side of the Lutheran church. It seems unrealistic to try to identify this phenomenon in the American church today, but there is one part of it that can be seen in Pless: A confessionally grounded ecumenism. Pless knows his own church but constantly engages beyond it. The books he reads, the invitations he accepts, and the company he keeps all point to this: John Pless is a biblically faithful confessional Lutheran, but he is not walled off from the rest of Christendom. The influence of not only Wilhelm Löhe but also Hermann Sasse shows itself here. I refer the reader to the *damnamus* essays in this volume. When Pless observes how Sasse was "an ecumenical confessionalist and a confessional ecumenist," he describes something he strives to emulate.

Luther's writings being collected during his lifetime gave occasion for one of Pless's favorite writings, on the *Oratio, Meditatio, Tentatio* triad. Luther put this guidance on reading the scriptures in the preface to his own writings, even though it probably belonged as a preface to his Bible translation work. But he seemed to know this because what he wrote was that most of his writings were not worth reading; in his view, one should turn straight to the scriptures. Perhaps, in submitting to publication anyhow, Luther knew that writing steeped in the scriptures also leads people into the scriptures. The same goes here. It would be strange and against the nature of a foreword for me to summarize and advise against reading the writings collected here in favor of simply picking up your Bible, but this may be said: You'll find in the pages, Pless, but behind him Luther, Löhe, Sasse, and a few others. And ultimately, all of these instruments of God want to be set aside, want to get out of the way to lead you to the scriptures and the Savior they reveal. In that vein, join me in giving thanks for Luther, Löhe, Sasse, and Pless.

Dr. Jacob Corzine
Assistant Professor of Theology
Concordia University Chicago

Abbreviations

AC—*Augsburg Confession*

AE—*Luther's Works*, American Edition, 1955ff.

AP—*Apology of the Augsburg Confession*, cited by article and section nos.

ELCA—The Evangelical Lutheran Church in America

FC-E—Epitome, *Formula of Concord*, cited by article and section nos.

FC-SD—Solid Declaration, *Formula of Concord*, cited by article and section nos.

GW—Wilhelm Löhe, *Gesammelte Werke* (GW), ed. Klaus Ganzert (Neuendettelsau: Freimund, 1951–1986)

K-W—Kolb and Wengert editon of *The Book of Concord* cited by article and section nos.

LC—*Large Catechism*

LCMS—Lutheran Church-Missouri Synod

LSB—*Lutheran Service Book*

LW—*Lutheran Worship*

SC—*Small Catechism*

SA—*Smalcald Articles*

Tappert—Tappert Edition of *The Book of Concord*

TR—*Treatise on Power and Primacy of the Pope*

WA—Weimarer Ausgabe: *D. Martin Luthers Werke: kritische Gesamtausgabe*, 1883ff., cited by volume no. (occasionally by section no. and also by page no. and line no.)

PART I
Sermons

PREACHING FOR PREACHERS

Ordination, Installation, and
Anniversary of Ordination Sermons

1

Ordination of Andy Wright

Sent with a Word

Romans 10:5-17

REDEEMER LUTHERAN CHURCH, LANCASTER, OH

Trinity VII / 22 July 2012

We are here today because God has answered a prayer. The Lord Jesus instructed His disciples, saying, "The harvest is plentiful, but the laborers are few. Therefore pray earnestly to the Lord of the harvest to send out laborers into his harvest" (Luke 10:2). Lord's Day after Lord's Day, throughout the world, congregations have implored the Lord to raise up faithful men for the ministry and equip them for their holy calling that the voice of the Good Shepherd might be heard in all the world. In the ordination service, the church receives an answer to that prayer with praise and thanksgiving. It is fitting that this ordination service is held here at Redeemer Lutheran Church, for it was in your midst that Andy aspired to the pastoral office. Here he was taught the faith and encouraged in his studies. You have prayed for him and supported him with your gifts. Now in a very real way, the Lord of the harvest is using you as His instrument to send Andy off to another congregation, St. John Lutheran Church in Keystone, Iowa, where he will shepherd the Lord's flock in that place.

All that is going on here today in this ordination service centers on the fact that it is the Lord who has answered His church's prayer in sending Andy as His servant to preach the Word and administer the sacraments. You have heard Jesus' words spoken to the men who would be His apostles—literally His sent ones—on Easter evening: "As the Father has sent Me, I also send you" (John 20:21 NKJV). And from our text in Romans 10, where Paul poses the rhetorical question, "And how are they to preach unless they are sent?" (Rom. 10:15). Ordination is the Lord's sending of a man to be a preacher of the Gospel, an ambassador of divine reconciliation and a messenger of the good news that in the blood of Jesus Christ, there is forgiveness of sins and peace with God.

The Apostle Paul writes that "If anyone aspires to the office of overseer, he desires a noble task" (I Tim. 3:1). But aspiration is not enough to put a man in the office. It is always dangerous to confuse the aspirations and desires of our fallible human hearts with the mind of God. Andy aspired to the office of the ministry. That's a good thing. Obviously, we would not be here this afternoon without Andy's aspiration to be a pastor. And we are grateful for the way that desire, that aspiration was confirmed and encouraged by his parents and family, by Rebecca, by the pastor and people of this congregation. But that is not what we are primarily gathered here to celebrate today. Nor is it mainly about Andy's abilities—though they are many and excellent gifts from God. It is not that a man's ordination day marks a goal accomplished. Ordination is not the marking of status achieved, but rather it is being set in place, being put under orders, an arduous trek into unknown territories; it is launching out on a venture of which you, Andy, cannot see the ending to borrow the language of a familiar old collect of the church.

Ordination is both gift and task. It is gift in that with prayers and the laying on of hands you are endowed with the same Holy Spirit who was given you in Baptism. That Spirit now equips and enables you to preach His Word and care for the flock of which He is making you an overseer—it's this Holy Spirit who intercedes for you with sighs and groans too deep for words. It is the Lord and Giver of Life who has called you to faith in the Gospel; He now strengthens you in your weakness to endure hardship as a good soldier of Christ Jesus.

To say that ordination is a gift is to confess that the Office of the Holy Ministry is not an entitlement. You have studied hard at Ann

Arbor and Fort Wayne. You have demonstrated perseverance and outstanding academic capacity, but these achievements do not alone qualify a man for the pastoral office. He must be sent. And the way the Lord sends a man is through the church, as the church calls a man to serve. Without this call, there is no ordination, no minister. Ordination attests to the fact that the Lord, through His church, has called you into the preaching office. To say that ordination is a gift is to confess that it is not about you but Christ. That is why Lutherans traditionally clothe their pastors with vestments, putting them in the uniform, so to speak, to demonstrate that when all is said and done, it is about Christ and His office; the man who is put there is secondary.

If ordination is gift, it is also task. Ordination puts a man under orders. You are given tasks to perform. They are outlined in the vows which you take. You are under orders to preach God's Word in season and out of season. You are to administer the sacraments in accordance with Christ's institution. Your teaching and preaching are pledged to be in conformity with the Holy Scriptures and the Lutheran Confessions. You are to watch over the flock of God purchased with His own blood. You are to do the work of an evangelist, a Gospel preacher. You are to admonish and instruct with great care and patience. With the law, you are to afflict the comfortable, and with the Gospel, you are to comfort the afflicted. Confronted by the enormity of the task, you might well step back, saying with Paul, "who is sufficient for these things?" (II Cor. 2:16). Or to use the words of that heroic teacher of the church that you have spent your graduate year studying, Hermann Sasse: "The deepest nature of this crisis [the crisis of the ministry] lies in the fact that God always demands from his servants something which is, humanly speaking, impossible" ("The Crisis of the Christian Ministry" *The Lonely Way*, Vol. 2, p. 356).

Your sufficiency does not come from yourself, from your own resources but from the Christ who is sending you. Ordination confirms what you already know. You belong to Him, who by His precious blood and innocent suffering and death has made you His own. In a few minutes, brother pastors will lay their hands on your head. There is a story about a young boy attending an ordination service with his father. When that solemn moment came for the laying on of hands with the pastors encircled around the candidate, the curious kid said to his Dad, "What are they doing?" The father replied, "They're taking out his brains." Well, ordination doesn't extract your brains, but it does commit your brains as well as your mouth, your eyes and ears, your hands and your feet—the whole of you—to this singular task of proclaiming Christ and Him crucified. How beautiful indeed are the feet of those who proclaim the good news.

Tomorrow with your earthly belongings in tow, you and Rebecca will head to Iowa. You are going there because that is where the Lord is sending you. What awaits you there, no one knows, save the omniscient Lord who sends you. No doubt, there will be times of great delight when you will be surprised by joy, to borrow a phrase from C.S. Lewis. No doubt, there will also be seasons of suffering and hours of disappointment. There will be exhilarating peaks and cavernous pits. But you go into that future as one who is sent. You go as one who travels at the direction of another with a message that is not your own. That is why the New Testament refers to those who hold the office of apostolic ministry as ambassadors. You are Christ's ambassador; His man sent to preach His Gospel. You do not wander aimlessly or stumble around in uncertainty exhausting yourself with expectations for effectiveness imposed by your own imagination or that of others. No, you march with a steady pace as a good soldier of Christ Jesus, whose Word alone directs your steps and sheds light on your path. You walk the road of ministry with determined steps and the sure-footedness of a man who is sent.

You go with His gift, with His promise that He will not abandon you. He will not leave you or forsake you. Just as He went with Moses to Pharaoh's throne, He goes with you. Just as He was in the mouth of the prophets, He puts His words in your mouth. Even as He was with the apostles whom He sent with His words of peace, so He is with you to bless and uphold your work. He sends you, Andy, with His words, words which are spirit and life. These are words that will not return empty but accomplish the purposes of the God who now commissions you to speak by His command and in His stead.

You are sent to proclaim Jesus Christ and Him crucified. You are sent into a dangerous and dying world. How dangerous and dying this world is, we were reminded by the tragic and senseless slaughter in a Colorado theater early on Friday. There are no guarantees of safety or of human success, but you do have the word of promise made certain by the fact that Jesus Christ is Lord. He is raised from the dead and He lives and reigns as Lord of His Church. No one who believes in Him will be put to shame. It is in that confidence that Andy is put into the office of preaching today. His future is with the Lord Jesus crucified and raised from the grave never to die again. So to paraphrase Sasse once more, the church has a future and the ministry has a future because Jesus Christ has a future. That future is yours, Andy. Amen.

2

Ordination of Aaron Hambleton

Ordination: The Answer to a Prayer

Matthew 9:35–38

REDEEMER LUTHERAN CHURCH, LISBON, ND

Trinity III / 21 June 2015

> O Spirit, who didst once restore
> Thy Church that it might be again
> The bringer of good news to all,
> Breathe on Thy cloven Church once more,
> That in these gray and latter days
> There may be men whose life is praise,
> Each life a high doxology
> To Father, Son, and unto Thee. (M. Franzmann)

We are here today because God has already answered this prayer. When He surveyed the crowds who wandered aimlessly, harassed and helpless like sheep without a shepherd, the Good Shepherd Himself commanded His people to "pray earnestly to the Lord of the harvest to send out labors into his harvest." At altars throughout Christendom that prayer has ascended. God, who is already more willing and eager to give than we are to ask, has once again looked in mercy on His church and He gives her yet another servant in the person of Aaron Hambleton, soon to be Pastor Hambleton.

The ordination service itself is one elongated AMEN to the Lord's answer to His people's prayer. The service itself indicates that Aaron has not put himself here in Lisbon, North Dakota. Neither did he come here because the congregation offered him a job, and after all these years of schooling and with Katie, Theresa, and John to take care of, he needed a job. He was sent by the Lord of the harvest. One teacher of our church (Jobst Schöne) has described the ordination service as the church's outstretched hand, open to receive the gift that the Lord gives when He provides a man to preach His Word and administer His sacraments.

Wherever the Lord answers prayer, there is rejoicing. So here today, there is much joy all around. Aaron, for you, this day marks the completion of a journey that started with an aspiration to be a pastor, which led you to the seminary. By prayer and careful study, you have prepared not only for this day but the work of the ministry, which will now begin in earnest and continue, please God, for decades to come. Others have prayed for you along the way, certainly your wife, parents, grandparents, and family members. And not only them but countless Christians who don't even know your name. It is for you as it is for all your brothers in office a humbling recognition that we have been and are so prayed for by Christ's people who have heeded Jesus' words: "Pray earnestly to the Lord of the harvest to send out labors into his harvest."

Jesus bids us to pray. Yes, to beg earnestly for laborers. Why the urgency? Jesus gives us the answer. The crowds are harassed and helpless. Sheep out of necessity need and require a shepherd. It is a matter of survival! Without a shepherd, the sheep are bound to scatter. Apart from a shepherd, they are susceptible to attacks from predators and easy prey for thieves. The Good Shepherd, who came to lay down His life for the sheep, now gives shepherds to tend His flock leading the sheep to the rich pastures of His Word, binding up the wounded, and protecting the helpless.

There is an urgency and necessity to this prayer because the sheep have enemies who are far more powerful than they. A shooting in a church in South Carolina where nine people were slaughtered is a vivid reminder of how real the enemy is as he seeks to kill, destroy, and scatter. The devil is prowling around like a roaring lion seeking who he may devour. There is the world that would lure the sheep into deep darkness and places of destruction. Then, there is the flesh, which is so easily enticed to believe that we can have life on our own terms, as though we could live without Jesus Christ. There is urgency to prayer as long as there is sin, death, and the devil. For as long as these exist, we cannot live without faith. And there is no faith without the Gospel, and the Gospel requires a preacher. That's the case which Paul makes in Romans 10: "And how can they hear without someone preaching, and how can they preach unless they are sent? . . . so, faith comes from hearing, and hearing through the word of Christ."

So we pray according to the Lord's will, imploring Him to send labors into His harvest. The Lord of the harvest has answered this prayer.

Dear Christians of Redeemer Lutheran congregation, you have prayed and waited these past months of the vacancy and now God has answered that prayer. Today, you receive this man that the Lord has sent you as an answer to that petition. In word and deed, you will honor him, love him, support him, and hear the Word of God, which he brings as the pastor God has sent you.

Brother Aaron, you placed yourself at the Lord's disposal. In aspiring to the office of overseer, a man makes himself available to wherever the Lord would send him, trusting that God in His infinite wisdom knows where He would have use of him. God has sent you here. Today you are ordained, and among other things, this means that now you see yourself and your being here in Lisbon as an answer to prayer.

God has put you here because there are sheep who are weary and worn out, harassed and helpless. The office of the holy ministry is here so that Jesus' work of preaching and the healing of souls might go on. By His obedient life and His innocent suffering and death, He has won the forgiveness of sins for the whole world. Now he desires that forgiveness to be announced and distributed. It is to be preached. That is where you come in. Your mouth is now His mouth for the words you speak are not yours, but His, and you declare them by His command and in His stead. Your ears become the Lord's ears as you hear the cries of the broken who lament their sins. Your hands are the Lord's hands, dipping into the water of Baptism, distributing Jesus' body and blood, and touching the heads of penitent sinners as you speak the absolution. In other words, the work you do is not yours but His. In your ordination, you are pledged to this work.

In this pulpit, from this altar, in the places where you teach God's Word, in the homes of your members, in hospital rooms and in front of the open grave, you are the Lord's man with His words on your lips: "Your sins are forgiven you!"

Your comfort in the days and years to come is anchored in the fact that you are an answer to prayer; that God has put you here. You may indeed be overwhelmed with all that is required of you as a shepherd in this old and dying world. It is, after all, an unending work that the Lord entrusts to you. There will always be sinners, and so the need for the work of the ministry of reconciliation will come to an end at the Last Day. With the Apostle Paul, you can only say, "Who is sufficient for these things?" Your sufficiency is not in yourself but in Christ Jesus, who has made you His servant. And because you have this ministry by the mercy of God, you do not lose heart (II Cor. 4:1).

You, Brother Aaron, are an answer to prayer. But there is yet more, the One who sends you as an answer to the prayers of His people also prays for you. In His great high priestly prayer of John 17, Jesus prays for His disciples. He implores His Holy Father to keep them from the evil one, to sanctify them in the truth, for His Word is truth. Jesus, who is the Yes and Amen to all the promises of God, prays for His church; He also prays for you.

In that confidence, go to the work which the Good Shepherd now gives you, knowing that because His blood has set you free and His resurrection has won the victory, the outcome of your life and work has already been secured. So be steadfast, immovable, always abounding in the work of the Lord, knowing that in Him, your labor is not in vain. Amen.

3

Ordination of Michael Daniels

The Ministry of the New Covenant

II Corinthians 3:4–6

SALEM LUTHERAN CHURCH, TAYLORSVILLE, NC

Trinity XI / 7 August 2016

This past month in Cleveland and then in Philadelphia, the attention of our nation and even the world was turned to decisions being made by the two leading political parties as to who would be put forward as their respective candidates for president of the United States. There were stirring speeches and rhetorical appeals. Those gatherings captured media coverage and commentary, and no doubt, the dust will not settle until the election takes place in November. By way of contrast, we are gathered here this afternoon not to put forward a man for political office with all the ruckus of a convention. Instead, we are here on this lazy August afternoon because Christ Jesus is putting a man in a spiritual office, the office of preaching, the office of the holy ministry of Word and Sacraments. This is not an office of worldly authority, but it is an authority for it is the office of the Spirit, the Lord and Giver of Life. So Dr. Luther says in one of his many sermons of John 20: "This was not Christ's mandate to His disciples, and He did not send them forth for secular government. Rather, He committed to them the preaching office, and the government over sin, so that the proper definition of the office of preaching is that one should preach the Gospel of Christ and forgive the sins of the crushed, fearful consciences, but retain those of the impenitent and secure, and bind them" (AE 69:383).

That is the office, Michael, into which you are placed today. The media might yawn at a church service, which seems so pale and insignificant when set alongside the commotion of a convention hall. Still, I would submit to you that what is taking place today will have a significance—yes, an eternal significance—long after the names of Donald Trump and Hilary Clinton are forgotten (and for that matter, even when your own name is no longer remembered). The kingdoms of men and nations rise up and pass away, but the Word of the Lord endures forever. It is an everlasting Gospel, this word of the cross, which you, Michael, are ordained, that is, put under orders to proclaim.

The person who is put into the office of president has weighty responsibility on their shoulders. The man who is put into the office of preaching has an even heavier burden to bear. Presidents and prime ministers, kings and emperors are given charge over things temporal. Pastors exercise an office with eternal consequences as they are charged to forgive the sins of the broken and retain the sins of the self-righteous—those who, in their fleshly security, refuse to repent.

Political candidates recommend themselves for secular offices even as they seek the approval and recommendation of others. But who can recommend himself for the office of preaching? As he writes II Corinthians, Paul does not commend himself, but Christ Jesus. So also with this young man, this son of Salem congregation, who is ordained today; it is finally not about Michael but about Jesus.

Indeed, there is much to celebrate and give thanks for this afternoon. It is fitting that the congregation has a godly pride in the fact that one of your own, taught the Holy Scriptures and the Catechism in your midst, nurtured in the fear, love, and trust in God above all things, confirmed in the faith at this altar and fed here with the body and blood of Christ has been led to prepare for the pastoral office. On behalf of the whole church, I speak a word of thanksgiving for the gift that you have given in providing Michael for the work of the ministry. It is good and right that his parents and family, who have supported and encourage him at each step along the way, now rejoice that Michael has come to this day. And Michael and Emily are no doubt relieved that the rigors of seminary education are in the rearview mirror and a big bright Texas-size future awaits them. There is eagerness and excitement now to get on to the work which you have been preparing for these past years. That is all well and good but there is more. There is one thing which you are to know and never forget. It is this: Jesus Christ, crucified and raised from the dead, is alone your sufficiency for preaching office.

Your confidence is finally not that you have a Master of Divinity degree from Concordia Theological Seminary, or that you have the set of skills required for effective ministry, or that Zion Lutheran Church in Tomball, Texas thinks that you will be a good fit to work with Pastor Hull. All of that may be helpful, but you have something greater. The Apostle puts it like this: "Such is the confidence that we have through Christ toward God." In a few minutes, Michael, you will make some God-sized vows, solemn promises that your teaching will be completely bound to the Holy Scriptures and the Lutheran Confessions, and that your life will adorn and reflect the doctrine of Christ you are sworn to deliver in season and out of season. These vows should cause you to tremble more than a little. You can finally give a full-throated and unqualified "yes" to these questions because your confidence is toward God through Christ.

That little phrase that Paul uses "through Christ" is the key. Paul's ministry was not validated by his cleverness or perseverance, by his eloquence or appearance, by his credentials of heritage or education but only through Christ. So it is with you, Michael. You are sufficient for this work only because your sufficiency is from God through Christ.

He has made you competent to be a minister of the new covenant. The Prophet Jeremiah spoke of the new covenant that God would make with His people. The old covenant made at Sinai was shattered by Israel's sin. There is no salvation there. The Law can only curb and condemn sin; it is powerless to forgive sin. Instead, Jeremiah proclaims a new covenant. That new covenant contains a promise absent in the old covenant. And the promise is this says Jeremiah: "I will forgive their iniquity, and I will remember their sin no more" (Jer. 31:34).

You are a minister not of the letter which kills (that's the Law) but of the Spirit who gives life (that's the Gospel). Yes, you will preach the Law in all of its sternness to those who are hardened in their unbelief, but that preaching will never take their sin away. You will preach the Law only so your hearers might come to hear the promise of the new covenant: "I will forgive their iniquity, and I will remember their sin no more." The letter kills, the Spirit gives life. The law never finds righteousness and it is powerless to create it. The Gospel only finds sinners, but it is the power of God, for salvation, for it bestows righteousness in the forgiveness of sins for the sake of Christ.

You, Michael, are today authorized to be an agent and ambassador of the new covenant—on your lips are the words of Jesus, the Lamb of God who takes away the sin of the world. His words are spirit and life (John 6:63). Your competence and your confidence are in them. Move away from Jesus' words, start referencing self, proclaiming something other than the Law and Gospel, or mixing and muddling the two, you will have neither competence nor confidence. For this reason, your confession, like that of the disciples, can only and ever be: "Lord, to whom shall we go? You have the words of eternal life."

Preach the Law? Yes, for it is necessary to bring secure sinners to repentance. Afflict those who are comfortable in and with their sin. To those who have been so afflicted, preach the comfort of Jesus Christ who atoned for the sins of the world, and by His resurrection gives forgiveness of sins to all you will receive it. That is the work of the minister of the new covenant. Today, Michael, it is the work committed to you.

Christ Jesus is sending you on your way today as a minister of the new covenant, not the letter that kills but the Spirit who gives life. You cannot see the ending of the path set before you. The Lord who sends you does not promise that the journey on which you are now embarking will be an easy one. This culture of death into which you are sent despises Christ. The ever-deceiving world, your own stubborn flesh, and the clever devil will always be on the attack. But you have a promise that is guaranteed by the Lord Jesus Christ, who has been raised from the dead never to die again. This is the lively and life-giving hope which will not disappoint you. In Him, your life and work are secure for, in this Jesus, your sufficiency is from God. He has made you competent to be a minister of the new covenant, not the letter which kills but the Spirit who gives life. You have His promise. That is enough. Amen.

4

Ordination of Michael Holman

The Confidence of a Minister of the New Testament

II Corinthians 3:4–6

PEACE LUTHERAN CHURCH, OELWEIN, IA

Trinity IV / 27 June 2010

Jesus says, "Blessed are those who hear the Word of God and keep it." Michael, you have heard the Word from pastors, your parents, and your teachers. That Word has laid claim over your heart and mind. It has deprived you of whatever freedom you might have claimed for yourself, wrestling you and pinning you just as surely as the angel of the Lord had Jacob in his grip back there at the ford of Jabbok in the Book of Genesis. And with the tenacity of Jacob, you have kept that Word, refusing to let go without a blessing. He has blessed you. Your fate is tied up with the destiny of His Word. It is a Word that has free course as it accomplishes the purpose for which God sent it. And in that Word's way with you, it was implanted in your thinking to desire that noble task of being a shepherd of God's flock. So today marks the culmination of years of study and preparation of hearing and keeping God's Word. These last years have been given to reading and reflection, disputation and discernment. The church has examined you and declared you ready and able to serve as a pastor. These congregations have called you to be their pastor, so you are to be ordained, set into the office to preach the Word and administer the sacraments.

But this day is not finally about you, Michael. There are two congregations here who have heard the Word of God. Over the years, God has sent you pastors, preachers to proclaim the Word of Christ, the words which are Spirit and life, words which create and sustain faith in the One who was crucified for our sins and raised again for our justification. You have been blessed through the preaching of Christ and Him crucified. Pastors come and pastors go, but the Word of the Lord endures forever. That you might continue to be blessed by the Word of our God, you have prayed that the Lord of the harvest would send you a preacher. He has answered that petition. And you are blessed!

In this service of ordination, the church rejoices to receive from the Lord the gift of a pastor, a preacher, and a servant of God's Word. Paul's Spirit-given words in II Corinthians anchor both pastor and congregation in the promise of Christ Jesus, the only sure and trustworthy foundation for the work you are undertaking, Michael, and for the life that you will have as pastor and people together.

Paul speaks of confidence, a confidence that we are given through Christ toward God. This is not the self-confidence of the old Adam, reliant on his own capacities, his own intellect, his own devices. A service of ordination is not so much the celebration of a goal achieved, like finishing a prescribed course of studies and passing a theological interview and now at long last beginning embarking on a paying career as pastor, as it is a confession that this man has no sufficiency in himself; his sufficiency is from God who has made him a competent minister of the New Testament. That is why the church insists that those called to be pastors are bound to the Holy Scriptures and the Lutheran Confessions. We don't need pastors who dazzle congregations with their own brilliance or impress the flock with their creativity or overwhelm the community with their charisma. God desires shepherds who can make no claim to self-sufficiency for their sufficiency is in Christ alone. Like the Apostle, they are men who do not preach themselves but have the courage and boldness to preach no other Savior than that Jew who was crucified as a blasphemer for claiming equality with God by forgiving sins. Ordination, Michael, is not so much about your competence or sufficiency, but about Jesus Christ, who has made you competent with something as simple as His promises!

Your competence is from the Lord. As surely as the Lord Jesus breathed on His disciples and by His Word and Spirit sent them to forgive the sins of all those who repent and retain the sins of the impenitent, He is today sending you. In a few minutes, we'll hang a stole around your neck to remind you and those who hear you of that fact. You have no other authority than that of Jesus' promise. Yours is not a legal authority that would force people to pray, pay, and obey. Yes, you will exercise the office of the law, but its letter can only kill. It is the Spirit, the Holy Spirit, who is the Lord and Giver of life. You have nothing to claim but Jesus' words, words of Spirit and life. You have the Gospel.

His words are more than sufficient for the task. Of course, it doesn't seem to be that impressive. The Corinthians didn't find Paul all that credible. His only credentials for apostolic ministry were the marks of his suffering, the bearing of the cross. Paul came to them, not with impressive speech or impeccable arguments; he came among them determined to know nothing else than Christ and Him crucified as the wisdom and power of God. That was Paul's apostolic competence. Michael, it is yours as well.

It is given you to stand in front of the text of Holy Scripture to hear it, and in hearing it, we repeat it in your reproof and exhortation, in your declaration of convicting law and your consoling proclamation of comfort in the wounds of Christ. It is not given to you to interpret the text so that it conforms to the pattern of your mind but to be interpreted by the text so that your mind is renewed and your lips unlocked to speak the oracles of God. You are finished with your seminary training, but you will forever remain a student. Luther said, "A Christian is an eternal pupil from infancy onwards" (WA 32, 136, 3f). This is doubly true for pastors. Cease being a student of the Scriptures and you are unqualified to preach. Your sufficiency is anchored in His Word alone.

Dear people of Peace and Our Redeemer Lutheran Churches, you are receiving today from the Lord, a servant of His sending. Christ is giving you a minister of the New Testament, not of the killing letter but of the Spirit who gives life. Because your minister speaks Christ's words from this pulpit, in the classroom, over a cup of coffee, at your bedside, before a gapping grave, and all the other places where you need to hear the voice of the Good Shepherd, you will have certainty, the certainty that you have a Savior who holds on to you in life and in death. You have a minister of the New Testament and he will not let you forget the good news that God was in Christ reconciling the world to Himself, making peace through the blood of the cross. Receive him as the man that the Lord has put here by His Spirit for your good and blessing.

Dear Brother Michael, soon to be Pastor Holmen, you are embarking today on a path of which you cannot see the ending. What will be in store for you and Jana here in northeast Iowa, in the midst of Peace and Our Redeemer congregations? Of course, we don't know the answer to that question. In all likelihood, the ministry here will embrace both seasons of wonderment and worry, times of deepest joy and profound disappointment. Come what may, face it in the confidence that you have through Christ toward God. The Word He has given you to preach in season and out of season will not return to Him empty. It will accomplish the purpose for which He sent it. Luther said that our theology is certain because it takes us outside of ourselves; it draws us into Christ crucified and risen from the dead. His future is your future. His future is the church's future. That is your confidence for ministry. Live in the freedom Christ Jesus gives, going to your work in joy, for your labor in the Lord is not in vain. Amen.

5

Ordination of Zachary Oedewaldt

The Wisdom for the Ministry:
The Word of the Cross

I Corinthians 1:18–25

ZION LUTHERAN CHURCH, DECATUR, IN

Trinity V / 12 July 2020

> O Spirit, who didst once restore
> Thy Church that it might be again
> The bringer of good news to all,
> Breathe on Thy cloven Church once more,
> That in these gray and latter days
> There may be men whose life is praise,
> Each life a high doxology
> To Father, Son, and unto Thee. (M. Franzmann)

God in His wise mercy has answered that prayer yet here again today. We are here rejoicing this afternoon that God has sent Zachary Oedewaldt to serve as pastor in His church. One teacher of the church described the ordination service as the church's out-stretched and open hand, eager to receive the gift from the Lord of a pastor, a preacher, an ambassador of His own sending. Just as surely as the risen Lord Jesus breathed on the fearful disciples on Easter evening and spoke to them His words of peace and commissioning, so He is now giving you a pastor. Today another man is put into apostolic ministry to preach the Word into the ears of sinners, the word of the cross. He will preach the word of the cross into the water so that those baptized into Jesus' death will have His name to call upon and so be saved. He will administer the Lord's Supper, and so, as the Apostle says, you will eat the Lord's body and drink His blood proclaiming the Lord's death until He comes.

No wonder then that the day of ordination is a time of high thanksgiving for both congregation and candidate. Good people of Zion, today you celebrate that your congregation will have another servant of God's Word to work alongside Pastor Voorman. And you are not getting a stranger. You know Zach and Amber from his year of vicarage. You've recognized his character and capacities, and you're glad to welcome him back, not as Vicar Oedewaldt but as Pastor Oedelwaldt.

And Zach, for you and Amber, this is also a day of celebration. The years of preparation and planning, first at Concordia-Irvine and then at Concordia Theological Seminary, have come to cul-mination. You have studied and you have prayed. The church has examined you and found you ready and fit to undertake this high and holy calling as a minister of Jesus Christ. As one of your teach-ers, I can gladly attest to your competence as a student.

But your competency is deeper and more substantial than the good grades or academic recognition you've received. Your confi-dence is in Christ crucified. The Apostle Paul came to Corinth not with the eloquence of high-sounding rhetoric or the wisdom of the philosophers but with the word of the cross on his lips.

It is this word of the cross that you believe and confess and that you are today pledging yourself to preach without compromise. This word of the cross is the message that God was in Christ, rec-onciling the world to Himself. It is the proclamation that God has redeemed the world of lost and condemned sons and daughters of Adam, who are born with his legacy of sin and death. The Son of God, Christ Jesus our Lord, did not come with gold or silver but with His holy and precious blood, His innocent suffering and death as the Catechism tells us. It is the announcement of this news that defies the wisdom of this world. The wisdom of this world dictates that you get what you deserve. The word of the cross declares that God justifies the ungodly, showing grace and mercy to those who don't merit it and are unworthy. The wisdom of the world sees suffering as an evil to be eradicated even if it means killing the one who suffers. The word of the cross declares that by His suffering, Christ has brought righteousness for the unrighteous, peace with God instead of condemnation, and life out of death. Jesus did not come to transform the world, to create a new social order or teach some self-evident ethical principles. He came to do what the Law weaken by sin, could not do. He came to suffer and die under the curse of our sin that in Him, we might have God's own righteousness.

The Apostle Paul recognized that he was preaching to an audience that had other expectations. Jews were looking for signs to validate his sermon. Greeks sought a message that could be verified by human wisdom, demonstrated to be logically consistent with their definitions of reality. Instead, Paul preaches the wisdom of the cross, foolishness to the world as it sinks deeper and deeper into blindness and death, but to those who are being rescued, those who are being saved, it is the power of God. God turns things upside down. He humbles the high and mighty. He exalts those who are casts down. He kills and He makes alive. He brings life out of death. This is what God does in Jesus, who was crucified for us. He was put to death for our sins and raised again for our justification.

It is all there in the word of the cross! The word of the cross is nothing less than the Gospel itself. This word of the cross needs a preacher. This Word doesn't lie static. It is not dormant between the closed covers of a book. It must be preached. It needs lips, a tongue, and a mouth. It is to be preached so that it can be heard and trusted for the promise that it is. Luther reminds us that Christ could die a thousand deaths on Calvary, but if the news is not proclaimed, it is like a buried treasure that benefits no one. It is given to preachers not merely to preach about the cross, but to preach the cross. That is to say that the death that Jesus died—He died FOR YOU—for the forgiveness of your sins. God sends preachers who preach this one thing: Christ and Him crucified. The preacher doesn't simply preach about the cross; he doesn't offer theories about what happened with Jesus' death. The preacher proclaims the word of the cross. That is, the preacher predicates the incredibly violent death of Jesus at the hands of sinners as the very work of God for you.

This does not mean that the sermon shrinks the church year into a perpetual Good Friday (Sasse) but rather that everything—Christ's incarnation, His resurrection, His Ascension, the sending of the Holy Spirit, and the Lord's return as judge—are seen through the lens of the cross. Paul has to deal with all kinds of things in the Corinthian congregation—factionalism, sexual sin, lawsuits between Christians, abuse of spiritual gifts, women preaching, bad communion practices, and even denials of the resurrection. But he addresses all of these in and through the word of the cross. He never moves away from his determination to preach Christ crucified and Him alone. Anything that would put Christ Jesus and His cross as second place must be swept aside. Paul fits Luther's definition of a theologian of the cross; he calls the thing what it is!

So also with you, dear brother Zach. You are ordained into the preaching office today. In doing all the things that need to be done in the congregation, whether it be visiting the sick, working with the youth, teaching in the school, reaching out to the community, planning for the future of the congregation, organizing and administering various aspects of congregational life, you are never to cease preaching the word of the cross. That's front and center, but it also underlies and shapes everything you are called to do.

The theologian Karl Barth wrote that when it comes to discipleship, all Christians remain amateurs. We might paraphrase that to say when it comes to the ministry all pastors remain amateurs. That is, we are always learning from the wisdom of the cross. We never cease being pupils of the Holy Spirit as He works through His Holy Scriptures to draw us to Christ the crucified. So my prayer for you today, Zach, is that you'll remain an amateur, continuing to study and grow ever deeper in the wisdom of the cross. Don't think of yourself as a professional—that would be fatal for the ministry. Remain an amateur, always learning God's foolishness. Let Christ crucified be your wisdom!

I need not tell you how challenging these times are for Christians and our congregations. You are entering the ministry at a time when the faith is mocked, and the future appears dark. But God has raised Jesus, the One who was crucified, from the grave never to die again.

Because He lives, the future of the church is secure. The gates of hell will not prevail against it. So also, Zach, is your future. The word of the cross guarantees it. Indeed, "The foolishness of God is wiser than men, and the weakness of God is stronger than men" (I Cor. 1:25). That is the Lord's sure and certain promise for the office and ministry into which you are placed today.

> From the cross Thy Wisdom shining,
> Breaketh forth in conquering might;
> From the cross forever beameth
> All Thy bright redeeming light.
> Alleluia, Alleluia! Praise to Thee who light dost send!
> Alleluia, Alleluia! Alleluia without end! Amen. (578:4 LSB)

6

Ordination of Paul Doellinger

In the Service of a Word That Stands Forever

Isaiah 40:8

ST. PAUL LUTHERAN CHURCH, CASSOPOLIS, MI

Trinity IX / 1 August 2010

"By the word of the LORD the heavens were made," said the Psalmist, and "by the breath of his mouth all their host" (Ps. 33:6). But we live in a world that is distrustful of words. Words are said to be slippery; only so much talk reduced to hot air. We want action, not words. Or as one cliché puts it, "walk the walk, don't talk the talk."

We are here this afternoon because words do matter. It is on account of words that your pastor-elect, Paul Doellinger, sits here in front of us. Like Timothy of old, from childhood, he has known the Holy Scriptures, which made him wise to salvation. His parents brought him to the font where words joined to water were spoken over him, forgiving him his sin and endowing him with the Holy Spirit. His mother and father brought him to the services of God's house, and as he grew in years, they placed into his hands the Holy Scriptures, teaching him the Ten Commandments, the Creed, and the Lord's Prayer. His pastors taught him the Catechism and faith was enlivened and solidified. It continued at Ann Arbor and at Fort Wayne with the study of Hebrew and Greek, more Scripture and God's doctrine deepening in him the saving knowledge of Jesus Christ and the desire to pursue what the Apostle calls "the noble task" of being a bishop, an overseer of God's flock. Words, Paul, have brought you to this time and place. For the way the words of God have been at work in your life through your parents and family, through pastors and teachers, we give thanks to God.

Today, we are here to ordain Paul Doellinger. That is, his life will now be bound to the Word of God as a preacher. In a few minutes, your pastor-elect will make some vows, some solemn promises. He will confess his allegiance to the canonical books of the Old and New Testaments as the inspired Word of God and the only infallible rule of faith and practice. He will confess the Creeds as faithful testimonies to the truth of Holy Scriptures and the Lutheran Confessions as the true exposition of the Scriptures. He will promise to continue to study these Scriptures and Confessions, to teach them to young and old, and to perform all the duties of his office in conformity with them. Your pastor is not a servant to his own opinion and assessment of things but to the Word of His Lord. Both he and you will be reminded of that every time he speaks to you as a "called and ordained servant of the Word."

This bed-rock fact gives comfort to both the congregation and the pastor. To you hearers of God's Word here in St. Paul's Lutheran Church, you are given the assurance that your pastor is put here to speak not his own words but the Word of the Lord that stands forever. You have a pastor who will not trim the Scriptures to fit his own agenda but instead will stand under those Scriptures to proclaim to you the living Word of the Lord. You can count on that!

My brother Paul, today Christ Jesus is making you a servant of His Word. You have prepared for this day through careful study and prayer. You have been examined and declared ready in doctrine and fit in life to assume this office. Through the call of this Christian congregation, God Himself has called you to this place. Days, months, and even years of anticipation are brought to fulfillment as now you are ordained into the office of the Holy Ministry. But the joy and excitement of this festive day dare not blind you to the cross that is laid upon you. All Christians, in one way or another, are given a cross to bear. Pastors are not exempt from life under the cross. The very Word you proclaim will bring you suffering for as Luther puts it, where the holy and precious Gospel is proclaimed there, the holy cross will follow. Sometimes the imprint of the cross is very public; most times, it is private, born in silence and secrecy. Sometimes the cross takes the form of persecution, ridicule, and rejection. The lives of prophets of the Old Testament and the Apostle Paul in the New Testament are eloquent but bloody reminders of that. But the cross that pastors bear also takes other shapes such as the agony that comes when Gospel is heard but not believed; when the cares and concerns of this life choke and strangle faith in the lives of people under his care.

But as you are yoked with the office, you have a sure and sturdy promise. Listen again to our text for Isaiah: "The grass withers, the flower fades, but the word of our God will stand forever." Without God's Word, the ministry is nothing. In fact, there would be no ministry and no need for pastors. The office exists for the sake of the Word, and it is that Word which will comfort and sustain you.

The very Word which you preach, the Word of the cross—the Word that is foolishness to those who are perishing but the very power of God to those who are being saved—is ultimately the only thing you have to offer your hearers for the forgiveness of their sins, for their life and peace. This is the Word which carries the Spirit who works to create faith in the hearts of those who hear it when and where it pleases Him. This is the Word that does not return to God empty but accomplishes His purpose. This is the Word that you are given to preach with undying patience, in season and out of season. This is the Word that the Apostle declares is not bound but has free course. Heaven and earth will pass away, but this Word endures forever. This Word is nothing less than the Word made flesh, Jesus Christ, crucified and risen from the dead. His words say what they do and do what they say. Preaching not yourself, but Him, you have the courage and confidence to step into the office today, knowing the outcome of your work is in His nail-pierced hands. You have the promise of His empty tomb that your labor in His name is not futile or in vain. You have the promise of the One who says, "Be of good cheer, I have overcome the world." The victory of our crucified and risen Lord over sin and unbelief gives you the boldness to preach, to recklessly sow the seed of the Gospel whether men like or like it not, to paraphrase the words of the hymn-writer, for that Word, shall endure and stand when flowers and men shall be forgotten.

When God makes a promise, He takes on the responsibility to fulfill it. He promises to be with you, Brother Paul, to use your mouth as His mouth, your hands as His hands. So go do the work the Lord is today giving you as one whose trust is in the promise which will not disappoint: "The grass withers, the flower fades, but the word of our God will stand forever." What more do you need than that? Amen.

7

Ordination of Ryan Cramer

Christ's Ordination Prayer for You

John 17:6–18

ST. ANDREW LUTHERAN CHURCH, ROCKTON, IL

Trinity XVIII / 3 October 2010

We are here today in answer to prayer. I know, Ryan, you have prayed for this day as you studied and prepared these past years at the seminary. With the lack of calls last April and the delay it brought about, no doubt the intensity of your praying increased. Certainly, others here at St. Andrew's, along with parents, family, and friends, have prayed for you. Indeed the whole church has prayed for you, Sunday after Sunday, imploring the Lord of the harvest to raise up faithful and able men who will count it pure joy to spend and be spent in the service of the Gospel. This service is a testimony to the faithfulness of the Lord as once again; He has in mercy heard the prayer of His church.

But there is yet another who has made and continues to make intercession for you, Ryan. It is the Lord Christ Himself. The great Lutheran theologian Hermann Sasse who lived through the ravages of World War II in Germany, comforted his hearers in the midst of that war with the reminder, "Jesus still prays for His church." In the text from John 17, part of Jesus' high priestly prayer on the night of His being handed over to die, we are given to eavesdrop on the prayer that Jesus makes for the men who will be His apostles, His sent ones, and by extension, His prayer for you, Ryan, as today you are sent as surely as the Lord Jesus Himself would send them on Easter evening.

There is comfort in hearing from the lips of a Christian friend the assuring words, "I will pray for you." How much more comforting it is to know that Jesus Christ, crucified as our Brother and risen from death to give us life in His name, is praying for you. Dr. Sasse says, "Here it is not a mere man who is praying—no human being can pray it after Him. Here prays the eternal Son. All other prayers are prayers of men to God, prayers of creatures to their Creator. But this one prayer is prayed by the eternal Son to the Father" (*We Confess the Church*, 13–14). Jesus includes you in His prayer. That is the confidence you are given as today the Lord puts you into the preaching office.

In view of the enormity of the tasks God lays on those who are called into His service as ministers of the Gospel, the Apostle Paul raises the question in II Corinthians 2: "Who is sufficient for these things?" Then he goes on to assert in the next chapter that we are not in ourselves sufficient to claim anything as coming from us, "but our sufficiency is from God" who made us competent to be ministers of the New Testament. Our sufficiency, your sufficiency is from God. How abundant this sufficiency is we hear in Jesus' prayer, and it all hinges on what we have been given by Jesus: God's name and Word!

Called by the Lord's name and signed with that name in Holy Baptism, Ryan belongs to this Lord. Nothing that we would say of Ryan overrides or says more than the fact that He belongs to the Father who created him, the Son who purchased him with His blood, and the Spirit who hallowed him to be His own in Baptism. It is in that same name—"In the name of the Father and of the Son and of the Holy Spirit" that Ryan will be ordained and consecrated to "the Office of the Holy Ministry of the Word and Sacrament in the one, holy, catholic and apostolic church" this afternoon. There is nothing here of the granting of a special power or an indelible character. There is no energy bestowed here that will move you into an estate different from that of a baptized sinner. Rather with His name, the Lord God now is sending and authorizing you to speak His words.

Like the apostles, Ryan, you are on the receiving end of the Lord's giving. Jesus' prayer for his apostles is more about their need than their capacities or achievements. The ordination service is more about the neediness of the candidate rather than his capability.

Our Lord held out no notions of a romanticized life for His apostles. He offers them no prospects of triumphalism in winning the world for the kingdom. Instead, He prays for them precisely because He has given them the Father's word: "I have given them your word, and the world has hated them because they are not of the world, just as I am not of the world." Jesus implores His Father to keep His apostles in His name and through that name in the oneness and unity of faith. Such is Jesus' prayer for you, Ryan. Jesus guards and keeps His own in His name and Word. He consecrated Himself to the death that was His alone to die to purchase and claim sinners as His own possession, alive in righteousness, innocence, and blessedness even as He is risen from the dead. So Jesus prays, "Sanctify them in the truth; your word is truth."

It is that word, Jesus' words, words of spirit and life that Ryan is sent to preach. Jesus says in our text that He has given His apostles this word. It is Jesus' word, not your own. The ministry is not about making it up as you go along but proclaiming the words of the One who send you. As Martin Franzmann's hymn puts it, we are to preach that word "to men who like or like it not" for this Word shall endure and stand "when flow'rs and men shall be forgot" (LSB 586:1). His Word stands. It will not be overcome by the powers of this or any age. It will continue to go forth from God's mouth and accomplish the purpose for which He sent it. Jesus gives you this Word to preach. You know that this Word is nothing less than the Word of the cross, and it is through this preaching that our God will rescue the lost, to bring salvation to sinners. God backs it up with His promise!

We can't pray Jesus' high priestly prayer for that prayer can only be uttered by the Son to His Father as it references the work that is uniquely His. But we can and do pray the prayer that He has taught us, the Lord's Prayer. And in a few minutes with brother pastors laying hands on Ryan, we will pray it. We will invoke Jesus' Holy Father, who is now our true and dear Father, to give Ryan boldness and confidence in his praying for the people committed to his care. We will call upon the Lord to hallow His name as Ryan teaches the

Word of God in truth and purity. We will pray that God will give His Holy Spirit so that those who hear the Gospel preached by Christ's servant will believe and live holy lives in time and eternity. We pray that God's good and gracious will is done in this new preacher and those who hear him. We pray that the Father would open His hand to give him daily bread—all that he needs for this body and life, and that He lavishes on him the same forgiveness of his trespasses that he speaks to others. We pray that the Lord would guard and keep him from every temptation to false belief, despair, and other great shame and vice. And finally, we pray that Good Lord would deliver him from every evil and grant him at the end of his days to come into the heavenly kingdom hearing the Father's approval "Well done, you good and faithful servant." Our High Priest has already put His "Amen" to this prayer.

Jesus prays for you, Ryan. The Father has answered His Son's prayer, and so we send you on your way to the work and ministry that is yours to do at St. Paul Lutheran Church in Foley, Alabama trusting in nothing other than the name and words of Him who is our life and joy, Christ Jesus the Lord. Amen.

8

Ordination of Jacob Gaugert

The Promise of the Resurrection
and the Work You Are Given Today

I Corinthians 15:58

DR. MARTIN LUTHER LUTHERAN CHURCH, CHICAGO, IL

Saturday in Easter II / 17 April 2010

We are here this morning in the glow of Easter. That is true chrono-logically as we celebrated Jesus' resurrection two weeks ago tomor-row. But more than that, we are gathered here because the Father raised His slaughtered Son from the grave and the Son alive with wounds to prove He was not a phantom of fatigued apostolic imag-ination, breathed out His Spirit on the men He had chosen, sending them to forgive sins. The sending that the Lord put in motion on that first Easter evening has not stopped. Today we are here on the receiving end of the Lord's sending. The Lord sends another servant, Jacob, to do what the apostles were given to do, to preach Christ Jesus, forgiving the sins of those who repent and retaining the sins of those who insist on keeping their sins for themselves.

When and where the Lord gives out His gifts, there is joy. John tells us that when the disciples heard Jesus speak His words of peace and when they saw His hands and side that they were glad. Certainly, there is joy and gladness to go around here today. There is joy for you, Jacob, as today marks the end of a long and winding road of education that would prepare you for this holy office: Undergraduate studies at Mequon, seminary in Fort Wayne and Oberursel, and vicarage in Berlin and Norman, Oklahoma. More than just receiving academic degrees, you have learned the Holy Scriptures, which are able to make you wise into the salvation that is in Christ Jesus. You have studied the Lutheran Confessions, and today, you will make them your own confession—a confession which you are not ashamed to make before the judgment seat of God's Son. You have mastered languages and delved deeply into church history. You gained a capacity to preach, conduct the liturgy, catechize, and counsel. You have been examined and declared ready by the church to undertake the office of Christ's under-shepherd, to be entrusted with the care of souls purchased and won by the Good Shepherd Himself. Surely today is a day of profound joy for you.

It is also a day of gladness for your parents and family who have supported you with their money and prayers, who have watched you grow as they anticipated this day.

Today is truly a continuation of Easter for the members of Dr. Martin Luther Congregation as you have prayed to the Lord to send you a pastor. You have waited, and now your prayer is answered, and your waiting is terminated. Your Easter gladness is deepened as this ordination service is a reminder that the Lord has not forsaken His flock or overlooked you but given you a man to be your pastor.

But ordination is not so much the celebration of a goal achieved as it is an anticipation of what is to come. So the Apostle Paul says in our text: "Therefore, my beloved brothers, be steadfast, immovable, always abounding in the work of the Lord, knowing that in the Lord your labor is not in vain" (I Cor. 15:58). These words, dear Brother Jacob, anchor you and work the Lord is giving you to do in the promise of His resurrection.

These words come at the end of I Corinthians 15, the great "resurrection chapter" of the New Testament. Paul has reminded the Corinthians of the Gospel which he preached, and they received: "For I delivered to you as of first importance what I also received: that Christ died for our sins in accordance with the Scriptures, that he was buried, that he was raised on the third day in accordance with the Scriptures" (I Cor. 15:3–4). This is the content of apostolic preaching; this is the message proclaimed by Paul as the Word which has the power to save. But if Christ has not been raised, Paul is quick to add, this preaching is vain, and our faith is in vain for we are left in our sins, of all men to be most pitied for this life is futile, and the future is without hope. But in fact, Christ has been raised from the dead. He has appeared to Cephas and then to the twelve and more than 500 brethren and finally to Paul himself. Paul goes on for the rest of the chapter to extol the resurrection of Jesus Christ, the Second Adam, the first fruits of those who sleep. By His death, He has defeated death. Death is swallowed up in victory. Yes, sin gives death its sting—its ouch—and sin gets its potency from the law. But listen to Paul's doxology: "But thanks be to God, who gives us the victory through our Lord Jesus Christ."

It is God who gives us the victory through His Son put to death for sin and raised again to give life to all who trust in His name. That is the message, Jacob, you are ordained to preach. C.F.W. Walther, in his evening lectures to theological students, transcribed and published under the familiar title, *The Proper Distinction Between Law and Gospel*, reminded future pastors: "Remember when you become ministers, you become helpers of the Christians' joy" (407). That is a good reminder for you, Jacob. God is today giving good news, glad tidings of great joy to preach: forgiveness of sins for real sinners, life in the midst of death, and hope when the future is dark. It is all true on account of Jesus, the One who died for the sins of the whole world and whose resurrection declares God's righteousness for all.

You have been taught this Gospel. You believe it. Today you will confess it once again. Today you are ordained to preach. You will announce it week in and week out from the pulpit. You will declare it in the absolution. You will administer it as the Lord uses you as His mouth and hand to wash away sin in Holy Baptism. You will serve it to open and hungry mouths around this altar as you feed them with Jesus' body and give them to drink of the cup of the New Testament in His blood. You will speak it at bedside and before open graves. It is a word that will pass from your lip into the ears of catechumens young and old. It is a Word that will carry you outside the walls of this church to the streets, workplaces, and homes of this community. It is a Word you will speak in English, and perhaps in Spanish or German. But whatever the setting and whatever the language, it remains ever the good news of Good Friday and Easter, of our Brother and Redeemer put to death for our trespasses and raised again for our justification.

You will sustain the weak and the weary with this Gospel. But this Gospel that you are given to preach will sustain you. For you see, the empty tomb of Jesus is God's own guarantee that your future is opened to God's favor and mercy. The words of the Apostle Paul apply to you: "Be steadfast, immovable, always abounding in the work of the Lord, knowing that in the Lord, your labor is not in vain." By God's grace, you will make such promises to "be steadfast, immovable, always abounding in the work of the Lord" as you pledge yourself to the Holy Scriptures and the Ecumenical Creeds, and the Lutheran Confessions in few minutes. You will freely and willingly give yourself to the work of the ministry, promising to preach the Word in season and out of season, to demonstrate to the church a constant and ready ministry centered in the Gospel. Big promises indeed! So large and daunting that they should cause you to tremble a bit! You would be foolish to make them were it not for the promise of God that your labor in the Lord is not in vain.

The specific challenges that the coming days will bring we know not. But this much is sure: your labor will not be in vain because Jesus is raised from the dead never to die again. You, Jacob, are beginning a new chapter today. No longer just Jacob, but Pastor Gaugert ordained for a work that will not be void of pain and tears. Yes, the cross and death itself. But you already know the end of the story. When the church in Stuttgart, where Pastor Helmut Thielicke was bombed out during the air raids of the Second World War, Thielicke preached to those who were left saying, "He who has the victory of the last hour, can endure the next few minutes." We have the victory of the last hour. Jacob, you have the victory of the last hour for Christ is raised, and death has no dominion over him or over you. So in the confidence of His resurrection victory, go to the work of the ministry with confidence and joy. You have Christ's promise—and that is more than enough. Amen.

9

Installation of Rev. Jason Lane

Preach One Thing: The Wisdom of the Cross

I Corinthians 1:18–2:5

CELEBRATION LUTHERAN CHURCH, JACKSONVILLE, FL

Trinity XXIV / 14 November 2010

> "For I decided to know nothing among you except Jesus Christ and him crucified." (I Cor. 2:2)

The Lutheran theologian, Hermann Sasse, who knew a thing or two about the cross and suffering, once said that everything we do in the church must be sterilized by the theology of the cross. That was true for the Apostle Paul, who came to the culturally diverse seaport city of Corinth rampant with superstitious spirituality, prostitution, and immorality. It will be true for you, Pastor Lane, as you commence your service in the pastoral office here in Jacksonville, your own version of Corinth. God has put you here for the same reason that He sent Paul to Corinth—to preach a wisdom that is foreign to this and every human culture, the wisdom of the cross. That is, through the preaching of Jesus Christ crucified, that God wills to bring an end to all the empty and dead-ended ways that people try to rescue their own lives. Paul's singular message is, "For I decided to know nothing among you except Jesus Christ and him crucified."

Now that might not seem to fit your new pastor. He knows a whole lot! After all, in addition to a Masters of Divinity degree, he has a Masters of Sacred Theology from our seminary in Fort Wayne and has spent the last two years in Germany working on a doctorate. But the Apostle is not speaking here as though the strength of faith means lack of learning. Remember, Paul was a master of rhetoric, well-trained by his mentor, Rabbi Gamaliel. Knowing nothing but Jesus Christ and Him crucified does not mean that you have an empty brain but that every thought is taken captive to this Lord. It means to confess, as we do in the Catechism, that "I cannot by my own reason or strength believe in Jesus Christ my Lord or come to Him, but the Holy Spirit has called me by the Gospel."

Human reason is always active, trying to secure knowledge of God by speculation. It will not rest in its never-ending search to devise its own projects that it deems would satisfy God. This fleshly wisdom concludes that God will be pleased with me if I develop a godly attitude or if I exhibit a lifestyle that is moral. The mind of the old Adam is creative and restless, forever an activist. That is why it cannot but assess the wisdom of the cross to be foolishness. Puffed up in its own pride, the wisdom of this age dismisses God's work of salvation as an embarrassment.

Paul does not come to Corinth to out-smart the Corinthians. He does not come to make God more attractive to them. He comes to preach Christ, a stumbling block to the Jews and folly to the Greeks. It is not with high-blown philosophies or electrifying entertainment that the Apostle seeks to take captive the minds and hearts of his hearers but with the proclamation of the cross, that is, the announcement that God was in Christ reconciling the world to Himself through the blood of His Son. So Paul came to the Corinthians, he will say a bit later, not as a peddler of the Word of God but as man commissioned to speak of Christ Jesus and for Christ Jesus.

Paul's own destiny is tied up with the Word of Christ, a Word that will suffer rejection and scorn to be sure. But it is a Word that will not be bound even though Paul finally finds himself in shackles. It is a Word that will grow and triumph because it is the Word of the crucified and risen Lord, a Word that does not return to Him empty or void. It is the Word of the Cross!

It is on account of this Word of the cross that the Lord Jesus Christ established the office of the holy ministry on Easter evening. Risen from the dead, He comes to His men huddled together in fear, behind locked doors. He shows them the marks of the nails and the scare of the spear. He speaks His words of peace and breathes on them His Spirit. As the Father sent Him into the world to redeem the world by His death, so now He sends His apostles: "If you forgive the sins of any they are forgiven them; if you retain the sins of any they are retained." The redemption done on the cross will not stay back there on Golgotha. It is no good to us there on that "green hill far away." The redemption accomplished by Christ on the cross must be delivered. The cross must be preached for it is through this preaching that the faith which receives Christ's forgiveness is created. God does not leave His church without the office whose work it is to preach, that is to proclaim and distribute the Word of the cross.

We are here today to install the Reverend Jason Lane as pastor of Celebration Lutheran Church. That is, of course, a reason for rejoicing on the part of both the pastor-elect and the congregation. The man who will be your new pastor has devoted himself to years of study, over and beyond what is required for certification and ordination. He and his family have waited, anticipated, and prayed for this day. The Lord has answered their prayers by bringing them here. It is no less a day of thanksgiving for the people of Celebration Lutheran Church as you also waited on the Lord for the gift of a new shepherd. You have prayed that the Lord would send you an ambassador of the cross, a servant of His Word. Your prayers are answered.

Today Pastor and congregation will be bound together in and under the Word of the cross. That is why your pastor will confess his submission to the Holy Scriptures as the only infallible rule of faith and practice. He will confess his allegiance to the Book of Concord as a true and correct exposition of the Word of God, and promise to let all of his preaching, teaching, and practice be guided, shaped, and corrected by these Confessions. And you as a congregation will receive your pastor according to these solemn promises, pledging to uphold him with your prayers and honoring him as the shepherd and teacher placed over you in the Lord.

Paul came to the Corinthians according to his own testimony with no small amount of fear and trembling, but he came to that congregation in the confidence that he was put there by the Lord, the Lord's servant. No pastor in his right mind would begin his work without fear and trembling. After all, both pastor and congregation are launching out on a venture of which they cannot see the ending, facing paths and perils unknown to paraphrase and old collect of the church. Where the gospel is preached, there the holy cross will follow, Luther reminds us. What crosses are to be borne by pastor and congregation here, we do not know. But together, pastor and congregation press on toward the future in the confidence that Christ alone gives in the wisdom and the word of the cross. For His cross is the guarantee that He will never leave or forsake you. It is the sure and certain pledge that you are given with His body and blood of the forgiveness of your sins and with that the promise of the final victory.

"Preach one thing—the wisdom of the cross" that was Martin Luther's admonition in an early sermon. That is what the church is bidding you to do today, in this place, Pastor Lane. "For the word of the cross is folly to those who are perishing, but to us who are being saved it is the power of God." Amen.

10

25th Anniversary of Ordination for Rev. Timothy J. Mech

Of Angels and Pastors

St. Luke 10:17–20

TRINITY LUTHERAN CHURCH, SHEBOYGAN, WI

Saint Michael & All Angels / 28 September 2014

A few years ago, the German Old Testament scholar Claus Westermann wrote a little book under the title, *God's Angels Need No Wings*. God's angels are His messengers; they are those creatures created to do His will without ceasing. As the Book of Hebrews puts it, they are "ministering spirits sent out to serve for the sake of those who are to inherit salvation" (Heb. 1:14). This is reflected in Luther's morning and evening prayers, where we pray that God would let "His holy angel be with me, that the evil foe may have no power over me." While sometimes these celestial creatures do appear to human beings and some do have wings as the bright and shining seraphim of Isaiah 6, there is no indication that all angels have wings, and for the most part, they remain hidden, not visible to the human eye.

Now today, we are celebrating the festival of St. Michael and All Angels but also the 25th anniversary of a man called to be your pastor. You may say, well, Professor, we know Tim Mech and Tim Mech is no angel! And of course, in one sense, you would be right but not entirely so. In the Collect for this day in the church year, we prayed in thanksgiving that the Everlasting God has "ordained and constituted the service of angels and men in a wonderful order," acknowledging that God uses men called and ordained as His servants to do angelic work. What is this angelic work? It is proclaiming His saving Gospel, guarding and keeping His children with Jesus Christ in the one true faith.

The men that the Lord Jesus sent out in our Gospel reading got a taste of this work. The 72 Jesus sent out return to Him exuberant and excited at the results of their mission: "Even the demons are subject to us in your name." But Jesus has more to say: "I saw Satan fall like lightning from heaven. Behold I have given you authority to tread on serpents and scorpions and over all the power of the enemy, and nothing shall hurt you." But you have an even more profound confidence and a deeper reason for rejoicing. So Jesus says, "Do not rejoice that the spirits are subject to you, but rejoice that your names are written in heaven."

The 72 men sent out by the Lord were given angelic work to do. Without any luggage, they are sent into the harvest field as lambs among wolves with a message to announce: "The kingdom of God has come near." The Kingdom of God is where Jesus is reigning. The kingdom of God is where there is forgiveness of sins, life and salvation. God uses angels as His announcers. Think of Christmas when the angel announced to the shepherds huddled on the prairies around Bethlehem that to them "a Son is born, a Savior is given." That is the preaching of the Gospel. Fast forward to Easter morning when the angel uses the empty tomb as a pulpit and preaches to the women: "Do not be afraid, for I know that you seek Jesus who was crucified. He is not here, for he has risen" (Mt. 28:5–6). Angels proclaim not themselves but Jesus!

Angels rejoice not in their cosmic powers that enable them to subdue demons and shut down Satanic attack, but in Christ, who is their King. But we are given even more for Christ did not come to redeem angels with His blood but human beings. He came to suffer a bitter passion and die a sinner's death on the cross and the third day be raised from the dead that your name might be etched in heaven, inscribed in His Book of Eternal life. It is the mission of angels to proclaim that good news, to guard and keep Christ's holy people from Satan's destructive rage, and finally escort us into the heavenly kingdom.

There is a lot of misunderstanding of the work of angels today. Often we hear of a person speaking of a dead loved one as somebody who is now an angel. Scriptures nowhere teach this notion. Or perhaps angels are thought as fat little infants, with wings fluttering around in the heavenly regions as decorative objects in the celestial court. When the Scriptures picture the angels for us, they portray them as mighty servants of the living God anything but ethereal and unsubstantial. They are God's strong warriors who serve Him without sleeping day and night. They are His living messengers and guardians of His people.

Now all of this brings us to the connection of St. Michael and All Angels, and this 25th anniversary of the ordination of your pastor for God has indeed "ordained and constituted the ministry of men and angels in a wonderful order." Pastor Mech has been doing the work for an angel these last 25 years. Like the angel at Bethlehem, he has announced to you from this very pulpit the good news that you have a Savior; that the child born to Mary was given into the flesh for you. Like the angel in front of the Lord's empty tomb, Pastor Mech has stood by the graves of your loved ones and declared the good news of Jesus resurrection, saying, "Do not be afraid, because Jesus is raised from the dead, your loved one who died in Christ will live." Pastor Mech might not have wings, but time and time again, he has flown into your homes to guard you against the tricks and temptations of the devil, to fight for you with the sword of the Spirit, which is the Word of God, and to console you with God's promises. Like Michael in the Epistle from the Book of Revelation, your pastor wields the true testimony of Jesus Christ against that ancient serpent who accuses you, for the blood of the Lamb triumphs over all his evil works and ways and gives you peace.

Brother Tim, it is the work of an angel you have been doing these last 25 years. Indeed it is a wonderful privilege to be made a steward of the mysteries of God, a servant of His Word authorized to speak by His command and in His stead. Indeed as the Apostle says, "We have this ministry by the mercy of God." Today you, Darlene, and your family recall the awesome, angelic privilege that has been given to proclaim Christ Jesus and Him crucified over all these years.

And, dear congregation, you rejoice to receive such a faithful servant as one of God's own angel to the church here in Sheboygan. But all of us together have something even greater to rejoice in today. Listen again to the words of Jesus: "Rejoice that your names are written in heaven."

That is the great and everlasting gift of the Gospel. You are baptized in the name of the Father and of the Son and of the Holy Spirit. With that name given to you, you are a sheep in the flock of the Good Shepherd who laid down His life for you and with His blood purchased and won you as His own. You belong to Him, and there is no higher status, no greater identity than that you are a baptized child of God whose name is written in heaven. So today, pastors and people together, preachers and hearers of the Word of God are gathered around the Lord's altar with angels, and archangels, and all the company of heaven to receive the body and blood of God's Son for the forgiveness of our sins and the strengthening of our feeble faith.

Having so received the Lord's promise and tasted of His goodness in the forgiveness of our sins, we are not left standing here simply recalling or contemplating the past but instead, our eyes are fixed toward what is yet to come. So we press on together toward the life, work, and beauty that Christ yet has in store for us, praising the One who is the King of angels but our Brother and Savior Jesus Christ. Indeed, "he will command his angels concerning you to guard you in all your ways" (Psalm 91:11), for He has written your name in heaven. Amen.

The peace of God which passes all understanding keep your hearts and minds in Christ Jesus to life everlasting.

CHAPEL SERMONS FROM CONCORDIA THEOLOGICAL SEMINARY

11

Living in Light of the End

II Peter 3:11–18

TUESDAY IN ADVENT III / 14 DECEMBER 2010

Yesterday's reading from II Peter ended with verse 10, which also sets the stage for today's text. I'll read it again: "But the day of the Lord will come like a thief, and then the heavens will pass away with a roar, and the heavenly bodies will be burned up and dissolved, and the earth and the works that are done on it will be exposed."

The day of the Lord will come like a thief. If you have ever had your home broken into, if you have been a victim of robbery, you no doubt recall a sense of violation. The broken window, the smashed lock signals the entrance of one who unexpectedly makes a way into your space, wreaking havoc as he plunders through your possessions and claims them for himself. A thief deprives you of more than things; he deprives you of security. Living in a parsonage in Minneapolis, I slept soundly through an intruder breaking a window and climbing into the house. I didn't discover the presence of this fellow until stripped naked and ready to step into the shower, I noticed a telephone cord out of place, leading to the hands of the intruder. I'm not sure who was most shocked—him or me!

Surprise! Startled! Caught unaware and off guard. That is how the New Testament in general and II Peter in particular picture the day of the Lord's second advent. In light of the fact that Jesus will come like a thief and with His coming dissolve the things of creation, our text raises the question: What sort of people ought are we be in light

of these things? We are not told to protect ourselves against this invad-
ing thief. It is not a matter of installing a more effective alarm system,
hiring around the clock guards, putting up more sensitive motions
detectors, or stronger doors and impenetrable gates. The day of the
Lord is coming like a thief; no amount of preparation will prevent His
intrusion. There are no precautionary measures to keep Him at bay.

Instead, II Peter focuses on those whose lives will be overtaken
by this Divine Robber, speaking of the character of those who wait.
Advent is all about waiting. We've heard that theme echoed throughout this season. And we hear it again in our text as we are told to wait
as those whose lives are characterized by holiness and godliness, to
wait as those who are anticipating that coming day when the heavens
will be ignited and the stars and planets melted by cosmic flames.

The day of Lord coming as a thief will rob you of every creaturely
support that invites your trust. No earthly refuge will suffice. There is
no place to run, no crevice to hide from this Lord who comes to judge
the living and the dead. Instead, Peter speaks of our waiting for and
hastening the day of God, being diligent to be found in Him, without spot or blemish, and at peace. In his first epistle, Peter spoke of
Christ as the lamb without blemish or spot who has cleansed us with
His own blood (I Peter 1:19); now he speaks of our living without
blemish or spot. The only way to be ready for that great and coming
day of the Lord, that day which will rob you of all that you have, is to
have that one treasure which will not leave or forsake you as earthly
treasures fly. It is to have Christ Jesus. So Peter says, "Grow in the
grace and knowledge of our Lord and Savior Jesus Christ."

Peter's advent exhortation to us, then, is a call to trust in the Lamb
of salvation, to live in Him, not carried away, blown off course, losing
our stability by adhering to shaky and uncertain teachings, but standing in Christ's own righteousness as those who are dead to sin and
alive to God through faith. For the Christian in this fading world, it is
always Advent. In the evening of this perishing world, God calls us to
the stability of faith, to patient endurance that is not blown off course
by the deceits of Satan, the allurement of the world, or the weakness of
the flesh. We live with the recognition that the day of the Lord is coming, approaching like a thief who leaves you utterly defenseless. He will
take away all your treasures. But look at what He gives through His
blood: A new heavens and a new earth in which righteousness dwells.

Amen! Come, Lord Jesus, come! Amen.

12

Lutheran Leadership
Development Homily

Psalm 46

**MONDAY IN 2ND LAST WEEK OF CHURCH YEAR /
18 NOVEMBER 2019**

Our text today is a familiar one. It is the psalm that was the basis for Luther's hymn, "A Mighty Fortress." It is indeed an appropriate psalm for the End of the Church Year as we are reminded that before the Lord Jesus returns in glory there will be great distress among the nations and in nature itself. In yesterday's Gospel, we heard that "Nation will rise up against nation, and kingdom against kingdom" and that "there will be great earthquakes, and in various places famines and pestilences. And there will be terrors and great signs from heaven. . . . And there will be signs in sun and moon and stars, and on the earth distress of nations in perplexity because of the roaring of the sea and the waves" (Luke 21:10, 11, 25). Such is the picture of life painted in Psalm 46 as the chaotic powers of nature and bloody progress of history with its seemingly endless chapters of blood-thirsty violence swirl around us.

Both nature and history are marked by uncertainty. We know of the surprise that overtakes people when an earthquake strikes and the mountains come tumbling down and cities are reduced to rubble. Or think of how one day a sea is so calm and peaceful only to rage with a typhoon or a hurricane. The quiet and gentle breezes of a summer's day are stirred into a tornado or a destructive dust storm.

Rains come and a river overflows, flooding villages and flushing human beings underneath its currents to drown. This is the world in which we live. No wonder that Luther says that in this fallen creation, the sound of even a rustling leaf can terrify us.

History is something of a meat grinder. Greed and aggression are ever-present and they fuel wars. Tribe goes against tribe. Hostility erupts and blood flows in the streets and corpses litter the fields and the stench of death fills the air. The world itself is reduced to one large, stinking cemetery. The cries of the wounded and the lament of the grieving are perpetually heard.

In nature and history, mercy is not evident and hope is elusive. But it is against this backdrop where nothing is safe, that God's Word speaks. Remember, dear brothers, that this is a Word that will endure even when the flower fades and the grass withers. This is a Word that will remain when the chiefs, presidents, kings, and prime ministers lie in dust. What does His Word declare? Listen once again: "God is our refuge and strength, a very present help in trouble" (Ps. 46:1). Indeed He is that castle strong whose fortress walls enfold us and protect us against every enemy for eternity.

"Therefore we will not fear though the earth gives way, though the mountains be moved into the heart of the sea, though the waters roar and foam, though the mountains tremble at its swelling." We need not fear for the Lord has called us by name in our Baptism where the promise of Isaiah 43 is personalized: "But now thus says the LORD, he who created you, O Jacob, he who formed you. O Israel: 'Fear not, for I have redeemed you; I have called you by name, you are mine. When you pass through the waters, I will be with you; and through the rivers, they shall not overwhelm you'" (Is. 43:1–2).

This is true, for there is another river, not the muddy, turbulent raging river that sucks victims into a watery death but a life-giving stream that vivifies. It is the river whose streams make glad the city of God, the holy habitations of the Most High. This is the river that flows from the side of the One who says let all who thirst come unto me and promises that those who drink this water will be refreshed for eternity. This is the river that irrigates and enlivens the new Jerusalem that will never be overrun by enemies and consigned to destruction. It is the holy Christian church, the place where Emmanuel dwells with His people. "God is in the midst of her, she shall not be moved;

God will help her when morning dawns." That morning has already dawned; it is Easter. And you know what happened that Easter dawn. The Lord Jesus, who was crucified for our trespasses was raised again for justification. He lives never to die again.

Yes, "the nations rage, the kingdoms totter, but he (that is, the crucified and risen Lord) utters his voice, and the earth melts." His Word has authority over chaotic waves. He says, "peace, be still," and it is so. Even more, His Word has authority over your sin and death. He says, "your sins are forgiven you," and they are taken away and the oppressive kingdom of Satan is defeated.

This is Jesus. He is the Lord of hosts. He is our fortress, this God of Jacob. So the Psalmist invites you to come and see what He has done: "Come, behold the works of the LORD, how he has brought desolations on the earth. He makes wars cease to the end of the earth; he breaks the bow and shatters the spear; he burns the chariots with fire" (Ps. 46:8–9). This is the Lord Jesus Christ, the Prince of Peace! He does His alien work of breaking and hindering "every evil plan and purpose of the devil, the world, and our sinful nature, which do not want us to hallow God's name or let His kingdom come" so that He may do His proper work of strengthening us and keeping us firm in His Word and faith until we die. He is the Lord who has reconciled us to His Father, making peace by the blood of His cross. There is no certainty in nature or history, but His cross, His death for you, for your forgiveness, that is the truth that is certain in this old world of change and decay.

God has yet one more thing to say to you in this psalm: "Be still, and know that I am God. I will be exalted among the nations, I will be exalted in the earth" (Ps. 46:10). This being still is not silence so you can listen to your own inner voice, but the silence that gives space for the Word of God, for faith comes by hearing and what is heard is the word of the cross of Christ Jesus. He is the Lord of hosts. He is the God of Jacob, who is your fortress. Be still and know that His mercy surrounds you, and He will bring the good work which He began in you to completion at the Day of His coming. Amen.

13

A Meeting of Mothers

Luke 1:39–45

THE VISITATION / 31 MAY 2019

Mother's Day was celebrated on the second Sunday of this month, and predictably irate preachers took to Facebook complaining about the expectation of their congregations for this Sunday to be observed as a high holy day of the calendar. It is a good thing to honor our mothers, giving thanks to God for the First Article gift that they are. Pastors can easily include such petitions in the Prayer of the Church and make appropriate references in the sermon. Remembering our mothers on the second Sunday of May is not a bad thing, but the church has another "Mother's Day" and it is today, May 31, the Visitation.

Luke tells us of the meeting of two mothers. It was more than a "Mom's Morning Out." They are relatives but yet very different from one another. One of these mothers is young and unmarried. The other is a woman long married to Zechariah, the priest, who finds herself pregnant after years of barrenness in her old age. What did these two women who seem to be so very different from each other talk about? Did they share stories about their pregnancies? Did they talk about their fears or the way that being pregnant impacted their own bodies? Did they wonder out loud about the future of their respective children? Did Elizabeth, old and wise, give comfort and assurance to little Mary in a pregnancy that surely qualifies as unplanned? Luke doesn't tell us. Instead, he speaks of a spirited exchange of greeting and blessing that goes on between these two women and centers on the baby in Mary's womb.

Yesterday was Ascension. We heard of the Lord Christ going up with the sound of a trumpet far above all heavens that He might fill all things. The One who ascended is the God who condescended to be our Savior, born of a virgin. It is a happy coincidence that this year, the Visitation falls on the day after Ascension. While like the apostles in Acts 1, we are tempted to look up into the heavens, to pierce the clouds to find the Lord, they and we would be gazing at the wrong place. The Visitation pulls us back down to earth, drawing us toward His birth in the flesh. We're on the way to Advent on this day after Ascension.

Luther's Christmas preaching is strikingly earthly. Commenting on the *Magnificat*, Luther speaks of God's work in the womb of Mary as a work that is done in the depths: "Thus God's work and His eyes are in the depths, but man's only in the heights" (AE 21:301). Christmas wrecks all attempts to penetrate God's hiddenness and seek Him out in heaven. He comes to us, clothed in our humanity. In obscure Bethlehem, God demonstrates His favor for sinners "by stepping down so deep into flesh and blood" (AE 52:12). The eternal Word of the Father is made flesh to dwell among us. The incarnation is not a sign that points us to an absent deity but the Creator of all things now Himself a creature without ceasing to be Creator!

In the fullness of time, God did not send a book, an ethicist, a vision statement, a mission plan, a liturgy, a mystical experience, or a church; He sent the Word. He sent His Son the Word made flesh, born of woman. It is this Word carried in Mary's belly that evokes Elizabeth's Spirit-filled blessing: "Blessed are you among women, and blessed is the fruit of your womb!" Mary had her own marveling question of how it could be that she, a virgin, could conceive and give birth to a son. It was not an inquiry shaped by doubt and unbelief but arising from faith itself. Likewise, Elizabeth is caught up in amazement. She recognizes that she is in the presence of the One who will be born as her Lord. Also, even in his prenatal state, Elizabeth's yet unnamed son, who will be known as John the Baptist, leaps with joy at Mary's greeting, hinting at the fact that his life will be spent in preparing Immanuel's way, pointing to Him who is the Lamb of God who takes away the sins of the world. Like Mary, she too raises a question shaped by wonderment: "And why should it be granted to me to that the mother of my Lord should come to me?"

There is much blessing going on in this meeting of mothers. Mary is acclaimed as blessed. She has the singular blessing of carrying Jesus in her flesh. There is yet more. Elizabeth says, "And blessed is she who believed that there would be a fulfillment of what was spoken to her from the Lord." Mary heard the word of the Lord and believed it. So Mary becomes the model of faith for all Christians as Jesus says, "Blessed are those who hear the Word of God and keep it."

The visitation was a meeting of mothers, but in that convocation, the Lord Himself was preparing to visit His people to redeem them. That redemption He accomplished by the shedding of His blood, His innocent suffering and death for us, for the forgiveness of our sins. He visits us with that forgiveness here today in His words preached and with His body and blood given us to eat and drink. His ancient promises fulfilled. Redemption done and delivered. Blessing here not just for Mary but for you. Blessed are you who believe that there is fulfillment of what the Lord has spoken. Let it be to you as you believe. Amen.

14

Get Your Mind Out of the Grave

Colossians 3:5–17

TUESDAY IN EPIPHANY I / 13 JANUARY 2012

There is a new business opening in Seattle. It is not another Starbucks or micro-brewery. It is a body recomposing firm. Now, in addition to ground burial, entombment, or cremation, this firm is offering an environmentally-friendly and sustainable way of disposing of the corpse. The body is placed in a bin with moistened wood chips, aerated, and allowed to decompose. Afterward, the human compose may be returned to loved ones for use in a family garden or spread in a park.

In today's text, Paul also has the disposing of the body in mind. Of course, he is not talking about this physical body of flesh, blood, and bone but the body of sin that asserts itself in opposition against its Creator. Our text is part and parcel of a bigger piece of apostolic fabric that runs back to Chapter 2, where Paul writes of Christ in whom the fullness of the Godhead dwells bodily. It is into Him that you were baptized. This baptism, the apostle describes as a circumcision made without hands. So "having been buried with him in baptism, in whom you were raised through faith in the powerful working of God, who raised him from the dead." And there is more. Not only did God raise Jesus from the dead, He has also raised you who were dead in trespasses and the uncircumcision of the flesh, giving you the forgiveness of your sins. The argument continues in Chapter 3:1, "If then you have been raised with Christ, seek the things that are above, where Christ is, seated at the right hand of God."

Get your mind out of the grave! "For you have died, and your life is hidden with Christ in God" (Col. 3:3). When He makes His final Epiphany, He will appear not merely before the three magi but before all nations. Then every eye will see Him. And then at that awesome Epiphany, you too will appear with Him in glory. The way of death is plain: sexual immortality, the defilement of what God has declared good, the passions of a pornographic heart, evil cravings, and covetousness which is idolatry. Avoidance of these vices does not make you a Christian. But they contradict the life you are given in Christ because they contradict Him. Left to flourish, they deliver only condemnation, God's wrath. Put them away. Strip them off like you would a contaminated coat. Leave them buried in Christ's tomb. Don't go back to exhume the corpse that was buried in baptism.

Paul describes the old nature by moving from the outward acts of fornication to impurity of body and mind to the unbridled passions of the soul, evil desires of the heart, and the covetousness which would rob God of His Lordship. These form a lethal catalog not merely of an impaired morality but sin, which provokes God's wrath—His ultimate NO to both sin and sinner. These are the expressions of the way of death. "You once were living in them." Now you are to put them away. The anger, the wrath which inflames the soul. The malice of a warped heart articulated with a mouth given to malicious speech that cannot speak the truth but is, instead, a fountain of lewd language. We are shocked and offended by a certain foul-mouthed female cleric, "rock star" of another church body and rightly so. But the Word of the Lord doesn't leave us untouched. Your orthodoxy doesn't give you a pass when it comes to the Eighth Commandment. Last time, I checked this Commandment was still in force for theologians, too.

You did not so learn Christ! You are to be rid of these things. The old self calls good evil and evil good. The old self lives the lie, unable to recognize the truth about itself or the Creator. Put it off. Leave it in the grave for you have died with Christ in your Baptism and have been raised from the dead even now to walk before Him in righteousness and holiness.

So the Apostle turns from an exhortation against the habits of hell or what Thielicke calls the impulses of the Babylonian heart to the new life which you are given in Christ Jesus. He does not say that you are to strive and struggle so that one day sooner or later, you might attain to this new existence. Rather, he declares what is already the case: You have put on the new self. You have put on Christ. He is the express image of the unseen God, and in Him, you are being renewed. In Him, the divisions of ethnicity, nationality, economic status and any other marker people might use to define who they are come to an end. Christ crucified and raised from the dead is all and in all. And He is for you in every way.

The Christian life, you see, is more than prohibition; it is more than the eradication of evil. No, the Christian life is the existence of a new creature brought into being through the Word of the Gospel that announces the forgiveness of sins for the sake of Jesus, who was put to death for your sins and raised again for your justification. It is this same Gospel that carries with it the promise of the resurrection. So the Apostle bids us as God's chosen ones, already holy and beloved to put on compassionate hearts, kindness, humility, meekness, and patience. It is given us to bear with each other even as God in Christ has exercised unending patience with us. Forgiven by Christ, we cannot but forgive those who sin against us. Binding it all together is love, which preserves us in the harmony found only in Christ Jesus. It is His peace which has the last word, literally refereeing the heart. Risen from the dead, He says, "peace be with you," and that settles it. Only one thing left to do. Be thankful.

Thanks be to God through our Lord Jesus Christ for in Him you are dead to sin and alive to righteousness. Amen.

OCCASIONAL SERMONS

15

A Lament from the Ruins

Job 30:16–24

LCMS LIFE CONFERENCE, WASHINGTON, DC

Conversion of St. Paul / 23 January 2013

This evening's text from the Book of Job puts us with Job in the midst of the ruins, teaching us how to lament—that is, how to cry out to God. In a day when worship is judged effective and meaningful if it is upbeat, inspirational, celebratory, and positive, there is not much room for lament. It is far too negative, too depressing, to meet our refined taste for liturgies that are affirming, creative, and exciting. But where the church lacks the capacity for lament, a fragile human optimism replaces the hope which does not disappoint, and the praise of God becomes shallow and empty. In fact, we may even praise ourselves under the guise of adoring God.

We stand with Job tonight, who knows that God's judgment and wrath cannot be evaporated by wishing them away. We stand with Job, tossed about by a God who plays rough with His children to paraphrase Luther. We stand with Job, who does not explain away the hidden work of God—His inscrutable ways which, as Luther said, often appear as those of a mad axeman let loose in the forest, chopping and hacking way. We stand with Job, slimy and muddy in the mire of our sin, ourselves like him "dust and ashes" and bound for death. We grieve over a wrecked society where the murder of children is considered a fundamental human right, and the elimination of the injured or aged is thought to be an act of compassion. We stand with Job, whose complaint is not merely about faceless forces of evil, a decadent culture, a cancerous secularism, or corrupted enemies; His complaint is directed to the Almighty God who he says "has turned cruel to me." We stand with Job, who is not asking for an answer to the riddle of evil but for the Lord's salvation.

Hence Job's lament: "Yet does not one in a heap of ruins stretch out his hand, and in disaster cry for help?" We know, of course, something about life in the middle of devastation. The ruins among which we live, move, and have our being is not a bombed-out Dresden of crumbling, charred buildings but a land where death is regularly administered under the most clinical of conditions. In fact, the ruins are hailed as monuments of enlightened progressiveness. We may indeed reflect on how we have come to such a time as this, where the weakest of our neighbors are the most endangered. We may look for reasons for the shifts in morality, and the denial of truths once held to be self-evident. We might well look at strategies to recover and restore the recognition of human life inherent and God-given dignity. We may seek venues for teaching and advocacy. This is all well and good. But tonight we are not here for that. Tonight we are here to stand with Job, with outstretched hands praying in the midst of a disaster.

Our prayer, like that of Job, is nothing other than a lament. It is a protracted *Kyrie Elesion*! It is a plea for God's own mercy, His compassion. Lament might be described as prayer in those times when God leaves "the wound open" to use the words of Oswald Bayer. It is not a self-directed whine, but a prayer addressed to God Himself. Job's lament is not the whimper of one who sees himself victimized by society or circumstances but one who has a God-sized problem. Listen again to his lament: "God has cast me into the mire, and I have become like dust and ashes. . . . You (that is, God) have turned cruel to me; with the might of your hand you persecute me. You lift me up on the wind, you make me ride on it, and you toss me about in the roar of the storm. For I know that you will bring me to death and to the house appointed for all the living." Job's lament is directed to God, who is his judge, his critic, who stands by, gazing on his shame but does not act, at least not yet.

Like Job, we lament before the God who leaves the wound open. We lament before the God, who certainly has the power to bring an end to all that contradicts His will. We lament before a God who has the power to put down the mighty from their thrones, close abortion clinics, and reverse the hearts and minds of those who institutionalize evil. God instead leaves the wound open.

In the fullness of time, Job's lament was answered. The Redeemer whom Job confessed that he would see in his own flesh and with his own eyes has come into this ruined world where we live. The Book of Hebrews tells us that this Jesus, God's own Son, was given to lament: "In the days of his flesh, Jesus offered up prayers and supplications, with loud cries and tears, to him who was able to save him from death" (Heb. 5:7). This Jesus is the Word of God come in our flesh to bare our sin and be our Savior. He is God's own answer of grace and truth, of life and salvation through the forgiveness of sins to God's wrath, revealed from heaven against all unrighteousness. Jesus' wounds—His side split open by a Roman spear, and His nailed pierced hands and feet—are forever the foundation of our confidence to live in a world where God leaves the wound open.

In that confidence, we live and work, repenting of frustration and weak resignation. Bringing our exhaustion, unbelief, and fatigue to His cross, we have His promise: "Come unto me, all you who labor and are heavy laden, and I will give you rest." Resting in the wounds of this Jesus and alive in the hope which His resurrection guarantees, we stand in the midst of the ruins calling upon the Lord in this troublesome day, knowing that He will hear and He will hear and that our lament will be answered, "for the Lamb who is in the midst of the throne will be **our** shepherd and he will guide **us** to the springs of living waters, and God will wipe away every tear from **our** eyes."

The peace of God which passes all understanding keep your hearts and minds in Christ Jesus to life everlasting. Amen.

16

Service of Humiliation and Supplication

In the Light

I John 1:5–2:2

IMMANUEL LUTHERAN CHURCH, ALEXANDRIA, VA

March for Life (Pre-March service) / 22 January 2010

The Psalmist prayed, "Yea, though I walk through the valley of the shadow of death, I will fear no evil." We are living in a world where the shadow of death seems ever to lengthen, casting its cruel shade over public and private existence. Last week in Haiti, an earthquake shattered the land, causing buildings to crumble down, delivering death to thousands or even hundreds of thousands, a grime reminder that nature itself groans in travail under the burden of our sin. Even as we are here this morning, the suffering that continues there is immeasurable, beyond calculation. We recoil in horror over the immensity of the casualties in Haiti. However, we cannot forget that whatever the body count from that devastating earthquake finally totals, it will still not come near the tally of the unborn whose lives ended not in a collapsing building but in a clinic in the nearly four decades since the passing of Roe v. Wade.

Add to that the way human bodies are treated as playthings to be quietly and efficiently disposed of once they are broken or have outlived their usefulness, and we perceive that deep darkness indeed has descended on our land. Marriage as a life-long, one-flesh union between man and woman is seen as antiquated as homosexuality, once barely mentionable, is now openly extolled and celebrated. Luther said that a theologian of the cross calls a thing what it is, yet our culture's theologians of glory call good evil and evil good. We call darkness light and light darkness.

In such an environment, it is easier than we recognize to accommodate ourselves to the darkness. I'm told that trout swimming in deep caverns never venturing in streams above ground finally become blind, their vision adjusted to their lightless waters. So too perhaps our spiritual sight becomes dim as the eyes of the soul can no longer distinguish between light and darkness. Like the subterranean trout, we become at home in the pitch black of our cultural darkness, so everything becomes a drab and dull shade of gray. Like the Pharisees, shocked and offended by our Lord's healing of the man born blind in John 9, we claim to have perfect vision, and yet we have become blind, insensitive to the light of God, which exposes the darkness of sin.

The darkness of which the Apostle John writes is more than the sum total of your misdeeds. It is more than the sins of abortion and euthanasia. It is more than the lusts of eyes and heart. It is more than our weak resignation to the evils we deplore. It is the inborn darkness of the human heart. It is what Luther identified as the primal sin from which every other sin is given birth and vitality. It is the sin against the First Commandment; the failure to fear, love and trust in God above all things. It is the unwillingness to let God be God. Like our first parents, we retreat into the shadows. We foolishly try to hide from the One who is Light Eternal. We fantasize that there is safety and security in the darkness, for there, we reason, we can take cover and live as though God did not matter and I mattered most, to paraphrase one of our confessional prayers.

The root of the problem is that we think we are more reliable, more trustworthy than God Himself. I don't know if God can be trusted, but I can trust myself. Pro-choice is not just a political slogan; it describes the old Adam. We are all pro-choice! We insist on having our say, making our choice, and exercising our free will. We might be persuaded to deliver our lives into God's hands, but God's absolute insistence that He is God in all that He does rob us of the freedom to do things our way. Instead, we are bound and determined to make a god that we can live with, a tamed deity who knows his place and will not interfere with our precious freedom. That is darkness.

No wonder that the atheistic philosopher Jean-Paul Satre once said that even if we knew the biblical God to exist, we would have to pretend He did not exist in order to be free in the way we think we want to be free! Despising the One who spoke calling light out of darkness, we want to be free to create our own light. Yet the more enlightened we become with self-knowledge, the more dreary and dark human life becomes. To paraphrase an earlier philosopher, if we are our own creator, there is nothing to stop us from becoming our own angel of death.

There is a temptation for us here today. We might quickly conclude that the darkness is only out there in this culture of death, only out there in this God-forsaking world. We may comfort ourselves that the darkness is out there in abortion clinics or court chambers where human laws seemingly displace divine commandments. The darkness is with those benighted physicians who use the gifts of medicine to destroy life rather than to provide care and healing.

Certainly, the Word of God calls for repentance from all who practice these deeds of darkness. But there is more. You are called to repent. We are called to repent. Listen again to the Apostle: "If we say we have no sin, we deceive ourselves and the truth is not in us." God calls us to repent of our failure to speak and act on behalf of the weak and helpless who cannot speak or defend themselves. He calls us to repent of our readiness to attempt a truce with the darkness; an easy accommodation to that which God abhors. But there is yet more. God also calls us to repent of our self-righteousness—a zeal in the rightness of our cause that too easily turns into a form of self-justification. "We are not like left-wing politicians and abortionists! Therefore God must be favorably impressed with me."

We are not saved by our ethics. Our morality does not bring us to bask in the radiance of holy light. There is no salvation in virtue, no matter how upright or enlightened it may be. There is only One whose blood cleanses us from all sin. His name is Jesus. He is the Light of the world, the light that has come into the world—the light that shines in the darkness of the world and yet is not overcome or extinguished by it.

Today is a day of humiliation and supplication, but it is not a day of gloomy darkness for our Lord's Epiphany beams on us. The heavenly star has guided us to the manger so that the words of the Prophet Isaiah are true of us: "The people who walked in darkness have seen a great light; those who dwelt in a land of deep darkness, on them has light shone" (Is. 9:2). I am here today and authorized to announce to you that this Jesus is the propitiation for your sin by His death on Calvary, and He forgives you all your sins by His blood, blood that He gives you to drink in the cup of His New Testament.

So walk in the light of His Word. Walk in the confidence that the Sun of Righteousness has dawned on us: This is the message we have heard from him and proclaim to you, that God is light, and in him there is no darkness at all. Amen.

17

Dedication of
University Lutheran Chapel

More Than Brick and Mortar

Ephesians 2:19–22

MINNEAPOLIS, MN

Trinity XII / 8 September 2019

"He who goes out weeping, bearing the seed for sowing, shall come home with shouts of joy, bringing his sheaves with him," so said the Psalmist in Psalm 126. We can't help recall today the tears when over seven years ago, this congregation was evicted from a building that had sheltered it for over fifty years. The Lord's people have endured longer exiles throughout history, but seven years is still a long time to live and wait with uncertainties and delays. But today, we can look back with thanksgiving that God has brought us to this hour and this place. He has given University Lutheran Chapel a building of its own. It is with profound thanksgiving today that we receive this building as a gift from God's hand. But in doing so, we also confess that we have never been homeless.

When you left the old building, there were no guarantees that you would have a new building or even that the congregation would hold together. God never promised that you would have a new building. But He did make a promise by which you have lived. He promised that He would never leave or forsake you. Jesus Himself made a promise to His disciples on the eve of His crucifixion that extends to you: "I will not leave you as orphans." You were without a building but never homeless.

So the Apostle Paul reminds us in our text from Ephesians. Being church, the Lord's own people has nothing to do with whether or not you possess a building. That old and now demolished chapel at 1101 University Avenue was never really our home. And this sparkling new building, one day, will also crumble into dust unless the Lord returns first. We sang of that in the hymn a few minutes ago:

> Built on the Rock, the Church shall stand
> Even when steeples are falling,
> Crumbled have spires in every land;
> Bells still are chiming and calling.
> Calling the young and the old to rest,
> But above all souls distressed,
> Longing for rest everlasting. (645:1 LSB)

We are members of the household of God. Washed by the Spirit in water and the Word, we are born anew into the Body of Christ. Our head, Jesus Christ, is risen from the dead, never to die again. His future is our future. Because His Word endures forever, so shall the church, His body, which is a creature of that Word. Those who belong to Jesus Christ are never without a home. Where His Gospel is preached, His Baptism administered, and His body and blood are distributed, there is His holy church.

You were without a building to call your own, but you were never homeless. Paul puts it like this: "You are no longer strangers and sojourners, but you are fellow citizens with the saints and members of the household of God, built upon the foundation of apostles and prophets with Jesus Christ himself being the cornerstone."

Paul draws some striking contrasts as he paints a picture of what we were apart from Christ and who we now are in the second half of Ephesians 2. We were "in the flesh" (2:11); now, we are "in the Lord . . . in the Spirit" (2:21–22). We were "separated from Christ" (2:12); now, we are "built on . . . Christ" (2:20). We were "alienated from the commonwealth of Israel" (2:12); now, we are "fellow citizens with the saints" (2:19). We were "strangers . . . and sojourners"

(2:12, 19); now, we are "members of the household of God" (2:19). We were "without God" (2:12); now, we have "access . . . to the Father" (2:18). We were "far off" (2:13, 17); now, we are "near" (2:13, 17). We were held in "hostility," and now, we have "peace" (2:14–17). We were living with a "dividing wall of hostility" (2:14) that imprisoned us in sin and death; now, we are "joined together . . . a holy temple" (2:21).

All that Paul says of the church is true only on account of Christ! By the blood of Christ, you have been purchased and won to be His own and live under Him in His kingdom and serve Him in everlasting righteousness, innocence, and blessedness. That redeeming work of Christ does not lie back there dormant in the distant past of history. It must be proclaimed. There needs to be a preacher who comes and proclaims that this Jesus is for you. Take away the "for you," and there is no Gospel. Where this Gospel of Jesus "for you" is proclaimed, there the Spirit is calling, gathering, and sanctifying a holy Christian people for Himself. That preaching, of course, can be done in a grove of trees in the wilderness, a storefront, barn, or garage. To paraphrase Luther in the Large Catechism, the place does not make the Word holy, but the Holy Word makes the place holy.

This beautiful chapel, which today we receive as a gift of the Triune God, is made holy by the Holy Gospel of Jesus Christ, which will be proclaimed here in sermon and sacrament. When Martin Luther preached a sermon for the dedication of the Torgau Chapel in 1545, he said, "Let nothing else happen here but that our dear Lord Jesus Christ speak to us in His Word and we answer Him in prayer and praise." God speaks, and His words bestow what they promise, and we confess Him as the Lord that He is. It is in and through His words received through prophets and apostles that His household lives from a solid foundation with Jesus Himself being the cornerstone.

Today we give thanks to God that a long, sometimes painful, and arduous exile is over. University Lutheran Chapel once again has a place where God's Word might be preached, and His sacraments administered. The glory is not unto us but Him, who is the Giver and Donor of every good and perfect gift. In his lectures on Psalm 82 from 1530, Luther noted that benefactors can build magnificent churches, but there is something even greater. Luther says:

To support and protect a poor, pious pastor is an act that makes no show and looks like a small thing. But to build a marble church, to give it gold ornaments, and serve dead stone and wood—that makes a show that glitters! That is a virtue worthy of a king or a prince! Well, let it make its show! Let it glitter. Meanwhile my pastor, who does not glitter, is practicing the virtue that increases God's kingdom, fills heaven with saints, plunders hell, robs the devil, wards off death, represses sin, instructs and comforts every man in the world according to his station in life, preserves peace and unity, raises fine young folk, and paints all kinds of virtue in the people. In a word, he is making a new world! He builds not a poor temporary house, but an eternal and beautiful Paradise, in which God is glad to dwell. (AE 13:52–53)

This is a house for the glory of the Lord. That downward glory of God, the glory of the Word made flesh, is pleased to dwell among us as His promise is preached. Through this ministry, the Lord Jesus is here present to build something greater than this new chapel. He is here to make of us a dwelling of God in the Spirit that will endure to eternity. For that indescribable gift, we give thanks this day.

"Now to him who is able to keep you from falling and to present you without blemish before the presence of his glory with rejoicing, to the only God, our Savior through Jesus Christ our Lord, be glory, majesty, dominion, and authority, before all time and now and for ever. Amen" (Jude 24–25 RSV).

18

A Good Confession and a Good Fight

I Timothy 6:11–16

LCMS LIFE CONFERENCE, CRYSTAL CITY, VA

St. Timothy, Pastor & Confessor / 24 January 2015

Back in 1936, living in the shadow of Nazism, Hermann Sasse wrote, "We come out of a time in which the Church was understood as a place of rest in a restless world" (*Witness*, 195). He noted that Christians of the previous generation had forgotten Jesus' words that He had "not come to bring peace, but a sword" (Mt. 10:34). Instead, Sasse asserted, "They wanted to have the peace of Christ without the harsh war he orders us to enter. They wanted a church where they could save their souls and live undisturbed by the noise of the world. But thereby, they forgot the deep peace that the Redeemer of the world alone can give us, and they forgot the real Church" (*Witness*, 196).

What Sasse said so many years ago still rings true today, perhaps even more so as now we clearly find ourselves on a battlefield. No longer does the Christian church enjoy a privileged place in North America. We are all too familiar with the ways that the presence of Christianity is marginalized, long-honored virtues dismissed, and religious conviction sequestered to the realm of a private and even toxic sentiment. A few years ago, it was popular to speak of the culture wars. But the conflict in which our Lord calls us to be engaged is deeper and more deadly than a clash of cultures. It is, as the Apostle says in Ephesians 6, a wrestling match not between flesh and blood, but against the rulers, against the authorities, against the cosmic powers over the present forces of evil in the heavenly places. It is to this battle that Timothy, "the man of God," is called to stand and to fight as a "good soldier of Christ Jesus."

As he had done in Ephesians 6, also in the Pastoral Epistles, Paul uses this military imagery. He is, Luther says, like a pious field commander addressing soldiers in battle admonishing them to be bold, courageous and confident. So Timothy is exhorted to lay aside every entangling sin that would ensnare and drag him into certain destruction, to be content and not glued by greed to the riches of this world. Instead, he is exhorted to pursue righteousness, godliness, faith, love, steadfastness, and gentleness. These are the weaponry of our warfare. Timothy is to lay hold of the eternal life to which He was called through the Gospel and confessed before the presence of many witnesses. Only in this confession can he fight the good fight of the faith. And it is only in this confession that you can fight the good fight of the faith.

This "good confession" was made by our Lord Jesus Christ before Pontius Pilate when He did not deny but confessed that He is the King whose kingdom is not of this world. A "good confession" is never made up, never merely the assertion of a subjective theological opinion; it is a speaking back to God and to the world the words which the Lord Himself has spoken to us. There is gravity, a weightiness to this confession for it is made *coram deo*, in the presence of God. The auditor of this confession is not just the ears of other people but of the living God Himself. So the question is not what will the world think or how will our unyielding stance be evaluated by the media, but what will the Lord who judges the living and dead hear from your lips? "Whoever confesses Me before men," Jesus says, "I will also confess before My Father who is in heaven. But whoever denies Me before men, I will also deny before My Father who is in heaven" (Mt. 10:32–33 NKJV).

Such confession is always a matter of the First Commandment. Will you fear, love, and trust in God above all things? To cling to the First Commandment is to invite conflict and attack, for even though there is but one true God—Father, Son, and Holy Spirit—there are gods and lords aplenty in this old dying world that vie to have you aligned with them, fearing, loving, and trusting in them rather than the Son of the Father, who was crucified for your sins and raised again for your justification.

Paul does not leave Timothy or you without comfort and consolation in our text. His words are far more than a rallying of the troops with a harangue to incite them to face the battle unflinchingly. Paul's exhortation is spoken against this eschatological horizon: "The appearing of our Lord Jesus Christ, which he will display at the proper time." He is the King of kings and Lord of Lords. He alone is the possessor of immortality. Light of Light, He is, and the darkness has not and will not overcome Him. This is to say that the outcome of this war is not in doubt for the Lord, who will come on what Luther called that dear Last Day, has already won the victory by His dying and rising. He has already purchased and won you with His precious blood and innocent suffering and death that as the Catechism confesses, you might live under Him in His kingdom and serve Him in everlasting righteousness, innocence, and blessedness even as He is risen from the dead and lives and reigns to all eternity. Amen.

19

Reformation Sunday

An Eternal Gospel to Proclaim

Revelation 14:6–7

**CIRCUIT REFORMATION SERVICE AT
GRACE LUTHERAN CHURCH, NAPLES, FL**

Reformation Sunday / 26 October 2014

We are here today to do what Lutherans have done for generations, that is, celebrate the Reformation of the church, which a 33-year-old priest ignited on October 31, 1517, when he tacked his 95 Theses to the door of the Castle Church in Wittenberg. Of course, whether you are a Christian or not, you can't escape the significance of the Reformation. It is an important chapter in western history; yes, in world history. The Lutheran theologian of the last century, Hermann Sasse, in his important book, *Here We Stand*, suggested that there are three inadequate interpretations of the Reformation. First, there is a **heroic interpretation** of the Reformation. In this view, Luther is regarded as a hero in much the same way as a George Washington or an Abraham Lincoln might be viewed. Focus is here placed on Luther's character, traits, inner struggles and personality. Second, there is what Sasse calls the **cultural-historical interpretation** of the Reformation. Here the Reformation is understood as a movement of liberation, a turn from the unenlightened darkness of the medieval world full of suppression and superstition to the bright dawn of a new world marked by the power of the intellect and the freedom of the individual. Third, there is the **nationalist interpretation** of the Reformation, and as you might imagine, this was quite popular in Germany, especially in the years leading up to the 400th anniversary of the Reformation in 1917. Here Luther is portrayed as the German Reformer who defied a Pope in distant Rome and a Spanish emperor, Charles V, to assert a German church with Bible and liturgy in the German language. Here Luther and the Reformation became a symbol of German identity and independence.

Now, Sasse tells us that each of these views the Reformation is inadequate. And he is right. The fourth view says Sasse is the correct view, and that is the understanding that the Reformation is an episode in the history of the one holy Christian and apostolic church. That is why we adorn the chancel with red paraments, and the pastors are wearing red stoles today. Red is the color of Pentecost, the festival of the Holy Spirit who calls, gathers, and enlightens a holy Christian people for Christ Jesus through the Gospel which forgives sin. The Reformation is an episode in the history of the church. We call it Reformation for the church was deformed by false and misleading teachings which were embodied in errant practices making Christ's holy bride almost unrecognizable under the papacy. This young Wittenberg professor spotted pastoral malpractice in the Roman church, and he sought to argue the case on behalf of Christian people living under the burden of demands which they could not fulfill by their own spiritual power. Luther was not about creating a new church, but restoring the Gospel to the church so that genuine repentance and true faith might be preached among every nation, tribe, language, and people might be brought to worship God as He wills to be worshipped in Christ Jesus.

That brings us to our text from Revelation 14:6–7 as John the Seer reports that he saw an angel flying overhead with an eternal gospel to proclaim to those who dwell on the earth. This was the text that Pastor Johannes Bugenhagen used in the funeral sermon at Luther's burial in 1546 where the preacher identified Luther as that angel who carried this "powerful, blessed, divine teaching" which would continue to live, overthrowing the Babylon of the pope's church (Brecht III:379). Well, the Gospel which Luther did preach was nothing other than that one eternal Gospel, which is the power of God unto the salvation of all who believe.

There is only one Gospel, and that is the good news that God was in Christ reconciling the world to Himself, not counting the trespasses of sinners against them but on account of the atoning work of the Son of God, setting sinners free from condemnation by the Word which forgives sins. It is that Word and that Word alone that Luther confessed and fought for in every aspect of His Reformation work. It is the Word of the Gospel, the Word of the Cross, the Word by which I became and remain a Christian as Luther put it.

Luther's confidence and our confidence is the Word of Christ, this eternal Gospel. In the early days of Lent in 1522, Luther came out of hiding in the Wartburg Castle to return to the pulpit in Wittenberg to rescue the Reformation from those whose fanaticism would turn it in a chaotic revolution. And it was on that occasion, Luther would confidently preach: "I simply taught, preached, and wrote God's Word; otherwise, I did nothing. And while I slept [cf. Mark 4:26–29], or drank Wittenberg beer with my friends Philip and Amsdorf, the Word so greatly weakened the papacy that no prince or emperor ever inflicted such loss upon it. I did nothing; the Word did everything" (AE 51:77).

Luther, like the Apostle Paul before him, knew that the Word of the Lord was not chained up or fettered but was living, loose and active. Luther knew and trusted in the promise of the Lord recorded in Isaiah 55: "For as the rain and the snow come down from heaven and do not return there but water the earth, making it bring forth and sprout, giving seed to the sower and bread to the eater, so shall my word be that goes out from my mouth; it shall not return to me empty, but it shall accomplish that which I purpose, and shall succeed in the thing for which I sent it" (Is. 55:10–11). God's Word is packed with the Lord's own power. It says what it does and does what it says because it is His Word, this eternal Gospel.

Jesus says that the heavens and earth will pass away, but my words will not pass away. So the slogan, *Verbum Domini Manet in Aeternum*, "The Word of the Lord endures forever" became a battle cry of the Reformation. Nations come and go. Princes rise up and fade away. But the Word of God remains. It is an anvil that hath worn out many a hammer, said one wise Christian. Persecutions ancient and contemporary have not been able to snuff it out. "Crumbled have spires in every land," we sing in that fine old Danish hymn, but the Church of Jesus Christ is kept secure in the eternal Gospel, which never loses its newness.

This eternal gospel has a history. It was promised to our first parents after the fall, proclaimed by the prophets, and in the fullness of time, it was fulfilled as the Incarnate Word suffered and died under Pontus Pilate for our trespasses and raised again on the third day for our justification. This eternal gospel was preached by the apostles, confessed by the creeds, and when it had been dimmed and diminished by human notions of salvation by works, it was restored to the church by the Lord through His servant, Martin Luther, who shouted where others merely mumbled, to paraphrase church historian Mark Noll. In season and out of season, this eternal gospel has a history.

Yes, humanly speaking, these present days might appear dark and threatening for God's flock. Luther once warned his dear Germans that the Gospel is like a summer rain shower. Therefore we are to be eager to hear Jesus' words while they are proclaimed in our midst. The Prophet Amos warns of a famine of the Word of God when through man's persistent rejection, God lets His Word move on to other places. There are places mentioned in the New Testament where once there were Christian congregations alive and thriving, but if you go there today, you will find none. Think also of the majestic European cathedrals, which today are nearly empty on a typical Sunday. Do you realize that on any given Sunday, more people are attending Lutheran Services in Africa then there are in all of North America and Europe combined? The eternal Gospel moves on!

Where this eternal gospel is received as God's own announcement that the ungodly are justified not by works of the law but by the atoning death of Jesus now received by faith alone, there is the true worship of God of which the angel speaks. There the Living God, the Maker of heaven and earth, the One who is the source of the vast oceans and bubbling little springs, is feared, loved, and trusted above all things. That is the true worship which, by God's grace, Luther restored to a deformed church so badly in need of reformation. In this worship, human beings do not seek to placate a holy God with the idolatry of their own sacrifices but learn rather to receive God's favor as He bestows it in His preached Word, in the waters of Baptism, and with His body and blood. That is why our confessions call faith the highest and holiest worship of God for faith looks to Christ alone for forgiveness of sins, comfort now in this life of suffering, and peace in that kingdom which is yet to come.

So we celebrate this Reformation Sunday not with a nostalgic recollection of a great and heroic man named Martin Luther or as a marker of a turning point in western civilization, or as a reminder of our German heritage. No, we celebrate this Reformation Sunday by repenting of our unbelief, confessing our slowness to treasure God's Word, and by faith laying hold of the eternal gospel which Luther preached, for in it, we have the forgiveness of our sins and peace with God now and forever. Amen.

20

Mission Festival

The Feast the Lord Has Prepared

St. Matthew 22:1–14

TRINITY LUTHERAN CHURCH, NORBORNE, MO

Trinity XX / 13 October 2013

The Lutheran theologian of the last century, Werner Elert, said, "Some live in the light of the Last Day, others in its shadow" (*The Last Things*, 28). That could well be the caption for the Gospel reading from Matthew 22, the parable of the wedding feast. Jesus compares the kingdom of heaven to King, who spared no expense in preparing a wedding dinner for his son. The fatted calves were killed, and his oxen were slaughtered. The meat was roasted, the tables were set. Only one thing was lacking—the guests.

The messengers are sent out into the village to announce to those who had been invited that dinner was ready. Don't delay; supper is going to get cold. The table is set. Come to the hall, for now is the time for eating and drinking. Now is the hour of celebration and song. But those invited did not come. They didn't even have the courtesy to send their regrets. They mocked the generosity and hospitality of their king by ignoring the invitation. In fact, to add insult to injury, they showed their hatred of the king by killing the servants who were sent out with the invitation. Theirs is no polite rejection to come to the royal wedding; it is the hostility that cannot tolerate the king. If they can't kill him, at least they will show him their hatred by the shameless and murderous way they treat his servants.

But the spiteful rejection of the king's invitation does not stop him. He wills to have a full house at his son's wedding, so servants are dispatched into the highways and out through the alleys with the commission to gather as many as they can find. All who will hear are invited, the good and the bad. The party will go on. The father's lavish generosity will not be wasted. There will be guests who sit at table and feast from the abundance of the king's provisions. His son will have a marriage feast.

Now the Lord Jesus Christ plainly tells us that this parable illustrates what the kingdom of heaven is, the kingdom that His Father has prepared for sinners. This is the first thing we should note in our Lord's teaching today. The kingdom is prepared not by human beings but by the Father. Martin Luther would put it like this: "The kingdom is not in the process of preparation but was prepared before, and the sons of the kingdom do not prepare the kingdom, but are in the process of being prepared themselves; that is, the kingdom merits the sons, not the sons the kingdom" (*The Bondage of the Will*, 182–183). The Father has prepared the kingdom; we do not build it or prepare it ourselves.

The Lord has prepared this kingdom for us from all eternity, and He established it in time by sending His Son to suffer and die in your place and then on the third day, be raised from the dead never to die again. This is the kingdom for which we pray when we say "Thy kingdom come" in the Lord's Prayer. Remember the words of the Catechism: "The kingdom of God certainly comes by itself without our prayer, but we pray in this petition that it may come to us also." Then the Catechism goes on to answer the question "How does God's kingdom come?" in this way: "God's kingdom comes when our heavenly Father gives us His Holy Spirit, so that by His grace we believe His holy Word and lead godly lives here in time and there in eternity."

God has prepared this kingdom for all the sons and daughters of Adam and Eve by sending His only Son into the world to be our Brother and Savior. You know those familiar words of John 3:16, "For God so loved the world, that he gave his only Son, that whoever believes in him should not perish but have eternal life." None were excluded. The blood of Jesus Christ was shed for all. That is the basis for mission. The Lord now sends His servants into all the world to call and gather not only those who were first invited—the Jews who rejected their Messiah but also the Gentiles—to the marriage feast. The kingdom is prepared, and so the invitation goes out into all the world. As Luther put it, the Gospel and Baptism must traverse the world. The message is ever the same. In the midst of the crumbling and decay of all the kingdoms of this world, in the face of government shutdowns and economic collapse, we are receiving a kingdom that cannot be shaken. We can sing with confidence the words of our Reformation hymn: "And take they our life, goods, fame, child, and wife, though these all be gone, our victory has been won; The kingdom ours remaineth."

We engage in mission because the Gospel is universal; that is, it shows forth God's unmerited favor in the blood of Christ for each and every human being. It is the good news that while we were still sinners, Christ died for us. While we were yet ungrateful enemies, God was in Christ reconciling us to Himself by the blood of His cross, His innocent suffering and death.

We engage in mission because the Gospel is omnipotent, all-powerful. It is the power—literally the dynamite—of God for the salvation of all who believe, as the Apostle testifies in Romans 1:16. The Word of the Lord that goes forth from His mouth does not return to Him empty but accomplishes the purpose for which He sent it.

Weddings are times for joy and festivity as family and friends come together to celebrate that a man and a woman are embracing each other in love, embarking on the life of being one flesh together until death separates them. It is indeed a once in a lifetime situation, and that is why parents spend so much money to have a memorable reception when children get married. So it was with the father in our parable. Yet there is a cloud of deep sadness that hangs over this parable. Those who were invited to delight in the lavish hospitality of the king would not come. They reject his generosity and go so far as to shamelessly slaughter the servants who bear the royal invitation.

There is yet more sadness in the final turn of Jesus' parable. One who is invited to the feast shows up but insults the host by not being clothed with a wedding garment. This guest treats the meal as ordinary and seeks to enjoy it on his own terms. He takes the generosity of the king for granted, and he is bound hand and foot and cast out into the place not of festivity and joy but the pit of weeping and gnashing of teeth, the place of outer darkness. That is hell, the kingdom of Satan. Hence the Lord's stern warning that even though the kingdom is prepared, one through unbelief can reject it and be left only with eternal condemnation. Indeed some do live not in the light of the Last Day, but its shadow!

This Mission Sunday reminds us that the Gospel is not static. It does not stay put. Luther once warned his dear Germans that the Gospel is like a summer rain shower. Therefore we are to be eager to hear Jesus' words while they are proclaimed in our midst. The Prophet Amos warns of a famine of the Word of God when through man's persistent rejection, God lets His Word move on to other places. There are places mentioned in the New Testament where once there were Christian congregations alive and thriving, but if you go there today, you will find none. Think also of the majestic European cathedrals, which today are nearly empty on a typical Sunday. Do you realize that on any given Sunday, more people are attending Lutheran Services in Africa then there are in all of North America and Europe combined? The Gospel moves on!

The Lord would have His wedding feast full, so today He sends His servants out into all the world to baptize and teach that many may be drawn to the wedding feast of the Lamb in His kingdom, clothed in the righteousness of Christ alone. Thanks be to God that His invitation has come to us. May He grant unto us all ears to hear, hearts to believe, and tongues to confess Him that by His grace we, too, might be found part of that great multitude, which no one can number, from every nation, tribe, and language gathered around the Lamb extolling Him alone. Even now, we live in the Light, not the shadow of the Last Day, and so we say: "Amen! Blessing and glory and wisdom and thanksgiving and honor and power and might be to our God forever and ever! Amen" (Rev. 7:12). Amen.

21

Ash Wednesday

Have Mercy on Me, O God

Psalm 51

ST. PAUL LUTHERAN CHURCH, PRETORIA, SOUTH AFRICA

Ash Wednesday / 1 March 2017

Poets and philosophers throughout the ages have given humanity the counsel, "Know yourself." Ash Wednesday is, in fact, about knowing yourself. But the knowledge of self that God would impart to you today is much deeper, more radical—knowledge that comes from introspection. Martin Luther, in his commentary on Psalm 51, observes that this psalm gives us two things: (1) a knowledge of self; and (2) a knowledge of God. The two always must go together. Luther remarks that if we have a knowledge of self without the knowledge of God, we would be left in despair. And on the other hand, if we would have a knowledge of God without the knowledge of self, we would end up with an arrogant presumption. God gives us the knowledge of ourselves as we really are, and He gives us the knowledge of Himself as He actually is, merciful to sinners for the sake of Jesus Christ.

David was inspired by the Holy Spirit to pray and write this psalm after the Prophet Nathan had confronted him with his sin, bringing him to repentance and then speaking the word of absolution. Remember the story: David, the great and powerful king of Israel, sins. The lust of his wandering eyes and the chaotic passions of his heart lead him away from God and to a woman, Bathsheba, who is not his wife. He beds Bathsheba in his own palace, and she becomes pregnant with his child. Now the king is in a predicament. Bathsheba's husband, Uriah, is away at war. It will not be too long until Bathsheba's growing belly will be a sign to all that she is pregnant, and gossip will soon spread through the streets of Jerusalem. David will make the best of this bad situation. He devises a plan to recall battle-weary Uriah back home for some rest and relaxation. Then the pregnancy can be pinned on him. But the plan doesn't work, for Uriah honoring the established protocol for soldiers, will not have sexual intercourse with his wife while his comrades are fighting and dying. This calls for drastic measures from a panicky king. David, in effect, signs Uriah's death warrant as he gives orders that this faithful soldier is to be dispatched to the front lines, and in the heat of the battle, the troops are to pull back, leaving Uriah exposed. It was sure and certain death. The plot works, and David takes Bathsheba to be his bride.

No doubt, David breathed a sigh of relief. He had salvaged his reputation, and now he could move forward with his life. David did not reckon with the fact that his secret sins were not so secret after all, for his life was lived before a God who is never in the dark regarding our sin. From Him no secrets are hid. He sees. He knows. This God sends to David the Prophet Nathan. Nathan tells David a parable. It's a simple story about a rich farmer with many herds of sheep and a poor man with only a pet lamb to his name. When the rich farmer has guests staying at his place, rather than taking a lamb from his own flocks for the braai, he steals and butchers the pet lamb of his poor neighbor. David is infuriated at the injustice, scandalized by the heartless greed of the wealthy rancher. So he blurts out, "The man who did this deserves to die!" Nathan says to David, "You are the man." David is caught and convicted. There is nothing he can say or do except repent: "I have sinned against the Lord." Nathan speaks the absolution: "The Lord has put away your sin; you shall not die."

David knows himself, and He knows His God. There is enough in this psalm for us to ponder throughout the forty days of this Lenten Season. In fact, Psalm 51 would be a good psalm for you to pray and meditate on each day between now and Easter. But tonight, we are focusing on the knowledge that God gives us of ourselves and the knowledge that He gives us of Himself.

We know ourselves to be sinners. It is not simply that we have made our share of mistakes or that we've, on occasion, violated this or that commandment of God. It runs deeper than that. Listen again to how David puts it: "Behold, I was brought forth in iniquity and in sin did my mother conceive me" (v.5). That is to say, before you committed any particular sin, before you first lied or had a hateful thought, before you did anything, you were a sinner. That is what we call original sin or the "root sin" as Luther put it. We have inherited it from Adam, and it sentences us to Adam's death. That is why we hear the words this Ash Wednesday: "Remember that you are dust and to dust you shall return." And from this root sin, there grows all manner of transgressions: murder, adultery, theft, lies, coveting what God has not given you, and all the rest.

Luther says that Psalm 51 makes two kinds of people manifest. The one type of person attempts to justify him or herself in attitude or by action. But in attempting to declare ourselves right, we accuse God. "If we say we have no sin," writes the Apostle John, "we deceive ourselves all the truth is not in us." We make God a liar. The other type of person, Luther observes, is the person who justifies God and in doing so condemns him or herself. This is what David does when he prays, "for I know my transgressions, and my sin is ever before me. Against you, you only have I sinned and done what is evil in your sight, so that you may be justified in your words and blameless in your judgment" (v.3–4). When you confess your sin, you cease lying to and about yourself. You cease lying to God. Instead, you agree with God's verdict. This is true knowledge of self.

If we were left there alone with the knowledge of self, that would be despair. It would indeed be the "hell of self-knowledge." Nathan did not leave David alone with the verdict of condemnation, "You are the man." David was not abandoned to the terrible truth that he had sinned against the Lord. Nathan speaks another word, a word of absolution: "the Lord also has put away your sin" (II Sam. 12:13).

Ash Wednesday does not abandon us with the knowledge that we are death-bound sinners. There is a sure and certain promise for you because of the Son of David, Jesus Christ. He is the Lamb of God who carried on his own shoulders David's sin and your sin. He carried it to His own death of the cross where He answered for it in His own body and with His own blood. His crucified body and shed blood proclaim to you this night a steadfast love and abundant mercy that will not let you go. You belong to Him, for He has redeemed you by His passion, purchased and won you not with gold or silver but with His innocent suffering and bloody death. From dust, you are to dust you shall return, but because of Jesus' death and resurrection, from dust, you shall rise again!

You are not left alone with uncertainty as to how God, the Creator whom you have sinned against, thinks of you. He has demonstrated His love for you in that while you were yet His enemy, He handed over His only Son to be your Savior. In His cross, the fatherly heart of God is revealed, and that heart beats with steadfast love and tender mercy. It is for you because Jesus is for you. Amen.

FUNERAL/MEMORIAL SERMONS

22

Funeral Sermon for
Rev. Dr. Lowell C. Green

Psalm 118:17; John 11:25

ST. PAUL LUTHERAN CHURCH, BUCYRUS, OH

Friday in Trinity VI / 1 August 2014

"I shall not die, but I shall live, and recount the deeds of the LORD" (Psalm 118:17) and "I am the resurrection and the life. Whoever believes in me, though he die, yet shall he live" (John 11:25).

Dear family and friends of Dr. Lowell C. Green: Grace, mercy, and peace be yours from God the Father and the Lord Jesus Christ!

I read recently that Disney World had been declared to be a "death-free zone." According to the report, employees were instructed never to record a death as actually taking place on the premises. Of course, there are no death-free zones anywhere to be found in this world where sin has entered the picture, for where there is sin, there is death. Lowell C. Green was a sinner, and so he too has died. The man that we cherished as husband, father, grandfather, brother, friend, and teacher has experienced the fate that is there for every descendant of Adam, one that also awaits you. These last few years, death often seemed close at hand for Lowell. So his passing from this life last Thursday was not a surprise. The frailty brought about by age and illness caused many of us to marvel that he hung on as long as he did. But finally, no amount of resilience can endure the Word of the Lord, which says, "Return, o children of man" sweeping us away like grass which fades and withers as we heard in Psalm 90.

Yet in the face of Lowell's death and our own forthcoming deaths, we are bold to say with Psalmist: "I shall not die, but I shall live, and recount the deeds of the Lord." We can make that confession with the Old Testament poet only because of what Jesus said to Martha in the cemetery at Bethany, "I am the resurrection and the life. Whoever believes in me though he die, yet shall he live." We are here today because we believe that Jesus' words are true for Lowell and for all who cling to the Savior in faith.

Now there is much that can be said of Lowell Green. He was a husband, father, grandfather, brother to his family. He was a pastor and a teacher of the church. His scholarship was precise and exacting, and many in my generation recall with gratitude the fruit that we received from his disciplined study of Luther and Lutheran theology. The life that he lived was remarkable in many ways. I think of his time as a student at Erlangen, where he drank deeply from his teachers Werner Elert and Paul Althaus and then returned to pass on what he had learned from them in classrooms and conferences in this country and Canada.

Lowell could be a demanding man with high expectations—and that might be something of an understatement. But let it not be forgotten that he demanded and expected much of himself. He knew that to those whom much is given, much will be required. Lowell was on the receiving end of a legacy of Lutheran theology and hymnody, and he recognized his responsibility to preserve and extend it to the next generation and beyond. That was not an easy task, especially in a day when so many are willfully ignorant or indifferent.

The sainted Martin Franzmann once said that grief is not a rare vegetable in the diet of a confessional theologian. So also with Lowell for he loved the Lutheran Church and was wounded when pastors and church leaders neglected, denied, or squandered the legacy of the Reformation. He was impatient with such human foolishness, for he knew that God has elected to save sinners through another foolishness—what the Apostle Paul calls the wisdom of the cross.

Whatever else may be said of Lowell's life, this we are compelled to say: He was a sinner justified by faith for the sake of Christ alone. Lowell was no antiquarian interested in musty tomes simply for academic self-satisfaction. He was a theologian of the cross, and his life was spent in the service of that everlasting Gospel. Martin Luther had a deep passion for Psalm 118. In fact, he called it his favorite psalm. He used our text from verse 17 as something of a personal motto, inscribing it on the wall of his room in the Castle Coburg in 1530. Luther wrote of this verse in a way that also frames Lowell's life and gives us comfort today. Listen to what the Reformer says:

> Though I die, I die not. Though I suffer, I suffer not. Though I fall, I am not down. Though I am disgraced, I am not dishonored. This is consolation. Furthermore, the psalmist says of the help: 'I shall live.' Isn't this amazing help? The dying live; the suffering rejoice; the fallen rise; the disgraced are honored. . . . These are all words that no human heart can comprehend. . . . And here you see this comfort and help is eternal life, which is the true, everlasting blessing of God. . . . If sins are forgiven, death is gone. And without fail there must be the comfort and confidence of eternal righteousness and everlasting life. (AE 14:86)

This little piece from his teacher, Dr. Luther, attests to the fact that Lowell's life and work were not in vain. Jesus crucified for our sins and raised again for our justification was his confidence in life and in death. The church which Lowell loved has a future. Lowell, though dead, has a future. You have a future because Christ Jesus has a future. He was put to death for your sins and raised from the dead, never to die again. He gives life to you. Your future is His future. Baptized into his death, you share in His resurrection.

Lowell was a theologian whose life was given to "recounting the deeds of the Lord." He did that as a father to his children in family devotions. He did that as a pastor to the congregations he served in Texas, Illinois, South Dakota, Minnesota, and New York. He did that as a teacher of the church, so students were molded by his rigorous thought, and through them, as well as through Lowell's writings, he will continue to recount the deeds of the Lord!

But there is much more than living on through one's loved ones or through the monument of one's scholarship. The Lord who shed His blood to redeem Lowell lives, and because He lives, Lowell lives in Him. Jesus says, "Let not your hearts be troubled. Believe in God; believe also in me. In my Father's house are many rooms. If it were not so, would I have told you that I go and prepare a place for you? And if I go and prepare a place for you, I will come again and will take you to myself, that where I am you may be also" (John 14:1–3). The Lord has now fulfilled that promise for Lowell, and so we can be at peace. His sins are forgiven. He has eternal life through the merits of Christ alone.

We now lay Lowell's body worn out and spent from a lifetime of living into the grave to await the resurrection even as we rejoice that he is even now with the Lord, who is the God not of the dead but of the living. "I shall not die, but I shall live, and recount the deeds of the Lord." Thanks be to God through our Lord Jesus Christ, who gives us the victory! Amen.

23

Committal for Rev. Dr. Kenneth F. Korby

We Have Only Done What Was Our Duty

> "So you also, when you have all that you were commanded, say, 'We are unworthy servants; we have only done what was our duty'" (Luke 17:10).

CONCORDIA CEMETERY, FORT WAYNE, IN

Friday in Easter II / 24 April 2009

Servants are there to do the will of the master, not vice versa. Servants know their place; they are not there to be served but to serve. No master waits on his own servants. No master says, "Now you sit down, and I'll serve you supper." No master, that is, except the Most High Son of God who humbled Himself to come to us as Servant, not to be served but to serve and give His life as a ransom for many.

To be served by Christ Jesus is to be taken captive by Him. That's what happened to Peter on Maundy Thursday evening as the Lord on His knees and girdled with a towel bathed Peter's feet. Peter's life was no longer his own. "Make me a captive, Lord, and then I shall be free," says an old hymn. If Christ sets you free, you are free indeed. Peter was set free to be the Lord's man, to live under Him in His kingdom, to be led in ways where he would never go on his own, to suffer all even to the point of death on account of his confession that this Jesus is the Christ, the Son of the living God.

Kenneth Korby was a free man. He knew his place for Christ Jesus had redeemed him that Kenneth might be "His own and live

under Him in His kingdom and serve Him in everlasting righteousness and innocence" even as Jesus is risen from the dead, lives and
reigns to all eternity. Kenneth knew his place; he knew himself a
servant of the One who first served him. For Kenneth, there was
magnificent freedom in slavery to Christ Jesus. It was the freedom to
be courageous in confession, to exhort and admonish, to teach and
to preach. It was the freedom to learn and then out of that treasury
of a lifetime of pondering the texts of Holy Scriptures, the Lutheran
Confessions, the writings of Luther, and countless teachers of the
church ancient and modern to give of that learning to others. He did
not see his pastoral and scholarly accomplishments as achievements
to be paraded before people. He did not see his sweat and labor as
triumphant trophies to be hauled up to heaven. He knew that all that
he was and all that he had was pure gift from the Father of lights.
And as these endowments were gifts freely given to him they were
gifts that he was duty-bound to share whether in study and prayers
with Jeanne and the children, lay folks in the congregations, students
at Valparaiso University and later at the seminaries, or literally hundreds of conferences.

But at the end of all the busyness for Kenneth was no cry for
recognition, no claim for accolades, just the confession of a heart set
free and a mouth opened by the Word of the Lord: "We are unworthy servants; we have only done what was our duty." Kenneth knew
it was his duty to thank, praise, serve and obey the Blessed Trinity,
who created, redeemed, and hallowed him to be His own. Today we
lay Kenneth's bodily remains into the earth in the sure and certain
confidence, the lively hope of the resurrection of the body when our
Lord will say to Kenneth and all who by faith are His: "Well done
thou good and faithful servant." Amen.

The peace of God which passes all understanding keep your
hearts and minds in Christ Jesus to life everlasting.

24

Memorial Service for Maggie Karner

Hidden with Christ in God

Col. 3:3–4

KRAMER CHAPEL, CTSFW

Saturday in Trinity XVII / 2 October 2015

Dear Brothers and Sisters of our Lord Jesus Christ and especially you, Kevin, Mary, Annie, and Heidi:

Death defined Maggie Karner. I'm not talking about the death that she experienced last Friday night but another death. The Apostle Paul writes to the Colossians who were very much still living and breathing, "you have died." Past tense. Maggie died to sin in her Baptism into Christ, and there her life was tucked away safe and secure in His wounds. Her life was hidden with Christ in God. And it still is, for the God and Father of our Lord Jesus Christ is not a God of the dead but of the living.

Maggie spent a lifetime living with death, not just these past few months. She was baptized into the death of Christ and given over to that one atoning death she daily died to sin and by the Gospel was raised to live before God in the newness of His saving righteousness.

Hidden with Christ in God, the life of the crucified and risen Lord was made manifest in Maggie's life. Maggie was a possessed woman. She was possessed by Jesus Christ. She belonged to Him. She still does. She learned and loved the Catechism which declares faith in Jesus Christ "who has redeemed me a lost and condemned person, purchased and won me from all sins, from death, and from the power of the devil; not with gold or silver but with His holy precious blood and with His innocent suffering and death, that I may be His own and live under Him in His kingdom, and serve Him in everlasting righteousness, innocence, and blessedness just as He is risen from the dead, lives and reigns to all eternity." That was most certainly true for Maggie. She belonged to Jesus Christ in this life. Now she belongs to Him for all eternity. Her life is hidden with Him in God.

Today we come together in this chapel to give thanks for the way that Christ's life was made in manifest in Maggie's living and dying. What can be said of her? She was a daughter to Robert and Marietta Sattler and a sister of David, John, Robert, and Karen. For thirty years, she was wife to Kevin. And she was mother to Mary, Annie, and Heidi. She was a tireless champion for the cause of the weak and unwanted, a passion that led her to devote her considerable energies to serve as Director of Life and Health Ministries in our church. All of this was given by our Lord to Maggie. It was her vocation, and in the comings and goings that made up her calling in this life, Christ was made manifest. You see, our Lord travels incognito. He hides Himself behind masks as Dr. Luther puts it. He is there behind the nascent life of the unborn, and He resides behind the disfigured faces of the sick and the dying. In word and deed, Maggie spoke for those who could not speak for themselves, and she spent this life the Lord had given her down to its last drops so that Christ might be made manifest.

In her living and her dying, the fact that she belonged to the Lord was put on display. Hearing and trusting in the voice of the Good Shepherd, she followed Him, recognizing that she had a calling even in dying. Paul Althaus, a Lutheran theologian of the last century, wrote:

> To die willingly means to accept God as God, to honor Him as the One who alone has immortality, who is God by the very fact that He gives us life and the right to take it back. We die to honor God. This is true all the more because He wants to be praised through our faith, and nothing calls for faith as much as dying. There is no other divine service like that in which man, with all his hopes and desires,

with all his thirst for life, obediently submits to God's call to die, and in his own end relies on God, commits himself into the hands of the Invisible when all things visible fade away. The perfection of the Son of God lies in His obedience to death. So we, too, must joyfully accept as God's grace that He calls us to the divine service of dying. By our death we are allowed to give praise to God.[1]

In her living and in her dying, Maggie did praise her God and Savior. She did not choose death as a way to claim dignity and bypass suffering, but heeding the Lord's voice, she followed Him through death to life.

Now her life is hidden with this same Christ in God. This is the Jesus who tells His disciples that in His Father's house there are many mansions and that He goes on ahead of them to prepare a place for them. Maggie is there in this place Jesus has prepared by His cross and resurrection. Maggie is there, her life hidden with Christ in God. There is yet more. Paul says that when Christ, who is our life, appears, we will appear with Him in glory. For Maggie and for all believers in Christ whose life is defined by His death, death is never the end of the story. Jesus' empty tomb is the guarantee that even though the grave hides our bodies for a time, when He appears, Maggie will appear with Him. No longer in a body worn out and bloated by cancer but in a body clothed in Christ's righteousness and remade in the likeness of the Lord's resurrected body.

Now Maggie's voice is silent, and we miss her face, but we will see her again for she is with the Lord, and on the Day of His appearing, our dear Maggie will show up as well. "Blessed are the dead who die in the Lord," says the voice from heaven in the Book of Revelation "that they may rest from their labors, for their deeds do follow them." Maggie is now enjoying that rest hidden away with Christ in God. And her deeds, well, they are certainly following her. She didn't take them to heaven where there is no need for them; she left them here on earth! Look around this chapel! The life that she lived in Christ will continue to bear fruits in the family that she leaves behind, in a church whose witness to mercy and life was so deeply enriched by her tireless efforts, and in ways beyond counting in places to the ends of the earth like Madagascar, India and Indonesia. She is at rest, but there is still work for you in this old dying world, plagued as it is with sin and suffering. We feebly struggle, she in glory shines. Let Maggie's life be an example and encouragement for your life, lived by faith in Christ, and fervent love for the neighbor.

You have died, and your life is hidden with Christ in God. There is no better place to be for Maggie or for you.

"Now to him who is able to keep you from stumbling and to present you blameless before the presence of his glory with great joy, to the only God, our Savior, through Jesus Christ our Lord, be glory, majesty, dominion, and authority, before all time and now and for ever. Amen" (Jude 24–25 RSV).

Note

1   Cited by Wenzel Lohff, "Paul Altaus" in *Theologians of our Times* ed. Leonhard Reinisch (Notre Dame: Notre Dame University Press, 1964), 63.

PART II

Theology is for Proclamation

Essays from the Craft of Preaching

All of these entries appeared on CraftOfPreaching.org (1517.org). The dates are listed under the titles. Some were parts of series and are combined here.

25

Advent Is for Preachers

Advent Accents Preaching, Making Known That It Is the Lord Who Comes to Bring Salvation, to Proclaim This in All the Earth.

11 JUNE 2018

Advent is for preachers. Well, of course, so is Christmas, Epiphany, Lent, Easter, Pentecost, and the whole of the church year. But Advent accents preaching, making known that it is the Lord who comes to bring salvation, to proclaim this in all the earth. Scholars point out that the Lutheran Reformation nuanced Advent preaching to give priority to proclamation; in contrast to medieval preaching, where the dominant theme was preparation.[1] Early Lutheran preachers accented proclamation, echoing the words of the Prophet Zechariah: "Behold, your king is coming to you; righteous and having salvation." Now that is a word to be proclaimed. The Palm Sunday crowds will not be quiet. They cry out as we hear in Luke's Gospel: "Blessed is the King who comes in the name of the Lord! Peace in heaven and glory in the highest" (Luke 19:38). The Pharisees who are unsettled by this ruckus get nowhere when they attempt to get Jesus to tone the commotion down. Jesus says that if His disciples were silent, the very stones would cry out.

Advent evokes proclamation and praise, for the Holy One of Israel comes to redeem sinners. If you have read the early chapters of Isaiah, you know that the coming and presence of God is not necessarily good news. For example, the Prophet Isaiah proclaims the comfort of God's salvation, deliverance and mercy in chapter 12. But these words are wedged in between oracles of woe and wrath; destruction meted out to all those who draw their life from dead idols and live in lethal unbelief acting as though the Lord God were powerless to call them to account. There is a dark side to Advent. Isaiah speaks of it as he preaches the alien work of God. He wields the ax against every outgrowth of sin, chopping through the thickets of our hearts entangled in the monotonous futility of exchanging God's truth for lies. The thorns and briars will crackle as they are kindled by sparks of divine judgment. Hungry flames will ravish Israel, the "remnant of the trees of his forest will be so few that a child can write them down" (Isaiah 10:19). But out of that charred earth, there comes forth a tender shoot from the stump of Jesse, the insignia of an unquenchable mercy and a divine favor for sinners that will not cease. In His wrath, God remembers His mercy. So, Isaiah proclaims the promise: "You will say in that day: I will give thanks to you, O LORD, for though you were angry with me, your anger turned away, that you might comfort me" (Isaiah 12:1).

God turns His wrath away from sinners and on to His Son. Wrath and mercy, repentance, and faith are the content of the preaching of Advent. God's alien work of deconstructing everything that stands in opposition to His good and gracious will rings through loud and clear in the preaching of the Old Testament prophets and John the Baptist. There is a highway to be prepared, rough places made smooth, and crooked paths made straight, so that in the end all flesh may see the salvation of our God (Isaiah 40:1–8). This preaching of the threat of the Law is not an end in itself; it is to be preached so that the proper work and Word of God, the glad news of God's reconciliation of the ungodly to Himself in Christ, might be heard. Condemnation gives way to consolation, so preachers comfort the afflicted and speak peace to those broken by their sins.

The promise of Advent makes room for lament[2] as preachers prompt hearers to call out to Emmanuel that He might come quickly to rescue us from the threatening perils of our sin and deliver us from the hopeless gloom that overshadows lives in the darkness of death:

O Morning Star, O radiant Sun,
When will our hearts behold Your dawn?
O Sun, arise, without Your light
We grope in gloom and dark of night. (LSB 355:5)

That's why Advent is for preachers. God is coming, but not in anger. His wrath has been turned from us and absorbed in the suffering and death of God's own Son, the Lamb of God who has answered for our sins on the cross. He came into His Zion, the holy city–the place of temple and sacrifice to suffer the fate of our unrighteousness, to bear our sin and be our Savior. Preachers are to proclaim Him for it is only in this Jesus that sinners find the comfort of which Isaiah speaks, the consolation of sins forgiven.

Preaching makes known what the Lord has done in all the earth. No wonder John the Baptist figures so prominently in Advent for he embodies the preaching of which Isaiah speaks. Yes, he gives voice to the Law as he swings the blade of God's judgment at sapless trees, withered in unbelief, and shriveled up in the death that is the fruit of sin. But his voice calling out in the wilderness calls the sinner to repentance and faith in the One who comes in the name of the Lord, the Lamb of God who takes away the sins of the world. Advent announces that this Lord is near. Luther says that we can't draw this Lord too deeply into the flesh. How deeply He is drawn into the flesh we know from Palm Sunday, from Bethlehem and finally from the Last Day when He will return as Judge, yet still our Brother. In the meantime, it is Advent. It's always Advent for the Christian, remarked Dietrich Bonhoeffer, for we lift our heads and cry out in eager expectation towards the redemption that draws near to us.[3] It is always Advent as we wait for what we already now receive by faith. The Lord who is coming is already here with a word of promise: "In your midst is the Holy One of Israel" (Isaiah 12:6b). His name is Jesus. Faith comes by hearing His words. Advent is for preachers. Proclaim His promises. We can't remain silent, lest the stones cry out.

Notes

1 Haemig, Mary Jane. "Sixteenth-Century Preachers on Advent as a Season of Proclamation or Preparation" *Lutheran Quarterly* (Summer 2002), 125–152.

2 Bayer writes "Lament and petitionary prayer are possible only on the basis of the promise."—*Living by Faith: Justification and Sanctification*, trans. G. Bromiley (Grand Rapids: Eerdmans, 2003), 72. For more on the place of lament, see Oswald Bayer, "Toward a Theology of Lament" in *Caritas et Reformatio: Essays on Church and Society in Honor of Carter Lindberg* edited by David M. Whitford (Saint Louis: Concordia Publishing House, 2002), 211–220. Also see Jeremiah Johnson, "Learning to Lament: Preaching to Suffering in the Lament Psalms" in *Feasting in a Famine of the Word: Lutheran Preaching in the Twenty-First Century* edited by M. Birkholz, J. Corzine, and J. Mumme (Eugene: Pickwick, 2016), 225–240.

3 See Bonhoeffer's sermon, "Come, O Rescue" in *The Collected Sermons of Dietrich Bonhoeffer*, edited and introduced by Isabel Best (Minneapolis: Fortress Press, 2012), 109–114.

26

From Advent to Christmas

Past, present, and future converge in Advent.[1] The historical coming of the Lord Jesus in the flesh, born of Mary to suffer and die for the world's redemption, is indicated by having the Palm Sunday account read on the First Sunday in Advent. All of the church year revolves around the cross. The movement of the church year is either toward Calvary or else it flows out of Calvary, coming to consummation in the return of the crucified Lord to judge the living and the dead. Advent proclaims that the Lord who rode into Jerusalem seated on a donkey with the humility of a "beggar king"[2] to use Luther's words, will come clothed in the splendor of His divine majesty to reign in glory everlasting.

Advent draws us back to Bethlehem and Jerusalem even as it pulls us toward what Luther called "the happy last day" (WA 49:731.5): "With Revelation 22:20—'Indeed, come, Lord Jesus'"—Luther prays that the Day of Judgment will come. It is the *extremus dies laeta* "we . . . wait for the arrival of the Lord and say: 'Come, Dear Lord Jesus.'" The Day of Judgment that one awaits is thus not to be understood in a neutral sense, but rather in a personal sense: it is the Lord who is expected. "We do not wait for an anonymous Last Thing, but for *the Last One*, whom we know by faith already. The anticipation of the beloved Day of Judgment is the anticipation of the 'beloved Lord.'"[3] The same Lord who came as our Brother and Savior will come again as our Judge.

An old collect of the church, appointed for use on Christmas Eve forges the link between the two advents of Jesus: "O God, You make us glad with the yearly remembrance of the birth of Your only-begotten Son, Jesus Christ. Grant that as we joyfully receive Him as our Redeemer, we may with sure confidence behold Him when He comes as our Judge; through the same . . ."[4] Only those who receive Him now by faith are ready to receive Him on the Last Day.

John the Baptist figures prominently in Advent's present tense, for he is the voice of the preached Word, calling all to repentance and faith. Luther called John the Baptist "an image, and a type, and also a pioneer, the first of all preachers of the Gospel,"[5] because he points to the Lamb of God who takes away the sin of the world. The Isenheim Altarpiece by Matthias Grunwald pictures John the Baptist standing by the cross with an open Bible in one hand and with the other hand pointing a larger than life finger toward the crucified Christ. John is that finger that points to the Lamb of God who takes away the sin of the world. John does his work by calling us to repent of our sins and calling us to faith in Jesus Christ, who has answered for our sin by His death on the cross. So Luther says in one of his Advent sermons, "Let us look to the mouth and finger of John with which he bears witness and points, so that we do not close our eyes and lose our Lord and Savior Jesus Christ; for to the present day John still very diligently, faithfully, and richly points and directs us here in order that we might be saved."[6]

With one foot clearly planted in the Old Testament and the other squarely standing in the terrain of the New Testament, John the Baptist is the prophetic voice brought to a single point and focused solely on Christ Jesus. As Martin Franzmann put it, "We who give ear to the voice of John, we who follow the pointing finger of John, the great Advent preacher, can never grow casual about Him and His mercy. Nor can we who have heard the Baptist's Advent cry ever think of repentance as a placid, pious exercise, a sort of routine religious daily dozen. It is the death of the old man and the creation of the new man as God's own."[7] The preaching of John the Baptist scrubs us, cleaning off the pretentious spirituality that we would use to defend ourselves against God's righteousness. His wilderness sermons are a homiletical laxative to cleanse us from being constipated with our putrid presumptions that the righteousness of our good intentions will suffice before God. His preaching levels mountains of pride and makes a straight way to the crib of Bethlehem and the cross of Golgotha.

Such preaching of the light displaces the lie, but it lands John in a dungeon and eventuates in his execution to satisfy the whim of Herodias' daughter. Before his decapitation, John's disciples are dispatched to Jesus with a question, "Are you the one who is to come, or shall we look for another?" (Luke 7:20/from the Holy Gospel for Advent III: Series C). This pericope and its parallel in Matthew 11:2–11 (the Holy Gospel for Advent III in the historic lectionary) has raised debate: Was John himself doubting the One whom he had proclaimed? Or was he asking this question for the sake of his disciples?[8]

John's whole life was given to the service of Jesus. He knew himself to be the one sent to prepare the Lord's way, to make ready a highway in the wilderness for our God. So John's very existence was spent on preaching repentance. His whole being was poured into the proclamation of the dawning of the Sun of Righteousness, the arrival of the Lamb of God promised by the prophets. John knew that he was not the Messiah but the forerunner, sent to announce His coming and prepare His way. But now John is locked away in jail. He will soon die. Where is the Messiah now? If God's Christ has come to give release to prisoners, yet is John still behind bars? "Are You the Coming One, or do we look for another?" Jesus sent word back to John. He says to John's disciples, "Go and tell John what you have seen and heard: the blind receive their sight, the lame walk, lepers are cleansed, and the deaf hear, the dead are raised up, the poor have the good news preached to them" (Luke 7:22–23). Jesus directs John to His *works*. He does what the Old Testament promised that Messiah would do. Jesus' works confirm that He is the Messiah sent from the Father. Then, Jesus adds a gentle rebuke: "And blessed is the one who is not offended by Me" (Luke 7:23). There is an offensive side to Advent, for it shows us a Savior who comes in such lowliness and weakness as to suffer His preacher's imprisonment, persecution, and entrance into His kingdom not by sidestepping death and the grave but going through it.

The Fourth Sunday in Advent brings us to the threshold of Christmas with the Annunciation and the Magnificat (Luke 1:39–55). Mary received quite a Christmas greeting from the Most High

God: "Rejoice, highly favored one, the Lord is with you; blessed are you among women" (Luke 1:28 NKJV). That Christmas salutation was delivered by that high angel of God, Gabriel—the same angel who years before had visited Daniel and spoke to him of the end of all things and the coming of God's kingdom of glory. Now Gabriel comes to a young girl in Galilee of Nazareth with news that is surprising as it is shocking. No wonder that Mary was troubled at this encounter and confused as to the meaning of this celestial message. There is no reason for Mary to be afraid for the work that God is about to perform in her is a work of His gracious favor: "Do not be afraid, Mary, for you have found favor with God."

God selected Mary to be the mother of His Son. She is blessed among all women, for she is given the unique privilege of carrying the Son of God in her womb. She is the instrument that God singles out to clothe His Eternal Word in the flesh. In the face of this awesome miracle, the Angel Gabriel says, "Do not be afraid." Then, the Angel goes on to unwrap this gift that God is giving to Mary and through her to the whole world: "And behold, you will conceive in your womb and bring forth a Son, and shall call His name Jesus. He will be great, and will be called the Son of the Highest; and the Lord God will give Him the throne of His father David. And He will reign over the house of Jacob forever and of His kingdom there will be no end." You see, the script for this Christmas greeting from heaven is the Old Testament itself. In these few words, the Angel summarizes the message of the Old Testament. It is a message that goes back to that promise God made to Adam and Eve in the Garden of Eden and echoed down through the halls of history in the testimony of the patriarchs and prophets. It is all coming to fulfillment as the angel speaks these words into the ear of the Virgin Mary.

This son conceived within the intimacy of Mary's womb is the God whom the universe cannot contain. True God, yet true Man, He is given the name "Jesus," the name that pledges us the Lord's salvation—the only name given under heaven by which we are saved from our sin, rescued from the grave, and redeemed from hell. To this embryo in Mary's body belongs the throne of David—that kingship which will have no end. He is the Alpha and the Omega, the beginning and the end. He is very God of very God, begotten not made as we confess in the Creed. His life did not begin in Mary's womb, nor did it end in the borrowed tomb. This little baby that is sheltered in Mary's flesh is the one eternal God.

We mark beginnings and endings. We live between birth and death. We cannot comprehend eternity. The Son born to Mary comes to us in the flesh, flesh which will suffer and die in our place to make us creatures of time, children of eternity. This little mass of flesh and blood that grows and develops in Mary's body is the God who comes to save us and make us citizens of His unending Kingdom.

Mary's response to the Angel's Christmas greeting is marked by its simplicity: "How can this be, since I do not know a man?" Mary's question is born of faith, not skepticism. She knows as we know, that it takes a man and a woman to produce a child. Unlike the scoffers of her day and ours, Mary's question is not fueled by unbelief. Rather, Mary's question is simple and child-like. Like a child, she is saying, "How is God going to do this?" And she gets an answer: "The Holy Spirit will come upon you, and the power of the Highest will over-shadow you; therefore, also, that Holy One who is to be born will be called the Son of God." Mary believes!

Martin Luther says that there are three miracles in this text from Holy Writ. The first is that a virgin should conceive without the aid of a male. For the God who created heaven and earth, this is but a trifle says Luther . . . a miracle that God could pull off with a twitch of His little finger. The second miracle is a little greater—that God would take on flesh and blood and house Himself within our frame. But the third miracle says Luther is the greatest, and it is this: that Mary believed the word of the Lord delivered to her by the angel. Luther goes on to say, "Had Mary not have believed she could not have conceived."[9]

Mary believes! She says: "Let it be to me according to your word." That is the Amen of faith. Faith does not dictate to God how He must act. Faith does not live by what can be seen with the eyes but by a Word spoken into the ears. Faith says, "Let it be to me according to your word." The proclamation of the Lord's three advents moves preaching from the cry, "Come, O Come, Emmanuel, and ransom captive Israel, that mourns in lonely exile here until the Son of God appear" (357:1 LSB) to the glad call, "Let the earth now praise the Lord, who has truly kept His word and at last to us did send Christ, the sinner's help and friend" (352:1 LSB). The movement from Advent to Christmas is the movement from promise to fulfillment.

Notes

1 See Mary Jane Haemig, "Putting the Advents back in Advent" *Lutheran Forum* (Summer 2012), 27–30.

2 For more on Luther's use of this imagery, see John T. Pless, "Learning to Preach in Advent and Christmas from Luther" *Concordia Theological Quarterly* (October, 1998), 269–286.

3 Oswald Bayer, *Martin Luther's Theology: A Contemporary Interpretation*, trans. Thomas H. Trapp (Grand Rapids: Eerdmans Publishing Company, 2008), 333–334.

4 *Pastoral Care Companion* (Saint Louis: Concordia Publishing House, 2007), 540.

5 *Sermons of Martin Luther*, Volume I, edited by John Nicholas Lenker (Grand Rapids: Baker Book House, 1983), 130.

6 *The House Postils*, Volume I, edited by Eugene Klug (Grand Rapids: Baker Book House, 1996), 91.

7 Martin Franzmann, "Fear Born of Forgiveness" in *Ha! Ha! Among the Trumpets* (Saint Louis: Concordia Publishing House, 1966), 23.

8 See the survey of opinions in Mary Jane Haemig, "Advent Preaching on 'Doubting John'" *Lutheran Quarterly* (Autumn, 2006), 348–361.

9 For the full citation, see Roland Bainton, *The Martin Luther Christmas Book* (Philadelphia: Fortress Press, 1967), 22–23.

27

Bright Valley of Love

A Story for Preachers as
Advent Turns Toward Christmas

22 DECEMBER 2019

As Advent takes a sharp turn toward Christmas, Edna Hong's gentle yet powerful, *Bright Valley of Love* comes to mind. Set in post-War World I Germany, it is the story of Gunther, a boy whose body was twisted and whose mind was strangled already in the womb. Forsaken by his mother and left to live his earliest years hidden away in a back room of his grandmother's house, Gunther is finally brought to Bethel, a Lutheran place of mercy where he is no longer seen as a shameful piece of human junk but a beloved child of the King of heaven. At Bethel, his ears are filled with the stories of Jesus, and the hymns of the church surround his feeble existence. Bethel was the house of God, and as such, it was also home to those that the world considered worthless: those seized with epilepsy, the crippled, the blind, and the mentally disabled. Here they were cared for by deaconesses with hearts and hands of mercy. Pastor Fritz (in real life Pastor Friedrich von Bodelschwingh the younger who stood in staunch opposition to National Socialism and with Hermann Sasse, Dietrich Bonhoeffer, Georg Merz, and Wilhlem Vischer was instrumental in producing the Bethel Confession of 1933[1]) is the director of Bethel who shepherds his congregation of misfits to the crib of One born to be their Savior.

Before coming to Bethel, Gunther did not know of Christmas. In that life, one day was no different from the next as each was dark and dirty. But now at Bethel, life for the whole community moved with the ever-changing rhythms of the church year. The season of Advent was permeated with Gerhardt's "O shall I receive Thee, How greet Thee Lord, aright?" Weissel's "Lift up your heads, ye mighty gates! Behold the King of glory waits," and Luther's "Ah, dearest Jesus, Holy Child, Make thee a bed, soft undefiled, within my heart, that it may be a quiet chamber kept for thee." Devotions around the Advent wreath and the Christmas crèche brought a new and undimmed world to the horizon of Bethel and its residents. The voice of praise was not silent here as the anticipation of the coming Savior brought light and love to the village. The promises of Advent were in the air.

All this was new to Gunther. So new and strange as to be contradicted by all that he experienced in his short life up to this point. In the glow of Advent candles and joyous songs exhorting mighty gates to fling open wide, little Gunther throws up his complaint: "There's a crack in everything!" Indeed "For Gunther, the joyous expectation of Christmas feeling was practically rubbed out by the other, the fear feeling. His complaint turned into a cry for help: 'What's so great about Christmas?" (59).

That is the question which the preacher must answer! Pastor Fritz enlists the other children to help him tell Gunther what is so great about Christmas. The answers are jumbled and not always coherent as the children reply with fragments of a hymn, like "to ransom captive Israel" or truisms like "Christmas is the 25th day of December" or "Christ is born in Bethlehem." Finally, one little girl, Leni, triumphantly repeats Gunther's initial complaint: "Because everything has a crack!"

Drawing close to Gunther's side, Pastor Fritz now answers the question: "It is true, Gunther, that there is a crack in everything. God sees the crack better than we do, and the crack is ever so much worse than we think it is. That is why God sent his Son from the heavenly home to our earthly home. Not to patch up the crack, but to make everything new. That is why Christmas is so great, Gunther" (61).

At Bethlehem, God did not inaugurate a repair job, plastering over the fissures of this broken world, working with the art of an embalmer to paint over the face of death with a cosmetic appearance of life. The Christmas gospel first preached by the angels is the announcement of the birth of a Savior who will bring heaven's peace to earth. From all eternity, the Father willed to send His Son, the eternal Word, into the flesh to tabernacle among those like Gunther that the world deemed unworthy of life. He was born not to reform this world but to redeem it by His blood. No longer veiled in poverty and shame, but forever clothed in our flesh, He now declares, "Behold, I am making all things new" (Rev. 21:5). He came not merely to deal with the symptoms of sin, but once and for all to break the grip of sin and defeat death. He comes to us at Christmas, Helmut Thielicke says, ". . . in the depths. I do not need first to have religious feelings, out of which I then produce some internal and external results, before he comes to me. He comes in the stable, to the disconsolate, the sick, and the despairing; he trudges in the long line of refugees; and if everyone and everything should desert me in my final hour, I can say, 'If I should have to depart, depart not from me.' Then he comes even to the dark valley of death. Crib and cross are of the same wood."[2] That is finally why Christmas is so great!

Oswald Bayer writes that we live in a world where "mercy is not self-evident."[3] That was certainly the case in the years leading up to World War II in Germany. It is no less true for us in 21st century North America. But in that "bright valley of love" called Bethel, the mercy that flows from crib and cross touched lives disfigured by the crack, which runs through all creation since our first parents' grabbed at the glory of their Creator in a vain attempt to make it their own. Christmas declares that there is mercy for the broken and those pushed aside as worthless. There is mercy for you now made evident in the fact that God became man, pleased with us to dwell.

> From the manger newborn light
> Shines in glory through the night
> Darkness there no more resides;
> In this light faith now abides. (332:7 LSB)

Notes

1 For more see, John T. Pless, "Bodelschwingh, Friedrich (the Elder) and Friedrich (the Younger) von" in *Dictionary of Luther and the Lutheran Traditions*, ed. Timothy J. Wengert (Grand Rapids: Baker Academic, 2017), 93.

2 Helmut Thielicke, *Being a Christian When the Chips are Down*, trans. H. George Anderson (Philadelphia: Fortress Press, 1979), 101.

3 Oswald Bayer, "Mercy from the Heart" in *The Mercy of God in the Cross of Christ* ed. By Ross Johnson and John T. Pless (St. Louis: The Lutheran Church-Missouri Synod, 2016), 192.

28

Preaching the Apostles' Creed in Advent

A Midweek Series

17 NOVEMBER 2019

At first glance, it might seem a bit strange to suggest a midweek series for Advent based on the Apostles' Creed. But if Advent has to do with God's gracious condescension to humanity, then the Apostles' Creed as Luther has taught us to confess it in the Catechisms makes perfect sense. Luther writes:

> For in all three articles God himself has revealed and opened to us the most profound depths of his fatherly heart and his pure, unutterable love. For this very purpose he created us so that he might redeem us and make us holy, and moreover, having granted and bestowed upon us everything in heaven and on earth, he has also given us his Son and the Holy Spirit, through whom he brings us to himself. For, as explained above, we could never come to recognize the Father's favor and grace were it not for the Lord Christ, who is a mirror of the Father's heart. Apart from him, we see nothing but an angry and terrible judge. But neither could we know anything of Christ, had it not been revealed by the Holy Spirit. (LC II:64–66, K-W, 439–440)

The sixteenth-century hymnist, Ludwig Helmbolt (1532–1598) provides us with a template that echoes Luther's words in the *Large Catechism*:

For thus the Father willed it, Who fashioned us from clay; And His own Son fulfilled it And brought eternal day. The Spirit now has come, To us true faith has given; He leads us home to heaven. O praise the Three in One! (713:7 LSB)

Each of the three midweek services will focus on an article of the Apostles' Creed.

Midweek Service in Advent I: "Out of His Fatherly, Divine Goodness and Mercy"

Advent is not about a path that we make for ourselves to God but about God coming to us. We see this in our creation. To say that God is our creator is to confess that my life comes from Him. Theologians speak of God creating out of nothing (*creatio ex nihilo*). That means He did not create out of any necessity but that He brought creation into existence as an act of His good and gracious will to bestow life. This is why Luther has us confess that God, the Father Almighty has created, sustained, and preserved us "out of fatherly, divine goodness and mercy, without any merit or worthiness in me." In the act of bringing us to life, our Father is bending down to us. He is the Giver and Donor of all that we have. Creation is not merely a prelude to redemption, but it is itself a gift received in Christ, who is the Word through whom all things were made. Given access to the Father through Christ Jesus, our eyes and ears are opened to see and hear the world not in fear but in the glad confidence that the Lord who made the stars of night is our Emmanuel.

Midweek Service in Advent II: "That I May be His Own"

Advent proclaims the coming of Jesus Christ, true God begotten of the Father from eternity and also true man born of the Virgin Mary. This Jesus, true God and true man in one person is my Lord. He came into the flesh to redeem human beings who had wandered from their Creator in unbelief and therefore stood under His condemnation. Jesus comes into the world not to condemn sinners but to reconcile them to His Father through the shedding of His blood on the cross. In His atonement for our sin, He is at once paying the price of our release and winning us from the jaws of sin, death, and hell. He does all this that we might be His own and live under Him in His Kingdom even as He is risen from the dead to live and reign forever as our Brother and Savior. We hear much about this Kingdom in the biblical texts associated with Advent as well as the hymns of this season. Jesus is the crucified and risen King. He is the Lord who has prepared for us the Kingdom. As Luther reminds us: "The Kingdom of God is not being prepared but has been prepared. Not preparing the Kingdom; that is to say, the Kingdom merits the sons, not the sons the Kingdom" (LW 33:153).

Midweek Service in Advent III: "Sanctified and Kept in the True Faith"

Dead in our trespasses and sins, we could not find our way back to God or come to Him. Free will is powerless over death. The Holy Spirit, who is confessed as the Lord and Giver of Life, calls us by the Gospel to saving faith in Christ Jesus. Sanctification is not about how we make ourselves righteous before God. Sanctification is what God has done for us in Christ. God makes us holy by forgiving our sins for the sake of Christ Jesus. Luther's Explanation of the Third Article begins not with a confession of faith but of our inability to believe. The focus is not on us but on the Holy Spirit, who has called us by the Gospel. This calling is ongoing as through the Gospel, He "daily and richly forgives all my sins and the sins of all believers." I could not believe in Christ even for a moment if the Holy Spirit were not continually calling me by the Gospel and keeping me with Jesus Christ in the one true faith. The Holy Spirit gives this promise through the Apostle: "And I am sure of this, that he who began a good work in you will bring it to completion at the day of Jesus Christ" (Phil. 1:6). Embedded in the absolution is the promise of the resurrection of the body and eternal life with Christ Jesus, our Lord. The road of Advent does not end in Bethlehem but on the Last Day.

The sermons for this Advent series will be based on Chapter 3, "Disciples Confess the Faith" in *Luther's Small Catechism: A Manual for Discipleship* by John T. Pless (CPH, 2019), pp. 49–74.

Midweek Service for Advent

SERVICE OF PRAYER AND PREACHING (LSB, p. 260)

Hymn:

> Week of Advent I: "Creator of the Stars of
> Night"—351 LSB
> Week of Advent II: "O Come, O Come
> Emmanuel"—357 LSB
> Week of Advent III: "Once He Came in
> Blessing"—333 LSB

Opening Versicles—Advent, p. 260

Catechetical Hymn: "We All Believe in One True
God"—954 LSB

Readings from Holy Scripture:

> *Week of Advent I*: Galatians 4:4–6
> (*God sent His Son born of woman to redeem us so that we
> are given the rights of sons by the Spirit*)
> *Week of Advent II*: Romans 15:7–13
> (*Christ the servant came to be the Savior of all*)
> *Week of Advent III*: John 15:24–16:15
> (*The Comforter is given to give us faith in Christ*)

Responsory for Advent
> Catechism, p. 264 (A Responsive Reading from the
> Catechism)
> > *Week of Advent I*: First Article and Explanation
> > *Week of Advent II*: Second Article and Explanation
> > *Week of Advent III*: Third Article and Explanation

Hymn

> *Week of Advent I*: "I Lie, O Lord, within Your
> Care"—885 LSB
> *Week of Advent II*: "Savior of the Nations
> Come"—332 LSB
> *Week of Advent III*: "On Jordan's Bank the Baptist's
> Cry"—344 LSB

Sermon

Offering

> During the offering, a hymn may be sung:
> Week of Advent I: "O Lord, How Shall I Meet
> You"—334 LSB
> Week of Advent II: "What Hope! An Eden
> Prophesied"—342 LSB
> Week of Advent III: "The Night Will Soon be
> Ending"—337 LSB

Prayer, p. 265

> Collect of the Week
> Collect for the Catechism
> Week of Advent I: Prayer for First Article, Praying
> Luther's Small Catechism, p. 37
> Week of Advent II: Prayer for Second Article,
> Praying Luther's Small Catechism, p. 43
> Week of Advent III: Prayer for Third Article, Praying
> Luther's Small Catechism, p. 48
> Collect for the Word, p. 265
> Evening Prayer, p. 266

Hymn Stanza

> "Prepare my heart, Lord Jesus, Turn not from me
> aside, And help me to receive You this blessed
> Adventide. From stall and manger low Come now
> to dwell within me; I'll sing Your praises gladly
> And forth Your glory show" (354:4 LSB)

Blessing, p. 267

Sermon 1: The First Article of the Apostles' Creed

24 NOVEMBER 2019

Advent draws us to the Lord who comes. We might even say that Advent really does begin in creation as the Father through His Eternal Word breathes His Spirit over the depths of darkness and calls into existence that the culmination of things that are not.

The well-loved hymn of Isaac Watts, which we associate with Christmas, announces, "Joy to the world, the Lord has come! Let earth receive her King" (387:1 LSB). Advent draws us to the Lord who comes. We might even say that Advent really does begin in creation as the Father through His Eternal Word breathes His Spirit over the depths of darkness and calls into existence that the culmination of things that are not. We did not create ourselves; rather, this God has made us along with all that exists. We read of it in Genesis: In the beginning, God spoke all creation into existence. There is beauty and order as over the six days, the Father creates light and separates it from darkness, brings land out of the waters, causes that earth to sprout vegetation small and large, and sets sun and moon in place. He fills the waters with living creatures and birds are made to fly in the air, animals of every description are made, and finally, on the sixth day, the culmination of creation week, He makes man, male and female, in His own image. And over it all, God speaks a benediction "it was very good."

But the sin of our first parents darkened this fresh and wondrous cosmos. They were given creation as a gift, but instead of trusting in the Giver, they believe the lie of the serpent. Their eyes are indeed now open, and they no longer see the world as gift; they see their own nakedness. Adam and Eve hide in shame. The world has become a fearful place. Luther said of Adam and Eve that now even the rustling of a dry leaf would have terrorized them. The world becomes one large, stinking cemetery. We may exalt in the glories of nature with high poetry praise, but the reality remains that majestic mountains do erupt, spewing volcanic death on those who live under their shadow. Serene seas can churn up reckless hurricanes, and calm breezes give way to tornadoes that sweep peaceful villages away. In the midst of life, there is death.

It is into this world that the Son of God comes born of woman, born to redeem those under the curse of the law. Born to ransom and rescue the whole human race. Born to give us a new genesis. Because the Father has sent His Son into this perishing world, creation can be received as a gift by those who know the truth. Recall the words of the Apostle Paul: "For everything created by God is good, and nothing is to be rejected if it is received with thanksgiving, for it is made holy by the word of God and prayer" (I Tim. 4:4–5).

What is this truth? It is nothing other than the fact that the Father who has made me and all that exists has sent His Son to redeem this world of lost and condemned sinners. In the blood of the One born of woman, God has reconciled the world to Himself. God's wrath poured out at Calvary has freed us from condemnation. In Christ Jesus, we receive all good things from the hand of a loving Father: body and soul, eyes, ears, and all my members, my reason and all my senses. And there is more. The Father takes care of them by giving clothing and shoes, food and drink, house and home, wife and children, land, animals, and all that I have. In other words, on account of Christ Jesus, "He richly and daily provides me with all that I need to support this body and life." In Christ, He "defends me against all danger and guards and protects me from all evil." In Christ, we can indeed answer the Apostle's rhetorical question in I Cor. 4:7, "What do you have that you did not receive?" with a resounding "NOTHING!" In Christ, we can see the generosity of the Father and confess with the Catechism that these gifts of the First Article are "all this purely out of His divine goodness and mercy without any merit or worthiness in me."

Yes, God gives daily bread to all people, even the unbelieving and wicked, but when those who know the truth of God's coming in the flesh pray, "Give us this day our daily bread," we are praying that the Father would open our eyes to the truth so that we "realize this and receive our daily bread with thanksgiving."

There is a certain kind of puritanical piety that often emerges in Advent, lamenting the materialism of the season. It is misplaced. God must like matter, for He created so much of it. After all, He made me and all creatures. And in the womb of the virgin Mary, He took on matter—flesh and blood. Christians need not cast a dark cloud over the wonderment that accompanies the sights, sounds, smells, and emotions of this season. They too can be embraced in the catalog of "every good gift and every perfect gift" that is "from above, coming down from the Father of lights, with whom there is no variation or shadow due to change" (James 1:17).

So we confess, "I believe in God, the Father Almighty maker of heaven and earth." The First Article of our Christian creed is good news, gospel, for the One who created us is the Father of the Son sent into the world to be our Brother and Savior. Therefore we can say with the hymn writer:

> Let the earth now praise the Lord
> Who has truly kept His word
> And at last to us did send
> Christ, the sinner's help and friend. (352:1 LSB)

Sermon 2: The Second Article of the Apostles' Creed

1 DECEMBER 2019

Under the lordship of the crucified and risen Emmanuel, our existence is one of blessedness. Blessedness means we are not under the condemnation of the Law, but the benediction of God's favor here in time and, hereafter, in eternity.

John the Baptist asked what one preacher describes as "Advent's ageless question." It was an inquiry made not out of idle speculation or academic curiosity; it was a desperate, life or death question. John said, "Are you the one who is to come, or shall we look for another" (Matthew 11:3)? The Second Article of the Apostles' Creed answers the incarcerated Baptist's query affirmatively. This Jesus, whose way John the Baptist prepared, is the One.

The Catechism's explanation of the Second Article centers its confession on Jesus Christ, true God, begotten of the Father from eternity, and true man, born of the virgin Mary, who is the Lord. With the title "Lord," Jesus is identified as Yahweh, God incarnate. The Catechism now takes this basic, Biblical truth to the next level. This Jesus is my Lord and my God. What is demanded in the First Commandment, "You shall have no other gods," is fulfilled through faith in Christ Jesus. He is my Lord.

To have a lord is to be possessed by another. In the ancient world, those who were called "lords" exercised power over their subjects, and sometimes oppressively. Think of slaves whose very bodies were claimed as the property of a master, a lord. Such was the case with the children of Israel subject to slavery in Egypt. In the New Testament, sin, death, and the Devil are pictured as lords. So, for example, Jesus says in John 8:34, "Truly, truly, I say to you, everyone who practices sin is a slave to sin." The Apostle Paul announces the flip side of this reality in Romans 6:14, "For sin will have no dominion [lordship] over you, since you are not under law but under grace." Likewise, Paul teaches us that, where sin is lord, death reigns: "Therefore, just as sin came into the world through one man, and death through sin, so death spread to all men because all sinned" (Romans 5:12). Sin pays off its slaves with the dividends of death, but there is more still. Dead in trespasses and sins (Ephesians 2:1), we were under condemnation, slaves beneath the mastery of Satan, ". . . children of wrath, like the rest of mankind" (Ephesians 2:3). Sin, death, and Satan are the only alternatives to the Lordship of Christ Jesus. You will be possessed by something or someone. If Jesus is not reigning over you with His grace and peace, be assured, you will not live a free and autonomous life. Sin, death, and the Devil will hold you fast in their all-embracing grip.

Luther's comforting confession of the Second Article tells us how Jesus Christ has "redeemed me, a lost and condemned person . . . that I may be His own, live under Him in His kingdom and serve Him in everlasting righteousness, innocence, and blessed, just as He is risen from the dead, and lives and reigns to all eternity." No wonder the theologian, Hermann Sasse, once exclaimed these words of Luther are the most beautiful words ever written in the German language and how sweet they are in English as well! For here, Luther is expressing the pulsating heart of the Gospel, echoing the Apostle Paul in Colossians 1:13: "He [the Father] has delivered us from the domain [lordship] of darkness and transferred us to the kingdom of his beloved Son." This is where we are located now— possessed by the Lord Jesus who purchased and won us from all sins, from death, and the power of the Devil, not with gold or silver but with His holy, precious blood and innocent suffering of death.

Here is life in a kingdom not governed by the sword of oppression and the ever-present threat of death, but by a King who reigns from the cross, exercising mercy and grace for broken sinners. Have you ever noticed how often our Advent hymns speak of this King and His Kingdom? For example, Charles Wesley has us sing in, "Come, Thou Long-Expected Jesus," these words:

> Born Thy people to deliver;
> Born a child and yet a king;
> Born to reign in us forever,
> Now Thy gracious kingdom brings.
> By Thine own eternal Spirit
> Rule in all our hearts alone;
> By Thine all sufficient merit
> Raise us to Thy glorious throne. (338:1 LSB)

Or the old Reformation era hymn, "Lift Up Your Heads, Ye Mighty Gates," beckons us with this royal call:

> Lift up your heads, ye mighty gates!
> Behold the King of glory waits.
> The King of kings is drawing near;
> The Savior of the world is here.
> Life and salvation, He doth bring;
> Therefore, rejoice and gladly sing.
> To God the Father raise
> Your joyful songs of praise. (340:1 LSB)

Or then there is "Prepare the Royal Highway," with its comforting announcement:

> His is no earthly kingdom;
> It comes from Heaven above.
> His rule is peace and freedom
> and justice, truth, and love.
> So, let your praise be sounding
> For kindness so abounding:
> Hosanna to the Lord,
> For He fulfills God's Word. (343:4 LSB)

We could go on and on with Advent hymns (and, on your own, you might want to page through the Advent section of your hymnal) to point out references to God's gracious Kingdom, which we are given in Christ Jesus our Lord. But these references will suffice to demonstrate how life in the Kingdom is given by the One who has made us His own out of His perfect righteousness, innocence, and blessedness. In His kingdom, we live, not in self-righteousness and, therefore, under condemnation, but under the righteousness of the Messiah by whose blood we are made His own. Under His righteousness, not achieved but given freely as a gift through faith, we live in innocence, for God does not hold our sin against us. Covered with His blood-bought forgiveness, our consciences are cleansed from guilt and our shame is covered. We have peace with God through faith in Christ. This innocence does not mean we never sin, but our sin is not held against us. Confessed and absolved it will not have lordship over us. God in the flesh is your Lord.

In His kingdom, we live, not in self-righteousness and, therefore, under condemnation, but under the righteousness of the Messiah by whose blood we are made His own.

Under the lordship of the crucified and risen Emmanuel, our existence is one of blessedness. Blessedness means we are not under the condemnation of the Law, but the benediction of God's favor here in time and, hereafter, in eternity.

Jesus' first Advent was greeted with cries of Jerusalem's citizens: "Blessed is the King who comes in the name of the Lord! Peace in Heaven and glory in the highest" (Luke 19:38)! Who is this King? It is Jesus Christ, my Lord, begotten of the Father from eternity, and true man, born of the virgin Mary. He has come so we might be His own and have life in His Kingdom. This is the glad news of the Advent season and our joyful confession. Amen.

Sermon 3: The Third Article of the Apostles' Creed

9 DECEMBER 2019

The Holy Spirit is fixated on Jesus, and it is the Spirit's mission to bring us to faith in Him for He is the way, the truth, and the life, and no one comes to the Father except through Him.

Unlike the previous two articles of the Creed, Luther begins his explanation of the Third Article, not with a confession of faith, but a statement of the inability to believe: "I believe that I cannot by my own reason or strength believe in Jesus Christ my Lord, or come to Him." Advent does not map our progress in coming to Christ. Rather, it is the story of God's condescension to us. He came and created us and all things out of the void of nothingness. And in the fullness of time, the same Lord who created the heavens and earth came from Heaven above to be our Savior, to suffer our sin and die our death. We might even call the Creed's Third Article, the third movement of Advent, for now, here in time, the Holy Spirit comes to us, bringing us to faith through the Gospel and keeping us in that faith to the very end.

The Holy Spirit, who breathes over the formlessness before there was a creation to bring into existence things that were not, does not sit idly by until the Day of Pentecost. He was there in the Old Testament, speaking by the prophets about the coming Messiah, the One of whom the Father said in Isaiah 42: "I have put my Spirit upon Him" (Isaiah 42:1). He is the Spirit who causes Mary to become pregnant, without the aid of a man, just as the angel said, "The Holy Spirit will come upon you, and the power of the Most High will overshadow you; therefore the child to be born will be called holy—the Son of God" (Luke 1:35). It is this same Holy Spirit who Jesus calls the Spirit of Truth, the Comforter. He is sent by the Father through the Son to bring to our remembrance all Jesus has said. "He will glorify me, for He will take what is mine and declare it to you. All that the Father has is mine; therefore I said he will take what is mine and declare it to you" (John 16:14–15).

Without the Spirit of Truth, we would still be held captive to the lies of Satan, prisoners of the grave, forever dead to God. Corpses cannot give life to themselves. The Catechism is simply echoing the truth of the Apostle Paul, who declared how no one can confess Jesus is Lord except by the Holy Spirit (see I Corinthians 12:3). The advent of the Holy Spirit brings Christ's work to us and brings us to Christ Jesus, who is our access to His Father.

We typically follow the structure of the Creed, moving from the Father to the Son and from the Son to the Holy Spirit. But the Creed also works in reverse. When by our own reason and strength we are powerless to come to Christ, the Spirit calls us by the Gospel, enlightens us with His gifts, and keeps us in the true faith. The Spirit does not promote Himself, but He preaches Christ. In fact, Luther says Jesus has made the Holy Spirit a preacher:

> Here Christ makes the Holy Spirit a Preacher. He does so to prevent one from gaping toward Heaven in search of Him, as the fluttering spirits and enthusiasts do, and from divorcing Him from the oral Word of the ministry. One should know and learn that He will be in and with the Word, and that it will guide us into all truth, in order that we may believe it, use it as a weapon, be preserved by it against all the lies and deceptions of the Devil, and prevail in all trials and temptations. . . . The Holy Spirit wants this truth which He is to impress into our hearts to be so firmly fixed that reason and all one's own thoughts and feelings are relegated to the background. He wants us to adhere solely to the Word and to regard it as the only truth. And through this Word alone He governs the Christian Church to the end. (AE 24:362)

The Holy Spirit is fixated on Jesus, and it is the Spirit's mission to bring us to faith in Him for He is the way, the truth, and the life, and no one comes to the Father except through Him. The Third Article takes us back to the Second Article and the Second Article to the First Article, where we recognize God for who He is, the Father Almighty, who has made me and all creatures.

Now, where and how is the Holy Spirit doing His work of calling, gathering, enlightening, and sanctifying me? Right here in His Church, where the Gospel is going on: "In this Christian Church He daily and richly forgives all my sins and the sins of all believers." The Advent of Christ Jesus in the flesh was a once and for all event. He was born once in Bethlehem. He suffered and died only once at Golgotha. He was raised from the dead, never to die again, only once. But the Advent of the Holy Spirit was not a one-time event limited to Pentecost Sunday. No, His advent is "daily and richly." The forgiveness of sins is the very air we breathe, and the Spirit continues to breathe it into us through the continual preaching of His Gospel. Spiritually, we cannot live without His words, which are truth and life continually coming into our ears and lodging in our hearts. Therefore, we hold God's Word sacred and gladly hear and learn it.

The Advent of the Spirit is ongoing, and it points to the Last Day when the anticipation and hope of Advent will give way to fulfillment. We will no longer wait and groan but, rather, we will forever be with Christ our Emmanuel. With our own ears, we will hear the voice of our Good Shepherd and follow Him to the feast that forever brings together Christmas and Easter. But even now, as we wait, the Advent of the Spirit gives us certainty and confidence. To paraphrase one theologian, every time the absolution is spoken, the verdict of the Last Day slips out ahead of time. Wherever the Spirit delivers Christ's blood-purchased goods, the forgiveness of sins is pronounced, and the Word is believed, there is life and salvation! So, now we wait, but not in anxiety or uncertainty, but in living hope, born of the Spirit. It is a hope which will never disappoint.

"The Spirit and the Bride say, 'Come.' And let the one who hears say, 'Come.' . . . He who testifies to these things says, 'Surely I am coming soon.' Amen. Come, Lord Jesus!" (Revelation 22:17, 20).

29

Midweek Advent Series

Oratio, Meditatio, Tentatio

27 NOVEMBER 2018

The order of service for this series is the **Service of Prayer and Preaching** *(LSB, p. 260).*

HYMN
> Midweek I: "O Come, O Come Emmanuel"—357 LSB
> Midweek II: "Creator of the Stars of Night"—351 LSB
> Midweek III: "Comfort, Comfort These My
>> People"—347 LSB

OPENING VERSICLES FOR ADVENT p. 260
OLD TESTAMENT CANTICLE "Sing Praise to the God of Israel"—936 LSB
READING FROM HOLY SCRIPTURE
> Midweek I: Psalm 119:12–16, 26–27
> Midweek II: Psalm 119: 97–104, 129–133
> Midweek III: Psalm 119:153–168

RESPONSORY FOR ADVENT p. 263
CATECHISM
> Ten Commandments/Apostles' Creed/Lord's Prayer
> Midweek I: Introduction/First Petition, p. 323 LSB
> Midweek II: Second Petition, p. 324 LSB
> Midweek III: Third Petition, p. 324 LSB

HYMN STANZA "For the Joy Thine Advent Gave Me"
548:3 LSB

SERMON
Midweek I *Oratio*
Midweek II *Meditatio*
Midweek III *Tentatio*
OFFERING
HYMN
Midweek I: "O Lord, How Shall I Meet You"—334 LSB
Midweek II: "Once He Came in Blessing"—333 LSB
Midweek III: "The Night Will Soon be
Ending"—337 LSB
PRAYER p. 263
COLLECT OF THE WEEK
Midweek I: Collect for Advent I
Midweek II: Collect for Advent II
Midweek III: Collect for Advent III

COLLECT FOR THE WORD p. 265
CATECHISM PRAYERS
Midweek I: Catechism Prayer for "Introduction"
(Pless, *Praying Luther's Small Catechism*, p. 54) and
Catechism Prayer for "First Petition" (Pless, p. 56)
Midweek II: Catechism Prayer for "Second Petition"
(Pless, p. 59)
Midweek III: Catechism Prayer for "Third Petition"
(Pless, p. 62)
EVENING PRAYER p. 267
HYMN STANZA "Arise, O Christian People"—354:4 LSB
BLESSING p. 267

Sermon Notes

Midweek I: Oratio

Oratio is prayer grounded in the Word of God. "When we use His
Word to pray, we pray by the Spirit" (Kleinig, 172). Like David, who

was given the words of the Lord and so prays that God would lead and guide Him, so our mouths are opened to call upon God for all that He promises. The *oratio* is embodied in the Introduction and First Petition of the Lord's Prayer in the Small Catechism. We can call God "our Father" because He has given us His Son. The Holy Spirit has brought us to faith in the Son through the Gospel. It is in this faith that we know that it is most certainly true that God is our Father.

The three articles of the Creed are also reversible. It is the Holy Spirit who brings us to Christ Jesus, our Lord, who has made us His own by His innocent suffering and death. We are located in His Kingdom, where we live under Him, serving Him in everlasting righteousness, innocence, and blessedness even as He is risen from the dead to live and reign for all eternity. In Him, we have boldness and confidence to enter into the presence of His Father.

The blessed One who comes in the name of the Lord gives us access to His Father. Luther reminds us that God's name is certainly holy in itself, but we pray that it may be kept holy among us. This is done when the Word of God is taught in its truth and purity, and we as His children lead holy lives according to it. Notice here how the Catechism's explanation resonate with the words of Psalm 119 where we implore God to "deal bountifully with your servant, that I may live and keep your word" (Ps. 119:17) and again, "Make me understand the way of your precepts, and I will meditate on your wondrous works" (Ps. 119:27). God's Word is heard and pondered in this Psalm so that "petition and confession, again and again, modulate into praise and thanksgiving" (H.J. Kraus, *Psalms* II:415). This modulation is also reflected in many of the hymns of Advent. For example:

> "Fling wide the portals of your heart; Make it a temple set apart from earthly use for heav'n's employ; Adorned with prayer and love and joy. So shall your Sovereign enter in and new and nobler life begin. To God alone be praise for word and deed and grace!" (340:4 LSB)

> "Enter now my waiting heart, glorious King and Lord most holy. Dwell in me and ne'er depart, though I am but poor and lowly. Ah, what riches will be mine when Thou art my guest divine! Hail! Hosanna, David's Son! Jesus hear our supplication! Let Thy kingdom, scepter, crown, Bring us blessing and salvation, that forever we may sing: Hail! Hosanna to our King." (350:2 & 4 LSB)

Also, "O Savior, Rend the Heavens Wide"—355 LSB, especially stanzas 6–7.

The posture of Advent is prayer, calling out to the Lord who has come, who comes to us now in His Word and will come again at the end to take us to Himself. In the meantime, we wait not as those who live in confusion and uncertainty but as dear children of God who have learned and continue to learn that God is our true Father and we are His true children so that we might make our petitions to Him as dear children coming before a dear father "with boldness and confidence."

The Lord has come to us. He is the Word made flesh. The Scriptures which His Spirit inspired prophets and apostles to write testify to Him. It is in and through the Holy Scriptures that Christ Jesus gives Himself to us. Without the Holy Scriptures, we would not know Him whose words are "spirit and life" (John 6:63). We listen to the Scriptures read and preached so that we might know Christ and His benefits. His words of promise give us the courage to call upon Him.

Bonhoeffer asserted, "The richness of the Word of God ought to determine our prayer, not the poverty of our heart" (*Psalms*, 15). It is for this reason that the Psalmist confesses his delight in the Lord's words (Ps. 16) and implores God to give him understanding that he may meditate on the Lord's wondrous works.

Our Advent *oratio* is ever "Come, Lord Jesus." He is near to all who call upon His name, and He has promised to hear us and save us.

Possible Outline

Introduction:

> Everything about Advent announces that the Lord is present to redeem and rescue His people. He has given us His holy name that we may call upon Him and live holy lives here in time and thereafter in eternity.

> I. God's Word gives us His Name.

> II. With His Name we Have His Promise: All Those who Call Upon His Name will be Saved.

III. God's Name is Kept Holy When we Call Upon His
     Name with our Lips and Honor it in Lives of Faith
     and Love.

Conclusion:

The Catechism reminds us that God's holy name is
given to us that we may call upon it in every trouble,
pray, praise, and give thanks. For the Christian, Advent
is much more than a hectic season of preparation for
the festivities of Christian. Advent is the Christian life
in miniature. It is listening to the words of the Lord and
learning ever again from His Word that we are His holy
children blessed with His name in Baptism. With His
name on our lips, we call upon Him in the midst of this
world's chaos, with our own lives lacerated by sin, and
in the face of death, trusting only in His promises for
the sake of the Son He sent to be our Brother and Savior.
Call upon Him now in this day of trouble. He will save
you, and you shall glorify Him.

Midweek II: Meditatio

"Intimate acquaintance with the word of Yahweh brings about superior prudence (cf. Deut. 4:6). It produces a careful walk (v.101) and
grants delightful enjoyment (v.103)" (H.J. Kraus, *Psalms* II:418). The
mediatio of Luther's triad is not self-reflective introspection, but a
life lived in the Word of God. Meditation is verbal as it engages the
words of the Lord. In the words of Cranmer's old collect, we "read,
mark, learn, and inwardly digest" God's Word. Note here the connections with Psalm 119. The Psalmist prays, "Oh how I love your
law! It is my meditation all the day" (v.97). Also, "How sweet are
your words to my taste, sweeter than honey to my mouth" (v.103).

Meditation is not an escape from the world into a monastic
cell where one is left alone with his or her thoughts. Rather it is life
in God's Word within the world. The kingdom for which we pray in
the second petition is not a Platonic sphere outside of temporal existence. God's kingdom comes with His Son, who entered this world

as the child of Mary. He brings His everlasting reign into human history, and history finds its ultimate fulfillment in Him, who is the author and finisher of our salvation. This kingdom comes to us now in time. How does this happen? Listen to the Catechism: "God's kingdom comes when our heavenly Father gives us His Holy Spirit so that by His grace we believe His holy Word and lead godly lives here in time and there in eternity."

No wonder then that Luther ties meditation to listening to sermons, remembering your Baptism, and engaging in the works of one's vocation like honoring parents according to the fourth commandments. We meditate on that which we love. To meditate rightly is to fear, love, and trust in God above all things and give oneself in love to the service of the neighbor according to God's commandments. Meditation is not spiritual introversion; it is extroverted, outside of oneself in Christ by faith and in the neighbor by love.

Possible Outline

Introduction:

> What do you think about when you hear the word, meditation? Buddha sitting cross-legged and gazing at his belly? Contemplative monks cloistered away with attention fixed on the rosaries in their hands? Spiritual techniques marketed with the promise of providing tranquility and stability to your life? The Bible gives us an altogether different picture of mediation. We meditate rightly by hearing and keeping God's Holy Word. We meditate on the things we love (here the preacher might give some examples). Loving the Word of the Lord, we meditate on it. Our hearts are occupied with God's Word.

>   I. To meditate on God's Word is to hear it, for faith comes by hearing the Word.

>   II. To meditate on God's Word is to take it to heart.

>   III. To meditate on God's Word is to live godly lives according to it.

Conclusion:

> As we have heard in the Catechism, "God's kingdom comes by itself without our prayer." We do not pull ourselves up into God's kingdom through our mediation. His kingdom is the kingdom of the ear, as Luther said in one of his sermons. We meditate when we, like Mary (recall Luke 1), hear and believe God's "Word and lead godly lives here in time and there in eternity."

Midweek III: Tentatio

Tentatio is the spiritual attack or affliction that comes when one meditates on the Word of God. Psalm 119:153 is a lament born out of this *tentatio*: "Look on my affliction and deliver me, for I do not forget your law." There is a parallel between this verse and the Catechism's explanation of the third petition: "God's will is done when He breaks and hinders every evil plan and purpose of the devil, the world, and our sinful nature which do not want us to hallow God's name or let His kingdom come; and when He strengthens and keeps us firm in His Word and faith until we die. This is His good and gracious will."

Advent reminds us that we do not pray the third petition as agnostics who do not know the will of God. God's good and gracious is revealed in the Blessed One, who comes in the name of the Lord. He is the Lamb of God, who takes away the sin of the world. His mercy is great (Psalm 119:156). Those who keep the words of this Savior will endure trial and persecution in one form or another. Think of the imprisonment of the great saint of Advent, John the Baptist (Matthew 11). Mary, who sings the *Magnificat* and ponders (meditates) on all that the God of her salvation has done (see Luke 2:19), will have her own soul pierced by a sword (Luke 2:35) as her Son is set for "the fall and rising of many in Israel" (Luke 2:34).

God's good and gracious will is our salvation. That, as Luther reminds us, is His "proper" work. But His proper work also entails His "alien" work, the work of breaking and hindering all that sets itself in opposition to His will: the devil, the world, and our sinful nature. Luther's prayer in the Large Catechism's explanation of the third petition is entirely consistent with Psalm 119: "Dear Father, your will be done and not the will of the devil or of our enemies; nor of those who would persecute and oppress your holy Word or prevent your kingdom from coming; and grant that we may bear patiently and overcome whatever we must suffer on its account, so that our poor flesh may not yield or fall away through weakness or sloth" (LC III:67, K-W, 449).

To hold fast the treasures of the first two petitions (God's holy name and the gift of His kingdom) means that there will be suffering in one form or another: "If we try to hold these treasures fast, we will have to suffer an astonishing number of attack and assaults from all who venture to hinder and thwart the fulfillment of the first two petitions" (LC III:61, K-W, 448).

Potential Outline

Introduction:

> How are you to pray "Thy will be done"? The German preacher, Helmut Thielicke, observed that this is a dangerous petition to pray for we are, in fact, praying against ourselves. We are not asking God to bring His will into alignment with our will. Just the opposite, we are imploring Him to bring our fickle and unpredictable wills into harmony with His good and gracious will. This is not without suffering, for we are asking God to "break and hinder" the will of the enemies: the devil, the world, and yes, our sinful nature.

> I. To meditate on God's Word is to become a target.

> II. Christians are under attack from the devil, the world, and our own flesh.

> III. God's Word sustains us to endure to the end.

Conclusion:

> Bonhoeffer has described the Christian life as one long Advent Season. We are waiting on a Savior who has

already come and comes even now. He has died in our place, defeated our enemies, and been raised for your justification. Clinging to His Word, we are set in spiritual warfare with all that stands in opposition to Him. Our confidence is not in ourselves but in His sure and certain testimonies, so we pray: "Give me life according to your steadfast love. The sum of your word is truth, and every one of your just and righteous decrees endures forever" (Psalm 119:159b–160).

30

Christmas from Below

23 DECEMBER 2018

"Whoever wants a gracious God must not bypass Jesus Christ, the proper mercy seat (Rom. 5:25); whoever seeks God apart from Christ will end up meeting the God, not of mercy but of wrath, as described by Moses as a 'devouring fire' (Deut. 4:24)."[1]

Luther's Christmas preaching is strikingly earthly. Commenting on the *Magnificat*, Luther speaks of God's work in the womb of Mary as a work that is done in the depths: "Thus God's work and His eyes are in the depths, but man's only in the heights" (AE 21:301). Christmas wrecks all attempts to penetrate God's hiddenness and seek Him out in heaven. He comes to us, clothed in our humanity. In obscure Bethlehem, God demonstrates His favor for sinners "by stepping down so deep into flesh and blood" (AE 52:12). The eternal Word of the Father is made flesh to dwell among us. The incarnation is not a sign that points us to an absent deity but the Creator of all things now Himself a creature without ceasing to be Creator!

This is no theoretical incarnation as if the message of Christmas was simply that God is like Jesus or that Jesus is a window through which we see God more clearly. No, this boy in the manger is God. More than that, He is God for us. If John the Baptist was the great preacher of Advent, then the angel of Luke 2:10ff is the first and greatest preacher of Christmas: "Fear not, for behold, I bring you good news of great joy that will be for all the people. For unto to you is born this day in the city of David a Savior, who is Christ the Lord."

Preaching the Gospel always hangs on the "for you." This simple phrase saves hearers from being subjected to only a lesson in history or chided with moralistic exhortations to strive for more joy or give more generously. Preachers imitate the angel announcing that this Savior born in Bethlehem, wrapped in swaddling clothes and resting in a manger, is for you. The boy lying in that crib is the Word made flesh for you.

In the fullness of time, God did not send a book, an ethicist, an action plan, a mystical experience, a liturgy, or a church. He sent the Word. Hermann Sasse helpfully explains that "the consummation of revelation, the incarnation of the only Son of God is described in this sentence: 'The *Word* became flesh and dwelt among us, and we *beheld* his glory' (John 1:14). The characteristic feature of biblical revelation is that it is *historical* revelation."[2] In Christ, God, "the King of kings and Lord of lords, who alone has immortality" steps out of His dwelling "in unapproachable light where no mortal can ever see or know Him" (cf. I Timothy 6:16) to be born of a woman located in what Martin Franzmann once referred to as "garden variety history" when Caesar Augustus ruled Rome (cf. Luke 2:1).

The preaching of Christmas brings us not to God in His majestic and terrifying hiddenness forever out of reach but to God hidden in flesh and blood so as to reveal Himself as our Savior. God condescends to be Emmanuel among and for sinners. Luther observes that if God were out to destroy us, He would have not taken on our flesh: "He has the power to cast us into hell yet he took soul and body like ours . . . If he were against us he would not have clothed himself in our flesh"[3]. In the weakness of Mary's baby and in the poverty of a cattle shed, the glory of the glory is revealed in the flesh for our flesh to see, touch, and hear. But Christmas is more than an object lesson, an iconic illustration of God's goodwill; it is God coming in the flesh to die for those who despised Him. The crib and the cross are of the same wood as Helmut Thielicke quipped.[4] The Lord takes on flesh and blood in order to be the Lamb of God who takes away the sin of the world by making Himself the once and for all sacrifice for sin. He was born to die that through His death, we are reconciled to our Creator (cf. II Corinthians 5:18–6:2).

The heavens were opened above the prairies of Bethlehem, not to give the shepherds a glimpse into the celestial sphere but to announce to them the birth of Him who was given for them and for us. God grant us preachers who mimic the angel in proclaiming the Savior as the Father's gift for you.

Notes

1 Dennis Ngien, *Luther's Theology of the Cross: Christ in Luther's Sermons on John* (Eugene: Cascade Books, 2018), 44.

2 Hermann Sasse, "The Church and the Word of God" in *The Lonely Way*, Vol. I (1927–1939), ed. Matthew C. Harrison (Saint Louis: Concordia Publishing House, 2001), 154. This is a very valuable essay for preaching as Sasse demonstrates that the Word made flesh is never to be separated from the revealed, proclaimed, and written Word. Just as the Son of God becomes man without ceasing to be God just so "the Word of God spoken in history becomes a human word, and yet it does not cease to be God's Word" (154–155).

3 Cited from a Luther sermon of 1527 (WA 23:731) by Norman Nagel in "Heresy, Doctor Luther, Heresy!" in *Dona Gratis Donta: Essays in Honor of Norman Nagel on his Ninetieth Birthday*, ed. J. Vieker, B. Day, and A. Collver (Manchester, MO: Nagel Festschrift Committee, 2015), 307.

4 Helmut Thielicke, *Being a Christian When the Chips are Down*, trans. H. George Anderson (Philadelphia: Fortress Press, 1979), 101.

31

Epiphany

The Father Unwraps the Gift of His Son

6 JANUARY 2019

If Christmas celebrates the Father's giving of the gift of Christ Jesus to us sinners, then Epiphany might be said to be the Father unwrapping this gift for us. Epiphany means "manifestation." In the three primary events of Epiphany—the visit of the magi (Matthew 2:1–12), the baptism of our Lord in the Jordan (Matthew 3:13–17), and the turning of water into wine at Cana's wedding (John 2:1–11)—the Father is making His Son known to the world. In the words of the Apostle, Paul kept secret for the ages is now revealed: "When you read this, you can perceive my insight into the mystery of Christ, which was not made known to the sons of men in other generations as it has now been revealed to his holy apostles and prophets by the Spirit. This mystery is that the Gentiles are fellow heirs, members of the same body, and partakers of the promise in Christ Jesus through the gospel" (Ephesians 3:4–6).

The coming of the magi, these strange pilgrims from the east who are guided by a star to the bed of the infant King, are the first of an unending procession of Gentiles who will come to worship Him, finding access to God's kindness and favor in Him. The gift of Christmas is intended for the whole world as the angel announced to the shepherds: "I bring you good news of great joy that will be for all the people. For unto you is born this day in the city of David a Savior, who is Christ the Lord" (Luke 2:10–11).

If the shepherds who came to Bethlehem to adore the newborn Lord represented the dregs of the culture-the untrustworthy and uneducated, then the wise men represent the other end of the spectrum. They are educated. They have reliable knowledge. They must have had wealth, or how would they have had the leisure to make the overland journey to Jerusalem and purchase expensive gifts for the One whom they seek?

But the contrast between the poverty of the shepherds and the wealth of the wise men is not the point of Epiphany. Epiphany has to do with manifestation or revelation. It is about the incarnation as one of our hymns puts "God in man-made manifest" (see LSB 394). Jesus is made manifest for the Savior that He is. This Lord is true God, begotten of the Father from all eternity and also true man born of the virgin Mary as the Catechism confesses. And in this manifestation given by God's Word to the wise men, we are given to see the contrast between the carnal wisdom of the world and the wisdom of the cross by which God confounds the wisdom of the wise.

The wise men followed what they had seen in the skies—this mysterious star—that they reckoned indicated the birth of the king of the Jews. They run the path of their logic: The king of the Jews must mean Jerusalem. So off to the holy city, they go with their treasures in tow. Coming to Jerusalem, they go to Herod's palace. This must be the place for a prince destined to David's throne. Their question—"Where is he who has been born king of the Jews?"—causes King Herod panic! Herod consults his court theologians. Bethlehem of Judea is the answer for the Prophet Micah said that out of this, Judean village would come a ruler who will shepherd God's people forever. The prophetic Scriptures will provide a course correction for the magi. Only when the Word of God is joined to the star are the magi led to Jesus. Without God's Word, there is no Epiphany, no manifestation of the mystery.[1]

This Jesus is the King revealed to the magi. The wise men do not find him by the compass of their own reason or strength. Human reason leads them astray. Human reason concludes that Israel's King must be born in the holy city, the seat of government. But Israel's King is not found within the halls of Herod but in Bethlehem. That is where the Scriptures point the wise men. The King of heaven and earth is bedded in a manger. The King of Glory is handed over to sinful men, crucified by sinners, and dies on a cross. There on the cross, He is epiphanied, revealed, and manifested as the Savior that he is. The authentic King of the Jews is not Herod but Jesus. That's what His cross proclaims!

Jesus' cross is for dull shepherds and bright magi. It is for the whole world. It is for you. In the events of the Epiphany, it is demonstrated that the magi do not find the one born King of the Jews by their own wisdom. No, in fact, the wise men will become what all believers finally are: little children. Little children for whom the Lord Christ gives thanks when He prays: "I thank you, Father, Lord of heaven and earth, that you have hidden these things from the wise and understanding and revealed them to little children; yes, Father, for such is your gracious will. All things have been handed over to me by my Father, and no one knows the Son except the Father, and no one knows the Father except the Son and anyone to whom the Son chooses to reveal him" (Matthew 11:25–27).

Jesus was revealed to the wise men. They are made to be like little children, capable only of receiving. And that is what Epiphany makes of us, children of the Heavenly Father who do not stand before God on the basis of our own wisdom or understanding but as those who live by faith alone. Living by faith, we look for the King only where He has promised to be found: In the manger of His Holy Scriptures, in the foolishness of preaching, in waters of Baptism, and under the bread and wine of the Holy Supper where He gives us His body to eat and His blood to drink for the forgiveness of our sins. It is here that the Father continues to unwrap His Christmas gifts given in His Son, declaring that they are for you.

Note

1 In other words, the wise men need a preacher. Here note Steven Paulson: "Without a preacher, one tries to stumble forward in life and in thinking within the limits of words as signs but always seeking to escape to a far-away freedom. The world becomes a spider web of signs pointing in some hopeful direction, but signs only end up pointing to other signs (as our postmodernists have proved) and fail to give the thing itself"—*Luther's Outlaw God*, Vol. I: Hiddenness, Evil, and Predestination (Minneapolis: Fortress Press, 2018), 6. Without the promised preached from the Prophet Micah, the star would have remained a riddle and Christ Jesus shrouded in darkness beyond their penetration.

32

Repentance and Faith from
the Penitential Psalms in Lent

9 FEBRUARY 2020

The penitential psalms (6, 32, 38, 51, 102, 130, 143) have long been associated with Lent. Pope Innocent III (1198–1216) ordered that all seven psalms were to be prayed each day, while kneeling, during the Lenten Season or if this proved unfeasible, at least on Fridays. In the Middle Ages, these psalms were associated with the seven deadly sins: Psalm 6 was said to address anger. Psalm 32 was associated with pride. Psalm 38 with gluttony. Psalm 51 with luxury. Psalm 130 was directed against envy and Psalm 143 against sloth.[1]

Luther lectured on the penitential psalms in 1517, and he revised these lectures and re-published them in 1525. Luther would provide a fuller exposition of Psalm 51 in 1532.[2] Luther would see sinfulness not merely as individual deeds but as a state of being that embraces all of man's existence, which he has inherited from Adam; this is the root sin from which man cannot deliver himself.[3] In this commentary, Luther observes that David confesses not simply his adultery and murderous plot against Uriah but the corruption of all his powers both inwardly and outwardly.[4] Luther writes,

> He [David] is not saying, 'My mother sinned when she conceived me'; nor is he saying, 'I sinned when I was conceived.' He is talking about the unformed seed itself and declaring that it is full of sin and a mass of perdition. Thus the true and proper meaning is this: 'I am

a sinner, not because I have committed adultery, nor because I have had Uriah murdered. But I have committed adultery and murder because I was born, indeed conceived and formed in the womb as a sinner.' So we are not sinners because we commit this or that sin, but we commit them because we are sinners first. That is, a bad tree and bad seed also bring forth bad fruit, and from a bad root, only a bad tree can grow. (AE 12:348)

Five years later, in the *Smalcald Articles*, Luther is insistent: "The foremost office or power of the law is that it reveals inherited sin and its fruits" (SA III:2, 4, K-W, 312). This statement is foundational for Luther's discussion of repentance. The law is retained, Luther says, in the New Testament in order to work repentance: "Now this is the thunderbolt of God, by means of which he destroys both the open sinner and the false saint and allows no one to be right but drives the whole lot of them into terror and despair" (SA III:3, 2, K-W, 312). Luther equates the law with the hammer of which Jeremiah speaks (Jer. 23:29). In opposition to papal theology, Luther asserts that "the law does not work an 'active contrition' or a 'contrived remorse' but a 'passive contrition,' true affliction of the heart, suffering, and pain of death" (SA III:3, 2, K-W, 312). Contrary to the Antinomians, Luther argues, repentance is produced by the law, not the Gospel. But to the office of the law, the New Testament immediately adds, "The consoling promise of grace through the gospel" (SA III:3, 4, K-W, 313). Where the law is preached without the Gospel, there is only death and hell. The law never provides consolation. Instead, as Mark A. Seifrid, in commenting on Romans 7:24–25, points out, "The law tells us a story about ourselves that we are unable to tell and unwilling to hear. It carries us on the 'journey to the hell of self-knowledge'—and in the knowledge of Christ back from there to heaven itself. Only those with ears to hear, who know the apostle's shout of thanksgiving, can listen to the story and see the image of our person reflected in the law."[5]

The papists do not preach genuine repentance, for they fail to see both the law and sin for what they are. They continue to hold out hope for some uncorrupted part of man retaining the capacity to will the good.[6] This leads to what Luther condemns as an "active contrition," where penance is parsed into three parts: contrition, confession, and satisfaction. "In this way, they directed the people who come to penance to place confidence in their own works" (SA III:3, 13, K-W, 314). This, Luther concludes, is a Christless procedure: "Here we see how blind reason gropes around in the things of God and seeks comfort in its own work, according to its own darkened opinions" (SA III:3, 18, K-W, 314).

Luther holds up John the Baptist as the model preacher of repentance for his preaching of the law condemns the totality of sin, whether it is inward or outward (see SA III:3, 30–32, K-W, 317). The repentance which John preaches is not uncertain or fragmentary (SA III, 3, 36, K-W, 318). Likewise, the forgiveness which John proclaims is inclusive, for he preaches Christ, the Lamb of God who takes away the sin of the world (SA III:3, 38, K-W, 318). This repentance is not confined to a single episode in the life of the Christian; it is ongoing: "This repentance endures among Christians until death because it struggles with the sin that remains in the flesh throughout this life" (SA III:3, 40, K-W, 318).

The understanding of repentance laid out by Luther in the *Smalcald Articles* is evident in his exposition of the Psalter.[7] Luther says that the Psalms might be called a "little Bible" for they show us Christ and His kingdom: "The Psalter ought to be a precious and beloved book, if for no other reason than this: it promises Christ's death and resurrection so clearly—and pictures his kingdom and the condition and nature of all Christendom–that it might be called a little Bible. In it is comprehended most beautifully and briefly everything that is in the entire Bible. It is really a fine enchiridion or handbook" (AE 35:254). Luther sees the Psalms as God's words to us; words which we, in turn, are authorized to speak to him in lament and praise, confession, and thanksgiving. Because the Psalms are God's Word, they give us certainty in our speaking.

Luther sees the Psalms as universal. They apply to all the saints: "Hence it is that the Psalter is the book of all saints; and everyone, in whatever situation he may be, finds in that situation psalms and words that fit his case, that suit him as if they were put there just for his sake, so that he could not put it better himself, or find anything better" (AE 35:256). When it comes to the preaching of repentance and faith, the Psalms are indispensable for, in them, Luther says, "There you have a fine, bright, pure mirror that will show you what

Christendom is. Indeed you will find in it also yourself and the true *gnothi seauton*, as well as God himself and all creatures" (AE 35:257).

Luther came to understand that the knowledge of self without the knowledge of God leads to despair and that knowledge of God without the knowledge of sin leads to presumption.[8] Psalm 51 gives us both. The preacher may wish to set the psalm in the context of II Samuel 11:1–12:15, unfolding the dynamic of Nathan's proclamation of God's law to David, which brings about the knowledge of self. See Ps. 51:3, "For I know my transgressions, and my sin is ever before me." Here the preacher could explore the connection what is entailed in this self-knowledge. Ash Wednesday is a day for self-examination. Recall the words of the Exhortation in Corporate Confession and Absolution (LSB, p. 290): ". . . it is proper that we diligently examine ourselves, as St. Paul urges us to do, for this holy Sacrament has been instituted for the special comfort of those who are troubled because of their sin and who humbly confess their sins, fear God's wrath, and hunger and thirst for righteousness. But when we examine our hearts and consciences, we find nothing in us but sin and death, from which we are incapable of delivering ourselves."[9]

The somber words of the Ash Wednesday liturgy announce to us what deep down we already know, that we are dust, and to dust we must return. But the problem is not merely mortality. It is not just that we die but that we die as sinners under God's judgment. It is a judgment that is not misplaced; it is justified (Ps. 51:4). It is a verdict of condemnation that falls not simply on miscalculated choices and perverse deeds; it falls on me, my person. It falls on the one who was a sinner before he first cursed, lusted, lied, hated, or killed. It falls on the one who was brought forth in iniquity and conceived in sin (Ps. 51:4).[10]

To confess your sin is to agree with God's evaluation of your life. To confess your sin is to cease the futile attempt to self-justify. Rather it is to join with David in saying to God: "Against you, you only, have I sinned and done what is evil in your sight, so that you may be justified in your words and blameless in your judgment" (Ps. 51:4). In confession, the sinner acknowledges that God is right. It is to agree with God's verdict: Guilty.[11]

But to speak of guilt requires some clarification today for another word has come to attach itself to guilt. So we speak of guilt feelings. Guilt is seen as the subjective reaction of the doer to the deed, i.e., how I feel about what I have done.[12] But this is not the case with the Scripture's use of the word guilt. In the Bible, guilt has not so much to do with emotions as it does with what happens in a court-room when a judge declares the defendant "guilty." The criminal may or may not have reactions of remorse, regret, or shame. It doesn't matter. The verdict of the judge establishes the reality. God's word of law unerring establishes His judgment. There is no appeal.

To deny the verdict means that the truth is not in us, says the Apostle John. But denial can never bring release. Only God's absolu-tion can release from the accusation of the law and unlock the sinner from his sins. Lutheran theology is nothing if it is not realistic![13] Like the Scriptures, Lutheran theology does not start with notions about human freedom and the potential (great or small) that human beings have. Theologies that start with assumptions about human freedom end up in bondage.[14] Lutheran theology begins with man's bond-age in sin and ends up with the glorious liberty of the Gospel. The bondage to sin is not a slight defect that can be corrected by appro-priate self-discipline. Neither is it a sickness that can be cured by the appropriation of the medication of regular doses of God's grace. Sin is enmity with the Creator that carries with it God's verdict of guilt and a divinely-imposed death sentence. To be a sinner is to be held captive in death and condemnation. The distance between God and humanity is not the gap between infinity and the finite but between a Holy God who is judge and man who is the guilty defendant.

Confession is the acknowledgment of this reality. The sin is named not in an effort to "get it off my chest" but to acknowledge it before the Lord to whom no secrets are hid. Where sin is not con-fessed, it remains festering and corrosive, addicting the sinner to yet another attempt at self-justification. Confession admits defeat and so leaves the penitent open for a word that declares righteousness, a verdict which justifies. That word is called absolution. It is absolution alone, says Gerhard Forde, that is the answer to the absolute claim of God who is inescapably present to the sinner.[15]

It is the absolution, the word by which God declares sinners righteous for Christ's sake, that the bones which God has broken with the hammer of His law are brought to rejoice. The Gospel alone puts joy and gladness into the ears of sinners (Ps. 51:8). For it is this verdict that the Judge of heaven and earth is hiding His face from our sins and scrubbing us clean from all iniquity (Ps. 51:9). The flip-side of God's hiding His face from our sins is His causing His face to shine on us (Numbers 6:24–26).[16]

This salvation is completely the work of the triune God. In forgiving sins, the God who created the heavens and the earth is bringing forth a new creation. Just as by His Word, God called all things into existence at the beginning, so now by His Word He is creating a clean heart and renewing a right spirit (Ps. 51:10; also see II Corinthians 4:6).[17] Hans-Joachim Kraus observes:

> The petitioner knows that he is entirely dependent on the merciful activity of God. From God's mercy alone he expects the blotting out of the guilt which is looked on as corruption (v.5) that totally perme-ates the human being. Only God can eliminate the threatening, dark wall of separation, sin, that separates God and human beings and blot out what is intolerable. Only by God's creative, renewing power can the heart be cleansed and led to a new obedience. Also the future is in the hands of God alone. If God sends the spirit of willingness and constancy, then the psalmist is saved from fickleness and unfaithful-ness. Even the witness of thanksgiving (v.15) is exclusively left in the hands of powers furnished by Yahweh. Everything is God's act. The sola gratia shines forth from every verse. No gift, no condition comes between God and man. No sacrifice has an effect on Yahweh. Only the pleading and trusting human being is the sacrifice, he who with body and life surrenders himself to God, who has nothing to offer but a heart that is bruised and broken (v.17). The human being presents himself to God for what he is. For him nothing remains except to plead for forgiveness and confess his guilt. In its extreme of knowledge and wisdom (v.6) which has been won from the prophetic word of the OT, Psalm 51 stands out in the Psalter. Its peak state-ments are unique. And its fullness of insights is incomprehensible.[18]

This salvation is completely the work of the triune God. In forgiving sins, the God who created the heavens and the earth is bringing forth a new creation.

Only where there is the forgiveness of sins can God be rightly honored and praised. Apart from God's forgiveness, we open our own mouths, and we know what spews forth. It is not the confession of Christ's righteousness, but blasphemous assertions of our own righteousness. The sin of the heart defiles the lips. Here the preacher may wish to draw out connections with the Second Commandment and its explanation in the Small Catechism.[19] Christ's absolution is the key which unlocks lips to praise His name by confession of His righteous deeds.

In Psalm 51, David links this praise of God with sacrifice (also see Hebrews 13:15–16). Sacrifice is not a means that we use to placate a wrathful God. On account of Christ's once and for all sacrifice for sin on the cross, the category of sacrifice gets relocated, as we see in Romans 12:1–2. Now by the mercies of God, the redeemed offer their bodies as living sacrifices not in order to achieve God's favor or to merit reconciliation with Him but for the sake of the neighbor. This is nicely put by Steven Paulson: "God is keeping his Christians and their churches in this old world as a sacrifice of the body for the neighbor. He does this along with the appeal that they endure suffering, not for their salvation, but for the sake of the old world, that it might be sustained for now, and that the preacher arrives in time to those who have not heard."[20] Here the preacher could draw out the implications of the Christian life as one of sacrifice as the answer or response of the one who is justified by faith. Good works are completely withdrawn from the equation of justification before God. They are relocated in the world for the well-being of the neighbor. God does not need or want your sacrifice (Ps. 51:16), but the neighbor needs it and so freed from the burden of self-justification, we are liberated to live for the sake of the world.

Luther sees both law and Gospel at work in Psalm 51. Through the law comes the knowledge of self, that is, a knowledge of sin which is always directed against God. Repentance is to be crushed with this knowledge imparted by the law. The law allows no space for self-justification. It is the Gospel, however, that gives broken sinners the knowledge of God's mercy in Christ Jesus. Preaching the Psalms give us a true knowledge of self (repentance) and a true knowledge of God (faith).[21] Luther recognized that in the penitential psalms, God gives us the words to cry out to Him in our distress, lament our sins, and confess trust in the promise of His righteousness in which alone is our sure and certain hope.[22] To preach the penitential psalms is to proclaim both the law and the promise. Luther's commentary on Psalm 51 provides preachers with an example of how this is done.

Passages and Hymns

Service	Psalm	Suggested Hymns
Ash Wednesday	51	"O Lord, throughout These Forty Days"—418 LSB "On My Heart Imprint Your Image"—422 LSB "To Thee, Omniscient Lord of All"—613 LSB "Your Heart, O God, Is Grieved"—945 LSB "As Rebels, Lord, who Foolishly Have Wandered"—612 LSB
Lent I	6	"Jesus, I Will Ponder Now"—440 LSB "O God, Forsake Me Not"—731 LSB "Thy Works, Not Mine, O Christ"—565 LSB "My Song is Love Unknown"—430 LSB
Lent 2	38	"Christ, the Life of All the Living"—420 LSB "Oh, How Great is Your Compassion"—559 LSB "Jesus, Thy Boundless Love to Me"—683 LSB "Cross of Jesus, Cross of Sorrow"—428 LSB
Lent 3	32	"Jesus, Grant That Balm and Healing"—421 LSB "Lord, to You I Make Confession"—608 LSB "I Lay My Sins on Jesus"—606 LSB "In Silent Pain the Eternal Son"—432 LSB
Lent 4	130	"When in the Hour of Deepest Need"—615 LSB "From Depths of Woe I Cry to Thee"—607 "Savior, When in Dust to Thee"—419 LSB "O Christ, You Walked the Road"—424 LSB
Lent 5	143	"Jesus, Refuge of the Weary"—423 LSB "Jesus Sinners Doth Receive"—609 LSB "Not Unto Us"—558 LSB "Stricken, Smitten, and Afflicted"—451 LSB "I Lie, O Lord, with Your Care"—885 LSB
Good Friday	102	"Lamb of God, Pure and Holy"—434 LSB "A Lamb Goes Uncomplaining Forth"—438 LSB "O Sacred Head, Now Wounded"—450 LSB "O Perfect Life of Love"—452 LSB

Liturgical Notes:

For Ash Wednesday, the order of service is in the *Lutheran Service Book: Altar Book* (pp. 483 ff). The lectionary is that appointed for Ash Wednesday.

Two services are provided for Good Friday in the *LSB Altar Book*, ("Good Friday-Chief Service" pp. 511ff and "Good Friday-Tenebrae Vespers" pp. 525 ff).

For the midweek services, there are several options (Vespers, Evening Prayer, Service of Prayer and Preaching in LSB). In keeping with the penitential nature of Lent (and this sermon series), "Corporate Confession and Absolution" pp. 290 LSB would also be appropriate.

For the midweek services, the passion history is the lectionary. See *LSB Altar Book*, pp. 487ff.

Collects fitting each of the psalms are available in the *Concordia Psalter*.

Notes

1 See Mark A. Throntveit, "The Penitential Psalms and Lenten Discipline" *Lutheran Quarterly* (Winter 1987), 495–512. Throntveit writes, "The connection between the psalms and these applications are tenuous, usually linked to a single word, and probably have more to do with the similarity in number between the psalms and the sins than with exegetical precision. More damaging in my opinion, is that such an application misses one of the crucial points these Psalms strive to make, namely the distinction between a cataloguing of specific sins, as in the individual laments and the recognition of sin as part of our human condition: 'Behold, I was brought forth in iniquity, and in sin did my mother conceive me.' (51:5), 'If thou, O Lord, shouldst mark iniquities, Lord, who could stand?' (130:3), 'for no man living is righteous before thee' (143:2b)" (500).

2 For background on Luther's 1532 exposition of Psalm 51, see Martin Brecht, *Martin Luther: Shaping and Defining the Reformation 1521–1532*, trans. James L. Schaaf (Minneapolis: Fortress Press, 1990), 456–458. Brecht says, "When confronted with the great Psalm 51 and its main thrust of repentance and justification, Luther felt that he was truly a student who needed the Holy Spirit as his schoolmaster. Nevertheless, his commentary may be called a masterpiece" (456).

3 Here see Robert Kolb, "The Lutheran Doctrine of Original Sin" in *Adam, the Fall, and Original Sin* ed. Hans Maduene and Michael Reeves (Grand Rapids: Baker Academic Press, 2014), 109–127. For an explicit treatment of

"root sin" in Luther's interpretation of Psalm 51, see Robert Kolb, *Luther and the Stories of God: Biblical Narratives as a Foundation for Christian Living* (Grand Rapids: Baker Academic, 2012), 104–106.

4 See Kolb, "In breaking the fifth and sixth commandments, David has defied and despised the Lord and thus has become guilty of blasphemy against the first commandment. David thus served as an excellent example of the interconnectedness of individual sinful acts and their root in the rejection of God and doubt of his Word"—*Luther and the Stories of God*, 104.

5 Mark A. Seifrid, "Romans 7: The Voice of the Law, the Cry of Lament, and the Shout of Thanksgiving" in *Perspectives on our Struggle with Sin: 3 Views of Romans 7*, ed. Terry L. Wilder (Nashville: B & H Academic, 2011), 114.

6 Here also see Article II in the *Augsburg Confession* and the *Apology*.

7 For an introduction to Luther on the Psalms, see Carl Axel Aurelius, "Luther on the Psalter" in *Harvesting Martin Luther's Reflections on Theology, Ethics, and the Church*, ed. Timothy J. Wengert (Grand Rapids: Eerdmans, 2004), 226–239.

8 On this point, see Dennis Ngien, *Fruit for the Soul: Luther on the Lament Psalms* (Minneapolis: Fortress Press, 2015), 29.

9 Note Hans-Joachim Iwand: "Our knowledge of God will only be true insofar as the essence of sin is taken into account and is understood. Likewise, our knowledge of sin will only be genuine if it is at the same time understood and recognized in connection with God's Being, for the one includes the other"—*The Righteousness of Faith According to Luther*, trans. Randi H. Lundell (Eugene, Oregon: Wipf and Stock Publishers, 2008), 26–27.

10 "Misleading are the statements of H. Gunkel that the OT does not recognize the total depravity of human nature but only affirms weakness vis-á-vis what is good, and that thus the OT statements are 'a preparation for the church's doctrine of original sin.' On the contrary, the OT emphasizes the total depravity, the degeneracy of guilt of human existence with an altogether different force than the church's doctrine of original sin"—Hans-Joachim Kraus *Psalms 1–59*, trans. Hilton C. Oswald (Minneapolis: Fortress Press, 1993), 503.

11 Here see Hans-Joachim Kraus: "In a confession of guilt over against God himself, the petitioner submits to the righteous judgment of Yahweh"—Kraus, *Psalms 1–59*, 503.

12 On this point see the discussion of Werner Elert, *The Christian Ethos*, trans. Carl Schindler (Philadelphia: Fortress Press, 1957), 163–173. Elert traces the subjective understanding of guilt to F. Schleiermacher.

13 Here note the German New Testament exegete, Udo Schnelle's comment on Pauline anthropology: "His view of human beings is not merely pessimistic, but realistic" in *Theology of the New Testament* trans. M. Eugene Boring (Grand Rapids: Baker Academic Press, 2009), 319.

14 On this point see Gerhard Forde, *The Captivation of the Will* (Grand Rapids: Eerdmans Publishing Company, 2005), 21.

15 Gerhard Forde, "Absolution: Systematic Considerations" in *The Preached God: Proclamation in Word and Sacrament*, edited by Mark C. Mattes and Steven Paulson (Grand Rapids: Eerdmans Publishing Company, 2007), 153.

16 For more on this point, see Claus Westermann, *The Living Psalms*, trans. J.R. Porter (Grand Rapids: Eerdmans Publishing Company, 1989), 98.

17 Here see Mark Seifrid on II Corinthians 4:16, "Paul simultaneously defines salvation as an act of creation and presents creation as an act of salvation. They are bound together not only in their like action but also in their form: just as the creation of light is the work of the word of God, so the Gospel is God's effective word that creates light in the darkness of the human heart. In this effective word, that performs what it says, God's person and work are revealed. Salvation is coming to know and confess God as the creator of our life."—*The Second Letter to the Corinthians* (Grand Rapids: Eerdmans Publishing Company, 2014), 200.

18 Hans-Joachim Kraus, *Psalms 1–59*, 507.

19 For more on this, see John T. Pless, *Praying Luther's Small Catechism* (Saint Louis: Concordia Publishing House, 2016), 19–21. Also see Albrecht Peters, *Commentary on Luther's Catechisms: Ten Commandments*, trans. Holger Sonntag (Saint Louis: Concordia Publishing House, 2009), 149–165.

20 Steven Paulson, "The Simul and the Two Kingdoms: The End of Time Twice" *Logia* (Reformation 2016), 20. The whole of Chapter 11, "The Fruit of Faith" based on Romans 12:1–2 in Paulson's book, *Lutheran Theology* (New York: T & T Clark, 2011), 228–243 is especially helpful in preaching the "new obedience" of which David speaks in Psalm 51:16–19.

21 A comprehensive guide to the preaching of the Psalms is to be found in Stanley Greidanus, *Preaching Christ from the Psalms* (Grand Rapids: Eerdmans, 2016). Greidanus includes extensive treatments of three of the penitential psalms (Psalm 51, pp. 240–271), Psalm 32 (pp.272–295), and Psalm 130 (pp. 364–379). Sample expository sermons are also included.

22 On Luther's understanding of the lament psalms, see Dennis Ngien, *Fruit for the Soul: Luther on the Lament Psalms* (Minneapolis: Fortress Press, 2015). For exegetical and historical treatments of these psalms see Philip Johnson, "The Psalms and Distress" in *Interpreting the Psalms: Issues and Approaches*, ed. David Firth and Philip Johnson (Downers Grove: IVP Academic Press, 2005), 63–84; Bruce Waltke, James Houston, and Erika Moore, *The Psalms as Christian Lament: A Historical Commentary* (Grand Rapids: Eerdmans, 2014); Claus Westermann, *Praise and Lament in the Psalms*, trans. Keith Crim and Richard Soulen (Atlanta: John Knox Press, 1981).

33

Preaching on Maundy Thursday

4 APRIL 2020

As I write these lines, it appears that many pulpits will be vacant, and most altars bare this Maundy Thursday. Yet faithful pastors will find ways to continue to preach, and, in some cases, small groups may be allowed to assemble in church to receive the Lord's body and blood even in the midst of this pandemic, proclaiming the Lord's death until He comes (I Corinthians 11:26). Others will need to wait for another opportunity to partake of the Lord's Supper. But in their waiting and yearning, preaching will remind them that "this holy Sacrament has been instituted for the special comfort of those who are troubled because of their sin and who humbly confess their sins, fear God's wrath, and hunger for righteousness" (Exhortation in "Corporate Confession and Absolution" LSB, p. 290). As the Commission on Theology and Church Relations document of The Lutheran Church Missouri Synod, "Communion and Covid-19," reminds us, we have certainty only as we stick to what the Lord has instituted (set in place and authorized) so we avoid clever ways of administering the Sacrament that would lead to doubt. Sometimes, as much as we hunger and thirst for the Sacrament, we must wait while still trusting in the Lord's promises. I think of my first teaching trip to the former Soviet Union in 1998, where I encountered Lutherans whose circumstances forced them to endure for decades without the Sacrament, living from the Scriptures, and the few sermon books that survived. Tears would fill their eyes when they told how after the collapse of Communism, a pastor finally arrived to administer the Lord's Supper. Their patience over many years of deprivation puts our impatience to shame when we are forced to go without the Lord's Supper for a few weeks. These circumstances invite the preacher to think more carefully about how we celebrate Maundy Thursday and especially how we preach on the Sacrament of the Altar.

Maundy Thursday does not transport worshipers back to the upper room, nor does it project Golgotha into the present as it is sometimes argued by certain twentieth-century theologians of liturgy following the trend set by Odo Casel[1]. In this view, Jesus transforms the ancient Passover rite making it a vehicle for the events of salvation history to be made present in the church's liturgy.

However, this approach fails to acknowledge the newness of the New Testament in what Christ bestows—His body and blood for disciples to eat and to drink. Norman Nagel would often point out that when we line up the Passover as described in Exodus with the narratives of the Lord's Supper's institution in the Synoptics and I Corinthians, the first and crucial question is not how are they similar but how are they different? This is also Luther's approach in the Large Catechism. To paraphrase Sasse, the Lord's Supper renders the old Passover obsolete.[2] Likewise, Mark Throntveit writes, "Jesus 'fulfills' the Old Testament Passover, but not by instituting the Lord's Supper in ritual continuity with the Old Testament seder. By dying on the cross, Jesus 'fulfills' the Old Testament Passover in the sense of bringing it to an end, thereby becoming the last paschal lamb, 'the Lamb of God who takes away the sin of the world.'"[3]

Here also see Luther in the Large Catechism where he argues that the Sacrament of the Altar is not like the old Passover bound to a special time but frequently where there is "opportunity and need" and not like "the pope (who) perverted it and turned it back into a Jewish feast" (LC V:47–48, K/W, 471–472). For Luther, the focus in the celebration of the Lord's Supper was squarely on the proclamation of the promise. This is nicely summarized by James Samuel Preus: "In Luther's reinterpretation, a different understanding of time is involved. We are no longer brought into 'ritual time,' in which the cross itself is mysteriously being 'actualized.' Rather, it is a matter of distribution, now, of a finished deed. The force, power, meaning of the deed of Christ is present not through 'representation,' but through the proclamation of words. Luther leaves Christ's death in irretrievable pastness, while the word of forgiveness—the distribution of the testament—is repeatable as often as the church gathers in obedience to, and in the presence of, the risen Testator."[4]

For Luther, redemption was accomplished at Calvary, but it is delivered in the Lord's Supper. In his 1525 treatise "Against the Heavenly Prophets," Luther asserted: "If now I seek the forgiveness of sins, I do not run to the cross, for I will not find it given there. Nor must I hold to the suffering of Christ, as Dr. Karlstadt trifles, in knowledge or remembrance, for I will not find it there either. But I will find in the sacrament or gospel of the word which distributes, presents, offers, and gives to me that forgiveness which was won on the cross" (AE 40: 213–214). This theme lies behind the Small Catechism's question on the benefit of eating and drinking in the Sacrament. It also echoed in the Large Catechism where Luther confesses the historical reality of Christ's death on the cross for sin and the distribution of this treasure by way of Christ's promise: "Although the work took place on the cross and the forgiveness of sins has been acquired, yet it cannot come to us in any other way than through the Word. How should we know that this took place or was given to us if it were not proclaimed by preaching, by the oral Word? From what source do they know of forgiveness, and how can they receive it, except by steadfastly believing the Scriptures and the gospel?" (LC V:31, K-W, 469–470). Luther sees in the Lord's Supper the most concentrated form of the Gospel[5] because in it, the death of Christ is proclaimed, and the benefits of that saving death are bestowed in His body and blood given us to eat and drink.

This is evident in Luther's sermon on Wednesday in Holy Week from 1529 where he says:

> These words of Christ spoken at the last supper, which are now spoken at the altar are as much the Gospel as if I were to say in the pulpit: I proclaim to you that Christ has died for you. The words at the altar are the same: 'Take, eat, drink etc.' Is this not Gospel? . . . The redemption and forgiveness of sins happened on the cross. But it must be proclaimed so that I may hear it. I will never experience it by simply looking at the cross. At the same time, many stood at the cross, but they did not know that there the forgiveness of sins would be gained until the voice came and directed them to the cross. If you take away

the word 'for you' from the cross, you see Christ as a thief on the gallows. But the words must teach you that he is the Savior.[6]

The "for you" is of the essence of the Gospel and, therefore, of the Lord's Supper. It needs to be accented loud and clear, especially on Maundy Thursday so that the testament and promise of Christ's body and blood remain the Lord's gift, not an enactment of our ritual piety. On this Maundy Thursday, in particular, let the "for you" of Christ's gifts dominate. Preach to create a hunger and thirst for this gift that your hearers may never take it for granted on the one hand or regard it as a matter of entitlement on the other hand. Listen again to Luther in 1529 sermon: "When the devil attacks, come for strength to the dear Word so that you may know Christ and long for the Sacrament! A soldier has his rations and must have food and drink to be strong. In the same way here: those who want to be Christians should not throw the Sacrament to the winds as if they did not need it."[7]

Notes

1 For a critique of these trends, see Oliver K. Olson, *Reclaiming the Lutheran Liturgical Heritage* (Minneapolis: Reclaim Resources, 2007), 13–85 and John T. Pless, "Liturgical Preaching: The Pitfalls and the Promise" in *Feasting in a Famine of the Word: Lutheran Preaching in the Twenty-first Century* ed. Mark Birkholz, Jacob Corzine, and Jonathan Mumme (Eugene: Pickwick Publications, 2016), 166–178.

2 Here see, Hermann Sasse, "The Lord's Supper in the New Testament" in *We Confess the Sacraments*, translated by Norman E. Nagel (Saint Louis: Concordia Publishing House, 1985), 49—97. Sasse observes that "all the details of the traditional Passover ritual, which Jesus doubtless observed, was irrelevant for the Lord's Supper itself" (64). And again since Jesus Himself is the Passover Lamb who gives His body and blood to be eaten and drunk, Sasse argues that, "There is no analogy to this fellowship, just as there are no parallels to this celebration. The Lord's Supper received this character as something unique, something remarkable from the Words of Institution" (66). Also see Otto Procksch, "Passa und Abenmahl" in *Vom Sakrament des Altars*, (Leipzig: Dörffling and Franke, 1941), 11–25.

3 Mark Throntveit, "The Lord's Super as New Testament, Not New Passover" *Lutheran Quarterly* (Autumn 1997), 284.

4 James Samuel Preus, "Neglected Problems in Eucharistic Dialogue," *Currents in Theology and Mission* 3 (1976), 182.

5 Also note Albrecht Peters: "For him [Luther], the Lord's Supper is not an offering and a good work performed by a human being in Christ before God; it is a testament and sacrament of God through Christ for us. As such it is the *summa et compendium Euangelii*"—Peters, *Commentary on Luther's Catechisms: Baptism and the Lord's Supper* (St. Louis: Concordia Publishing House, 2012), 21.

6 Martin Luther, "Sermon on Wednesday of Holy Week" in *The 1529 Holy Week and Easter Sermons of Dr. Martin Luther*, translated by Irving L. Sandberg (St. Louis: Concordia Publishing House, 1999), 68.

7 Ibid., 78.

34

Using Easter

21 APRIL 2019

Hermann Sasse referred to the Sundays between Easter and Pentecost as "the Church's Time of Rejoicing."[1] The Lord, who was crucified for our sins and raised for our righteousness, now distributes the gifts He has won for us. The readings from the farewell discourse in John's Gospel draw us toward Ascension and Pentecost with the promise of the Comforter who will give perpetual joy in the midst of suffering and death for Jesus has gone to the Father.

Easter is not confined to a single Sunday. Each Sunday in the Great Fifty Days of Easter brings into focus how the gifts of Easter are put to use. Evangelical preaching of the Lord's resurrection is not merely an apologetic proposal to believe that the tomb was empty, and Jesus was really raised from the dead. Rather the preaching of the resurrection is from the reality of the vacated grave and Jesus appearing bodily to His disciples and others.

Luther was a master of this preaching of the resurrection as can be seen especially from his numerous sermons on the traditional Gospel for the Sunday after Easter, John 20:19–31, happily now available in Vol. 69 of Concordia Publishing House's extension to the American Edition of Luther's Works. In these sermons, Luther's focus is on the distribution of the fruit of Jesus' passion and resurrection, namely, the forgiveness of sins. The Reformer certainly does not neglect the fact that our Lord's bodily resurrection happened in history; it is no fable. But in these sermons, his attention is drawn to how Easter is put to use. Gerhard Sauter provides an apt description:

The proclamation of the resurrection of the dead as the promise of life with God is the heart of every sermon; it is not one theme among others, which may be brought forth when the need arises. The evangelical sermon is not meant to teach a more successful way of life, or better management of one's life, or mastery of responsibility for others. These things reasonable people can find of their own accord; for such things, no preaching is needed. Preaching is needed because it leads us out of the 'vale of tears' into the future life. If this does not happen, then preaching is wasted time and a useless or even damaging enterprise.[2]

Using Easter means that the peace of Christ is to be preached into the conscience of those held captive by sin and death. The risen Lord Jesus comes into the midst of His disciples huddled together behind locked doors to make of them preachers of this peace. In a sermon for Easter Tuesday, preached in Wittenberg in 1529, Luther says, "Their office is to preach repentance and the forgiveness of sins in Christ's name, that is, they are to rebuke the world for sin so that people may acknowledge what sinners they are; and on the other hand, they should teach how they are to become free of their sins through Christ" (AE 69:368). Then Luther goes on to chide the false preachers of the Pope who burden Christendom with new laws about clothing vows, food and the like making sin where there is none. But the Gospel is a different message: "The Gospel, which Christ committed to the apostles and preachers, makes human consciences free from all laws, even the Law of God" (AE 69:368). Luther uses Easter to deconstruct the false forgiveness of the papal penitential apparatus and replace with the evangelical forgiveness accomplished by Christ's sacrificial death and declared in His resurrection.[3]

Preaching puts Easter to use when the sermon delivers comfort to those who tremble at the reality of their own sin and with it, death. This happens when the preacher does actually absolve sin. The absolution, whether pronounced individually or corporately in a liturgical formula or in the way of the sermon, is God's own declaration that the sinner's future will not be determined by his or her past. The absolution carries the promise of the resurrection. Christ Jesus, who forgives our sins, will not contradict Himself by abandoning us to death and the grave. As Luther puts it in stanza 6 of his Easter hymn, "Christ Jesus Lay in Death's Strong Bands": "Now His grace to us imparts Eternal sunshine to our hearts; the night of sin is ended. Alleluia!" (LSB 458:6).

Luther does not separate the forgiveness of sins from the resurrection of the body. They are joined together in the creedal language: "I believe in . . . the forgiveness of sins, the resurrection of the body, and the life everlasting." Luther can say without contradicting himself that the forgiveness of sins is the most difficult article of faith to believe, as he does in a sermon on John 19, "For no article of faith is more difficult to believe than 'I believe in the forgiveness of sins'" (AE 69:185) and again that the resurrection is the most difficult thing to believe as he does in a sermon on John 20, "For this [resurrection] has been and still is the most offensive article and hardest to believe" (AE 69:286). The difficulty entailed in both is actually the same for Luther in that they contradict human experience. We live in a world where sin is affirmed and even celebrated but not forgiven. Luther says in the John 19 sermon that the reason the evangelist devotes so much time to the report of Peter's denial and restoration is that we do not see such "boundless comfort afforded to sinners" (AE 69:185) in the day to day workings of the world. And when it comes to the resurrection, we see "before eyes that the entire world is being snatched away by death and dying. Emperors, kings, great and small, young and old—in sum, all the children of men—are laid in the grave and covered one after the other" (AE 69:286). Forgiveness of sins and resurrection from the dead go together in defying human reason or expectation. Neither can be taken for granted. They must be preached, and that means the preacher predicates them FOR YOU. Without the "for you," Easter remains in the past tense, and forgiveness of sins no more than an elusive dream, a desire without fulfillment.

In the Anglican tradition, it became customary to refer to the Sunday after Easter (now Easter II) as "Low Sunday," presumably because the ceremony and festivity of this Sunday was low in comparison with liturgical and musical heights of Easter Sunday. In North America, "Low Sunday" takes on another connotation. The bulging pews of the previous Sunday empty out. But for Luther, there was nothing "low" about the Gospel for the Sunday after Easter, for it demonstrates Christ Jesus risen from the dead but still marked with the scars of nails and spear, breathing out His words, which are giving peace in the forgiveness of sins.

Notes

1   Hermann Sasse, "The Church's Time of Rejoicing" in *Letters to Lutheran Pastors*, Vol. II: 1951–1956, ed. Matthew C. Harrison (Saint Louis: Concordia Publishing House, 2014), 355–368.

2   Gerhard Sauter, "Luther on the Resurrection" in *Harvesting Martin Luther's Reflections on Theology, Ethics, and the Church*, ed. Timothy J. Wengert (Grand Rapids: Eerdmans, 2004), 100.

3   For Luther's extensive treatment of the resurrection, see his lectures on I Corinthians 15 in *AE* 28:59–213. Helpful secondary literature includes Dennis Ngien, *Luther's Theology of the Cross: Christ in Luther's Sermons on John* (Eugene: Cascade Books, 2018), 271–290 and Ian Siggins, *Martin Luther's Doctrine of Christ* (New Haven: Yale University Press, 1970), 164–172. Both Ngien and Siggins offer rich and robust insights from Luther for preaching in the season of Easter.

35

Preaching I Peter

12, 19 APRIL 2020

> "In a word St. John's Gospel and his epistle, St. Paul's epistles, especially Romans, Galatians, and Ephesians, and St. Peter's first epistle are the books that show you Christ and teach you all that is necessary and salvatory for you to know even if you were never to see or know any other book or doctrine"—Martin Luther, "Prefaces to the New Testament" (AE 35:362).

Texts from I Peter are read as the continuing lectionary for the Sundays of Easter this year. In this season of a global pandemic, Peter's little letter is especially potent as he writes to sustain the hope born of Christ's resurrection in scattered believers whose lives were marked by suffering.

Probably written around 61 or 62 AD, I Peter addresses disciples in the diaspora, identified in 1:1 as "exiles" living in Pontus, Galatia, Cappadocia, Asia, and Bithynia. Leonhardt Goppelt describes the context of I Peter: "Christians were discriminated against by slanderous accusations. . . . This verbal hostility against the Christians comes from their fellow citizens, also and precisely from their relatives, colleagues, and acquaintances. It is more than personal insult: It takes from them the public respect on which existence in society depended, even more than in our time, and public officials have found action against them appropriate."[1]

Peter's salutation is Trinitarian as he speaks of God the Father calling and giving the destiny to His disciples as those sanctified by the Spirit for "obedience to Jesus Christ and sprinkling with blood." They are recipients of grace and peace.[2]

Discipleship in I Peter

The doxological prologue of 1:3–12 takes the form of a Trinitarian blessing: "Like the salutation, this apostolic descant is structured around the three Persons of the Trinity."[3] The God and Father of our Lord Jesus Christ has given us a new birth to a living hope through Jesus' resurrection from the dead. With this birth comes an inheritance which is "imperishable, undefiled, and unfading, kept in heaven for you" (1:4). God's power is keeping and guarding disciples through faith for the eschatological outcome of discipleship. Peter's language is echoed in Luther's Explanation of the Third Article of the Creed in the Small Catechism.

Discipleship lives under the holy and blessed cross. The Apostle mentions the suffering of various trials that faith genuineness may be tested. *Tentatio*. But the outcome of this faith is salvation. This is the salvation inquired about by the prophets who proclaimed it (1:10) by the Holy Spirit, who inspired their speaking and writing. Their prophetic message is now announced through preachers sent by the same Spirit.

The doxology of 1:3–12 leads to an exposition of the life of discipleship as set apart by the blood of Christ, lived in the obedience of faith, anchored in hope secured by Jesus' resurrection. In verse 1:13 (KJV), the Apostle exhorts disciples to "gird up" their minds, which echoes Ex. 12:11; they are be prepared for rigorous travel with a sober hope fixed in Christ. Not conformed to the passions of the old eon with its deceptive lusts, disciples lived in the holiness borrowed from the Lord who redeemed them not with silver or gold but the precious blood of the Lamb. I Peter's language here is recalled in Luther's Explanation of the Second Article. Disciples find the confidence for obedience in the God who raised Jesus from the dead. The language of ransom, Martin Franzmann observes, is "a call to holy fear in the Christian life."[4]

In 1:23, the Apostle returns to the new birth that takes place not through "perishable seed" but the imperishable seed of the Word of

God, citing Isaiah 40:6–9. Disciples live by this Word of the Lord, which has given them a new life set apart and cleansed for the sincere love of the children of God. Bo Reicke notes the parallel to Titus 3:5, where Baptism is spoken of as the new birth noting that Peter links the power for Baptismal regeneration in the word of God. He then goes on to observe that this word, which remains forever, is exactly the "word which has now been 'evangelized,' that is proclaimed as a message of joy to the recipients of the epistle. They depended previously on perishable 'flesh' and its seed that is on human interest and propaganda. Now they have been born anew to eternal seed, God's word."[5]

I Peter 2:1–8 describes repentance as a "putting away" of the traits of the old life: malice, guile, insincerity, envy, and slander. Instead of nurturing these destructive cravings, disciples remain "newborn babes" (2:2 RSV) with an appetite for the pure spiritual milk of the Word now that they have "tasted the kindness of the Lord" (2:3 RSV; see Ps. 34:8).

Repentance is a turning from unbelief to faith. In verses 4–8, Peter speaks of the life of faith as being built on Christ, the living stone rejected by men but chosen and precious by God. Built on this unshakeable foundation, disciples are joined together as a spiritual house and a royal priesthood. Discipleship is never a solo. Luther describes it: "The house of stone or wood is not His house. He wants to have a spiritual building, that is, the Christian congregation, in which we are all equal in one faith, one like the other, and all are placed and fitted on one another and joined together through love without malice, guile, hypocrisy, hatred, and slander, as the apostle has said" (LW 30:52).

To be a disciple of Jesus is to share in a "holy priesthood" that offers "spiritual sacrifices acceptable to God through Jesus Christ" (2:5). These spiritual sacrifices are the broken and contrite heart (see Ps. 51:17), the praise of God, lips that confess His works and lives that are given to service of those in need (see Heb. 13:15–16); and bodies as living sacrifices (see Rom. 12:1–2).[6]

I Peter 2:9–10 describes the identity of disciples as a chosen race, a royal priesthood, a holy nation, God's own people[7]. Underlying this pericope are several OT texts: Ex. 19:5–6 ("and you shall be to me a kingdom of priests and a holy nation"), Deut. 7:6 ("you are a people holy to the LORD"), Is. 43:21 ("the people whom I formed for myself that they might declare my praise"), Is. 45:4–6 ("I call you by your name, I name you, though you do not know me"), and Is. 61:6 ("you shall be called priests of the LORD"). What God had prophetically promised to Israel is now given to the church of Jesus Christ, the new Israel of God (see Gal. 6:16) as the recipients of God's mercy in Christ. Once without identity ("no people"), now they are God's people, possessed by Him (see Hos. 2:23). Previously without mercy, they have received mercy (see Hos. 1:9).

The Table of Duties

The Apostle provides a "table of duties" for disciples who live as "sojourners and exiles" in 2:11–3:7. Paradoxically, disciples are at one and the same time those called to live in God's holiness, strangers to the ways of the perishing world, and yet given responsibility for life in various earthly callings. Disciples maintain good conduct among unbelievers so that their blameless behavior guards them against accusations of evil.[8] Instead, the good works of disciples draw the Gentiles to glorify God on the day of His visitation (compare with Matt. 5:16). Here vocation and mission go together. Bo Riecke states, "Here, the epistle's remarkable theory of missions is expressed. The gospel will be promulgated to the extent that believers everywhere show such extraordinary patience and loyalty, in spite of the ill will of non-Christians, that every observer will be astonished and converted. This is also one of the basic thoughts in the Sermon on the Mount (Matt. 5:16, 47). What follows in First Peter is largely characterized by an unshakeable confidence in the success of such a practical demonstration of Christianity."[9]

The ethical content of this section of I Peter is intertwined with the Apostle's proclamation of Christ. "Our letter's *proclamation of Christ* is completely interwoven with its paraclesis. It presents Christ as savior of the world, as a comforting example for all who suffer, and as Lord and coming judge. The individual formulations depend on previous texts about Christ that bear a hymnic and confessional stamp and develop their statements with a paraenetic interest."[10]

The Apostle turns first to discipleship in view of governing authorities (2:13–17). This section finds a parallel in Romans 13:1–7 and Titus 3:1. Christians are not anarchists but willingly submit to temporal rulers "for the Lord's sake" (v.13), recognizing the God-ordained authority which upholds these offices. Freedom in Christ is not a pretext for evil. The civic community is an arena where the disciple lives as servants of God (see AC XVI).

Next, the Apostle turns to servants and masters (2:18–25)[11], setting this aspect of his table of duties in a Christological context, demonstrating the credibility of Stuhlmacher's assertion that the paraclesis is bound up with the proclamation of Christ. There are numerous parallels in this text to shorter passages in Ephesians 5:5–9 and Colossians 3:18–4:1. Disciples are to submit to earthly masters even when this involves suffering. The Suffering Servant (Is. 53) is also the Shepherd of His sheep enables such humility even as His sacrificial life is the example for those who are His by faith. Christ is not an example or pattern that disciples follow in order to attain salvation. Recall here Luther's insistence that Christ is foremost God's gift or sacrament. He is an example in the sense that He is a pattern for the horizontal life, the life that is lived in love toward the neighbor. Here the disciple follows in his Lord's steps, indeed being a little Christ to the neighbor even when it means enduring insult and injury.

Husbands are exhorted to love and be considerate toward their wives on the basis of I Peter 3:7. Physically, the wife is the weaker partner, but spiritually she is bound with him in the common calling to faith and the inheritance of the gift of life in Christ. This is a union that is to be tended and guarded so that the life of prayer is not impeded.[12] Adornment does not consist of outward decorations but the decorum of a quiet spirit. The marriage of Sarah and Abraham is lifted up as a model for disciples living in wedlock according to God's design.

The New Life in the Old World

Having addressed the particular estates or places of life, now Peter swings back in 3:8ff to virtues which should characterize all disciples regardless of their station in life. His exhortation includes a call to express unity of spirit, sympathy and love, and "a tender heart, and a humble mind" (3:8). In words reminiscent of Romans 12:14–21, in verse 9, Peter reminds his readers disciples are to bless as they have been called to receive a blessing, thus drawing them back to the God who called them in 1:3–9 and 2:9–10. This leads to his citation of Psalm 34:13–16 in 3:10–12, where the Psalmist admonishes those who love life to turn from evil and do right. Those who suffer for righteousness will be blessed.

In the face of those who would do evil to them, disciples live in confidence without fearful or troubled hearts. This stance is taken by reverencing Christ as Lord in the heart. Echoes here perhaps of Jesus' words in John 14:27 ("Let not your hearts be troubled"). Christ gives His disciples a "good conscience" (3:16) so that they may not stand accused in the midst of those who revile their good works. With this knowledge, disciples are to be prepared for the apologetic task.

Peter had already characterized the Christian as possessing and being possessed by a living hope (1:3). Now he calls on disciples to be ready to give an account for this hope (3:15). Living in a world where belief in the old gods was fading, and notions of post-mortem existence were shadowy at best, the disciples of Jesus lived with the confident expectation that there is destiny beyond death through the resurrection of Jesus. Ethically, their lives were lived in marked contrast to their pagan neighbors. The lives of disciples were not spent in denial of the dark reality of fate by intoxicating themselves with carnal pleasures. When reviled or attack, these Christians do not respond in kind. Peter anticipates that others will see the lives of Christians as different from their own and that this difference will prompt inquiry. This passage, often taken as something of a "proof text" for the enterprise of apologetics, reminds disciples that these questions which are put to them are an occasion for confession of the faith. This confession is made in the context of suffering for doing right.

The Descent into Hell

Once again, Peter draws his exhortation back to Christ and his death for sins, the righteous for the unrighteous (3:18)[13]. This passage is an extension of 1:18–21 and 2:21–24. Here Peter locates the "descent into hell" after Christ's vivification. To use the traditional language of classical dogmatics, Christ descent into hell falls under the heading of His exaltation, not his humiliation. Although 3:18–20 is not directly cited in Article IX ("Concerning Christ's Descent into Hell") or in Luther's 1533 Torgau sermon, which lies behind it, the confession that Jesus Christ, true God and true man, descended into hell not to suffer but to proclaim His victory over death and the devil. In a helpful essay that broadly recounts the history of the interpretation of this text, Martin Scharlemann concludes, "By way of summary it may be said therefore that I Peter 3:18–20 quite evidently tells us that Christ, according to His glorified body descended into hell to make proclamation there of Himself as the Messiah. This was the first step in His exaltation by which He 'disarmed principalities and dominions and displayed them openly, triumphing over them through the cross'" (Col. 2:15).[14]

Baptism

We have observed allusions to Baptism in Peter's language of rebirth; now, in 3:21–22, he is explicit with the declaration that Baptism, corresponding to God's saving of Noah and family through the flood, now saves. Just as the flood delivered death to the unrighteous of Noah's day and yet brought deliverance to Noah, so Baptism now puts to death our unrighteousness and delivers us alive in Christ. It is not ritual cleansing of dirt from the body but the acquisition of a good conscience through Christ redeeming work. There is a contrast between Baptism and the ablutions of Judaism.[15] Baptism saves because it is God's eschatological act of deliverance from sin, death, and hell.

Baptism does not exempt disciples from suffering, but rather they are outfitted with Christ, who suffered in the flesh for us (4:1). Faith in the crucified Christ means death to the carnal passions whose lethal impulse characterizes paganism in its attempt to escape from the ever-present wrath under which they live. They stand under divine judgment. Rather than living in the light of the Last Day, they live in its ever-deepening shadow. But to these who were dead in sin (see Eph. 2:1–9) the Gospel was preached that they might have the life of God.

The Disciple's Life Before the End

Disciples live in view of the eschatological horizon. The reality that the end is at hand calls for sanity and sobriety in contrast to the intoxicating debauchery that blinds those given to idolatry to impending destruction. Rather than the ego-centric sensual celebrations cataloged in 4:3, the life of the disciple is marked by an openness to the other in love that covers a multitude of sins and the practice of hospitality (4:9). Varied gifts are deployed for the well-being of the body in 4:10–11, bringing to mind the language of Paul, once again in Romans 12. "There is no basis for personal pride or envy on account of the gifts of grace. It is to be noted that the author does not enumerate gifts of tongues or other extreme manifestations as illustrations of this grace, but only such basis church activities as preaching, stewardship, and works of mercy. Common practices and ordinary deeds are regarded by the author as holy gifts of God's grace."[16] This section ends with a doxology to God through Jesus Christ.

The Disciple's Life Under the Cross

In 4:12–19, Peter returns to the theme of the inevitable suffering that awaits disciples as a "fiery trial" not to be seen as something strange or extraordinary. Such suffering is a fruit on sharing in Christ's suffering. John H. Elliot writes, "Not only is suffering innocently a divine test of faith (v. 12), a sign of solidarity with the suffering of Christ (v. 13a), a cause for rejoicing (v. 13bc), and a mark of the Spirit's presence (v. 14); it also an opportunity for actively glorifying God. Reproached believers who are honored by God (v. 14bc), honor God in return."[17]

Suffering can result from wrongdoing. Criminals suffer on account of their misdeeds. Christians suffer not from crimes but for a righteous confession. The judgment that awaits the world first begins in "the household of God" (4:17) and will come to a profound climax in the judgment of the world. Yet suffering is also tied to rejoicing for in it, God's glory is being revealed (4:13). In the face of all this, Peter calls on disciples to entrust themselves to the hands of a Faithful Creator (see Psalm 31:5; Luke 23:46). This language is picked up in Luther's morning and evening prayers in the Small Catechism.[18]

The Pastor's Call

An exhortation to the elders comes from Peter, who identifies himself as an elder and witness of the sufferings of Christ (5:1). The nature of the oversight given to those who bear the office is summarized in the command to "shepherd the flock of God" (also see John 21:15–17; Acts 20:28). This work is not done by compulsion or out of greed for gain but willingly. It is not an opportunity for domineering or lordship but for service born out of humility patterned on the basis of the Chief Shepherd who laid down His life for the sheep (compare with Philippians 2:5–11). Pastors are to be examples of such humility for the sheep under their curacy.

Ending on the Promises

The final section, 5:6–11, is packed full of promise to sustain faithful endurance in light of Satan's attack. He is to be resisted firm in the faith. Peter reminds his readers yet again that this experience of suffering is not unique but is catholic, required of the Christian brotherhood throughout the world (5:9). The "little while" of suffering will finally give way to the weight of an eternal glory. It is in this light that Peter concludes the body of his letter with a doxological blessing, confident that the God of grace will give His disciples endurance to the end even as He restores, establishes, and strengthens them along the way. For this reason, disciples are invited to cast all anxieties on the Lord for He cares about them (5:7; also see Ps. 55:22; Matt. 6:25–32; Lk. 12:22–31).

Appended to the epistle is a greeting coupled with a final admonition to stand firm. The holy kiss and the blessing of peace in 5:14 may reflect the liturgical reading of the letter[19].

Postscript: I Peter as Catechetical Preaching

Prior to the Second World War, the Anglican early church historian, Philip Carrington wrote *The Primitive Christian Catechism* in which he identified I Peter as a catechetical document.[20] More recently, the Australian Lutheran theologian, Andrew Pfeiffer has suggested that I Peter along with Ephesians and Colossians provide a template for catechesis centered in thanksgiving and praise, witness, watchfulness against the devil, and service to the neighbor in one's station in life that integrates well with the Small Catechism.[21] The most recent version of *Luther's Small Catechism with Explanation* published by the LCMS in 2017 makes use of 25 citations from this epistle. We see a connection between I Peter and central themes in the Small Catechism, including the Ten Commandments, the work of the Triune God, the atonement of Christ, the life of repentance and faith, prayer, Baptism, and the table of duties. Not only is there a parallel between I Peter and the Small Catechism in terms of content but also in practice. Oswald Bayer has contrasted Luther's approach to theology with that of Anselm. For Anselm, theology was faith seeking understanding. For Luther, it was faith enduring attack.[22] Luther's own words in the Large Catechism could well be taken as a summary of I Peter: "For where God's Word is preached, accepted, or believed, and bears fruit, there the holy and blessed cross will not be far behind. And let no one think that he will have peace; rather, we must sacrifice all we have on earth—possessions, honor, house and farm, spouse, children, body and life. Now this grieves the old creature, for it means that we must remain steadfast, suffer patiently whatever befalls us, and let go of whatever is taken from us" (LC III 65–66; K-W, 448–449). Yet under this suffering, there is the inexpressible joy of a living hope that sustains those who belong to Christ Jesus (1:6–9).

Notes

1 Leonhard Goppelt, *A Commentary on I Peter*, trans. John E. Alsup (Grand Rapids: Eerdmans, 1993), 39–40. Compare with: "The First Letter of Peter occupies a special position within the New Testament, because it is the first witness to the fundamental conflict between emerging Christianity's Christological monotheism and sacrally grounded ancient Roman society. The letter deals with a theological theme of its time that will become central for Christianity of the twenty-first century: being a Christian minority in an increasingly hostile world"—Udo Schnelle, p. 603; Also: "The trials besetting the readers of I Peter were spasmodic and particular rather than organized on a universal scale, a matter of incidents rather than policy. A matter of incidents rather than policy, at once ubiquitous and incalculable."—E.G. Selwyn, *The First Epistle of St. Peter*, 55.

2 On the salutation, see Martin Scharlemann, "An Apostolic Salutation: An Exegetical Study of I Peter 1:1–2" *Concordia Journal* (June 1975), 108–118. Scharlemann notes that Peter's use of "grace and peace" indicates "that the old aeon had passed and that his readers now enjoyed what kings and prophets

of old had longed to see and hear but could not because they had only God's promises and did not experience their fulfillment" (109).

3 Martin Scharlemann, "An Apostolic Descant: An Exegetical Study of I Peter 1:3–12" *Concordia Journal* (January 1976), 9.

4 Martin Franzmann, "A Ransom for Many: *Satisfactio Vicara*" *Concordia Theological Monthly* (July 1954), 514.

5 Bo Riecke, *The Anchor Bible: The Epistles of James, Peter, and Jude* (Garden City: Doubleday & Company, 1964), 87.

6 On the Romans 12:1–2 text, see Steven D. Paulson, *Lutheran Theology* (New York; T & T Clark, 2011), 228–243, especially his statement, "Christ is the end of all that old worship because he is the end of the law so that worship must now be in spirit and truth (John 4:24). Yet sacrifice does not disappear, it takes on an entirely new direction. Before Christ's arrival the direction of sacrifice was from the sinner up to God–vertically: 'But now.' It is made horizontal, and a sacrifice *acceptable* to God—but *made* to the neighbor. The sacrifice does not give in order to get back; those who have died in a death like Christ's do not need to hoard merit so that God's wrath will end. God's wrath is over, so that sacrifice has become love that gives itself over to the other" (231–232).

7 This passage, of course, is the basis for the Lutheran teaching on the Royal Priesthood of All Believers. The literature here is extensive. A few selected resources are *The Royal Priesthood: Identity & Mission* by the Commission on Theology and Church Relations (LCMS, 2018); Kenneth Korby, "The Pastoral Office and the Priesthood of Believers" in *Lord Jesus Christ, Will You Not Stay: Essays in Honor of Ronald Feuerhahn on the Occasion of his Sixty-fifth Birthday*, ed. Bart Day et al (Houston: Feuerhahn Festscrift Committee, 2002), 333–372; Norman Nagel, "Luther on the Priesthood of All Believers" *Concordia Theological Quarterly* (October 1997), 277–298; John T. Pless, "Catechesis for Life in the Royal Priesthood" in *Luther's Small Catechism: A Manual for Discipleship* (St. Louis: CPH, 2018), 171–195; John T. Pless "Reflections on the Life of the Royal Priesthood: Vocation and Evangelism" in *Shepherd the Church: Essays in Pastoral Theology Honoring Bishop Roger D. Pittelko* ed. Frederic W. Baue et al (Fort Wayne: CTS Press, 2002), 271–286; Roland Ziegler, "Priesthood and Office" *Logia* (Epiphany 2019), 25–34. Also see "2016 Res. 13–01A Task Force Report on Priesthood and Office" (LCMS, October 2018).

8 For a sociological reading of how Christians were both seen as outsiders and how they dealt with those outside the faith, see John H. Elliot, *A Home for the Homeless: A Sociological Exegesis of I Peter, Its Situation and Strategy* (Philadelphia: Fortress Press, 1981), especially Chapter 3, pp. 101–164.

9 Reicke, 94.

10 Peter Stuhlmacher, *Biblical Theology of the New Testament*, trans. Daniel P. Bailey (Grand Rapids: Eerdmans, 2018), 511.

11   Here note Reicke: "The admonition is not due to the political or social conservatism of the author, or out of respect for the rich. His interest centers exclusively on the eternal well-being of Christian workers" (98). They are to fulfill their worldly calling with faith in Christ and love for the neighbor.

12   Here also see Leonhard Goppelt, *A Commentary on I Peter*, 226–228. Goppelt notes that, "'Your prayers' are certainly not those of the husband alone, but the common prayers of husband and wife. Jesus himself taught that prayer is impeded when a relationship with a fellow human being is troubled. Whenever the most intimate human relationship—marriage—is not lived out satisfactorily the prayers of those involved are 'hindered'; they do not achieve the proper stature and do not reach oneness with God's will and provision" (228).

13   On the atonement in I Peter, see David R. Nienhus, "I–II Peter" in *T & T Clark Companion to the Atonement*, ed. Adam J. Johnson (London: Bloomsbury/T & T Clark, 2017), 689–692.

14   Martin Scharlemann, "He Descended into Hell" in *Toward Tomorrow* (St. Louis: CPH, n.d.), 111.

15   See Reicke: "This sacrament does not consist in putting off the uncleanness of the flesh, as purifications were occasionally regarded in Judaism" (114). Also see Edmund Schlink: "The forgiveness which is imparted through Baptism is determined by the fact that the baptized is assigned to the Crucified as the living, present, and active Lord. Therefore in this forgiveness it is not simply a matter of removing a purely cultic impurity, nor of pardoning isolated transgressions of divine precepts, nor of the cancelation of a specific individual guilt. Baptism is a change of dominion. Through Baptism a man is removed from the dominion of sin and placed under the rule of Christ"—*The Doctrine of Baptism*, trans. Herbert J.A. Bouman (St. Louis: CPH, 1972), 44–45.

16   Reicke, 123.

17   John H. Elliott, *The Anchor Bible: I Peter* (New York: Doubleday, 2000), 797.

18   See John T. Pless, *Praying Luther's Small Catechism* (St. Louis: CPH, 2016), 119–123.

19   For more on this, see Paul A.J. Achtemeier, *Hermeneia: A Commentary on First Peter* (Minneapolis: Fortress Press, 1996), 355–356; also Goppelt, 377–378 and Eliott, *The Anchor Bible: I Peter*, 890–892.

20   Philip Carrington, *The Primitive Christian Catechism* (Cambridge: Cambridge University Press, 1940). Chapter Three deals explicitly with I Peter.

21   Andrew Pfeiffer, "A Comparative Study of Ephesians, Colossians, and First Peter: Implications for the Evangelization of Adults" *Lutheran Theological Journal* (August 2000), 61–72.

22   Oswald Bayer, *Theology the Lutheran Way*, trans. Jeffrey Silcock and Mark Mattes (Grand Rapids: Eerdmans, 2007), 210–213. Also see Pless, *Luther's Small Catechism: A Manual for Discipleship*, 11ff.

36

Preaching Pentecost

13 MAY 2018

Commenting on John 16, Luther writes,

> Here Christ makes the Holy Spirit a Preacher. He does so to prevent
> one from gaping toward heaven in search of Him, as the fluttering spir-
> its and enthusiasts do, and from divorcing Him from the oral Word of
> the ministry. One should know and learn that He will be in and with the
> Word, and that it will guide us into all truth, in order that we may
> believe it, use it as a weapon, be preserved by it against all the lies and
> deceptions of the devil, and prevail in all trials and temptations. . . . The
> Holy Spirit wants this truth which He is to impress into our hearts to
> be so firmly fixed that reason and all one's own thoughts and feelings
> are relegated to the background. He wants us to adhere solely to the
> Word and to regard it as the only truth. And through this Word alone
> He governs the Christian Church to the end. (AE 24:362)

Pentecost preachers will remember that the Spirit is inseparably
bound to the Word.[1] To look for the Spirit outside of the Word is
to be lured into the realm of uncertainty where human or demonic
impulses are confused with the Lord and Giver of Life[2]. Rather we
follow the example of Peter preaching on the first Pentecost in Acts 2.
When the Apostle preaches, he proclaims the fulfillment of the Old
Testament (Joel and the Psalms) in Jesus crucified and risen.

The Holy Spirit has been called "the shy member of the Trinity."
In one way, of course, the Holy Spirit is anything but shy as He

empowers the prophets and apostles to speak with unparalleled boldness, giving them resilient courage in the face of persecution. But in another sense, the Holy Spirit is indeed "shy" in that He does not promote Himself but Christ Jesus as He takes what the Son has done for us and delivers it to us so that we have access to the Father. Any talk of the Spirit that is not cruciform in shape, devoid of Christ, is suspect. The work of the Spirit is also filtered through the lens of the cross. Hermann Sasse (1895–1976) knew this well. His preaching on the Holy Spirit remains a fine primer for our preaching on Pentecost.

This *theologia crucis* shines through Sasse's sermon, "The Comforter," based on John 15:26–16:4 preached on *Exaudi* Sunday (29 May 1938). In this sermon, Sasse develops the biblical understanding of the Holy Spirit as the comforter, the *paraclete* noting that it is the Spirit's office to console the "despairing heart in an hour of deep disappointment and bereavement."[3] Sasse illustrates this with a reference to Luther and the Reformation:

> Where the word 'comforter' stands in our Bible, there it stands as a powerful, living witness of him, who as the Reformer of the church, and the church with him, had experienced in the days of the Reformation because the Reformation was not well known as a shining triumph, but as a chain of very strenuous fights inside the church. For many at that time, it looked like the breakdown of the church. At that, the church hardly saw anything else. In such times, Luther learned to confess: 'I believe in the Holy Ghost'—and he experienced what kind of comfort this faith could be.[4]

It is the Comforter, the Spirit of truth, who makes the promise that the witness of Christ will not fail, "The Pentecost endeavors to equip Christians in a country on the brink of war (1938!) with a courage not born of trust in princes but in Christ who has overcome the world. He is not absent from His church but is with them through the Spirit, who contends against every false and lying Spirit." This means that "the Church's witness to Christ is not merely the witness of men. It is the witness of the Holy Ghost."[5] He is no naked Spirit, but the Spirit wrapped up with and permeating God's Word, both preached and written. Thus this sermon has a polemical edge against those like Schleiermacher would see the Scriptures as "only a mausoleum of religion"[6] in need of an injection of the Holy Spirit to become effective in our time. In Sasse's preaching, there is no divorce between Word and Spirit.

The Spirit works *sub contraio*, under opposites, to sustain and build up in the face of weakness and defeat. Sasse uses a similar approach in a Pentecost sermon based on Acts 2:1–14, "The Miracle of Pentecost," preached two years later (12 May 1940). Here Sasse contrasts cultural celebrations of Pentecost as the festival of springtime and new life with the grim realities of war, but the Holy Spirit, the Lord and Giver of Life comes in the promise of the Gospel to call and gather a holy, Christian people for Christ through the forgiveness of sins. The miracle of Pentecost is not obvious; it is the miracle of faith created through the preaching of the word of the cross.

Here Sasse demonstrates a sharp declaration of the Law as he engages the devastation brought about by "the spirit of man" who has turned God's good earth into a "huge cemetery." This, he says, is "what the spirit of man has brought about."[7] As preacher, Sasse shuts down any and all romantic notions of what the "nobility" of the human spirit might achieve! Then as incisively as he has preached the Law, he skillfully unleashes the miracle of Pentecost as the condescension of God's Spirit to sinful man. He reminds his hearers that the Holy Spirit is not a thing but a person and then goes on to proclaim the Spirit's work. He is the One who brought order out of chaos in creation, and He has spoken by the prophets. He is the One who descended on Christ in His Baptism and then was promised to the disciples by the Lord prior to the passion. The promise was fulfilled at Pentecost. Through his vivid recapitulation of the biblical account of the Spirit's work, Sasse proclaims that is this Spirit who is given to us and for us. The work of the Spirit is to give us Jesus.

We do not soar to the heights of heaven through some burst of divine or cosmic energy. No, the Spirit comes not to "heroes of the faith" but confused and trembling disciples: "The Holy Spirit comes to the place where men despair of their own wisdom and strength."[8] Luther's explanation of the Third Article in the *Small Catechism* that we cannot by our own reason or strength believe in Jesus Christ or come to Him but that the Holy Spirit has called us by the Gospel leaves an indelible imprint on Sasse's sermon. The message of Pentecost is not an addendum to the Gospel; it is the Gospel: "The Holy Gospel is the message that there is forgiveness of sins in Jesus Christ and in him alone. It is completely free, wherever this message is heard, that God the Holy Spirit is at work calling men and giving them the faith that goes to the heart."[9]

As a Lutheran theologian, Sasse confessed, "As God outside of Christ always remains the hidden God, so His Holy Spirit remains hidden from us unless we find Him in the Word and in the Sacraments. And just as the revelation of God in Christ is at the same time God's hiding in the human nature of Christ, so the Holy Spirit is deeply hidden in the means of grace. He is always an object of faith, not of sight."[10] We believe in the Holy Spirit only as He gives Himself in the words of Jesus (see John 14:26). Just so in his preaching on Pentecost, Sasse does not simply preach about the Spirit but proclaims he proclaims the message of reconciliation achieved by the suffering and death of the Son of God and now made ours in His words which are "spirit and life" (John 6:63).

Notes

1 "The Holy Spirit in his freedom has bound himself to the letters of the Bible so that any demonstration of the Spirit and power today (I Cor. 2:4) will happen in no other way that than '*in* and *through* the prophetic and apostolic Word that is sure, certain, and utterly reliable' (Bayer)" Jeffrey Silcock, "Luther on the Holy Spirit and His Use of God's Word" in *The Oxford Handbook of Martin Luther's Theology*, ed. Robert Kolb et al (Oxford: Oxford University Press, 2014), 306.

2 In the memorable words of Oswald Bayer: "Those who want to search for the Holy Spirit deep inside themselves, in a realm too deep for words to express, will find ghosts, not God. They will only be amusing themselves with baseless thoughts" Oswald Bayer, *Theology the Lutheran Way*, trans. Jeffrey Silcock and Mark Mattes (Grand Rapids: Eerdmans, 2007), 55.

3 Sermon: "The Comforter" preached on 29 May 1938 in *Wittness: Erlangen Sermons and Essays for the Church: 1933–1944*, translated by Bror Erickson (Saginaw: Magdeburg Press, 2013): 130. For Sasse's earlier exegetical work on the *paraklete*, see Norman Nagel, "Hermann Sasse Identifies the Paralete" *Lutheran Quarterly* (Spring 1996): 3–23.

4 "The Comforter," 131.

5 "The Comforter," 134.

6 "The Comforter," 134.

7 "The Miracle of Pentecost," 141.

8 "The Miracle of Pentecost," 144.

9 "The Miracle of Pentecost," 148.

10 Hermann Sasse, "On the Doctrine of the Holy Spirit" in *Letters to Lutheran Pastors*, Vol. III: (1957–1969), 209.

37

Preaching Trinity Sunday

20 MAY 2018

One Trinity Sunday, a pastor introduced the Athanasian Creed by telling the congregation that we are now going to confess together the incomprehensible doctrine of the Holy and Blessed Trinity. Upon hearing that creed, a young boy blurted out, "the whole thing incomprehensible." No doubt that lad speaks for many. The Trinity is thought of as confused and confusing dogma that is unessential to Christianity.

Thomas Jefferson still speaks for many:

> When we shall have done away with the incomprehensible jargon of the Trinitarian arithmetic, that three are one, and one is three; when we shall have knocked down the artificial scaffolding, reared to mask from view the very simple structure of Jesus; when, in short, we shall have unlearned everything which has been taught since his day, and got back to the pure and simple doctrines he inculcated, we shall then be truly and worthily his disciples.[1]

Jefferson rejected the doctrine of the Trinity because he could not accept the fact that Jesus Christ is both true God begotten of the Father from all eternity and true man born of the Virgin Mary. Jefferson's own version of the New Testament excises all reference to our Lord's deity. He leaves us with a Christ who is a moralistic teacher but not a Savior. Unitarians and, more recently, Jehovah's Witnesses, like Jefferson, claim that the teaching of the Trinity is a fabrication invented by those who corrupted the message of Jesus.

The celebration of Trinity Sunday–the only church festival specifically dedicated to a doctrine–reminds us of the necessity of confessing that the one God exists in three persons, Father, Son, and Holy Spirit. Luther offers good advice to preachers. He did not see the Trinity as a problem to be solved or a mystery to be unraveled, but the truth of God's revelation of Himself to be proclaimed and confessed.[2] Writing late in his life (1543), in the treatise on "The Last Words of David," Luther takes up the doctrine of the Trinity: "Thus it is useful and proper that there be some, both among the laity and the educated, particularly pastors, preachers, schoolmasters, who think it important to learn about such centrally important articles of our faith and to speak of them in German. . . . But for the one for whom this is too difficult, that person should stay with the children by using the catechism and should pray against the devil and his nonsense."[3] Neither the *Small Catechism* nor the *Large Catechism* provide a dogmatic discussion of the Trinity. Instead, Luther assumes the biblical and creedal truth of doctrine and proceeds to confess and teach not on the basis of abstractions but God's revelation of Himself in Christ.

Writing in 1528, Luther writes at the end of his *Confession Concerning Christ's Supper*:

> These are the three persons and one God, who has given himself to us all wholly and completely, with all that he is and has. The Father gives himself to us, with heaven and earth all creatures, in order that they may serve us and benefit us. But this gift has become obscured and useless through Adam's fall. Therefore the Son himself has subsequently gave himself and bestowed all his works, sufferings, wisdom, and righteousness, and reconciled us to the Father, in order that restored to life and righteousness, we might also know and have the Father and his gifts. But because this grace would benefit no one and could not come to us, the Holy Spirit comes and gives himself to us wholly and completely. (*AE 37:366*)

For Luther, the doctrine of the Trinity was not an incomprehensible abstraction for endless speculation but a comforting reality that evokes praise. In the *Large Catechism*, he writes: "For here we see how the Father has given us himself with all creation and has abundantly provided for us in this life, apart from the fact that he has showered us with inexpressible eternal blessings through the Son and the Holy Spirit" (LC II:24, K-W, 433). The Father who has created us wills our salvation in His Son sent into the world to die and rise again for us, and the Holy Spirit delivers this salvation in the Gospel for the forgiveness of our sins.

Thomas Jefferson was wrong. Far from being this "artificial scaffolding, reared to mask from view the very simple structure of Jesus," the doctrine of the Trinity is absolutely necessary if we are to confess that Jesus Christ is Lord by the power of the Spirit to the glory of God the Father. "Blessed be the Holy Trinity and the undivided Unity. Let us give glory to Him because He has shown his mercy to us."

Notes

1 Thomas Jefferson cited by Allister McGrath in *Understanding the Trinity* (Grand Rapids: Zondervan, 1988), 110.

2 For more on Luther on the Trinity, see Christine Helmer, *The Trinity and Martin Luther* (Bellingham, Washington: Lexham Press, 2017); Steven Paulson, "Luther's Doctrine of God" in *The Oxford Handbook of Martin Luther's Theology*, ed. Robert Kolb, Irene Dingel, Ľubomí Baatka (New York: Oxford University Press, 2014), 187–200; and Hans Schwarz, *The Trinity: The Central Mystery of Christianity* (Minneapolis: Fortress Press, 2017), 91–93.

3 Cited in Albrecht Peters, *Commentary on Luther's Catechisms: Creed*, trans. Thomas Trapp (St. Louis: Concordia Publishing House, 2011), 36.

38

Preparing to Preach on Reformation Sunday

Thoughts from Hermann Sasse

21 OCTOBER 2019

Each year, on the last Sunday of October, we celebrate the Reformation of the church which a 33-year-old priest ignited on October 31, 1517 when he tacked his 95 Theses to the door of the Castle Church in Wittenberg. Of course, whether you are a Christian or not, you can't escape the significance of the Reformation. It is an important chapter in western history; yes, in world history. The Lutheran theologian of the last century, Hermann Sasse, in his important book, *Here We Stand*, suggested that there are three inadequate interpretations of the Reformation. First, there is a **heroic interpretation** of the Reformation. In this view, Luther is regarded as a hero in much the same way as a George Washington or an Abraham Lincoln might be viewed. Focus is here placed on Luther's character, traits, inner struggles and personality. Second, there is what Sasse calls the **cultural-historical interpretation** of the Reformation. Here the Reformation is understood as a movement of liberation, a turn from the unenlightened darkness of the medieval world full of suppression and superstition to the bright dawn of a new world marked by the power of the intellect and the freedom of the individual. Third, there is the **nationalist interpretation** of the Reformation, and as you might imagine, this was quite popular in German, especially in the years leading up to the 400th anniversary of the Reformation in 1917. Here Luther is portrayed as the German Reformer who defied a Pope in distant Rome and a Spanish emperor, Charles V, to assert that a German church with Bible and liturgy in the German language. Here Luther and the Reformation became a symbol of German identity and independence.

Now, Sasse tells us that each of these views of the Reformation is inadequate. And he is right. The fourth view says Sasse is the correct view, and that is the understanding that the Reformation is an episode in the history of the one holy Christian and apostolic church. That is why we adorn the chancel with red paraments, and the pastors wear red stoles on Reformation Sunday. Red is the color of Pentecost, the festival of the Holy Spirit who calls, gathers, and enlightens a holy Christian people for Christ Jesus through the Gospel which forgives sin. The Reformation is an episode in the history of the church. We call it Reformation for the church was deformed by false and misleading teachings which were embodied in errant practices making Christ's holy bride almost unrecognizable under the papacy. This young Wittenberg professor spotted pastoral malpractice in the Roman church, and he sought to argue the case on behalf of Christian people living under the burden of demands which they could not fulfill by their own spiritual power. Luther was not about creating a new church, but restoring the Gospel to the church so that genuine repentance and true faith might be preached among every nation, tribe, language, and people might be brought to worship God as He wills to be worshipped in Christ Jesus.

Not only is Sasse's *Here We Stand* well-worth reading as you get ready to preach on Reformation Sunday, but there are also several other Sasse essays that might prime the homiletical pump. In a short essay from 1937, "Luther and the Teaching of the Reformation," Sasse demonstrates how the Reformation was sparked by Luther's pastoral duty of hearing confession. It was his time in the confessional box that "led him to draw up his theses on indulgences."[1] It was the Roman Church's teaching indulgences could substitute for fruits of repentance that prompted Luther toward the discovery that the word of absolution did not merely signify that the conditions for forgiveness had been met but instead was the very word of the Living

Christ that delivered the forgiveness of sins into the ears and hearts of the broken. Luther did not set out to change the church or much less establish a new one. Instead, he sought to reform that which had become deformed, namely preaching and pastoral care.

Luther's Reformation, Sasse contends, sought to give the Word of the Lord free course in the church. Of this Word, Sasse writes: "The Word discloses man as a sinner. It tears every mask from his face, even the mask of piety. It shows us that our religion, in our moral striving, we seek not God but ourselves. It shows us that there is no righteousness which can be attained by man's own efforts: 'There is none righteous, no, not one' (Rom. 3:10 KJV). But moreover, Luther found in the Scriptures what he henceforth understood as the real meaning of the Gospel."[2] This Gospel was not a theological theory for Luther: "The Gospel was for him not a doctrine about the possibilities of the forgiveness of sins but the message of God to the sinner to desire the forgiveness of sins and the promise of this forgiveness."[3] Asceticism, morality, sanctification, and the hope of immortality can be found in other religions. "But forgiveness of sins is found only in Jesus Christ."[4] Without the preaching of Christ's forgiveness, the church would remain deformed.

A second essay is from just after the World War in 1946, "Luther's Legacy to Christianity." In this work, Sasse observes, "The legacy which Luther left behind can properly be grasped only by one who realizes that this legacy applies to all of Christendom on earth."[5] This is the case for Luther sought to restore the pure preaching of God's justification of the ungodly to the church, for it is only in this message of divine reconciliation that the church can claim the right to exist. Sasse maintains that the note found in Luther's pocket after his death with the words scribbled, "We are beggars; that is true" defined the entirety of the Reformer's work. Where human beings cease to be beggars before God, there can only be unrelenting despair or pompous self-righteousness. Rome can speak of the *sola gratia*, but not the *sola fide*. Our righteousness is forever and always the righteous that comes by faith alone. "He [Luther] knew that the *sola gratia* must be enlarged by the *sola fide*, that to 'by grace alone' must be added 'through faith alone.'"[6] Only where this is done can the Christian remain a beggar before a gracious Lord.

Luther understood this, says Sasse, like no teacher before him. Luther's confession is set in stark contrast with that of Aquinas. For Aquinas, Christ cannot enter into living communion with a sinner. Luther asserted the very opposite: "Christ dwells only among sinners."[7] This Luther holds is the Gospel, which is inexhaustible for broken, beggarly sinners.

A third essay that holds promise to provoke deeper and substantial preaching on Reformation Sunday is a piece Sasse wrote relatively late in his life (1968), "Erasmus, Luther, and Modern Christendom." Here Sasse argues that the great dispute between Erasmus and Luther has never really come to an end. It continues down to the present day as both secularists and the religious hold out a place for the freedom of the human will. Erasmus was troubled by Luther's assertiveness when it came to both sin and faith. According to Sasse, Luther "saw behind Erasmus' concept of an undogmatic Christianity, the coming neo-paganism of the modern world."[8] In this sense, Sasse concludes that Erasmus "believes in God, but he has not entirely lost his belief in man. He is fighting for the dignity of man who is not totally lost, who has retained his free will and can cooperate with the divine grace. He has never been able to understand the depth of human sin."[9] Erasmus recognized moral and administrative defects in the Roman Church, but it was Luther who became the Reformer for he not Erasmus recognized the problem of human bondage to sin and preached a Gospel which was not about renovation of character but resurrection from the dead.

There is much homiletical fodder for preachers in these and the many other essays, letters, and sermons of Sasse to ponder the joyful task of preaching on Reformation Sunday. Unlike his contemporary, Rudolf Bultmann, who insisted that preachers must demythologize the text of Holy Scriptures for successful preaching, Sasse recognized the need to demythologize, not the text, but the hearer. This recognition relies on Luther's understanding of the human being's captivity to idolatry. It is the preaching of Christ crucified that sets captives free and makes of beggars princes and princesses in the kingdom of grace. This freedom is the theme of Reformation Sunday, and we may learn from Sasse how to use Luther's legacy to proclaim it.[10]

Notes

1   Hermann Sasse, "Luther on the Teaching of the Reformation" in *The Lonely Way*, Vol. I edited by Matthew C. Harrison (Saint Louis: Concordia Publishing House, 2001), 322.

2   Sasse, "Luther and the Teaching of the Reformation," 327.

3   Sasse, "Luther and the Teaching of the Reformation," 328.

4   Sasse, "Luther and the Teaching of the Reformation," 328.

5   Hermann Sasse, "Luther's Legacy to Christianity" in *The Lonely Way*, Vol. II edited by Matthew C. Harrison (Saint Louis: Concordia Publishing House, 2002), 172.

6   Sasse, "Luther's Legacy to Christianity," 174.

7   Sasse, "Luther's Legacy to Christianity," 176.

8   Sasse, "Erasmus, Luther, and Modern Christendom," in *The Lonely Way*, Vol. II, 381.

9   Sasse, "Erasmus, Luther, and Modern Christendom," 383.

10   For more on this, see John T. Pless, "Hermann Sasse the Preacher" in *Witness: Erlangen Sermons and Essays for the Church 1933–1944*, trans. Bror Erickson (Saginaw: Magdeburg Press, 2013), 7–30.

39

Remembering the Dead

Preaching on All Saints Sunday

27 OCTOBER 2019

November 1 is All Saints' Day; many congregations transfer the celebration to the following Sunday. It is good and fitting that Christian congregations keep this festival that also serves as something of a portal into the last Sundays of the church year with their emphasis on the last things: death, Christ's return to judgement, heaven and hell, and the promise of a new heaven and a new earth. The Lord Jesus Christ will bring His redemptive work to culmination. On All Saints' Sunday, we remember with thanksgiving, those blessed fellow-believers who died in the Lord and are now at rest even as we wait with them for the Last Day and the resurrection of the body to eternal life with Christ.

The *Augsburg Confession* sets the observance of All Saints' Sunday in evangelical perspective:

Concerning the cult of the saints they teach that the saints may be remembered in order that we imitate their faith and good works, according to our calling. Thus, the emperor can imitate the example of David in waging war to drive out the Turks from our native land. For both of them are kings. However, Scripture does not teach calling on the saints or pleading help from them. For it sets before us Christ alone as mediator, atoning sacrifice, high priest, and intercessor. He is to be called upon, and he has promised that our prayers will be heard. Furthermore, he strongly approves this worship most of all, namely, that he be called upon in all afflictions. I John 2 (:1): 'But if anyone does sin, we have an advocate with the Father . . . (AC XXI:1–4, BOC, Kolb/Wengert, 59)

We give thanks for the way of God's grace in Christ in their particular lives even as we imitate their faithfulness in our various vocations.

Preachers preparing to preach on All Saints' Sunday would do well to read and ponder a 1957 essay by Hermann Sasse, "Remembrance of the Dead in the Liturgy." In this article, Sasse deftly moves through the history of dogma, noting how remembrances of the dead as part of the church's prayers of thanksgiving, shifted to intercession for their eternal fate. Sasse notes that prayers for the dead developed in light of theories regarding postmortem cleansing of souls in Origen.[1] Later on the development of the doctrine of purgatory would accentuate the practice of prayers for the deceased. These prayers would find a home in the Canon of the Mass as the Sacrament would come to be seen as a sacrifice for the sins of the living and the dead. This practice is both unbiblical and contrary to the central doctrine of justification by faith alone.

Lutherans rightly reject the invocation of the saints. Sasse reminds us, Apology XXIV:94, which is sometimes romantically cited as an endorsement of intercessions for the dead is actually about the remembrance of deceased Christians in prayers which are a sacrifice of thanksgiving. Yet Sasse notes that Evangelical-Lutherans do rightly remember the blessed dead in the liturgy. We do this every Lord's Day as we are gathered around the altar with "angels, archangels, and with all the company of heaven" to acclaim Him who comes to us in His body and blood. On All Saints' Sunday we are especially reminded that "the church of the New Testament knows itself to be a colony of the citizens of heaven."[2] With our citizenship in heaven (Phil. 3:20), we are pilgrims who have no abiding city in this old dying world but look forward to an enduring *polis* which is yet to come (see Heb. 13:14). Yet even now Sasse recalls we have come to Mount Zion, the city of the living God with multitudes of angels, the assembly of the first born, and the congregation of the spirits of the righteous ones made perfect through the blood of our meditator, Jesus (see Heb. 12:22–25). We on earth sing the

Sanctus with the heavenly choirs. Heaven and earth are united in Christ Jesus.

Therefore Sasse says, "It is from this understanding of the church and the Divine Service that we are to understand the earliest form of the remembrance of the dead. If the *ecclesia* scattered abroad in the world are spoken of under the image of the ancient world order as 'colonies' of the *ecclesia* in heaven, then the church on earth and the Church in heaven is one, as Heb. 12:22 puts it, 'the church in an alien land' (*paroikia*) and 'the Church in the homeland' (*patris*)."[3] Wearied by the changes and chances of this life, wounded by our own sin, and hounded by the attacks of the evil one, we do indeed feebly struggle as those who have completed the race now dazzle in the glory of a light that has no ending. But we colonists still living as exiles on earth are one community with those who are forever alive in the homeland. "We feebly struggle, they in glory shine; Yet all are one in Thee, for all are Thine" (LSB 677:4).

So, "One can only speak of thanksgiving for those who have finished their course and of the prayer that the Lord strengthen the living for martyrdom. This is the form the remembrance of the dead takes throughout the second century. It corresponds precisely with what Luther and the Lutheran Confessions teach concerning the remembrance of the dead in prayer."[4] We give thanks to the Lord for His victory over death and the grave both for those who are now with Him in glory and for ourselves even as we press forward in faithfulness awaiting that Day when our eyes will see Him. Surrounded by so great a cloud of witnesses (Heb. 12:1) we wait with eager anticipation as we eat and drink Christ's body and blood acknowledging that in this Sacrament we are given the forgiveness of sins which carries with it the promise of the resurrection of our bodies. In this communion we are therefore bold to pray: "Gracious God, our heavenly Father, You have given us a foretaste of the feast to come in the Holy Supper of Your Son's body and blood. Keep us firm in the days of pilgrimage that, on the day of His coming, we may together with all Your saints, celebrate the marriage feast of the Lamb in His kingdom which has no end; through Jesus Christ, Your Son, our Lord, who lives and reigns with you and the Holy Spirit, one God, now and forever" (LSB, p. 212).

Notes

1 Hermann Sasse, "Remembrance of the Dead in the Liturgy" in *Letters to Lutheran Pastors*, Vol. III, edited by Matthew C. Harrison (St. Louis: Concordia Publishing House, 2015), 34.

2 Sasse, "Remembrance of the Dead in the Liturgy," 37.

3 Sasse, "Remembrance of the Dead in the Liturgy," 38.

4 Sasse, "Remembrance of the Dead in the Liturgy," 39.

40

Preaching Hope

Theological Reflections on
the Last Sundays of the Church Year

10 NOVEMBER 2019

> "The joylessness of much of our preaching could have
> its deepest root in the hopelessness of so much of our
> theology"—Hermann Sasse[1]

The final Sundays of the Church Year (Pentecost 22/November 10,
Pentecost 23/November 17, and the Last Sunday of the Church Year/
November 24) invite the preacher to think more deeply and speak
more clearly on hope. Hope is different from optimism. Optimism
as is its opposite—pessimism is grounded in human potential or lack
thereof. Hope is given in Christ, and it is dependent on Him. Oswald
Bayer notes that hope is tied up with Baptism:

> Baptism marks the intersection of the old world and the new. Ethical
> progress is only possible by returning to Baptism. That progress
> which promises us good things, and not just good things, but the
> very best, is converting and returning to Baptism, and therefore a
> new perception of the world in which we no longer have to choose
> between optimism and pessimism, between shrill anxiety about the
> future and euphoric hope regarding the further evolution of the cos-
> mos and the enhancement of its possibilities; all the same it remains
> true that God the Creator unceasingly does new things. Luther's

courage, which goes beyond optimism and pessimism, is grounded in Baptism. It may be seen in a saying that was not his own, although it fits his understanding very well: 'Even though the world perish tomorrow, today I will still plant a little apple tree.'[2]

This courage anchored in Baptism is what the Bible defines as "hope." Sasse engages the question of "What is Christian hope?" responding,

> It is given by God, by Christ, by the Holy Spirit. God, and especially Christ, is its content. It belongs to the great *charismata* that God the Holy Spirit gives to those who believe in Christ. It belongs together with faith and love and constitutes with them the triad that Paul mentions repeatedly, not only in I Corinthians 13, but also I Thessalonians 1:3 and Ephesians 4:16 [while other *charismata* may be lacking, these three are always present in every true believer]. Faith cannot be without hope, hope not without faith. And love belongs inseparably together with them. The formula is, so to speak, the shortest description of the Christian life.[3]

The triad also comes to the fore in Paul's doxological thanksgiving at the beginning of Colossians 1, where he recalls the faith and love of the Colossians in verse 4 and their hope reserved in heaven (v. 5). This doxology becomes the platform for the Apostle's launching of the great Christological confession of verses 13–20 (the Epistle for the Last Sunday of the Church Year). In this text, he proclaims the preeminence of Christ Jesus through whom all things were created and hold together. It is this Christ who has reconciled to himself all things, making peace by the blood of His cross. Hence Paul can say of this Christ that He is our "hope" (Colossians 1:27) and later on in 3:4, that "when Christ who is your life appears, then you also will appear with him in glory."

Jesus gives hope in the midst of death, as we see in Luke 23:27–43 (Holy Gospel for the Last Sunday of the Church Year). A dying thief pinned down on a Roman cross for his crimes cries out to Jesus with the petition that the Lord remember him in His kingdom. The Lord meets that prayer with a sure answer: "Today you will be with me in paradise." Here is man whose life did not merit the Kingdom. Hopeless were it not for Jesus. Recall Luther's words: "The Kingdom of God is not being prepared but has been prepared, while the sons of the Kingdom are being prepared, not preparing the Kingdom; that is to say, the Kingdom merits the sons, not the sons the Kingdom."[4] The thief was born anew to a living hope (see I Peter 1:3) where all human hope had perished, and optimism about the future was not an option.

These final Sundays of the Church Year directly draw us not toward optimistic or pessimistic speculation for as Johann Georg Hamann reminds us, the Day of the Lord "will come as a thief in the night and therefore there is no time for either political arithmetic or prophetic chronology to bring light."[5] The signs of the end, spoken of by Jesus in Luke 21:5–28 (Gospel for Pentecost 23), do not invite calculation but repentance and faith so that bent over bodies with downward gaze might "straighten up" for redemption draws near (Luke 21:28). These signs that "announce the coming of the kingdom as the first dim light of dawn announces the coming of the new day. But the day is not yet there."[6] Hope is faith-focused toward the future God has promised, enduring this old world with love that gives of itself freely to the neighbor.

Hope is neither apathetic nor fanatical. It is marked by a particular sobriety that looks to the future while engaging the present. The Epistle for Pentecost 23 (II Thessalonians 3:1–13) with Paul's exhortation that Christians are not to be given to idleness, and if a man does not work, he is not to eat, demonstrates that hope is no excuse for lazy indifference to the things of the world. Once again, listen to Sasse:

All the saints of God, all believers, share the hope that according to the wisdom of all nations belongs to the very nature of man, because man lives by hope (e.g., Ecclesiastes 9:4) and cannot live without hope. The hope of the sick for the restoration to health, the hope of the prisoner for freedom, the hope for social justice in a nation and for peace between the nations of the world—all these human hopes are common to Christians and non-Christians, and no Christian should disassociate himself from the hopes of his fellow-men, as long as these hopes are justified. It would be a grave violation of the great commandment to love our neighbor if we failed to understand these human hopes and if we refused our active participation in the lawful attempts to realize them under the pretext that there are higher things to hope for.[7]

Hope gives Christians the equilibrium to stand firmly in this world while waiting on the blessed Last Day without becoming intoxicated by dreams of heaven, whether in the hereafter or in some renewed society of ecological wholeness where peace and justice reign on this planet.

The Lord has given us a sure and certain promise: A hope that does not disappoint on account of Jesus' death and resurrection. It is in the midst of a world marked by empty and deceptive hopes that have broken hearts and lives that we are sent to deliver the promise of a future that has as its last chapter the resurrection of the body to eternal life with the Lamb who was slain but is alive forevermore. We who are preachers of hope might very well make Melanchthon's prayer are own:

> To hope grown dim, to hearts turned cold
> Speak tongues of fire and make us bold
> To shine Your Word of saving grace
> Into each dark and loveless place (585:3 LSB)

Notes

1 Hermann Sasse, "Some Thoughts on Christian Hope" in *The Journal Articles of Hermann Sasse*, ed. Bror Erickson (Irvine: New Reformation Publications, 2016), 226. Also see Hermann Sasse, "The Last Things: Church and Antichrist" in *Letters to Lutheran Pastors*, Vol. II, ed. Matthew C. Harrison (St. Louis: Concordia Publishing House, 2014), 98–115. This essay will be especially helpful if the preacher decides to preach on II Thessalonians 2:1–8, 13–17 with "the man of lawlessness" on Pentecost 22.

2 Oswald Bayer, *Living by Faith: Justification and Sanctification*, trans. G.W. Bromiley (Grand Rapids: Eerdmans, 2003), 66. For a fine and instructive treatment of Luther's confession of the Christian hope in Luther's theology, see Jeffrey Silcock, "Hope and Eternal Life" in *The Oxford Encyclopedia of Martin Luther*, Vol. I, ed. Derek R. Nelson and Paul R. Hinlicky (Oxford: Oxford University Press, 2017), 636–655.

3 Sasse, 230.

4 Luther (LW 33:153) cited in Bayer, 76–77.

5 Cited in Bayer, 67.

6 Sasse, 227.

7 Sasse, 227.

41

Eschatology

The Last Sundays of the Church Year

Writing in 1952, Hermann Sasse stated,

> In our day the Biblical doctrine of the Last Things has come alive for us as a gift given in the midst of what the church has had to endure. At the beginning of this century, a complacent church regarded the Last Things as an element of the first Christian proclamation which more or less belonged to that first period, a form of the Gospel which was for us only of historical interest. Or alternately, it was thought of as something that might be of significance for the future, at the end of our lives, or at the end of the world, something we needed to study only in preparation for such an end. That there is for the church no more vitally relevant doctrine than that of the Last Things was brought home to Christians by all they were called upon to endure.[1]

In the over six decades since Sasse penned those words, eschatology has a major theme in both academic theology and popular spirituality, albeit the term is freighted with variegated definitions.[2]

The last Sundays of the Church Year bring eschatology into focus with the lectionary's emphasis on death, the final judgment, and the promise of the new heaven and the new earth. These Sundays bring us to the conclusion of the Nicene Creed, "And He will come again with glory to judge both the living and the dead." We've said those words so often, but what do they mean?

Truth be told, we are more concerned about the judgment that comes from other human beings. We fret about how others will evaluate us. Sometimes it has to do with lesser things like how we dress or the way our lawn looks. Other times it might be more profound worries like an employee who is anxious over an annual performance review or a student taking an entrance exam that may determine which academic paths are opened or closed to him. The stresses and strains of this life seem enough to keep us preoccupied with the here and now. The judgment which will come at the end seems distant and abstract, far removed from all the things that call the worth of our lives into question right now. So we may ask the question not with skepticism but with honesty: what does the return of the Lord Jesus in judgment mean for me now in the face of all the real-life verdicts that I have to face?

The answer to that question is found in God's Word appointed to be read in the churches on these last Sundays of the Church Year. These are the Sundays of the end times. They point us to the sober reality that life will not go on as usual. These gray and increasingly winter-like days of November bear all the signs of death. The dazzling red and gold leaves of autumn give way to brown and barren branches. So also in the Church Year, these November Sundays have the chill of death. The year hastens to a close and with it the reminder that our lives hasten on as well. The Scripture readings appointed for these Sundays are a wake-up call. Think of the readings from Mark 13. Jesus says learn from the fig tree. When it begins to blossom, you know that summer is at hand. Wake up to the reality that the Son of Man is at the gate.

Jesus speaks of cosmic signs. The sun will be darkened, and the moon will not share its beams. Stars tumble from the skies and the heavenly powers are shaken. Then the Son of Man comes on the clouds with power and great glory. He dispatches His holy angels to gather a harvest from the seeds that were sown, and so they reap the elect from north and south, from east and west. None that belong to Jesus will be lost. That great cloud of witnesses will be complete; they will forever be with Jesus, the pioneer, and perfect of their faith. He endured the cross, triumphed over death by dying, and now He is seated at the Father's right hand. It is the Jesus who is near the gate, standing at the door.

Of course Jesus spoke these words just after He had entered through the gate on Palm Sunday. He was in Jerusalem moving ever closer to Calvary, where sun and moon would be darkened, and the powers of heaven shaken as the sinless Son of God endured all that our sin deserved—God's wrath and death itself. You see, Judgment Day really does begin on Good Friday, for it is there that Jesus is judged with our sins, the righteous for the unrighteous! Indeed the generation that Jesus spoke to would not pass away until these things had taken place. The time of God's visitation was upon them. They would see the Son of Man scorned and blasphemed. They would see Him handed over to wicked men, sentenced and spit upon, beaten, and bloody. They would see Him suffering and dying. They would hear Him cry out in His dying breath, "It is finished." God is finished with sin in Jesus for Jesus is the Lamb of God who takes away the sin of the world in His own body, pinned to a Roman cross. With His blood, He drains away the pollutant of your unbelief.

It is this Jesus who will come again to judge the living and the dead. The last days are not out there in the future somewhere. You are in them now. The church has been living in the last days every since Good Friday. To live in the last days is to live on the threshold between time and eternity. How close we are, we do not know. Life can be and is deceptive. It is easy to think that life just meanders on, that the comfortable routines that we have established for ourselves will continue uninterrupted. We can so easily be lulled into the fleshly security of the man in Jesus' parable who surveyed his filled to overflowing barns and concluded that his soul could be at rest for he had laid up for himself a bounty of wealth that would supply his needs for years to come. Jesus calls this man a fool, for the abundance of his riches blinded him to the fact that his soul would be required of him that very night.

You see, the things by which we evaluate our lives are transient and deceptive. Wealth and health are not permanent. There is a Judge who is standing at the door. He is not removed in some far distant realm of the future. He is near now even as one day—a day that is hidden from—He will come on clouds, and every eye will see Him and every tongue confess either in eternal joy or perpetual shame that He is Lord. Faith is not preoccupied with futile attempts to calculate the day or hour. Faith lives by the precious promises that Jesus makes right now. "Heaven and earth," Jesus says, "will pass away, but my words will not pass away."

That means that even though we always live as those who walk under the shadow of death, we can live in confidence and peace. The believer in Jesus Christ does not have to fret about the final judgment, living in uncertainty and fear. Why? Because you have already heard God's final verdict ahead of time. God let it slip out early. It is no longer a secret. It is called the absolution. God says, "I forgive you all your sin." It is as sure and certain here on earth as it is in heaven!

A Lutheran pastor of the last century once said that a Christian should go to the Lord's Supper as though he were going to his death. And that a Christian then may go to his death as though he were going to the Lord's Supper. When we go to the Lord's Supper, the Apostle Paul tells us, we proclaim the Lord's death until He comes. When we go to our death, then we will confess that Jesus' death for our sins is our confidence. His blood is our righteousness and the forgiveness of our sins, the promise of an open heaven. Werner Elert once said the "Day of Judgment . . . is just as close to us as the Judge is."[3]

Faith rejoices to receive this Lord ever-near; unbelief is terrified. So again, Elert, "Some live in the light of the Last Day, others in its shadow."[4] It is the office of preaching to proclaim that the One who comes at the End, is the Lord who came in the flesh to be our Brother and Savior that those broken by their sin might live not in the long shadows of the Last Day but in the brilliance of the light of the face of Christ Jesus our Lord.

Notes

1 Hermann Sasse, "Last Things: Church and Antichrist" in *We Confess the Church*, trans. Norman E. Nagel (Saint Louis: Concordia Publishing House, 1986), 108.

2 For an overview, see Reinhard Slenczka, *Ziel und End* (Neuendettelsau: Freidmund-Verlag, 2008), 67–115 and "Last Things" in *Confessing the Gospel Today*, Vol. II ed. Samuel Nafzger (Saint Louis: Concordia Publishing House, 2017), 1109–1194; also see Steven Paulson, "The Place of Eschatology in Modern Theology" *Lutheran Quarterly* (Winter 1998), 327–353 and Jeffrey Silcock, "A Lutheran Approach to Eschatology" *Lutheran Quarterly* (Winter 2017), 373–395.

3 Werner Elert, *The Last Things*, trans. Martin Bertram (St. Louis: Concordia Publishing House, 1974), 28.

4 Elert, 28.

42

Catechetical Preaching

11 AUGUST 2019

It might be said without too much exaggeration that Luther's *Small Catechism* was born in the pulpit. Years before its publication in 1529, Luther was preaching on the catechism: the Ten Commandments, the Creed, the Lord's Prayer, and the sacraments. We have an example of the Reformer's catechetical preaching in the ten sermons he preached in Wittenberg between November 30 and December 18, 1528 (see AE 51:133–193) just weeks before he finished his first draft of the *Small Catechism*. Luther's catechetical preaching was at once didactic and kerygmatic as he sought to teach the basics of the faith while at the same time strengthening believers to live by God's promises in Christ. Luther envisioned the catechism as a hermeneutic for both preachers and hearers.

Preaching asserts the First Commandment: "You shall have no other gods." This commandment calls for faith so that the God and Father of our Lord Jesus Christ is feared, loved, and trusted above all things. That is to say, the God who created all that exists—and there is no other God—makes a particular claim on His creatures. In His holy jealousy, He will not share them with counterfeit deities that promise heaven but deliver hell. Running through each of the remaining nine commandments is the First Commandment. God's commandments guard and protect the lives of His creatures in this fallen world. When and where they are broken, there is accusation that carries with it God's own wrath against sin. Catechetical preaching on the Decalogue is anchored in the First Commandment and tied to the threat and promise of the Conclusion: "God threatens to punish all who break these commandments. Therefore, we should fear His wrath and not do anything against them. But He promises grace and every blessing to all who keep these commandments. Therefore, we should also love and trust in Him and gladly do what He commands." Luther's explanations of the individual commandments are not only prohibitive but also prescriptive; God identifies the evil works which we are to avoid even as He shows us the works which He delights in. Our failure to fear, love, and trust in Him above all things is demonstrated in our loving what God hates and our abhorring what God desires. So God's Law is always and forever damning everything that is not in Christ. To be sure, God's commandments are the path of life and blessing, but the only thing that they can do with sin and the sinner is condemn. The Law is to be preached for repentance, not self-empowered renovation.

The First Commandment overlaps with the First Article of the Creed. To paraphrase Luther, the First Commandment forbids all false gods; the First Article shows us who the true God is. He is not a distant "supreme being" or an unnamed deity. He is the Father, the almighty maker of heaven and earth. In confessing that the creator is Father, we are not speaking by analogy or metaphor. The Creator is Father because He has an eternally begotten Son, the Lord Jesus Christ. The First Article is preached through the lens of the Second Article. Hence Luther would have us realize that all that God does for us in creation is done exclusively "out of fatherly, divine goodness, without any merit and worthiness in me." Even in the First Article, Luther is confessing justification by faith alone.

The beating heart of the Small Catechism is the Reformer's priceless confession of the Second Article. In concise poetic prose, Luther tells us who Jesus is and what He has done to become our Lord. He is true God begotten of the Father from eternity and true man born of the Virgin Mary. With clarity and utter simplicity, Luther summarizes the Chalcedonian confession of the two natures in Christ, rendering it preachable!

What has this Christ done? He has purchased and won me, lost and condemned person, from all sins, death, and the power of the devil not with gold or silver but His holy blood and innocent suffering and death. Luther is not bound to one picture of the atonement but brings together the biblical motifs of ransom (purchased) and victory (won), thus demonstrating how the work of Christ is to be preached not as a theoretical transaction framed by the Law, but as an evangelical necessity of the Christ who actually reconciles humanity to God and God to humanity by dying under the condemnation of the Law on a Roman cross. The outcome of this work is that the crucified and risen Jesus is "my Lord." He has redeemed me from the curse of the Law and snatched me from the grip of Satan and the jaws of death. Jesus' lordship means that I am now in His possession, located in His kingdom to serve Him in everlasting righteousness, innocence, and blessedness.

The redemption accomplished in the Second Article is delivered in the Third Article as the Holy Spirit calls lost and condemned persons—dead in trespasses and sins—to faith in Christ through the Gospel. The Third Article teaches preachers that this Gospel can never be left in the rearview mirror. It is always and ever proclaimed anew as sin, death, and despair are never absent on this side of the resurrection. For this reason, Luther asserts that, "In this Christian church he daily and richly forgives all my sins and the sins of all believers." Luther says elsewhere that the Christian preacher can't open his mouth without speaking an absolution. Conversely, a sermon that does not absolve is not a Christian sermon!

Christian preaching echoes Luther's "This is most certainly true." The conclusion of each article of the Creed is the foundation for addressing God as "Our Father" with all boldness and confidence as dear children speak to a dear father. Preaching evokes such prayer as it equips believers to call not upon an unknown and hidden deity but in God whose fatherly heart is revealed in Christ. The Lord's Prayer is the template of the Christian's life of beggarly neediness, even as it is an exposition of the Father's merciful provision for His children. Luther's exposition of the Lord's Prayer demonstrates the necessity of the *simul et peccator* in preaching. Through the Law, God is putting the old Adam to death, "breaking and hindering every evil plan and purpose of the devil, the world, and our sinful nature which do not want us to hallow God's name or let His kingdom come." But it is through the Gospel that God "strengthens and keeps us firm in this faith until we die." The outcome of preaching like the Lord's Prayer itself is that we may say, "yes, yes, it shall be so."

The Small Catechism keeps Baptism present tense in our preaching. It is not merely that I was baptized but I am baptized. The name of the Father and of the Son and of the Holy Spirit sticks. Baptism delivers the gifts of the Second Article, working forgiveness of sins, rescue from death, and the devil by the Holy Spirit's word in and with the water. Faith lays hold of what the Spirit gives, dying daily to sin and daily rising by the promise of the Gospel to the newness of life.

Baptismal death and resurrection is enacted in confession and absolution. Here preaching brings the hearer to examine his or her life in light of the Ten Commandments and his/her station in life where sin is anything but generic. Confession of sin is not an end in and of itself. The goal is the absolution, that is, the forgiveness of sins. Christ's words placed on the lips of the pastor are not merely descriptive of a forgiveness of sins located elsewhere; they are words that do what they say. They give the forgiveness of sins here on earth.

The Catechism also teaches us how to preach the Lord's Supper. On the basis of Jesus' words, Luther confesses that this Sacrament is "the true body and blood of our Lord Jesus Christ under bread and wine instituted by Christ Himself for us Christians to eat and drink." The Lord's Supper is not an extension of Golgotha into the present, nor is it the Christian's "time travel" back to Calvary. Rather, the body and blood of the One who suffered for our sins is now given us to eat and drink under bread and wine for the forgiveness of our sins. In preaching and in the Sacrament, the "for you" is indispensable. The Gospel is not merely a recollection of the past; preaching is not simply the retelling of a historical narrative but the announcement that what the Lord did when He suffered and died under Pontus Pilate was "for you." The forgiveness of sins was achieved in the unrepeatable event of Jesus' death on Good Friday, but it was not delivered there. Forgiveness of sins is not achieved or accomplished in the Lord's Supper but it is delivered in this Sacrament with Christ's word of promise: "given and shed for you for the forgiveness of your sins." The Catechism's exposition of the Lord's Supper serves to guard and keep preaching evangelical so that benefits of Christ's atoning death are predicated to the hearer. His death is for you. The Sacrament makes the promise of preaching explicit.

Luther appended to the six chief parts of Christian doctrine, the daily prayers, and the table of duties. These take us back to the conclusion of his explanation of the First Article of the Creed: "For all this, it is my duty to thank and praise, serve and obey Him." God is to be "thanked and praised" in the rhythms of daily life as He "richly and daily provides me with all that I need to support this body and life." Morning and evening. Rising up from sleep and going to bed at night. Mealtime. We acknowledge the Father as the One who opens His hand to donate daily bread to sustain our creaturely lives. Catechetical preaching confronts hearers with the Apostle's rhetorical question in I Corinthians 4:7, "What do you have that you did not receive?"

God is served and obeyed not by leaving the world behind but rather in the midst of the world where we now live in the places of life that the Creator has so arranged: in the congregation, in the civic community, and in the household. Christians are not drawn out of the mundane but called instead to live in creation according to God's commandments in love and service to the neighbor. Declared righteous by the word of Christ, we now live righteously in the world, daily dying to sin and living in the newness of life as we give of ourselves to the benefit and well-being of those people God has placed in our lives.

Paying attention to the connection of the Table of Duties to the First Article will clarify the preaching of sanctification. For Luther, the location of sanctification (as the response of the believer) is not in the Third Article but in the First Article. God carries the action of all the verbs in Luther's Explanation of the Third Article. The Third Articles takes us to the Second Article, where we are made the possession of the Lord's Jesus by His suffering and death and given to live under Him in His kingdom and serve Him in everlasting righteousness, innocence, and blessedness. It is from the Second Article that we then go to the First Article confessing God as Father through His Son our Lord Jesus Christ. Sanctification, then, is getting use to the status we have as sons of God through faith in Christ who now recognize and joyful engage the duty to thank, praise, serve, and obey Him not under the compulsion of the Law but from the "free and merit spirit" created by the Gospel.

As we said at the beginning of this little essay, the Catechism was born in the pulpit. We might also say that the Catechism is also at home in the evangelical pulpit guiding and shaping what the preacher says so that faith might be created and love given direction.

43

Revisiting an Overlooked Classic

Franzmann on the Gospel According to Matthew

24 NOVEMBER 2019

Shortly after Marin Franzmann's (1907–1976) death, Kenneth Korby referred to his teacher as "the sweet singer of the Missouri Synod." Indeed that was an apt description of Franzmann, who was destined to be remembered for his contribution to 20th-century Christian hymnody. He is less remembered for his exegetical work and that is a shame for Franzmann knew that theology must sing. It is no dry and pedantic pursuit chasing after dogmatic trivia but a vibrant art that listens intently to the Holy Scriptures, "the breathing space of the Holy Spirit" as Oswald Bayer has called them so that Christ Jesus is proclaimed to lacerated sinners in all of His crucified beauty and resurrected favor. A chief and abiding exegetical contribution of Franzmann is his 1961 book, *Follow Me: Discipleship According to Saint Matthew* (CPH, 1961). A couple of weeks ago, a friend asked me, "What's with this revival of Franzmann?" I'm not sure that there is a Franzmann revival going on, although the recent book by Matthew E. Borrasso, *The Art of Exegesis: An Analysis of the Life and Work of Martin Hans Franzmann* (Wipf & Stock, 2019) has helpfully reminded us of his multifaceted life.[1] A Franzmann revival would not be a bad thing. My goals here, though, are much more modest. With Year A (the Year of Matthew) in the LSB Three-Year Lectionary fast approaching, I simply want to commend *Follow Me: Discipleship According to Matthew* to preachers as a devotional companion as they read, mark, learn, inwardly digest and finally proclaim Christ from the inspired pages of this gospel.

Franzmann sees the theme of discipleship woven into the tapestry of Matthew's narrative. Unlike disciples of the rabbis, disciples of Christ, Jesus do not elect their Lord and Teacher. He elects them, calling them to a cruciform life, molding their erratic wills to fit His own good and gracious will. In fact, as Franzmann puts it, "Jesus is singularly brusque with enthusiastic volunteers" (2). Like the prophets of the Old Testament, disciples are called and compelled by the Word of the Lord who came to them. The One who calls and claims mundane men from fishing nets and tax collecting stations to be His disciples is no mere rabbi, but Israel's Messiah (8).

Matthew highlights the continuity between the Old Testament and the New Testament. Franzmann observes how tirelessly Matthew demonstrates that the Scriptures are fulfilled in this Jesus. From his recital of Jesus' genealogy through to the emergence of the voice of John the Baptist crying in the wilderness, Matthew demonstrates how Jesus is the promised Emmanuel born in Bethlehem, the son called out of Egypt whose advent is the occasion of Rachel's lamentation for her slaughtered children.

As John the Baptist looms so large in the lectionary for Advent, preachers would do well to study Franzmann's exposition of the life and message of the man identified as the Voice crying in the wilderness (see pp. 15–32). The Baptist proclaims that God's Kingdom is at hand. Franzmann says of the King and His kingdom: "His kingship is no longer merely a reign over the history of men and nations; it has, in a sense, become incarnate" (19). The preaching of Advent proclaims that the Kingdom is here in the person of the King! In Him, the promises made to David are not annulled.

John's preaching heralds this King and His coming Kingdom. In view of the arrival of the King, "John demanded a repentance as radical as it was universal, as deep as it was wide. His appeal was more categorical even than that of the prophets, for it was made under the urgency of the last days, in the shadow of the coming final revelation of God" (28). In the singular voice of the Baptist, all the words spoken of old by the prophets are brought to a point with John's preaching of repentance. So John the Baptist stands one foot in the Old Testament, the other in the New as he announces that the light of God's new and final revelation has come in the Christ whose way he has given to prepare.

Franzmann was a master at shaping exquisite word pictures from his exegetical lathe. In the section on the Beatitudes, he writes of Christ Jesus: "As Messianic Giver He gives absolutely, into emptiness" (36). Disciples remain beggars, capable only of being given to out of the generosity of a Donor whose benefits do not cease. Franzmann's writing is coherently crisp and unerringly evangelical: "He is promising and giving to those who have nothing and need everything, that which answers their every need. He is pointing men to the present fact and future hope of God acting for men and for their salvation" (38). Jesus is the One who is greater than Moses, so Franzmann writes, "It is plain: Jesus is not urging upon His disciples a more strenuous moralism; He is bidding them spell out in their lives the implications of their new existence" (45). Jesus does what the Law is powerless to do; He saves. Jesus gives what the Law is impotent to bestow: freedom to live in the forgiveness of sins.

Jesus' miracles or "mighty deeds," as Matthew calls them, figure large in Franzmann's treatment of this gospel. Franzmann observes the "embarrassed fumbling with the miraculous, which is characteristic of so much present-day theology" (68). In place of such dogmatic timidity, Franzmann shows preachers a more excellent way that does not apologize for the text but actually has the boldness to say what the text says. "In the miracles of the beggary of man and the largesse of God were strikingly and unmistakably delineated, so that each miracle became the Gospel in miniature and was so proclaimed" (68).

Along the way, Franzmann also offers sober and sane counsel for who bear the authority of the preaching office: "Only the compassionate can bear the burden of authority without being either bent or twisted or broken by it" (81).

Franzmann reads the parables as expositions of the "mysteries of God" as the Lord, who tells them, confounds the wise and gives understanding to the simple. All of the parables, for Franzmann, are to be heard under the cross: "God's ultimate 'parable' (in this sense) is the cross, where the Godhead is both impenetrably veiled in flesh and fully revealed in the splendor of a love which surpasses the highest reach of human love that men can only call it divine and believe it and adore it. The cross, above all else, is God's revelation, gives to him who has and takes away from him who has not, at the cross men say either, 'Jesus be cursed' or, 'Jesus is Lord' (I Cor. 12:3)" (113).

Faith clings to what is given from the Lord; it is always a beggarly faith; it looks to God who fills the hungry with good things. This faith itself is a gift, not something that the believer creates himself. The divine origin of this faith is demonstrated in the diabolical attack that it must suffer: "Proof of the divine origin of faith is seen in the fact that Satan attacks all good works of God; and he attacks it in characteristically satanic fashion, by imitative perversion of it" (139).

The church for Franzmann is not a club of self-sanctified saints but a holy company of beggars who live by trust in the electing and consoling word of absolution: "Forgiveness is the ground the disciple walks on, and the air he breathes; he exists only on the terms of forgiveness. The word of the forgiveness which the church hears fills the church with forgiveness" (154). Forgiveness of sins is not just the first step, which sets the disciple on a path which sooner or later allows him to leave the absolution behind and demonstrate his own spiritual capacities.

The cross and resurrection are not just the climax of Matthew's evangelical narrative. Franzmann spots that the imprint of the passion and the victory of "the suffering Servant of prophecy is woven into the texture of all the Gospels" (190). It is in this light Franzmann observes that the "Transfiguration does not lose touch with the world of history and fact" (141). The Transfiguration is the confirmation of Peter's confession that Jesus is the Christ and the Lord's subsequent reprimanding reminder to Peter that He will be delivered over to death on the cross.

Throughout Franzmann's exposition of Matthew's Gospel, judgment and grace, law and gospel, wrath and mercy in the words and actions of Jesus ring through loud and clear. The cross and resurrection, atonement and divine vindication stand in view of the eschatological horizon. The fate of Jerusalem portends the tribulation to befall the world. "All history is a sign for the eyes of faith; all history alerts the disciples to the end of history" (179). At the end of the history is the cross itself: "In a very real sense, the cross was a last judgment on man and did usher in the Day of the Lord" (213).

In the technical sense of the word, *Follow Me* is not a commentary. It lacks detailed exegetical notes, word studies, grammatical analysis, and the like. The fact that it is not a commentary does not lessen its usefulness to preachers in the least. Instead, Franzmann walks alongside readers of the Gospel according to Matthew, like a sharp-eyed and knowledgeable tour guide pointing out features of the evangelical landscape that invite and provoke deeper reflection, which, in turn, cannot but help make preaching more interesting and robust.

Note

1 Also see Ronald Feuerhahn, "Martin H. Franzmann: An Exegetical Preacher" in *Concordia Pulpit Resources* (December 1, 1996–February 9, 1997), 2–4.

PART III

Theological Essays

OFFICE OF THE MINISTRY

44

The Office of the Ministry in Global Lutheranism

PREVIOUSLY PUBLISHED IN THE REFORMATION 2019 ISSUE OF *LOGIA*, PP. 23-28

Given the ongoing disputes and dialogue on the nature of the office of the holy ministry in global Lutheranism, it would be interesting to examine works by recent Lutheran theologians such as Edmund Schlink,[1] Peter Brunner,[2] Wilfried Harle,[3] Wolfhart Pannenberg,[4] and Hermann Sasse. Each of these men has made a contribution to the place of the office of the ministry in contemporary Lutheran dogmatics, and to a greater or lesser degree, their work has made an impact on the way the office of the ministry is understood in world Lutheranism. Such a survey, though, would end up only skimming the surface, giving a taste of aspects of similarity and distinctiveness in these theologians. Schlink and Brunner represent a broad Lutheran consensus on the office of the ministry during the middle part of the last century. Pannenberg's work would have more wide-ranging significance in that he drew from ecumenical sources and, in turn, his work would leave its imprint on *Baptism, Eucharist, and Ministry*, the so-called Lima document produced by the World Council of Churches in 1982. Härle's book is widely used in German universities as an introductory textbook in systematic theology, so it is, at least, to that degree representative of contemporary approaches. Instead, I have decided to focus on the work of only one of these theologians, Hermann Sasse (1895–1976). Not only did

Sasse frequently address questions of church and office in his writings, he was, in many ways, a global Lutheran theologian. Born in Germany, he studied for a year in the United States. He traveled throughout Europe as an active player in the Ecumenical Movement prior to World War II. After the war, he immigrated to Australia, where he would teach but also continue an active correspondence with both Lutheran and other Christian theologians throughout the world. It was from the Australian years that Sasse would circulate his "letters to Lutheran pastors." Geographically isolated from both Europe and North America, rather remarkably, Sasse remained in constant literary contact with a range of both Lutheran and non-Lutheran theologians and churchmen abroad. His letters reflect his theological commentary on significant doctrinal and ecclesiological issues. These letters are collected in three volumes, *Letters to Lutheran Pastors*, edited by Matthew Harrison.

To understand why the work of Hermann Sasse is a fitting window through which we get a glimpse of the doctrine of the ministry in global Lutheranism, it is helpful to understand something of his own biography.[5] Educated at Berlin with Karl Holl, Adolf von Harnack, Reinhold Seeberg, and Adolf Deissmann as his teachers, his student days were interrupted by World War I. He enlisted in the army and endured the hardships of war. He was one of only six survivors in his unit in a battle fought in Flanders. After the war, he returned to his studies with his perspective, tempered by the life-and-death realities of combat. Sasse completed a postdoctoral year (1925–26) at Hartford Seminary in the United States.[6] He was called to the faculty at Erlangen in 1933, a position he held until 1948. Sasse collaborated with Dietrich Bonhoeffer, Georg Merz, Wilhelm Vischer, and Friederich von Bodelschwingh in the drafting of the Bethel Confession of 1933. He would refuse to sign the Barmen Declaration of 1934 on confessional grounds, understanding it to be a unionistic document. Sasse's protest against unionizing tendencies within German Lutheranism came to a head in 1948 when he resigned his membership in the Bavarian Church. The next year he received a call to teach at Immanuel Seminary in North Adelaide, Australia, where he would serve for the remainder of his life until he died from smoke inhalation in a house fire in August of 1976.

Staunchly Lutheran, Sasse was tirelessly involved in ecumenical discussion throughout his career, including service on official delegations, such as that of the Lausanne Conference in 1927 and numerous personal contacts in the Roman Catholic and Reformed churches. Sasse was instrumental in the merger of the two Lutheran bodies in Australia into the Lutheran Church of Australia in 1966. He made several visits to the United States, where he had ties to a wide range of theologians in all major Lutheran bodies.

It was during his year at Hartford Seminary that Sasse read Wilhelm Löhe's Three Books about the Church. It was this book, Sasse asserted, that made of him a confessional Lutheran. Sasse's critical appreciation for Löhe would prevent him from making the Bavarian pastor an infallible icon. Rather Sasse sought to understand Löhe in the context of the nineteenth century.

The nineteenth century was characterized by Sasse as that time when European Christianity experienced an awakening after "the icy winter of Rationalism"[7] and with this, a questing after the true church. The quest was exemplified across confessional borders. Johann Adam Mohler (1796–1838), a German Roman Catholic theologian, advocated an ecclesiology that understood the church as a Spirit-filled organism pulsating with the life of the risen Christ rather than an institution. Before converting to the Roman Catholic Church, the Anglican theologian John Henry Newman (1801–1890) proposed a developmental understanding of doctrine and church. Reformed theologians such as Alexandre Vinet (1797–1847) and Hermann Friedrich Kohlbrügge (1803–1875) sought to recover a more robust ecclesiology among the Reformed in Europe, as did the so-called Mercersburg theologians John Nevin and Philip Schaff in the United States. The Irvingites and the Disciples of Christ were representative of Restorationist attempts to claim an alleged New Testament form of the church. Lutherans were not exempt from this quest. Sasse situates Löhe squarely within this context along with other prominent Lutheran figures, including Johann Gottfried Scheibel (1783–1843), August F.C. Vilmar (1800–1868), and C.F.W. Walther (1811–1887).

As heir of the confessional reawakening of the nineteenth century, Löhe embraced the Lutheran Confessions as the clear exposition of the Holy Scriptures. This led him to reject the Prussian Union and all that it entailed. Löhe's confessionalism may be described as a "sacramental confessionalism," in that Löhe understood all of Lutheran doctrine drawn together in the sacrament of the altar. This sacramental confessionalism had both ecclesiological and pastoral consequences. Ecclesiastically it meant that for Löhe, there could be no intercommunion with those of another confession.[8] Pastorally it meant that the Confessions are embraced to keep the Lutheran Church centered in the purity of evangelical proclamation and administration of the Lord's Supper. For Löhe, the Confessions prevented involvement in interconfessional mission societies and the embrace of what he identified as "Methodistic" tactics of evangelization and pastoral care.

Sasse honored Löhe as a churchman with the courage of conviction, who, along with others of the nineteenth century, contended for the Lutheran Confessions.[9] He recognized Löhe along with August Vilmar as representative of both a true confessionalism and a genuine ecumenism.[10] Löhe's recognition of the place of the sacrament of the altar in the life of the church echoes throughout Sasse's own massive writings on the Lord's Supper. Like Löhe, Sasse recognizes that the church is a pilgrim people who have no earthly home apart from this sacrament.[11]

While deeply indebted to Löhe and appreciative of his struggle for the confessional integrity of the Lutheran Church as well as his churchly piety, Sasse is also critical. Even though he had profound respect for the Lutherans of the confessional revival of the nineteenth century, Sasse recognized their limitations. He observes that the awakening took on two forms. One, he describes "as in the direction of Spener" and the other toward Quenstedt.[12] In Sasse's mind, the theologians of the nineteenth century, Löhe included, did not go far enough:

> Perhaps the Awakening of the Lutheran Church from the fatal stupor of Rationalism had to begin with an Awakening in the direction of the Lutheranism of Spener, or that of Quenstedt. But these two types of the Lutheranism of the Awakening could and can only be transitional stages toward an Awakening of the Lutheran Church in the sense of the Lutheran Confessions, which, as the Formula of Concord states explicitly, are to be interpreted according to the doctrine of Luther "as the leading teacher of the Augsburg Confession," [FC SD VII 34] and not according to Quenstedt or Spener.[13]

While Löhe stood in the dogmatic tradition of Lutheran Orthodoxy, his work would also bear the imprint of Pietism.[14] He made relatively sparse use of Luther's writings. Löhe's writings on pastoral theology draw significantly on the pastoral theologies of August Hermann Francke and Johann Ludwig Hartmann.[15]

Like Löhe, Sasse will accent the oneness of the church. Löhe sought to preserve the essential unity of the "visible church" with the "invisible church" by means of the body/soul analogy. According to Sasse, neither Walther nor Löhe escaped the danger which he saw as inherent to the distinction. Sasse offered a more probing critique calling for a return to Luther's language of the "hidden church."[16]

Affirming Löhe's fundamental definition of mission as "nothing but the one church of God in motion, the actualization of the one, universal, catholic church,"[17] Sasse observes that Löhe was not exempt from the Romanticism of his day, which gave rise to the description of the Body of Christ as an organism. The conceptuality of an "organism" gives rise in Sasse's thinking to an understanding of the church as a living entity of multiple parts in need of coordination. Rather than grounding the church's oneness in the marks of the pure preaching of the gospel and right administration of the sacraments (AC VII), this model is sociological. Sasse concludes that "Vilmar and Löhe read the romantic concept of society as an organism into the Lutheran doctrine of the church, while Walther without knowing it, understood the Lutheran doctrine of the church through the eyes of the Enlightenment's concept of society."[18]

Sasse sees the conflict between Walther and Löhe as a great tragedy in nineteenth-century Lutheranism.[19] Both men were opposed to the subjectivity of the Erlangen school but came to opposing conclusions regarding the nature of the church and the office:

There was and is no way of reconciling Löhe's and Walther's concepts of the church with each other. But when both sides began to understand that Löhe's concept of the church was determined by the non-biblical idea of the social organism, and Walther's by the non-biblical concept of the religious society, was it not possible then to recognize the real church of the New Testament, of which through the spectacles of his own worldview each one had seen something that was true?[20]

Sasse asserts that the church is neither a democracy nor an aristocracy.[21] For him, the office is set not above the congregation but within it. Article VII of the Augsburg Confession guards the Lutheran Church from attempting to fix, as Löhe and Walther did, a biblical form of the church. Here Sasse argues that Luther's position of freedom in matters of church structure is confirmed by recent New Testament exegetical studies.[22]

Sasse recognizes in Löhe a genuine Lutheranism that will not erase confessional boundaries. Nevertheless, he sees a danger within the Bavarian pastor's conceptuality of the church as an organism a parallel with Anglicanism's via media, which would bear bitter fruit in the involvement of Lutheran churches in various proposals for church unity. While Löhe is adamant in his rejection of unionism, he speaks of the Lutheran Church as the true church, which is a union of opposite extremes.[23] Löhe argues that the Reformation is partly complete and partly incomplete: "It is complete in doctrine but incomplete in the consequences of doctrine."[24]

In Sasse's view, Löhe's position is strikingly similar to John Henry Newman's articulation of the via media, which ultimately led him to Rome.[25] The Lutheran Church is no synthesis between Catholicism and Reformed Protestantism. Sasse can only conclude that Löhe's way was a dangerous path, a trajectory leading into a Lutheranism that sought to be inclusive but whose destiny would be compromise.[26]

In the end, Sasse could express high praise for Löhe on many fronts ranging from his reverence for the sacrament of the altar in teaching and liturgical practice, his rejection of rationalism, his zeal for mission, and his opposition to the territorial government's attempt to monitor ecclesiastical life. But Sasse believed that to honor the fathers of the Lutheran Church was also to subject them to the binding authority of the Holy Scriptures and the Lutheran Confessions. Some of Löhe's failings are seen as characteristics of the age in which he lived, that is, Romanticism. Others, Sasse believed, were weaknesses in Löhe's failure to articulate a doctrine of the church in conformity with Article VII of the Augsburg Confession. In short, Löhe is received as a church father who is to be honored without being blindly emulated.

Grateful for the heritage of the nineteenth-century confessional revival though he is, Sasse does not blindly follow these Lutheran fathers. Instead, he seeks to chart a course following the Lutheran Confessions. The anchor point in Sasse's theological method is Article VII of the Augsburg Confession:

> Likewise, they teach that the one holy church will remain forever. The church is the assembly of saints in which the gospel is taught purely and the sacraments are administered rightly. And it is enough for the true unity of the church to agree concerning the teaching of the gospel and the administration of the sacraments. It is not necessary that human traditions, rites, or ceremonies instituted by human beings be alike everywhere. As Paul says (Eph 4:5, 6): "One faith, one baptism, one God and Father of all." (Kolb-Wengert, 43)

In many ways, his essay from 1943–1944, "The Lutheran Doctrine of the Office of the Holy Ministry," is both foundational and representative of Sasse's thinking about the ministerial office. In this essay, Sasse notes the distinctiveness of the Lutheran doctrine in contrast to both Rome and the Reformed, who see the ministry in terms of an ordo, whereas the Lutheran Confessions understand the ministry as an office established by the Lord's own mandate. Christ has not instituted a particular polity or form of ecclesiastical governance but rather the office of the ministry.

The Lutheran Confessions see the office of the ministry in terms of gospel rather than the law. Forms of church government may vary—congregational, episcopal, synodical, presbyterial are the basis for and source of Article V of the Augsburg Confession: "To obtain justifying faith God has instituted the preaching office, providing for the proclamation of the saving Gospel and the administration of the sacraments." Sasse writes: "The doctrine of the office of the ministry is very closely connected with the doctrine of justification."[27]

The office exists for the sake of and service of the gospel. While the law is to be preached by those who bear the office, Sasse does not see it as standing on equal footing with the gospel. The relationship of law and gospel in the office is that of God's alien work to his proper work:

The more seriously we take the immutable, eternal, divine command-ments, the more we also know that the preaching of the Law is not yet the final and highest thing that has been given committed to us. The final and highest task of our office is this: that we lead penitent sinners to the one who is their Savior, because he has borne the sin of the world.[28]

This gospel is nothing less than God's reconciliation of the world to himself. Sasse cites II Corinthians 5:19–21, asserting that the "basic melody of the eternal Gospel must ring through the vari-ation and fullness of our preaching with an illustrious consistency."[29]

As the office of the gospel, the office of the ministry is one. The office of preaching/teaching the gospel and administering the sacra-ments is a single office. Sasse comments: "The two are inseparable."[30] Distinctions within the one office are of human origin. It is through this one office that Christ is governing his church with the forgive-ness of sins. Sasse observes that the "external" government of the church simply guarantees this "real" church government "the full-est opportunity to work."[31] The external government of the church must exist, Sasse argues, echoing Apology VII and VIII, because the church is not only "an association of faith and the Holy Spirit in hearts" but always and at the same time "an association of external things and rites."

Since the office of the ministry is the office of the gospel, Luther and subsequently the Lutheran Confessions are fighting a two-sided battle against both Rome and the spiritualists. This is an aspect of Luther's "lonely way," as Sasse likes to put it. Contra Rome, Luther asserted that the office is not one of sacrifice. Sasse observes that the New Testament does not apply the term priest to those in the min-isterial office. On the other side, there are the Enthusiasts who draw the conclusion that any and all Christians may preach without a call.

Sasse concludes this essay with an examination of Luther's 1523 *Concerning the Instituting of the Ministry of the Church*, sent to the congregations in Prague. Luther is seeking to answer the question of how the church obtains pastors if there are no bishops to ordain them. According to Sasse, this "is the most fundamental treatment of the doctrine of the office of the ministry from Luther's pen."[32] In such cases of necessity, the congregation may appoint men to the office. Sasse notes that even the most "high church" of nineteenth-century Lutheran theologians, August Vilmar, "emphatically agreed with Luther, even though he regarded the case of Christians in the wilderness as a fictitious borderline case."[33]

While affirming Luther's basic principle, Sasse is quick to point out how this teaching is misused if it is taken in an exclusively congregational sense. The advice, after all, to the Bohemians, was not to an individual congregation but to the entire church in that country.[34]

Sasse observes that the Lutheran Confessions did not run with Luther's view that the *ministerium ecclesiasticum* is the exercise of the general priesthood. Rather, as we see in the *Treatise on the Power and Primacy of the Pope*, the church is the royal priesthood of I Peter 2 and has the right to elect and ordain ministers. The pastor is called by the church and bears the office instituted by God. In Sasse's discussion of Article XIV of the Augsburg Confession, he points out that there is a distinction between the public proclamation of the word that "is bound to the commission given in ordination"[35] and the speaking of God's word to the neighbor, catechetical and devotional instruction in the home, and the absolution that occurs in the context of the mutual consolation of Christians.

The Ecumenical Movement brought to the surface latent questions about the doctrine of the ministry. In his 1956 essay *Successio Apostolica* Sasse addresses the issue of the apostolicity of the office. Observing that the Roman theologians speak of the apostolicity of origin, doctrine, and succession, it was Anglicans in the nineteenth century who would draw out the implications of apostolic succession and insisting on it as a condition for full communion. Yet the claims to an unbroken chain of ordinations under the condition of apostolic succession, Sasse finds dubious:

> When the Church of England and its daughter churches (recently also certain Lutheran churches, and union churches such as that of South India) make so much of their apostolic succession, one is prompted to ponder the fact that we are most apt to speak of those virtues which we do not possess. It is hardly by chance that this overemphasis on apostolic succession emerged in a church that indeed claims to be catholic and to possess the three offices of bishop, priest, and deacon, and yet is unable to say what these offices actually are.[36]

The notion that something more is given by apostolic succession than is given to the office of the ministry runs counter to Augsburg Confession V. Lutherans value apostolic succession in doctrine, not in a lineage of unbroken episcopal ordinations.

Attention to the office of the ministry resurfaces in a number of Sasse's essays and letters on ecclesiology, confessional subscription, church fellowship, missions, and ecumenism. Essays in 1963 and 1971 will address women's ordination, arguing that the practice is outside of the Lord's institution of the office. It is forbidden by the apostle and hence divisive of church fellowship.

In 1968, late in his career, Sasse authored an article on "The Crisis of Christian Ministry." In this piece, he makes a distinction between "the crisis that belongs to the nature of our office" and "that which is conditioned by the church in a certain age."[37] In the early church, there was the crisis occasioned by the death of the apostles, the threat of paganism in the rising Gnostic movement, and the emergence of christological heresies. Living in the shadow of Bultmann and his program of demythologizing the New Testament, Sasse sees the crisis of his day as one of the truthfulness of the scriptural gospel. If the gospel is not true, the office is vacant of any significance, and ministers will seek to create other tasks to validate their professional existence as ecclesiastical managers or spiritual therapists. The crisis that belongs to the nature of the office is that God sends sinners to remit sins. The solution to this crisis, as well as the specific ones which fluctuate from age to age, Sasse sees in the promise of Isaiah 55 that the word of the Lord will accomplish the purpose for which he sent it. Because Jesus is risen from the dead, the future of the church is secure.

Certainly, Sasse was disappointed with the course of events in world Lutheranism during the last half of the twentieth century. It was his confidence in the Lord's word that guarded him from cynicism, bitterness, and despair. If it is true that the pastoral office is brotherly *Amt*, to use the words of Ulrich Asendorf, Sasse's essays and letters on the pastoral office were not just dogmatic treatises but a lively application of the doctrine to sustain Lutheran pastors in the lonely way. Like all genuine theology, Sasse understood that the doctrine of the office must be seen through the lens of the theology of the cross.[38] Without triumphalism, he sought to champion the

Lutheran way, confessing the office of the ministry as instituted by Christ to serve the gospel. His careful work on this topic commends itself to confessing Lutherans throughout the world in these gray and latter days.

Notes

1 Edmund Schlink (1903–1984), an ecumenically involved Lutheran professor at Heidelberg, wrote extensively on the office of the ministry. See his "The Coming Christ and Church Traditions: Essays for Dialogue among Separated Churches," in *Ecumenical and Confessional Writings*, ed. and trans. Matthew Becker (Gottingen: Vanderhoeck & Ruprecht, 2017–), 1:135–65, 211–48; also see his *Theology of the Lutheran Confessions*, trans. Paul Koehneke and Herbert J.A. Bouman (Philadelphia, PA: Fortress Press, 1961), 194–269.

2 Peter Brunner (1900–1981), Lutheran systematic theologian and liturgical scholar at Heidelberg. Brunner's work on the ministry includes "Salvation and the Office of the Ministry," *Lutheran Quarterly* 15 (1963): 99–117; and "The Ministry and the Ministry of Women," in *Women Pastors? The Ordination of Women in Biblical Lutheran Perspective*, ed. Matthew C. Harrison and John T. Pless (St. Louis, MO: Concordia Publishing House, 2012), 263–94.

3 Wilfried Harle (b. 1941), emeritus professor of systematic theology and ethics at Heidelberg. See his *Outline of Christian Doctrine: An Evangelical Dogmatics*, trans. Ruth Yule and Nicholas Sagovsky (Grand Rapids, MI: Eerdmans, 2015), 474–84.

4 Wolthart Pannenberg (1928–2014) taught at Munich and was deeply engaged with issues of ecumenical theology. See his *Systematic Theology*, trans. G.W. Bromiley (Grand Rapids, MI: Eerdmans, 1991–1998), 3:370–434.

5 See John T. Pless, "Hermann Sasse," in *Twentieth-Century Lutheran Theologians*, ed. Mark C. Mattes (Gottingen: Vandenhoeck: & Ruprecht, 2013), 155–77; John T. Pless, "Sasse, Hermann," in *Dictionary of Luther and the Lutheran Traditions*, ed. Timothy J. Wengert (Grand Rapids: Baker Academic, 2017), 661–62; also Lowell C. Green, *The Erlangen School of Theology: Its History, Teaching and Practice* (Fort Wayne: Lutheran Legacy Press, 2010), 289–98; and *Hermann Sasse: A Man for Our Times?* ed. John R. Stephenson and Thomas M. Winger (St. Louis, MO: Concordia Academic Press, 1998).

6 Sasse documents his American experience the year after he returns to Germany (1927) in a short monograph, "American Christianity and the Church," in *The Lonely Way: Selected Essays and Letters*, trans. Matthew C. Harrison (St. Louis, MO: Concordia Publishing House, 2001–2002), 1:23–60. Among other things, Sasse notes the activism of American churches and their clergy when it comes to programs and business techniques that are driven, he believes, by notions of effectiveness. He observes the impact of the Social

Gospel Movement, the lack of interest in doctrine, and the drive to outward unity. For more here, see John T. Pless, "A Conversation between Mark Noll and Hermann Sasse," *LOGIA* 22, no. 1 (Epiphany 2013): 5–7 also published in this volume as ch. 47.

7 Hermann Sasse, "The Ecumenical Movement," in *The Journal Articles of Hermann Sasse*, ed. Matthew C. Harrison, Bror Erickson, and Joel A. Brondos (Irvine, CA: NRP Books, 2016), 454.

8 Here see "Löhe Correspondence on Unionistic Communion Practice in the Bavarian Church," and Wilhelm Löhe, "Opinion Concerning Communion Fellowship," in *Closed Communion? Admission to the Lord's Supper in Biblical Lutheran Perspective*, ed. Matthew C. Harrison and John T. Pless (St. Louis, MO: Concordia Publishing House, 2017), 145–50, 17 7–200.

9 "German Protestantism and world Lutheranism are obviously lacking today men with the power of faith and strength of character, with understanding for things theological and ecclesiastical and with the courage of conviction of a Scheibel, and a Löhe, of a Vilmar and a Walther, of a Harms and a Petri, a Rochholl, and a Bezzel." Hermann Sasse, "On the Relation of the Universal Church and the Individual Congregation in the New Testament," in *Letters to Lutheran Pastors*, trans. Matthew C. Harrison (St. Louis, MO: Concordia Publishing House, 2013–2015), 1:137.

10 "In their theological thinking as well as their ecclesiastical action, men like Vilmar and Löhe represent both true confessionalism and true ecumenicity." Hermann Sasse, "On the Problem of the Union of the Lutheran Churches," in *Letters to Lutheran Pastors*, 1:153.

11 Writing in 1949 shortly after his immigration to Australia, Sasse said, "This Church [the United Evangelical Lutheran Church in Australia], founded by Lutheran emigrants from Prussia in 1838, closely connected with old Breslau, with Hermannsburg, with the Neuendettelsau of Wilhelm Löhe, shall henceforth be my church home. For us Christians (as Löhe ever again has reminded us) partake of the Passover of our Lord as pilgrims with staff in hand, our earthly home is there and only there where stands the altar of our Church." Sasse, "Universal Church and the Individual Congregation," 1:137.

12 Hermann Sasse, "The Results of the Lutheran Awakening of the Nineteenth Century," in *Letters to Lutheran Pastors*, 1:329.

13 *Ibid.*

14 Sasse observes, "Also in the case of Löhe the pietistic heritage was a powerful influence which helped shape his Lutheranism." Hermann Sasse, "Confession and Theology in the Missouri Synod," in *Letters to Lutheran Pastors*, 2:10. Sasse is also critical of Löhe's "pietistic chiliasm" (*Letters to Lutheran Pastors*, 2:174). For more on this aspect of Löhe's eschatology, see Jacob Corzine, "Löhe as an Example of nineteenth century Lutheran Chiliasm," in *Wilhelm Löhe: Tlieologie und Geschichte*, ed. Dietrich Blaufuß (Neuendettelsau: Freidmund-Verlag, 2013), 87–103.

15 See, for example, Wilhelm Löhe's *Tlie Pastor*, trans. Wolf Dietrich Knappe and Charles Schaum (St. Louis, MO: Concordia Publishing House, 2015), 9–12.

16 Here note Sasse: "The situation [in the nineteenth century] is similar to that of orthodoxy, which frequently permitted Calvinism or Catholicism to pose the problems without observing the false formulation of the question. Thus, for example, the problem of the visible and invisible church plays a troublesome role down to our own day. The fathers of the period of orthodoxy and also those of the nineteenth century failed to note that Luther's *ecclesia abscondita* ['hidden church'] is not simply to be equated with the *ecclesia invisibilis* of Reformed theologians. And it would have been well not simply to take over the Reformed terminology, but rather abide by the expressions of Luther and the Confessions. The church, of course, is not something to be seen but an 'article of faith.' Our eyes are not able to behold it since it is the *regnum Christi* which, in this world, is *cruce tectum* ['hidden under the cross'], as the Apology says with Luther in his commentary on Article VII and VIII of the *Augustana*. No human eye sees the church as the Body of Christ. It is an eschatological reality [*Tatbestand*] that must be distinguished from the temporal and historical entity of the *societas externarum rerum et rituum* ['association of outward things and rites']. In this respect one may indeed call the church invisible. But the term *ecclesia invisibilis* has by Augustine and by Reformed theology been encumbered with additional implications, which we cannot recognize. Why did not one stay with Luther's simple teaching: ['*Absconditia est* via saints concealed']. At this point, as in many others, old Lutheran orthodoxy remained entirely too dependent upon its opponents. And the theologians of the nineteenth century, who possessed no better works on dogmatics than those of the era of orthodoxy (where should they have gotten them?), simply took over these attitudes." Hermann Sasse, "On the Problem of the Relation between the [Office of the] Ministry and the Congregation," in *Letters to Lutheran Pastors*, 1:124–25.

17 Wilhelm Löhe, *Three Books about the Church*, trans. and ed. James L. Schaaf, Seminar Editions (Philadelphia, PA: Fortress Press, 1969), 59.

18 Hermann Sasse, "Unity and Division within Lutheranism," in *Letters to Lutheran Pastors*, 2:398.

19 See Sasse, "Relation between Ministry and Congregation," 1:121.

20 Sasse, "Lutheran Awakening," 1:328.

21 Sasse, "Relation between Ministry and Congregation," 1:120.

22 *Ibid.*, 1:125–31.

23 Löhe states: "In an age when 'union' is everyone's slogan, the children of the true church are obligated to make it very clear that, by virtue of the doctrine it confesses, their church is a union of opposite extremes and it is the great task of the pure church always to testify anew to this true union before opposing churches, to prove that what they seek (correctly understood)

is comprehended in the doctrine of our church and is brought to life by the living of this doctrine." Löhe, *Three Books*, 157.

24 *Ibid.*, 152.

25 Sasse states: "It should be warning to Lutheranism, especially those who perpetually toy with the romantic notion of the Lutheran Church as the 'uniting center of the denominations,' such as we find in Claus Harms [1778–1855] and Wilhelm Löhe [18081872] as a contemporary parallel to [John Henry] Newman's [1801–90] doctrine of the *via media*, 'the middle way,' which always leads to Rome." Hermann Sasse, "Remembrance of the Dead in the Liturgy," in *Letters to Lutheran Pastors*, 3:52.

26 Here see Sasse's 1966 essay, "Inclusive Lutheranism," in *The Lonely Way*, 2:341–45.

27 Hermann Sasse, "The Lutheran Doctrine of the Office of the Ministry," in *The Lonely Way*, 2:124.

28 *Ibid.*, 2:125.

29 *Ibid.*

30 *Ibid.*, 2:126.

31 *Ibid.*, 2:129.

32 *Ibid.*, 2:133.

33 *Ibid.*

34 Here also see Sasse, "Universal Church and the Individual Congregations," 1:136–48. In this essay, Sasse identifies five uses of *ecclesia* in the New Testament: (1) the *una sancta*; (2) the congregation—like the church in Jerusalem as seen in Acts 2:47; 5:11, etc.; (3) all Christians in a particular region—like Judea or Samaria; (4) the church in a particular place such as Corinth or Philippi; and (5) the congregation gathered in some house as in Rom. 16:6; I Cor. 16:19.

35 Sasse, "Office of the Ministry," in *The Lonely Way*, 2:136.

36 Hermann Sasse, "*Succesio Apostolica*," in *Letters to Lutheran Pastors*, 2:427. Sasse was a keen observer of the developments leading to the formation of the Church of South India in 1947 and its attempts to find footing within the Anglican community. See Hermann Sasse, "The Union of South India as a Question for the Lutheran Church," in *Letters to Lutheran Pastors*, 3:321–39. For the prehistory of the Church of South India, see Bengt Sundkler, *Church of South India: The Movement Towards Union*, 1900–1947 (London: Lutterworth Press, 1954).

37 Hermann Sasse, "The Crisis of the Christian Ministry," in *The Lonely Way*, 2:356.

38 See Hermann Sasse, "*Theologia Crucis*," in *Letters to Lutheran Pastors*, 1:385–402.

45

Luther's *Oratio, Meditatio,* and *Tentatio* as the Shape of Pastoral Care for Pastors

PREVIOUSLY PUBLISHED IN THE JANUARY-APRIL, 2016 ISSUE OF *CONCORDIA THEOLOGICAL QUARTERLY,* PP. 37–48

The fact that pastors also need pastoral care is inherent in the nature of the office itself. In a 1968 essay under the title, "The Crisis of the Christian Ministry," Hermann Sasse puts it like this: "God always demands from his servants something which is, humanly speaking, impossible."[1] The language of crisis was common back in 1968. Racial unrest in the United States, student protests in Europe, and the Vietnam War captured public attention. The church, of course, was not exempt; there was sweated anxiety regarding the future of the church. Things were described as being in a "crisis." It was in this period that we heard of the crisis of biblical authority, the crisis of preaching, the liturgical crisis, the crisis of church unity, and the like. There was a restlessness for new forms, and everyone was convinced that the present crisis would be resolved only by innovation and creativity. Sasse weighed in with his own essay on the crisis of the Christian ministry. What he says is instructive.

Sasse notes that we must distinguish between the "crisis which belongs to the nature of our office" and "the crisis which is conditioned by the situation of the church in a certain age."[2] We tend to fixate on the second crisis and can form our own catalog of issues that might be seen as crises today: projected clergy shortage, maltreatment of pastors, clerical burnout, moral failure of pastors, lack of public trust of the clergy, and the like. More often than not, these issues are addressed programmatically or administratively in the church. That is not bad, but if that is the only approach, it is inadequate and incomplete. These are certainly real problems, but they can only be adequately addressed from the perspective of the primal crisis that belongs to the nature of the office itself. This crisis is occasioned by the word of God itself, namely, that God uses sinners to remit the sins of sinners. Here Luther's triad of *oratio*, *meditatio*, and *tentatio* comes into play, providing an orientation for how we understand the pastoral care of pastors.

Luther describes the making of theologians who can distinguish the law from the gospel in his 1539 "Preface to the Wittenberg Edition of Luther's German Writings." He uses these three Latin terms (*oratio*, *meditatio*, and *tentatio*) to describe this process. His framework was a distinct break from the popular medieval scheme for theology as *lectio*, *oratio*, and *contemplatio*. Westhelle observes:

> Luther's schema begins with *oratio*, which is more than prayer; it is all God-talk, talk of and to God when one knows that reason will not suffice. Second is *meditatio*—in which he includes *lectio*—which is not limited to meditation in the internal sense but also "external," hence engaging others in reflection. Luther does not follow the third medieval rule, *contemplatio*, but instead he brings up a very different and original concept, *tentatio*, which becomes the foremost—the "touch-stone" he calls it—and the last characteristic of theological reflection.[3]

Thus Luther moves away from the speculative theology of scholasticism and the contemplative spirituality of mysticism. For Luther, the *telos* of the Christian life on this side of the Last Day is not a beatific beholding of the divine but suffering under the cross, which conforms the one who meditates on the Scriptures to the image of Christ crucified.

I. *Oratio*

For Luther, "Holy Scriptures constitute a book which turns the wisdom of all other books into foolishness, because not one teaches about eternal life except this one alone."[4] *Oratio* is anchored in the reading and hearing of these Scriptures, which create faith in Christ Jesus and kindle prayer. According to Luther, this is the prayer that David models in Psalm 119:

> 'Teach me, Lord, instruct me, lead me, show me,' and many more words like these. Although he well knew and daily heard and read the text of Moses and other books besides, still he wants to lay hold of the real teacher of the Scriptures himself, so he may not seize upon them pell-mell with his reason and become his own teacher. For such practice gives rise to factious spirits who allow themselves to nurture the delusion that the Scriptures are subject to them and can be easily grasped with their reason, as if they were Markolf or Aesop's Fables, for which no Holy Spirit and no prayers are needed.[5]

Concerning Luther on Psalm 119, Oswald Bayer comments,

> Almost from the outset, Psalm 119 takes on fundamental significance for Luther's battle with the pope, who wants to prevent him from remaining with the word through which "I became a Christian": the word of absolution. From the beginning of the Reformation, this psalm is seen as a prayer for the victory of God's word against its enemies. In fact, it is seen as a double prayer that was turned into a hymn verse in 1543: Lord, keep us steadfast in your word and curb the pope's and the Turk's sword.[6]

The Scriptures are, to use the words of Oswald Bayer, the breathing space of the Holy Spirit.[7] Not only did the Spirit breathe his words through the prophets and apostles, but he continues to breathe in and through the Scriptures so that faith in Christ Jesus is created and sustained. In contrast to Schleiermacher, who described the Holy Scriptures as a "mausoleum of religion, a monument to a great spirit once there but no longer,"[8] Luther understood the Scriptures as the living and life-giving word of God, the dwelling place of the Spirit.

There was a shift in 1758 when Johann Salmo Semler (1725–1791) denounced Luther's use of *oratio, meditatio*, and *tentatio* as unscientific and antiquated monastic theology that must be replaced by what he claimed as a historical reading of the Scriptures.[9] Semler forgot that "the exegesis of Holy Scripture cannot contradict their inspiration."[10] Now Scriptures are to be read and mastered without prayer and meditation. They are also rendered as ineffective weapons in the face of spiritual attack. Studied this way, they can no longer be proclaimed as words of Spirit and life. Sermons become commentaries on the text rather than proclamation of the text, occasions for the edification of religious consciousness, or fortification in morality.

It is easy to see the contrast with Luther. In his Genesis lectures, for example, Luther writes, "I am content with this gift which I have, Holy Scripture, which abundantly teaches and supplies all things necessary both for this life and also for the life to come."[11] Luther believed the Scriptures to possess clarity, for they are illuminated by the Christ to whom they bear witness. The Scriptures are also sufficient to make us wise for the salvation that is in Christ alone. Far from being a dead letter in need of being vivified by the Spirit, the Scriptures that were inspired by the Spirit are now the instrument of his work to create and sustain faith.

II. *Meditatio*

The word of God is heard with the ear, engaging the hearts and the minds of those who receive it in faith. With the lips, this implanted word is confessed, proclaimed, and prayed. *Oratio* leads to *meditatio*, which is meditation on the word of God. For Luther, this meditation is not an exercise of spirituality that turns the believer inward in silent reflection; *meditatio* is grounded in the *externum verbum* (the external word), to use the language of the Smalcald Articles (SA III VIII 7). For Luther, *meditatio* is oral and outward, so in his Genesis lectures, he states,

> Let him who wants to contemplate in the right way reflect on his Baptism; let him read his Bible, hear sermons, honor father and mother, and come to the aid of a brother in distress. But let him not shut himself up in a nook . . . and there entertain himself with his devotions and thus suppose that he is sitting in God's bosom and has fellowship with God without Christ, without the Word, without the sacraments.[12]

Evangelical meditation draws one outside of himself into the promises of Christ (faith) and into the need of the neighbor (love):

"Such meditation does not just involve gazing at one's spiritual navel; it does not eavesdrop on the inner self."[13] Luther, therefore, is dead set against any and all forms of enthusiasm[14] that would rely on visions or miraculous appearances.

> Christ once appeared visible here on earth and showed his glory, and according to the divine purpose of God finished the work of redemption and deliverance of mankind. I do not desire he should come to me once more in the same manner, neither would I should he send an angel unto me. Nay, though an angel should appear before mine eyes from heaven, yet it would not add to my belief; for I have of my Saviour Christ Jesus bond and seal; I have his Word, Spirit, and sacrament; thereon I depend, and desire no new revelations. And the more steadfastly to confirm me in this resolution, to hold solely to God's Word, and not to give credit to any visions or revelations, I shall relate the following circumstance: On Good Friday last, I being in my chamber in fervent prayer, contemplating with myself, how Christ my Saviour on the cross suffered and died for our sins, there suddenly appeared on the wall a bright vision of our Saviour Christ, with the five wounds, steadfastly looking upon me, as if had been Christ himself corporeally. At first sight, I thought it had been some celestial revelation, but I reflected that it must needs be an illusion and juggling of the devil, for Christ appeared to us in his Word, and in a meaner and more humble form; therefore I spake to the vision thus: Avoid thee, confounded devil: I know no other Christ than he who was crucified, and who in his Word is pictured and presented unto me. Whereupon the image vanished, clearly showing of whom it came.[15]

Visions are deceptive and deceiving; Holy Scripture is not.

Meditation is immersion into the text of Holy Scripture. It is the ongoing hearing of God's word that is read and preached so that the one who hears Christ is enlivened to trust his promises and equipped to respond to the needs of the neighbor in his calling in the world. Luther likened meditation to a cow, chewing its cud. In his 1525 commentary on Deuteronomy 14:1, he writes: "To chew the cud, however, is to take up the Word with delight and meditate with supreme diligence, so that (according to the proverb) one does not permit it to go into one ear and out the other, but holds it firmly in the heart, swallows it, and absorbs it into the intestines."[16]

Luther provides a practical tool for such meditation in his celebrated devotional booklet, "A Simple Way to Pray," written in 1535 for the Wittenberg barber, Peter Beskendorf. Here he suggests that a person meditate on each commandment of the Decalogue "in their fourfold aspect, namely, as a school text, song book, penitential book, and prayer book."[17] In Luther's way of meditation, one is encouraged to dwell on the text and to engage in various dimensions, including the didactic, doxological, diagnostic, and intercessory. Those who stand in front of the text are taught, brought to praise God, have their sins uncovered, and are given material for their praying.

While Luther prepared this tract for a layman, it certainly has application for the pastor whose life is given to the service of the text of Holy Scripture for the sake of proclamation and pastoral care. The Psalms, in Luther's estimation, were an especially fertile place for meditation for preachers. In his lectures on Psalm 1 (1519–1521), he states,

> Therefore it is the office of a man whose proper duty it is to converse on something, to discourse on the Law of the Lord. For this meditation consists first in close attention to the words of the Law, and then drawing together the various parts of Scripture. And this is a pleasant hunt, a game rather like the play of stags in the forest, where "the Lord arouses the stags, and uncovers the forests" (Ps. 29:2). For out of this will proceed a sermon to the people which is well informed in the Law of the Lord.[18]

The preacher is not meditating on the word simply for his own spiritual wellbeing but for those placed under his curacy in the church. He meditates on the word so that he may have something to say from the Lord to the people he is given to serve.

III. *Tentatio*

For Luther, meditation does not take place in a spiritual vacuum in isolation from the temptations of the world, the flesh, and the devil. God uses *tentatio* (spiritual affliction, trial, and temptation) to drive away from the self and toward his promises alone. Bayer captures Luther's thought:

Anyone who meditates can expect to suffer. Luther once again also allows Psalm 119 to prescribe this experience. Therefore in light of this third rule, he expects students of theology also to see themselves in the role of the psalmist who "complains so often about all kinds of enemies . . . that he has to put up with because he meditates, that is, because he is occupied with God's word (as has been said) in all manner of ways."[19]

For Luther, meditation is anchored in the First Commandment. To use the words of Albrecht Peters, "God's First Commandment, however, confiscates this center of our entire human nature for itself. God, as our Creator, calls our heart out of clinging to what is created and demands it for itself in an exclusive and undivided way. Here the First Commandment and the Creed interlock."[20] It is only this confiscated heart, fearing, loving, and trusting in God above all things that is free to pray in the fashion that God commands and promises to hear. Such prayer is not easy; it involves struggle, for "when we meditate on the first commandment we are involved in a battle between the one Lord and the many lords (cf. I Cor. 8:5f)."[21] To meditate on the First Commandment and to pray from it is to let God be God, but for the flesh, the world, and the devil, such meditation is a declaration of war.

Tentatio is no stranger to those who serve in the pastoral office. Luther understands this *tentatio* as a spiritual affliction that drives faithful servants to rely on the sure and certain promises of Christ alone. Commenting on Genesis 32:32, Luther says, "our Lord Jesus Christ, tested Jacob not to destroy him but to confirm and strengthen him and that in his fight he might more correctly learn the might of the promise."[22] God does his work under opposites: "When God works, He turns His face away at first and seems to be the devil, not God."[23]

Temptation, which is entailed in the *tentatio,* is necessary for the Christian life in general but especially for preachers of the word. Luther says in a "Table Talk" of 1532,

> I did not learn my theology all at once, but had to search constantly deeper and deeper for it. My temptations did that for me, for no one can understand Holy Scripture without practice and temptations. That is what the enthusiasts and sects lack. They don't have the right critic, the devil, who is the best teacher of theology. If we don't have

that kind of devil, then we become nothing but speculative theologians, who do nothing but walk around in our own thoughts and speculate with our reason alone as to whether things should be like this, or like that.[24]

The experience of temptation prepares and equips the pastor to serve as an "instructor of consciences" in the sense that he must have the capacity to distinguish the law from the gospel, directing the afflicted away from the erratic and errant movement of the conscience from excuse-making to accusation. A conscience ceases to rationalize sin or be terrorized by the law only when it comes to rest in the forgiveness of sins:

> Therefore I admonish you, especially those of you who are to become instructors of consciences, as well as each of you individually, that you exercise yourselves continually by study, by reading, by meditation and by prayer, so that in temptation you will be able to instruct consciences, both your own and others, and take them from the law to grace, from active righteous to passive righteousness, in short from Moses to Christ. In affliction and in the conflict of conscience, it is the devil's habit to frighten us with the law and to set against us the consciousness of sin, our wicked past, the wrath and judgment of God, hell, and eternal death, so that he may drive us into despair, subject us to himself, and pluck us from Christ.[25]

Like the apostle Paul in II Corinthians 1:3–4, who speaks of the comfort that we give to others in their afflictions as flowing from the comfort that we ourselves have received from Christ, Luther speaks out of the *tentatio* that he himself had experienced. The judgment of Walther von Loewenich is on target: "The secret of Luther's proficiency in pastoral care was that he himself had known what it was like to experience attacks of despair [*Anfechtung*]."[26] Only as one who himself was comforted by the gospel could Luther be a comforter to the afflicted and despairing.

Oratio, Meditatio, and *Tentatio* in the Pastor's Life

Luther's triad of *oratio, meditatio,* and *tentatio* shapes the ongoing life of the pastor as he is forever dependent on the power of God's promises. The crosses and afflictions of the pastoral life drive the pastor to meditate on the words of the Lord, and God's word opens his lips for confession, prayer, praise, and proclamation, with the confidence that the divine word accomplishes God's purposes and does not return to him empty.

Here we see that Luther's triad is also reversible. The *tentatio* drives us to the *meditatio,* which in turn enables the *oratio,* the calling on the name of the Lord. Spiritual attack disables and deconstructs all of our own resources; we are left without anything but Christ and his absolving word. In that word, the conscience takes refuge, delighting in it day and night, to use the language of Psalm 1, and finding in it a gift more precious than gold and silver and sweeter to the taste than honey, to use the imagery of Psalm 119:72, 103. It is this word that opens the lips for prayer and proclamation.

At this point, it might also be observed that the catechetical core—the Ten Commandments, Creed, and Lord's Prayer—follows the contours of the *oratio, meditatio,* and *tentatio.* Robert Kolb has observed that the Decalogue sets the agenda for Christian praying and the Lord's Prayer for Christian living.[27] Along these lines, we might also say that *oratio* encompasses the prayer that grows from God's command and promise. *Meditatio* is a meditation on the works of the Triune God, and *tentatio* is that life lived under the cross, which is characterized by the Lord's Prayer, where we pray the seven petitions that describe our wretchedness and promise God's mercy. Luther's theology of prayer is a reflection of the theology of the cross. James Nestingen writes:

> The Ten Commandments set out the requirements of the creaturely life, incumbent by creation; the Creed declares the gifts of the Triune God; the Lord's Prayer gives voice to the circumstances of the believer living in a world of the nomos (law) in the hope of the resurrection. Luther's explanations of the Lord's Prayer arise from such an analysis of the situation of faith. Barraged by the relentless demands of the law, under assault by the powers of this age yet gripped in the hope of the gospel, the believer learns "where to seek and obtain that aid." So, while exposing the Lord's Prayer at its first level, as instruction in how to pray, Luther is at the same time describing the contention in which faith lives, giving language for the rhythm of death and resurrection that is the hallmark of life in Christ. At this level, the Lord's Prayer is

a cry wrung from the crucible, an exposition of the shape of life lived under the sign of the cross in the hope of the resurrection.[28]

Each petition of the Lord's Prayer is a diagnosis of our neediness and a promise of God's mercy.[29]

What are the implications for the pastoral care of pastors? First, Luther did not understand this triad as individualistic or private. Broadly speaking, they take place within the context of the life of the church. Bayer has pointed out the parallel between Luther's ordering of the seven marks of the church enumerated in Luther's treatise "On the Councils and the Church" and the *oratio, meditatio,* and *tentatio* of the Wittenberg Preface, both of which were written in the same year. The *oratio* and *meditatio* are embraced in the first six marks: the holy word of God, Baptism, the Sacrament of the Altar, the office of the keys, the calling of ministers, and prayer/public praise/thanksgiving to God. The seventh external sign is "the possession of the sacred cross."[30] This sign is the *tentatio.* For Luther, it means that Christian people:

> must endure every misfortune and persecution, all kinds of trials and evil from the devil, the world, and the flesh (as the Lord's Prayer indicates) by inward sadness, timidity, fear, outward poverty, contempt, illness, and weakness in order to become like their head, Christ. And the only reason they must suffer is that they steadfastly adhere to Christ and God's word, enduring this for the sake of Christ.[31]

More narrowly, we see the triad in the context of the ministerium.

While our spiritual fathers spoke more frequently than we commonly do of the "ministerium," it is a word in our collective vocabulary that we would do well to recover, especially when we think of the pastoral care of pastors. Years ago, Ulrich Asendorf spoke of the pastoral office as a brotherly *Amt.* We are not isolated spiritual entrepreneurs, but we are brothers bound together under the Holy Scriptures and the Lutheran Confessions. And under their regency, we are accountable to one another. We are to have one another's backs, to use the slang. This is not a hermeneutic of mutual pastoral suspicion, nor is it a matter of mouthing the mantra "we've got to trust one another."[32] It is a watching out for the brother, but not something that would make his fulfilling the responsibilities given to him unnecessarily difficult. It is also being there for him with the courage to call him to repentance and the compassion to console him with word of the cross. In this way, pastors are also comforting one another with the comfort that they have received from Christ, to paraphrase Paul's language in II Corinthians.[33]

The *tentatio* is sure to come for the pastor, but he need not face it alone. God gives us brothers and fathers in the office, not simply as companions to dispel loneliness, but as men who will be for us the ears and mouth of Christ Jesus. Such mutual conversation of the brethren is not an occasion for a mutual pity-party, but it exists for the exercise of God's law and his gospel so that we are called to repentance and faith even as we bear the cross in our various callings. Churchly implications of this are to be found in the practice of visitation, for which we have circuit visitors. The change in nomenclature is a welcome one. Counselors are called in when people are in crisis. Visitors look in to see how things are going not only in times of difficulty or in a period of transition but in the ongoing life of the pastor. Whether it is the circuit visitor or another brother in office, pastors also need a father confessor.

Second, *oratio, meditatio,* and *tentatio* frame the pastor's life of prayer, study, and suffering. The pastor lives with Holy Scriptures as a child in a cradle, to borrow Luther's language.[34] It is here that we learn how to listen to God and to call upon him. It is being nestled in the Scriptures that we learn how to preach and to pray and to suffer. It is this study to which the Apostle beckons Timothy when in II Timothy 2:15, he urges him to present himself as a workman who has no need to be ashamed, "rightly handling the word of truth." This is what Bayer calls "*askesis*" or the exercise of faith.[35] It is essential for the spiritual soundness of the pastor. Such study and prayer are not leisure-time activities, a retreat from the world of supposedly "real ministry," but instead, they are essential for both the pastor and his hearers, and they cannot be divorced from the cross that is borne for the sake of the office.

Pastoral care of pastors will shepherd pastors to live within Luther's triad: *oratio, meditatio,* and *tentatio* rather than seeking alternative ways, self-chosen and self-directed, of serving God's holy people.

Notes

1 Hermann Sasse, "The Crisis of the Christian Ministry," in *The Lonely Way, Selected Essays and Letters, Volume 2 (1941–1976)*, ed. Matthew Harrison (St. Louis: Concordia Publishing House, 2002), 356.

2 Sasse, "The Crisis of the Christian Ministry," 356.

3 Vitor Westhelle, *The Scandalous Cross* (Minneapolis: Fortress Press, 2006), 35–36. See also John Kleinig, "*Oratio, Meditatio, Tentatio*: What Makes a Theologian?," *CTQ* 66, no. 3 (July 2002): 255–267, and John T. Pless, *Martin Luther: Preacher of the Cross: A Study of Luther's Pastoral Theology* (St. Louis: Concordia, 2013), 17–25.

4 Martin Luther, *Luther's Works*, American Edition, 55 vols., ed. Jaroslav Pelican, Hilton C. Oswald, and Helmut T. Lehmann (Philadelphia: Fortress Press; St. Louis: Concordia, 1955–1986), 34:285; hereafter AE.

5 AE 34:286.

6 Oswald Bayer, *Theology the Lutheran Way*, trans. Jeffery G. Silcock and Mark C. Mattes (Grand Rapids: Wm. B. Eerdmans Publishing Co., 2007), 40.

7 Oswald Bayer, "Theology as *Askesis*," in *Gudstankens aktualitet: Festskrift til Peter Widmann*, ed. Marie Wiberg Pedersen, Bo Kristian Holm, and Anders-Christian Jacobsen (Copenhagen: Forlaget Anis, 2010), 46.

8 Cited by Bayer in "Theology as Askesis," 38.

9 See Bayer, "Theology as *Askesis*," 38. For more on Semler's significance, see Roy A. Harrisville, *Pandora's Box Opened: An Examination and Defense of the Historical-Critical Method and Its Master Practitioners* (Grand Rapids: Eerdmans, 2014), 105–113.

10 Bayer, "Theology as *Askesis*," 49.

11 AE 6:329. Also, for more examples of how Luther cherishes the Holy Scriptures as God's word, see Mark D. Thompson, *A Sure Ground on Which to Stand: The Relationship of Authority and Interpretative Method in Luther's Approach to Scripture* (Waynesboro, GA: Paternoster Press, 2004), 249–282; Robert Kolb, "Nowhere More Present and Active Than in the Holy Letters: Luther's Understanding of God's Presence in Scripture," *Lutheran Theological Journal* 49, no. 1 (May 2015): 4–16.

12 AE 3:275.

13 Oswald Bayer, *Martin Luther's Theology: A Contemporary Interpretation*, trans. Thomas Trapp (Grand Rapids: Eerdmans, 2008), 35.

14 See Bayer, *Theology the Lutheran Way*, 40. Here Bayer quotes a December 1520 Luther sermon on Genesis 28, "If they bore their way into heaven with their heads and look around they will find no one, because Christ lies in a crib and in a woman's lap. So let them fall back down again and break their necks." Bayer also writes, "Those who want to search for the Holy Spirit deep inside themselves, in a realm too deep for words to express, will find only ghosts, not God" (55).

15 Cited in Hugh T. Kerr, *A Compend of Luther's Theology* (Philadelphia: Westminster Press, 1943), 57.

16 AE 9:136.

17 AE 43:209. Also note Brecht's observation: "Nowhere is the connection between order and freedom in Luther's practice of prayer so clearly seen as in his advice for Master Peter." Martin Brecht, Martin Luther: The Preservation of the Church 1532–1546, trans. James L. Schaaf (Minneapolis: Fortress, 1993), 14.

18 AE 14:296.

19 Bayer, *Theology the Lutheran Way,* 60.

20 Albrecht Peters, *Commentary on Luther's Catechisms: Ten Commandments,* trans. Holger Sonntag (St. Louis: Concordia, 2009), 118. Also see John Maxfield: "For Luther idolatry is the self-enslaving false worship of a heart turned in on itself, of religious piety shaped by self-will and thus works righteousness in any number of ways, of substituting human reason for the revelation of God in the divine Word." John Maxfield, "Luther and Idolatry," in *The Reformation as Christianization: Essays on Scott Hendrix's Christianization Thesis* (Tübingen: Mohr Siebeck, 2012), 168.

21 Bayer, *Theology the Lutheran Way,* 62.

22 AE 6:144. Here see Mary Jane Haemig, "Prayer as Talking Back to God," *Lutheran Quarterly* 23 (Autumn 2009): 270–295.

23 AE 7:103.

24 AE 54:50.

25 AE 26:10.

26 Walther von Loewenich, *Martin Luther: The Man and His Work,* trans. Lawrence Denef (Minneapolis: Augsburg Publishing House, 1982), 359–360. See also Lennart Pinomaa, "The Problem of Affliction," in *Faith Victorious: An Introduction to Luther's Theology,* trans. Walter J. Kukkonen (Philadelphia: Fortress, 1963), 89–100; Mark D. Thompson, "Luther on Despair," in *The Consolations of Theology,* ed. Brian S. Rosner (Grand Rapids: Eerdmans, 2008), 51–74.

27 Robert A. Kolb, *Teaching God's Children His Teaching: A Guide for the Study of Luther's Catechism* (Saint Louis: Concordia Seminary Press, 2012), 103.

28 James Nestingen, "The Lord's Prayer in Luther's Catechism," *Word & World* 22, no. 1 (2002): 39–40.

29 In his *Explanation of the Lord's Prayer for Simple Laymen (1519),* Luther described the Lord's Prayer as "seven reminders of our wretchedness and poverty by means of which man, led to a knowledge of self, can see what a miserable and perilous life he leads on earth" (AE 42:27).

30 AE 41:164.

31 AE 41:164–165.

32 In the New Testament, Christians are never directed to trust one another. We are instructed to love, forgive, edify, admonish, encourage, restore, and bear with one another but never to trust one another. Trust is reserved for God alone.

33 See the excellent discussion of this comfort in Mark Seifrid, *The Second Letter to the Corinthians* (Grand Rapids: Eerdmans, 2014), 22–30.

34 Cited by Bayer, "Theology as *Askesis*," 46.

35 Bayer, "Theology as *Askesis*," 35.

HERMANN SASSE

46

Wayward Students of Harnack

Hermann Sasse and Dietrich Bonhoeffer on the Word of God

PREVIOUSLY PUBLISHED IN THE
TRINITY 2017 ISSUE OF *LOGIA*, PP. 31-35

The early careers of Hermann Sasse[1] (1895–1976) and Dietrich Bonhoeffer[2] (1906–1945), in many ways, ran parallel and often intersected with one another. They collaborated in the production of the Bethel Confession only to part ways over the Barmen Declaration.[3] Both were sons of the Prussian Union. Both men would travel for studies in the United States.[4] Each was involved in resistance to National Socialism. Most significant for this essay is the fact that Sasse and Bonhoeffer were students in Berlin and had a common teacher in the person of Adolf von Harnack[5] (1851–1930), and both would move substantially and decisively away from the liberalism of this revered professor in their own articulations of the doctrine of the word of God.

No other theologian since Friedrich Schleiermacher (1768–1834) had exerted such influence on Protestant theology as had Harnack. He came to the Berlin faculty in 1888 after a series of appointments in Leipzig, Giessen, and Marburg, and he would set the theological tone of the university until his death in 1930. Drastically distancing himself from the confessionalism of his father, Theodosius Harnack (1817–1889), he became the icon of classical liberalism as reflected in his *Essence of Christendom* (1900), which along with his skepticism about the doctrine of the Apostles' Creed, stirred a storm of conflict. His three-volume history of Christian doctrine represented what was widely recognized as a scientific and critical investigation of the development of doctrine. Hailed by the academy but seen as an apostate by many in the church, Harnack was a tireless teacher and an attractive mentor for many in the first three decades of the twentieth century.

Hermann Sasse

In 1913 Sasse matriculated at the University of Berlin, simultaneously studying both theology and philology. Berlin at the time was a showcase of theological heavyweights: Adolph von Harnack, Karl Holl, Reinhold Seeberg, Julius Kaftan, and Adolph Deissmann. Deissmann would become his *Doktorvater*, while Holl instilled in Sasse a deep interest in Luther. In a 1965 article, Sasse recalls: "We who had been students of Holl suddenly began to realize that the Lutheran Reformation meant something also for modern mankind: 'Man is nothing, and nothing is left to us but to despair of ourselves and hope in Christ.' . . . We began to study Luther, the Confessions and the Bible."[6]

But Harnack would also leave an imprint on Sasse, as can be seen in his 1936 essay "The Theologian of the Second Reich: Thoughts on the Biography of Adolph von Harnack." The essay, written six years after Harnack's death, was an extended review essay of Agnes von Zahn-Harnack's biography of her father. Sasse counted Karl Holl and Harnack as his major teachers of church history at Berlin, even though his own doctrinal position will be set in stark contrast to these two giants of the theological arena of his youth. Viewing Harnack against the backdrop of German Idealism, Sasse saw in his teacher a fading brilliance as the sureties of the nineteenth century collapsed with the coming of the First World War. It was unfortunate, Sasse opines that Harnack became a theologian:

> That he became a theologian was really a mistake, even if a productive one. For what theology is in its deepest essence, Harnack never understood, though he could have learned from his father, Theodosius Harnack, who was a real theologian. The tragedy of his

[Adolf Harnack's] life is in the fact that he who studied so many theologians of all eras, of whom he possessed an intimate and personal knowledge, never was able to grasp what makes a theologian a theologian and distinguishes him from a scholar of religion.[7]

There is no lack of pathos in Sasse's words of admiration and disappointment:

Perhaps one needs to have been his student and have experienced for years the charm of his personality, the brilliance of his thought, and his gift for teaching in order to understand the depth of this tragedy. Thus he will not live on as a theologian—what remains of his work are important historical discoveries, but all his theological ideas are today already antiquated.[8]

Harnack sought to capture the "essence of Christendom," but he could only reconstruct a Jesus who is no longer the coming Messiah, the Son of God. Sasse penetratingly observes that what Harnack extols as the essence of Christianity is merely an elusive reflection of his own shadow. Harnack attempted to dismiss the dogmaticians, assigning their writings to the sphere of beautiful devotional literature, but Sasse notes, "Today the dogmaticians exact their own revenge from him when they relegate *The Essence of Christendom* to the realm of the devotional literature of liberalism."[9]

Echoing throughout Sasse's writings is a polemic against the antidogmatic nature of liberal theology embodied in Harnack but showing residual effects in other sectors of modern Christianity. The antidogmatic bias cannot but undercut the authority of the Scriptures. Where the authority of the Holy Scriptures is sacrificed, some other authority will fill the vacuum. Instructive here are two essays from 1968, "The Crisis of the Christian Ministry" and "Erasmus, Luther, and Modern Christendom."

In "The Crisis of the Christian Ministry," Sasse observes the lethal effects of "the new hermeneutic" occasioned by Bultmann on preaching, recalling a German candidate who refused ordination, saying, "I could perhaps preach on ordinary Sundays, but I cannot preach at Christmas and Easter; I cannot preach on myths."[10] When the word of God is lost, the church is lost. While he does not directly cite Harnack in this essay, Sasse clearly sees a resurgence of his teacher's theology in the middle part of the twentieth century in those theologians who can no longer preach from the confession that the Scriptures are the word of God.

Recalling the correspondence between Barth and Harnack, Sasse sees Luther's confrontation with Erasmus as preliminary to the contemporary struggle: "He [Luther] saw behind Erasmus' concept of an undogmatic Christianity the coming neo-paganism of the modern world."[11] Sasse's critique of Harnack's quaint ethical Christianity without dogma is here applied to Erasmus: "Erasmus, who was always preoccupied with the practical, ethical aspects of his philosophy of Christ, had no sense whatever for the dogma of the church."[12] In contrast to Harnack's rejection of the Apostles' Creed, Sasse asserts:

> There is no such thing as an "undogmatic Christianity"—no faith in Christ without a definite Christology. There are assertions concerning Christ in which the Christian rejoices, and for which he is prepared to die. What these assertions are is clearly stated in the sentence that precedes the "Take away Christ from the Scriptures . . .": "What solemn truth can the Scriptures still be concealing, now that the seals are broken, the stone rolled away from the door of the tomb, and the greatest of mysteries brought to light—that Christ, God's Son, became man, that God is Three in One, that Christ suffered for us, and will reign forever." In other words, the great Trinitarian and Christological dogmas of the church, the blessed Trinity, the incarnation of the eternal Son, his atoning death "for us," his bodily resurrection, and his reign in glory: this saving Gospel is the content proper of the Holy Scripture.[13]

Whatever difficulties Sasse[14] had with definitions of inspiration and inerrancy forged in Aristotelian categories in the seventeenth century and hardened by so-called repristination theologians of the late nineteenth and twentieth centuries, he was miles apart from Hartack's undogmatic approach to the Scriptures.

Dietrich Bonhoeffer

Bonhoeffer's relationship with Harnack was marked by respect.[15] Michael Dejonge observes:

[I] Bonhoeffer rebelled against his intellectual fathers, his rebellion took the form of quiet distrust manifested in critical intellectual distance. Temperamentally, Bonhoeffer was worlds apart from Barth and Gogarten, never failing to show deference and respect to his elders. Unlike the dialectical theologians themselves, Bonhoeffer continued to sit at the feet of the old masters. Despite his omnivorous consumption of Barth's theology, Bonhoeffer dutifully attended the seminars of Berlin's theological old guard: Reinhold Seeberg, Karl Holl, and Adolf von Harnack. If, as subsequent generations of theological students have been taught, Karl Barth's second edition of Romans sounded the death-knell of liberal theology, then Bonhoeffer was apparently content to live at least a little while longer among the corpses.[16]

When Harnack died in the summer of 1930, Bonhoeffer gave the eulogy on behalf of his students. The address, as might be expected, is a demonstration of filial affection from a student for an honored teacher. Speaking largely of his academic craftsmanship, Bonhoeffer recalls his mentor's consistent drive for clarity, authenticity, and intellectual rigor:

He stood beside us with questions and across from us with superior judgment. The sessions of intense work in ancient church history, for which he assembled us in his house during his later years, allowed us to get to know his unerring striving for truth and clarity. Empty ways of speaking were alien to the spirit of the seminar. Clarity had to reign at all costs, though that did not exclude the possibility that questions of the most inward and personal nature also had a place and might expect to find in him an ever-ready listener and adviser who was always concerned with one thing: the authenticity of his response.[17]

In the eulogy itself, Bonhoeffer devotes only a paragraph to Harnack's theology. Unlike Sasse, who would not recognize Harnack as a genuine theologian, Bonhoeffer offers this assessment:

But Adolf von Harnack—and this was the greatest thing for us—was a theologian, and we believed we could understand him only from this perspective, and that is why this should be stated clearly once more in this circle. Theologian—that means first of all not only that he wrote a history of dogma. Theology means speaking about God. The work of the theologian is concerned with nothing less. In Harnack the theologian we saw the unity of the world of his intellect; here truth and freedom found the true and unifying bonds, without which they become arbitrary.[18]

For Bonhoeffer, Hartack's theology is summarized in the conclusion of the paragraph:

He believed that the Zeitgeist was always determined through the Holy Spirit of Christianity, and the message of the Father God and the Son of Man held eternal rights and thus also rights to us. It is here we find Hartack's legacy to us. True freedom of research, of work, of life, and the most profound support by, and commitment to, the eternal ground of all thought and life.[19]

From his deceased teacher, Bonhoeffer would carry into his own life openness to the world and a spirit of critical inquiry, but his attitude toward the Holy Scriptures would be markedly different. The liberal, cultural Protestantism of which Harnack was the icon would be precisely the target of Bonhoeffer's attack.

Bonhoeffer's great teacher had not only marginalized the Old Testament but suggested that it was theologically dead weight to be abandoned by an enlightened church. Harnack declared,

To reject the Old Testament in the second century was a mistake which the church rightly repudiated; to retain it in the sixteenth century was a fate which the Reformation could not yet avoid; but to continue to keep it in Protestantism as a canonical document after the nineteenth century is the consequence of religious and ecclesiastical paralysis.[20]

Bonhoeffer's insistence that the Psalms be maintained in the church and understood as Scripture that bears Christ, is fulfilled by him, and is prayed by him so as to incorporate the church into these petitions of supplication and doxology, cut against reigning exegetical and dogmatic opinion, earning him the label of a "Biblicist."[21]

In contrast to this dismissive tagging of Bonhoeffer, John Webster offers a salutary corrective:

> In interpreting Bonhoeffer's work, it is fatally easy to take insufficient account of the fact that most of Bonhoeffer's work is biblical exposition (E.G. Wendel, Studien zur Homiletik Dietrich Bonhoeffers) apart from his two dissertations, *Sanctorum Communio* and *Act and Being*. Most scholars of Bonhoeffer have gravitated towards other issues: sociality and ethical, most of all. One result of this is the over-theorized picture of Bonhoeffer: the practical directness of Bonhoeffer's biblical writings and the sense that biblical exposition is the task of the theologian in which theory may be a hindrance has been lost from view.[22]

In his work on Psalm 119, we see Bonhoeffer the biblical expositor working pastorally with the scriptural text for the sake of the life of the church created by the word of God and Christians called to the life of discipleship, which is sustained by God's word.

In contrast to the prevailing liberalism of the early twentieth century, Bonhoeffer demonstrated a reverence for the Scriptures, for in them, he heard the voice of God, though he did not have the view of Scripture held within Lutheran Orthodoxy. One example will suffice. In the autumn of 1933, while lecturing at the University of Berlin, Bonhoeffer wrote a short essay entitled "What Should a Student of Theology Do Today?" In a few pages, Bonhoeffer reflected on what is entailed in the study of theology in a manner quite different than his own liberal teachers, Harnack included. The study of theology requires more than a scientific and detached attitude. Bonhoeffer gives this blunt but salutary advice to students:

> A student who is simply gripped by the subject matter of theology and cannot turn away from it can consider that a calling. But certainly, it must be what theology is really about that enthralls the student—a real readiness to think about God, the Word, and the will of God, a "delight in the law of the Lord" and readiness to meditate on it "day and night"; a real willingness to work seriously, to study, and to think. It is not the experience of a call but the determination to do sober, earnest, and responsible theological work that is the gateway to the study of theology.[23]

Bonhoeffer goes on to speak of the formation of the theological student not by cultivating his own subjective spirituality, developing his people skills, or increasing his capacities for ministerial performance. Rather, Bonhoeffer says:

> [T]he real study of *theologia sacra* begins when, in the midst of questioning and seeking, human beings encounter the cross; when they recognize the endpoint of all their own passions in the suffering of God at the hands of humankind, and realize that their entire vitality stands under judgment. This is the great turnaround, which for the course of study means the turn toward theological objectivity. Theological study no longer means revealing the passions of one's ego; it is no longer a monologue, no longer religious self-fulfillment. Rather, it is about responsible study and listening, becoming attentive to the Word of God, which has been revealed right here in this world; it is toning down one's self in the face of what is far and away the most important matter.[24]

Such study, Bonhoeffer suggests, is marked by the humility to learn from those who have gone before us. It is not a sign of maturity to dismiss the legacy we have received from our fathers in the faith: "How can such a facile setting aside of issues that were important to wiser and more serious people be evidence of anything but poorly concealed ignorance?"[25] Theological study does not seek novelty only to end in idolatry. Instead, the aim of the study of theology is finally to confess with clarity that Jesus Christ is Lord, knowing the difference between the truth and the lie, between true doctrine and false doctrine. Bonhoeffer continues:

> that under no circumstances are tactical considerations the way to serve one's church or the aim of theology; only the purest, most refined truth will do. Even with the best will in the world, tactical solutions only cloud and obscure the situation. The student of theology is the last one who should be thinking tactically and should carry on working with purely theological objectivity, in service to God.[26]

Finally, Bonhoeffer says that the student of theology "should know where the wellspring of the church's life is found, and how it can become clogged and poisoned"[27] so that in times of confusion, he may return to the true wellsprings of the Scriptures and the Confessions to be strengthened like the man the first Psalm calls blessed.

Conclusion

Both Sasse and Bonhoeffer would chart paths that would take them in very different directions from that of their teacher on the word of God. The roads taken by these two students of Harnack would not be identical. Bonhoeffer's understanding of the word of God will carry the imprint of his encounter with Barth, although he is not without criticism of this leading Reformed theologian. In contrast, Sasse is thoroughly Lutheran in his understanding of the necessity for the proper distinction of law and gospel in the reading of the Scriptures; his critique of Barth is early and unrelenting.[28] Bonhoeffer never attempted a systematic exposition of the doctrine of Scripture, per se. Sasse worked at developing a dogmatic definition of Holy Scriptures as the word of God in human form in an attempt to avoid nineteenth-century liberalism and its offspring in Bultmann's program of demythologizing the New Testament as well as in modern fundamentalism.[29] However, a fully worked out understanding of inspiration and inerrancy remained elusive, and his anticipated major work on the sacred Scriptures was never completed. Perhaps the final demonstration of how far Sasse and Bonhoeffer moved away from Harnack can be recognized in their preaching.[30] With both men, the task of the sermon was not to lecture on the word of God or develop from it an application of ethical principles. Both viewed the sermon as a proclamation of Christ crucified and raised for sinners as attested to by the Holy Scriptures, which continue to carry him into the ears and hearts of those for whom he died.

Notes

1 For an overview of Sasse's life and work, see John T. Pless, "Hermann Sasse," in *Twentieth-Century Lutheran Theologians*, ed. Mark C. Mattes (Göttingen: Vandenhoeck & Ruprecht, 2013), 155–77.

2 For an overview of Bonhoeffer's life and work, see Richard H. Bliese, "Dietrich Bonhoeffer," in *Twentieth-Century Lutheran Theologians*, 223–48.

3 See David Jay Webber, "Bonhoeffer and Sasse as Confessors and Churchmen: The Bethel Confession and Its Intended but Unfulfilled Purpose," *Logia* 21, no. 4 (Reformation 2012): 13–20.

4 Sasse studied at Hartford Seminary during the 1925–26 academic year. After his return to Germany, he wrote "American Christianity and the Church" (see *The Lonely Way*, 1:23–60) in 1927. Bonhoeffer read Sasse's book before coming to Union Seminary for his own studies a few years later. See Eberhard Bethge, *Dietrich Bonhoeffer: Theologian, Christian, Man for His Times: A Biography*, trans. Eric Mosbacher [and others] (Minneapolis: Fortress Press, 2000), 143. Also see John T. Pless, "A Conversation between Mark Noll and Hermann Sasse," *Logia* 22, no. 1 (Epiphany 2013): 5–7. It was in the United States that Sasse and Bonhoeffer would observe yet another variety of an undogmatic Christianity, which provoked a negative reaction from both men.

5 For an overview of Harnack's life and work, see Andreas Mühling, "Harnack, Adoph von," in *The Encyclopedia of Protestantism*, ed. Hans Hillerbrand (New York: Routledge, 2004), 2:844–47. On Harnack's place within the Berlin faculty, see Thomas Albert Howard, *Protestant Theology and the Making of the Modern German University* (Oxford: Oxford University Press, 2006), 391–402.

6 Hermann Sasse, "The Impact of Bultmannism on American Lutheranism, with Special Reference to His Demythologization of the New Testament," *Lutheran Synod Quarterly* 5, no. 4 (June 1965): 5.

7 Hermann Sasse, "The Theologian of the Second Reich: Thoughts on the Biography of Adolf von Harnack," in *The Lonely Way*, ed. Matthew C. Harrison (St. Louis: Concordia Publishing House, 2001–2002), 1:312.

8 Ibid.

9 Ibid., 1:318.

10 Hermann Sasse, "The Crisis of Christian Ministry," in *The Lonely Way*, 1:369.

11 Hermann Sasse, "Erasmus, Luther, and Modern Christendom," in *The Lonely Way*, 1:381.

12 Ibid.

13 Ibid., 1:383.

14 For a discussion of Sasse's evolving confession of the doctrine of Holy Scripture, see Kurt Marquart, "Hermann Sasse and the Mystery of Sacred Scripture," in *Hermann Sasse: A Man for Our Times?* ed. John R. Stephens (St. Louis: Concordia Academic Press, 1998), 167–93.

15 For a helpful overview of the long-standing relationship of Bonhoeffer to Harnack, which takes into account deep familial connections, see Martin Rumscheidt, "The Significance of Adolf von Harnack and Reinhold Seeberg for Dietrich Bonhoeffer," in *Bonhoeffers Intellectual Formation*, ed. Peter Frick (Tübingen: Mohr Siebeck, 2008), 201–24.

16 Michael P. DeJonge, *Bonhoeffers Theological Formation: Berlin, Barth, and Protestant Theology* (Oxford: Oxford University Press, 2012), 3–4.

17 Dietrich Bonhoeffer, "Eulogy for Adolf von Harnack," in *Dietrich Bonhoeffer Works* [hereafter abbreviated DBW], trans. Daniel W. Bloesch and James H. Burtness (Minneapolis: Fortress Press, 1996–2014), 10:380.

18 Ibid., 10:381.

19 Ibid.

20 Cited by Martin Kuske, *The Old Testament as the Book of Christ: An Appraisal of Bonhoeffers Interpretation*, trans. S.T. Kimbrough Jr. (Philadelphia: Westminster Press, 1976), 9.

21 Such is the judgment of Wolf Krötke, "Bonhoeffer and Luther," in *Bonhoeffer's Intellectual Formation*, 59. Krötke writes: "Bonhoeffer seems to accept unquestioningly the word of Scripture—which he now identifies with Jesus Christ himself—and thus assigns it priority in the act of understanding before the Spirit of Christ. Hence he falls prey to Biblicism."

22 John Webster, *Holy Scripture: A Dogmatic Sketch* (Cambridge: Cambridge University Press, 2003), 78–79. Also note Bonhoeffer's striking comments in a letter written on 8 April 1936 to his brother-in-law, Rudiger Schleicher, whose theological position was more reflective of the older liberalism of Adolph von Harnack. After explaining to his brother-in-law that God's word reveals the cross, thus spelling death and judgment of all our ways before God, Bonhoeffer says: "Does this perspective somehow make it understandable to you that I do not want to give up the Bible as this strange Word of God at any point, that I intend with all my powers to ask what God wants to say to us here? Any other place outside the Bible has become too uncertain for me. I fear that I will only encounter some divine double of myself there. Does this somehow help you understand why I am prepared for a *sacrificium intellectus*—just in these matters, and only in these matters, with respect to the one, true God! And who does not bring to some passages his sacrifice of the intellect, in the confession that he does not yet understand this or that passage in Scripture, but is certain that even they will be revealed one day as God's own Word? I would rather make that confession than try to say according to my own opinion: this is divine, that is human" (Dietrich Bonhoeffer, *Meditating on the Word*, trans. David McI. Grace [Cambridge, MA: Cowley Publications, 2000], 37). In a following paragraph, Bonhoeffer describes how this approach has opened the Scriptures to him: "And now let me tell you quite personally that since I learned to read the Bible in this way—and that was not so long ago—it has become daily more wonderful to me. I read it mornings and evenings, often also during the day. And each day I take up a text, which I have before me the entire week, and I attempt to immerse myself in it completely, in order to really listen to it. I know that without this I could no longer rightly live, let alone believe" (37–38). This newfound approach to reading and

meditating on the Scriptures is evident in Bonhoeffer's work with Psalm 119 less than two years after writing this letter. Here see John T. Pless, "Bonhoeffer on Psalm 119," in *The Restoration of Creation in Christ: Essays in Honor of Dean O. Wenthe*, ed. Arthur A. Just Jr. and Paul J. Grime (St. Louis: Concordia Publishing House, 2014), 227–40.

23 Dietrich Bonhoeffer, "What Should a Student of Theology Do Today?" DBW 12:432–33.

24 Ibid., 12:433.

25 Ibid.

26 Ibid., 12:435.

27 Ibid., 12:434.

28 While there are frequent critiques of Barth in Sasse's essays and letters beginning in the early 1930s and continuing for the rest of his literary career, perhaps the most succinct statement of the fundamental theological difference is found in "Lutheran Doctrine and Modern Reformed Theology of Karl Barth," in *Here We Stand*, trans. Theodore G. Tappert (Adelaide: Lutheran Publishing House, 1979), 161–78. First published in Germany in 1934 under the title *Was heißt lutherisch?* this book was used by Bonhoeffer in Finkenwalde, even though he would disagree with significant aspects of Sasse's treatment of the confessional question in light of Barmen.

29 Here see H. Sasse, "Luther and the Word of God," in *Accents in Luthers Theology: Essays in Commemoration of the 450th Anniversary of the Reformation*, ed. Heino O. Kadai (St. Louis: Concordia Publishing House, 1967), 47–98; also note Jeffrey J. Kloha, "Hermann Sasse Confesses the Doctrine *de Scriptura*," in *Scripture and the Church: Selected Essays of Hermann Sasse*, ed. Jeffrey J. Kloha and Ronald R. Feuerhahn (St. Louis: Concordia Seminary Press, 1995), 337–423.

30 Here see John T. Pless, "Bonhoeffer as Preacher," *Concordia Pulpit Resources* 16, part 4 (17 September-26 November 2006): 7–10; and John T. Pless, "Hermann Sasse as Preacher," in *Witness: Sermons Preached in Erlangen and Congregational Lectures*, by Hermann Sasse, trans. Bror Erickson (Saginaw, MI: Magdeburg Press, 2013), 7–30.

47

A Conversation between
Mark Noll and Hermann Sasse

**PREVIOUSLY PUBLISHED IN THE
EPIPHANY 2013 ISSUE OF *LOGIA*, PP. 3–23**

Mark Noll is a sharp-eyed watcher of American Lutheranism from the outside. In numerous essays, he has spoken of the ambiguity surrounding what it means to be Lutheran in America. In "American Lutherans Yesterday and Today," Noll observes: "The history of Lutheranism in America is complex primarily because Lutherans seem to have both easily accommodated to American ways of life, including religious ways of life, and never accommodated to American ways."[1] How about that for the proverbial Lutheran paradox? A new twist on the *simul*—American and un-American!

Actually, Noll was not the first to make this observation about American Lutheranism. In the academic year 1925–26, a young German pastor from the Prussian Union came to the United States to study at Hartford Theological Seminary in Connecticut. His name was Hermann Sasse. It was during his time in the States that Sasse came to embrace confessional Lutheranism through his reading of Wilhelm Löhe's *Three Books about the Church*. After returning to Germany, in 1927, he published a short book, *American Christianity and the Church*. It is this book that Dietrich Bonhoeffer would read in preparation for his coming to Union Seminary in New York.

Sasse saw American Lutheranism in the 1920s as not yet accommodating to American ways but living in a religious environment where such an accommodation would be very difficult to avoid. He also saw a great deal of promise for American Lutheranism. He was bemused by what he saw happening in other American Protestant churches in terms of worship. He writes:

> Consider, further, all the attempts at reinvigorating dead congregations. What proposals and experiments are made today in order to develop "artistic" unity in the Divine Service where possible! What an absurd idea to make the Word of God, which has become ineffective, now effective by showing a film about Christ in the church. The holy spectacle of the Roman Mass would be preferable![2]

But then Sasse had never heard of the Transforming Churches Network in the Missouri Synod or whatever counterparts there may be in the Evangelical Lutheran Church in America (ELCA) and the Wisconsin Evangelical Lutheran Synod. Sasse wrote of how churches advertised themselves:

> There are advertisements which seek to bait the public. Why should colorful billboards and psychologically designed newspaper advertisement not serve the church? They are all organizations which are part of the American church, from the kitchen to the bowling alley. Why should the church not offer what a secular club offers? And these things progressively force their way into religious life itself. Worship (Gottesdienst) has been as we say, "developed." There must always be something new, and everything must be effective: lighting effect, musical effect, and effective liturgy.[3]

Sasse recounted attending a service in a large Baptist church, where as soon as the preacher knelt to pray, the attendant switched off the lights so that darkness filled the sanctuary, creating the desired mood for the edification of the worshippers.

In those days, American Lutherans were mostly preserved from such things, or at least Sasse didn't encounter them on what would be the first of numerous visits to the United States. In contrast to the unionizing, liberal Protestantism Sasse knew from Germany, his first exposure to American Lutheranism was positive and even cautiously optimistic. Subsequent contacts in the United States would win for Sasse friends in all branches of American Lutheranism, from Theodore Tappert at the Philadelphia seminary to the men of the Wisconsin Synod who first published his letters in English; also J. Michel Reu in Dubuque, Herman Preus in St. Paul, and J.A.O. and Robert Preus in the Missouri Synod. In addition, Sasse was the first lecturer at Bethany Lutheran Seminary's Reformation Lectures. He also had his criticisms of trends within all of these American Lutheran configurations. But that would be another story.

Sasse recognized the complexity of the Lutheran way in America for many of the reasons identified by Noll. While Noll writes as a historian looking in retrospect at the winding and, more often than not, conflicting paths Lutheranism has taken, Sasse helps us see something of the theological challenges that confronted American Christianity in the 1920s and would impact all branches of American Lutheranism in one way or another down to the present day.

The so-called Social Gospel Movement is tagged by Sasse as a particularly American expression, although through Walter Rauschenbusch, it was grounded in the theology of the German Albrecht Ritschl. As Sasse saw it, the Social Gospel was the embodiment of a theology of works fueled by a free will. In this vision, Sasse said, "The perfection of the church coincides with the perfection of culture."[4] Contemporary examples might be found in any number of "peace and justice" pronouncements coming from the ELCA.

Sasse observed that American Christianity was by nature ecumenical and denominational, not confessional. "It is a church," he said, "which has renounced the idea that it is possible to possess the truth and the requirements necessitated by that truth for carrying out its work."[5] He was somewhat bemused that a fellow student at Hartford, a Quaker who was not baptized, could take a call to minister in a Congregational church where he would happily baptize both children and adults by either sprinkling or immersion given the choice of the parents or baptismal candidate. He noted, "At the edge of America's historical horizon stand the silhouettes of the Reformers, but they are fading fast. Calvin is hardly read by the average theologian. Luther still lives in the Lutheran Church through his catechism."[6]

In 1927 Sasse held out hope for Lutherans in America. Largely spared the skirmishes of the so-called Modernist-Fundamentalist debate over the Bible, the works-righteousness of the Social Gospel Movement, and the suspicion that creeds and liturgy were detrimental to growth and unity, Lutherans were not institutionally united, and they were something of wallflowers in the American religious garden. Here Sasse resonates with Noll. Sasse wrote:

> And the Lutherans are not united, leading an isolated life, having little influence on the intellectual life of the nation. But they are living and growing churches. If the movement toward unity (the first great consequence of which was the formation of the United Lutheran Church in 1918) continues and leads to the unification of all Lutherans it will be one of the most significant churches in America. The life of these churches dispels the notion that Lutheranism's doctrine of justification necessarily leads to quietism. There is in America perhaps no more active a church than the Missouri Synod, which is the most dogmatically rigorous Lutheran Church in the country. The history of the organization of this church demonstrates that Lutheranism can exist in forms other than a state church or dependent upon the state (as we hear happily repeated time and time again in Europe). Lutheranism is never more vibrant than where it is free from guardianship by a secular authority.[7]

Sasse's optimism for American Lutheranism would wane in later years as he detected movements leading not simply to polarization over questions of biblical inspiration and inerrancy, but a loss of nerve in confessing, Perhaps there is something of a parallel here to Noll's diagnosis as well. However, I would suggest that in a 1968 essay, "Erasmus, Luther, and Modern Christendom," Sasse takes us deeper than Noll.[8] In this essay, Sasse is no longer the young postdoctoral exchange student fascinated with his study abroad. He is a church theologian seasoned by suffering and disappointment, having left his Erlangen chair for a post at a small and seemingly insignificant seminary in Adelaide, Australia. His life had been spent as a keen observer and participant in ecumenical conversations and developments throughout Christendom, but with special attention to American Lutheranism.

In this essay, Sasse sees that the controversy between Erasmus and Luther has not come to an end. Sasse wrote that Luther "saw behind Erasmus' concept of an undogmatic Christianity the coming neo-paganism of the modern world."[9] Synergism is integral to American Christianity. We live in a country where, as one pundit put it, even Roman Catholics think like Southern Baptists. Of Erasmus, Sasse said, "He believes in God but has not entirely lost his belief in man."[10] That seems to characterize the religious environment of North America in these early years of the twenty-first century. Erasmus's notion of the freedom of the will and democratic assertions of liberty make the remark of Isaac Singer completely understandable: "We must believe in free will, we have no choice!"[11] That is the reason Sasse's famous line in his 1934 book *Here We Stand* should be sobering for American Lutherans: "The Evangelical Lutheran Church is a church which has been sentenced to death by the world."[12]

I think Sasse hits on something that is expressed so well by Gerhard Forde in his fine little book, *The Captivation of the Will*, when he said, "If one starts from the premise and defense of freedom of the will one will end in bondage."[13] Sasse suggests that Lutheran theology must start where Luther started, with human enslavement to sin, in order to end with freedom. Coupled with Forde's book, I find Sasse's essay instructive as we look at the Lutheran landscape in North America today. Perhaps the fault line is not so much between Lutherans who have different views of inspiration, Lutherans who are politically liberal versus those who are social conservatives, Lutherans who are said to be liturgical or nonliturgical, or Lutherans who accent the ministerial office as opposed to those who champion the congregation. Just maybe the fault line in American Lutheranism is at the point of the enslaved will. How one comes down on that question will, no doubt, have implications for all those other debates as well. That would be a conversation worth having, and perhaps Hermann Sasse might bring us to better clarity in answering the questions raised by Mark Noll's essay.

Notes

1 Mark Noll, "American Lutherans Yesterday and Today," In *Lutherans Today: American Lutheran Identity in the Twenty-first Century*, ed. Richard Cimino (Grand Rapids: Eerdmans, 2003), 4. Also see Mark Noll, "The Lutheran Difference," *First Things* no. 20 (February 1992): 31–40; and his chapter on "The Fate of European Traditions—Lutherans and Roman Catholics," in

The Old Religion in a New World: The History of North American Christianity (Grand Rapids: Eerdmans, 2002), 235–52.

2   Hermann Sasse, "American Christianity and the Church," in *The Lonely Way*, trans. Matthew C. Harrison (St. Louis: Concordia Publishing House, 2001–2002), 1:30.

3   Sasse, "American Christianity," 1:29.

4   Sasse, "American Christianity," 1:31.

5   Sasse, "American Christianity," 1:47.

6   Sasse, "American Christianity," 1:36.

7   Sasse, "American Christianity," 1:55.

8   Hermann Sasse, "Erasmus, Luther, and Modern Christendom," in *The Lonely Way*, 2:373–84.

9   Sasse, "Erasmus," 2:381.

10   Sasse, "Erasmus," 2:383.

11   Isaac Singer, quoted by Gerhard Forde, *The Captivation of the Will: Luther vs. Erasmus on Freedom and Bondage*, ed. Steven Faulson (Grand Rapids: Eerdmans, 2005), 49.

12   Hermann Sasse, *Here We Stand*, trans. Theodore Tappert (Adelaide: Lutheran Publishing House, 1979), 187.

13   Forde, Captivation, 44. Also instructive is Gerhard Forde's essay, "Lutheran Faith and American Freedom," in *The Preached God*, ed. Mark C. Mattes and Steven D. Paulson (Grand Rapids: Eerdmans, 2007), 195–203.

CARE OF SOULS

48

Your Pastor Is Not Your Therapist

Private Confession—
The Ministry of Repentance and Faith

PREVIOUSLY PUBLISHED IN THE EASTERTIDE 2001 ISSUE
OF *LOGIA*, PP. 21-26

"The prevailing theories in contemporary pastoral psychology are not in harmony with our confessional Lutheran understanding of the care of souls (*Seelsorge*)," writes Carl Braaten.[1] Pastoral theology has become pastoral psychology. E. Brooks Holifield's fascinating study *A History of Pastoral Care in America: From Salvation to Self-Realization* traces the story of how theology gave way to psychology. Mainline liberal theology, with its eagerness to be relevant, made space for courses in the psychology of religion and counseling in seminary catalogs. Anton Boisen began to train a small group of seminarians in pastoral care at the Worchester State Hospital in the summer of 1925, and thus the modern Clinical Pastoral Education (CPE) Movement was born.

Educated at Union Seminary in New York, Boisen believed that theological seminaries needed a thorough revamping in order to incorporate the scientific study of religious experience. No longer was theological education to be limited to literary texts. Boisen urged that seminarians engage in the study of "living human documents" in a clinical environment. Having himself been hospitalized for mental illness on two occasions, Boisen maintained that this experience served to equip him for pastoral work. While Boisen himself was committed to rather rigorous moral standards, those who came after him tended to place the blame for emotional distress at authoritarian religious preachments, especially as they related to sexuality. "Understanding" was the watchword for the generation of clinical pastoral educators that followed Boisen. Understanding "connoted tolerance, an acceptance of feelings; of the body, the senses, and sexuality; and opposition to rigidity and to condemnation. Understanding implied an ethical attitude, a willingness to sympathize with people rather than idolize conventions and rules."[2]

The theological contours of pastoral care became increasingly hard to discern. Attempting to integrate psychological insights into Christian theology and pastoral practice resulted in a theology that was forced to fit into the categories of current psychological theories. The gospel was reinterpreted in psychological terms. With the rise in popularity of Paul Tillich's theological method of correlation, it was held that Christian theology was compatible with depth psychology. Tillichian language of grace as unconditional acceptance and faith as "accepting that you are accepted" was thought to adequately convey the biblical message in psychological terms. Braaten summarizes the outcome of this approach:

> Many of the new professionals thought of themselves as critics of an authoritarian church, opponents of repressive moralism, and enemies of dogmatism. Persons should be free—and freeing of others—from moral authoritarianism and institutional impositions. Carl Rogers' book, *Counseling and Psychotherapy*, became a standard text among clinical groups and in theological seminaries. One of the reasons for its popularity was that the counselor could satisfy the impulses of the client seeking self-acceptance and self-realization.[3]

While the CPE Movement had its genesis within liberal Protestantism, its influence eventually reached beyond these churches into churches that were noted for their theological conservatism. By the 1960s, every major seminary, regardless of theological stripe, had incorporated courses in the psychology of religion, counseling, and programs of Clinical Pastoral Education into the curriculum. Within conservative evangelical denominations, there emerged those such as lay Adams and James Dobson, who advocated "Christian counseling," hoping to avoid the secular humanism that dominated the social sciences. Nevertheless, they, like their liberal counterparts, cast the gospel in the mold of the therapeutic. While conservative doctrinal assertions are given ascent, and traditional moral values are upheld, theology takes second place to psychology. Whether liberal or conservative, the minister is now given a place among the helping professions with all the rights and privileges that such an exalted station obtains.

The psychological domination of theology in the churches and the subsequent move to transform the pastor into a therapist have not gone unchallenged. One of the first to challenge pastors to attend to their calling as ministers of the gospel was Paul Pruyser, a clinical psychologist associated with the Menninger Foundation. In 1976 Pruyser authored a book entitled *The Minister as Diagnostician*, in which he argued that the Christian clergy "possess a body of theoretical and practical knowledge that is uniquely their own."[4] While Pruyser maintains that pastors may benefit from the insights of the psychological sciences, these insights ought not overshadow or diminish the integrity of the theological knowledge that is the foundation for pastoral work. Pruyser worries that many clergy have become uncertain of their unique calling and have restlessly looked to psychology for guidance rather than utilizing the legacy of Christian theology. The language of the church is jettisoned for the language of the clinic. In striving to be like counselors, ministers are rendered incapable of providing genuine pastoral care, that is, the care of souls, using the means that reside in the pastoral office.

Two United Methodists, William Willimon of Duke University and Thomas Oden of Drew University have weighed in with their critique of the church's uncritical embrace of the tools and techniques of the therapist. Willimon recognizes that counseling will be part of the pastoral task, but he laments the reduction of pastoral care to counseling. Observing that the "dialogue between psychology and theology has been a mostly unilateral affair, with psychology doing most of the talking,"[5] Willimon identifies the CPE Movement as a form of "liberal pietism" that is individualistic and anti-intellectual. Above all, Willimon notes that CPE fails to recognize the churchly context for pastoral care. Pastors become indistinguishable from physicians, social workers, psychiatrists, and other clinicians.

In his book *Worship as Pastoral Care*, Willimon echoes the reflection of the Jesuit liturgical scholar Josef Jungmann that "for centuries, the liturgy, actively celebrated, has been the most important form for pastoral care."[6] The pastoral care of the individual is done in the context of the congregation gathered around word and sacrament. Willimon is to be credited for calling pastors back to the liturgy as the primary and ordinary means of pastoral care.

Like Willimon, Thomas Oden was also deeply involved in the counseling movement of the 1960s. In fact, Oden writes of his own pilgrimage through the client-centered therapy movement and Transactional Analysis as well as dabbling in parapsychology before coming to embrace what he describes as classical Christianity:

> I have spent most of my career working span by span on a bridge between psychology and religion. Just how incessantly preoccupied I have been with this theological bridge is clear if from nothing else, from the titles of my previous books: *Kerygma and Counseling*, *Contemporary Theology and Psychotherapy*, *The Structure of Awareness*, *The Intensive Group Experience*, *After Therapy What?*, *Game Free*, and *TAG: The Transactional Awareness Game*. After two decades of bridge building, however, it is finally dawning on me that the traffic is moving on the bridge only one way: from psychological speculation to rapt religious attentiveness. The conversation has become completely one-sided. Theology's listening to psychology has been far more accurate, empathic, and attentive than has psychology's listening to theology. I do not cease to hope for a viable two-way dialogue, but there is as little evidence that theology is ready to speak out in such a dialogue as there is that psychology is ready to listen. The bridge will not be built by the complete acquiescence of theology to the reductionistic assumptions of psychology, or by relinquishing such key religious postulates as providence and resurrection.[7]

Since writing those words in his 1979 book *Agenda for Theology: Recovering Christian Roots*, Oden has gone on to write a pastoral theology as well as a multi-volume set entitled *Classical Pastoral Care* and a study of the pastoral theology of Gregory the Great, *Care of*

Souls in the Classic Tradition. In each of these works, Oden attempts to reconnect day-to-day pastoral work with classical Christian theology rather than psychological theories or managerial techniques.

Braaten, Pruyser, Willimon, and Oden write in light of the collapse of theology and practice in the so-called mainline, liberal churches. David Wells turns his attention to a similar failure within conservative or evangelical circles. In a series of three books, *No Place for Truth, or Whatever Happened to Evangelical Theology?* (1993), *God in the Wasteland: The Reality of Truth in a World of Fading Dreams* (1994), and *Losing Our Virtue: Why the Church Must Recover Its Moral Vision* (1998), Wells provides an analysis of the state of theology and church life among American Evangelicals. Wells notes that "many evangelicals believe in the innocence of modern culture and for that reason exploit it and are exploited by it so that they are unable to believe in all the truth that once characterized this Protestant orthodoxy."[8]

For our purposes here, it is worth noting Wells's criticism of the understanding of ministry within contemporary evangelicalism as it is shaped by therapeutic and/or managerial categories. Within evangelicalism, as within liberalism, the training of pastors has become biased against theology and oriented toward the imparting of professional skills. Witness the claims of the Pastoral Leadership Institute in our own circles! Wells writes,

> It is not hard to see why clergy should have embarked on their own movement toward professionalization. After all, that is how other professionals acquired their standing in society. It was by gaining control over their specialized fields that medical doctors, lawyers, architects, accountants, and engineers secured their own space and social standing for themselves. Professionalization, however, is itself a culture, and the values by which it operates are not always friendly to pastoral calling and character. For the most part, American clergy have not understood this. They grabbed at professionalization like a drowning man might grab at a life jacket, but having been thus saved, they must now live by its limitations and dictates.[9]

My colleague at Concordia Seminary in Fort Wayne, Dr. Roger Pittelko, says that the Missouri Synod has become the garbage collector of American Christianity. As fads run their course in other denominations, we seem to pick them up in the LCMS. The Oden and Willimon critiques of the CPE Movement are not that new; they were written over twenty years ago. Yet this model seems to have gained prominence in the LCMS only recently. Likewise, the professionalization of the ministry denounced by David Wells, a theologian at Gordon Conwell, a leading evangelical seminary, is eagerly embraced as innovative, creative, and "cutting-edge" by some within our synod. In collecting the theological hand-me-downs from other denominations, we are apt to clutter our churches with junk that others have already discovered not to be that useful anyway. In doing so, we also run the risk of displacing or losing altogether the gifts that we are called to set before the world.

I have devoted a substantial section of this essay to an overview of the critiques that others have offered of current, mostly clinically based models of pastoral care and ministerial practice. My point in providing this survey is to contrast the therapeutic model with the understanding of pastoral theology that undergirds the ongoing practice of confession and absolution in the Evangelical Lutheran congregation. To put it another way, you can't patch old cloth with new; you can't pour new wine into old wineskins. The therapeutic model of pastoral ministry is incapable of sustaining the practice of confession and absolution evangelically understood. In the remainder of this essay, we shall consider how the practice of confession and absolution might be used in the Lutheran parish, not as a therapeutic tool but as the locus of genuine pastoral care.

Our practice of confession and absolution must grow out of Evangelical Lutheran theology. "It is taught among us that private absolution should be retained and not allowed to fall into disuse," says Article XI of the Augsburg Confession. Martin Luther was no less adamant in the Large Catechism: "If you are a Christian, you should be glad to run more than a hundred miles for confession, not under compulsion but rather coming and compelling us to offer it. . . . Therefore, when I urge you to go to confession, I am simply urging you to be a Christian" (LC, "A Brief Exhortation to Confession"; Tappert, 460). In spite of these and other clear statements in the Lutheran Confessions, the practice of private confession and absolution is regarded by many as an archaic relic left behind by the Reformation and replaced by more relevant and psychologically sound methods of pastoral care.

A recovery of private confession and absolution entails a rediscovery of the evangelical Lutheran doctrine of repentance. In the Augustana, the practice of confession and absolution (Article XI) is joined to the doctrine of repentance (Article XII). The Lutheran Reformation has been characterized as a struggle over the doctrine of repentance. Already in the first of his Ninety-Five Theses, Luther writes: "When our Lord and Master Jesus Christ said 'Repent,' [Matt. 4:17] he willed the entire life of believers to be one of repentance" (AE 31: 25). Reacting against Rome's doctrine of repentance as an occasional activity that Christians were required to engage in, and the subsequent practice of selling indulgences, Luther taught that repentance is the natural rhythm of the Christian life set in motion at baptism and continuing until baptism's completion in the resurrection of the body.

Luther's insight is reflected in Article XII of the *Augsburg Confession*, where true repentance is defined as "nothing else than to have contrition and sorrow, or terror, on account of sin, and yet at the same time to believe the Gospel and absolution." Repentance is not the self-contrived sorrow of the penitent, but the "true sorrow of the heart, suffering, and pain of death" (SA III, III; Tappert, 304) produced by the hammer of God's law along with "faith, which is born of the Gospel" (AC XII; Tappert, 34).

This Lutheran doctrine of repentance refocuses the practice of confession and absolution. Gone is the insistence that all sins be enumerated. Freed from coercion and fear, confession was retained for the sake of the absolution. Thus the Large Catechism:

> We urge you, however, to confess and express your needs, not for the purpose of performing a work but to hear what God wishes to say to you. The Word of absolution, I say, is what you should concentrate on, magnifying and cherishing it as a great and wonderful treasure to be accepted with all praise and gratitude. (Tappert, 459)

Article XII rejoices in the absolution. All that diminishes absolution is rejected. Perfectionists, who claim that real Christians cannot fall into sin, are rejected. The Novatians, who denied absolution to those who sin after Baptism, are condemned because their false teaching undermines the forgiveness of sins won by Christ and bestowed in his word. Finally, Article XII rejects the opinion that remission of sins is obtained by human satisfaction rather than through faith in Christ.

Absolution is nothing less than the very voice of God himself. Article XXV expands upon Article XII: "We also teach that God requires us to believe this absolution as much as if we heard God's voice from heaven, that we should joyfully comfort ourselves with absolution, and that we should know that through such faith we obtain forgiveness of sins" (Tappert, 62). Spoken from the human lips of a pastor, the absolution is the very word of the Lord himself. More than a mere "assurance," absolution is "the very voice of the Gospel" (Ap XII, 2; Tappert, 182). It is on account of the absolution that the Augsburg Confession holds private confession in such high esteem and insists that it "not be allowed to fall into disuse." The fact of the matter is that private confession has fallen into disuse in our churches. It is beyond the parameters of this paper to review and analyze the causes of this displacement. The studies of others such as Paul Lang and Fred Precht trace the history of the loss. A survey of the treatment of private confession or lack thereof in the textbooks of pastoral theology in the Missouri Synod might also prove revealing. The same could be said for the catechesis for the Fifth Chief Part in the various synodical expositions of the Small Catechism. But this too will need to wait for another time. Rather, I would like to reflect on how we might work toward the recovery of private confession in our parishes on account of the treasure of holy absolution.

A salutary restoration of private confession will be anchored in preaching and catechesis. Marsha Witten's study of sermons on the parable of the prodigal son preached in Presbyterian, and Southern Baptist pulpits demonstrates how the language of secularity has overcome such biblical motifs as atonement, repentance, and faith.[10] Fulfillment of self is substituted for the forgiveness of sins. Sin is spoken of only in a most general sense, with preachers carefully crafting their language to cushion the blow of judgment. Secular categories such as victimization and alienation replace biblical categories of depravity, death, hell, and wrath. With such a muted preachment of the law, it comes as no surprise that the gospel is likewise reduced to a generic message of divine love that opens the way for self-acceptance. Preaching itself becomes therapeutic in its aims as it seeks either to soothe psychological hurts or to give wise counsel for sanctified living.

Against such a homiletical backdrop, private confession will be seen at best as one of many helpful techniques to relieve guilt; at worst, it will be seen as irrelevant and perhaps harmful to a well-balanced, integrated spiritual life that can be achieved by following prescribed principles.

Over against the kind of preaching observed and described by Witten, Evangelical Lutheranism understands preaching as that dual work of God by which he both kills and enlivens. God's words are performative. The words of God's law bring death to the sinner, stripping him of all excuses and taking away every idol that he would use for self-justification. The words of the gospel actually bestow deliverance from sin, death, and hell. Law preaching not only condemns the evil deeds of the flesh; it brings our good works under divine judgment, as Luther made clear in his Heidelberg Theses.[11] Gospel preaching moves beyond assurance and encouragement to actually deliver the benefits of Christ's atonement to those who live under the law's death sentence. Such preaching is never merely descriptive. It is not that preachers preach about law and gospel, but rather that they preach law and gospel.

Only in the context of law-gospel preaching will the value of private confession be appreciated, and the gift of holy absolution be treasured. The practice of private confession is actually an extension of such preaching. Genuine evangelical preaching proclaims a "located God." God is for us where he puts himself for us—in the water of baptism, in the body and blood present and distributed in the Lord's Supper, and in the words proclaimed in the sermon and spoken in the absolution. It is not that the forgiving words proclaimed in the sermon are somehow less than the words of absolution spoken to the individual penitent. The gifts of Christ are never piecemeal. Forgiveness of sins does not come in bits and pieces. There are no levels of forgiveness. Rather, the Smalcald Articles confess that the gospel "offers counsel and help against sin in more than one way, for God is surpassingly rich in his grace" (SA III, IV, Tappert, 310). The forgiveness of sins proclaimed in the sermon is not to be played off against the forgiveness of sins proclaimed in absolution to the individual penitent. In the abundance of his merciful will to save sinners, God has given us both sermon and absolution. The great value of individual absolution is that in the words of absolution, God would give to the penitent the certainty that this forgiveness is indeed "for you."

Following the example of Luther's "A Brief Exhortation to Confession" in the Large Catechism, pastors will extol confession in their preaching: "Thus we teach what a wonderful, precious, and comforting thing confession is, and we urge that such a precious blessing should not be despised, especially when we consider our great need" (Tappert, 460). Very practically, this means that pastors ought to look for those places in the lectionary where the text invites (and yes, even compels) that we give exposition to the benefits of confession for the sake of the absolution. To begin with, pay special attention to the Sundays in Advent and Lent. The penitential seasons especially afford bountiful opportunities for the preacher to set before the congregation the blessings of confession and absolution. A midweek Lenten series on the penitential psalms or a series devoted to Psalm 51 alone would provide another opportunity to proclaim confession and absolution as the concrete expression of the life of repentance and faith.

Careful and continuous catechesis of confession and absolution is essential. Fortunately, the 1986 translation of the Small Catechism restores Luther's "A Short Form of Confession" to the Fifth Chief Part. Here the catechist will follow the path of the catechism itself in teaching both what confession is and how confession is to be made. This catechization ought to continue in other contexts within the congregation, such as youth retreats, adult Bible classes, or study sessions built into regularly scheduled meetings of the board of elders and/or the church council. Peter Bender's *Lutheran Catechesis* and Harold Senkbeil's *Dying to Live: The Power of Forgiveness* provide excellent and accessible material for such teaching. Jobst Schöne's short monograph *The Christological Character of the Office of the Ministry and the Royal Priesthood* lends itself well for use as a study document with the board of elders or other lay leaders in the congregation in helping them to understand God's ordering of the office of the ministry and the function of that office in delivering Christ's forgiveness.

In catechizing his people, the pastor will make it clear that confession and absolution is the ordinary means of pastoral care in the church. It need not be reserved only for extraordinary circumstances or situations. Therefore it is salutary to establish and announce set times when the pastor will be available for confession and absolution.

Setting aside a period of time each week for confession and absolution has several advantages. First, it says to the congregation that confession and absolution is indeed a natural part of the church's life and the ordinary means of pastoral care. Confession and absolution is not reserved for desperate cases or extraordinary expressions of sinfulness. Second, it provides an avenue for those who have never taken advantage of this gift to approach their pastor without awkwardness. Third, it reminds our people that confession and absolution is there for them. The weekly announcement in the church bulletin or on the sign in front of the building gently reminds parishioners of this gift. Knowing that confession and absolution is regularly offered often prompts people who do not come at the scheduled time to seek out confession and absolution at other times when they are pressed hard by their sin and tormented by Satan.

One of the issues that the pastor must face is the question of which rite to use. At this point, there are basically two choices. First, there is Luther's "Short Form of Confession" in the Small Catechism. The advantages of this form are its brevity and evangelical clarity. It quickly moves the penitent to the point of confessing his sins and receiving absolution. A disadvantage of this form is that Luther provides something of a sample confession that is helpful for teaching but cumbersome for the penitent who attempts to put it in his own words. Second, there is the order for individual confession and absolution in *Lutheran Worship*. Much longer than Luther's simple form, the LW rite is wordy and ends up with three confessions of sin. Somewhat problematic also is the placement of rubric 5 after the naming of the sins but before the absolution. This rubric states that "the pastor may then offer admonition and comfort from Holy Scripture." A more fitting place for such pastoral speaking would be after the absolution as to catechize the penitent on how to embrace the word of forgiveness and use that word against the assaults of the devil. Peter Bender offers an order of private confession and absolution adapted from the Small Catechism and *Lutheran Worship* that avoids the wordiness of the LW rite while providing a structure that is easily followed by the penitent.[12]

The rite itself ought to take place in the chancel when possible. If the pastor is engaged in pastoral conversation or counseling with someone in his study, and that conversation leads to a request for confession and absolution, I suggest that the pastor and penitent move from the study to the chancel. This, along with the fact that the pastor is vested in surplice or alb with stole, serves to indicate the churchly nature of confession and absolution.

A few things need to be said about the actual hearing of confession. The pastor best learns how to listen to confession by being a penitent himself under the care of a father confessor. Often—especially in the case of a first-time penitent—the pastor will need to guide the penitent gently in making confession. Here the Small Catechism provides direction:

> *What sins should we confess?*
> Before God we should plead guilty of all sins, even those we are unaware of, as we do in the Lord's Prayer; but before the pastor we should confess only those sins which we know and feel in our hearts.

> *Which are these?*
> Consider your place in life according to the Ten Commandments: Are you a father, mother, son, daughter, husband, wife, or worker? Have you been disobedient, unfaithful, or lazy? Have you been hot-tempered, rude, or quarrelsome? Have you hurt someone by your words or deeds? Have you stolen, been negligent, wasted anything, or done any harm?

The diagnostic key is self-examination in view of one's vocation or place in life according to the Ten Commandments. Here the pastor does not unduly probe or coerce; he is not a moral detective. Rather, he bids the penitent to stand before the mirror of God's law that the inbred sin is brought to light, to paraphrase the words of the hymn. Here the pastor will need to be attentive to the words of the penitent, guiding the penitent away from complaining about his sins to actually confessing them, naming them. When there is confusion or lack of clarity here, the pastor may need to press the penitent to identify which commandment of

God he or she has sinned against. Likewise, the pastor will be on guard lest the penitent slip into the Adamic mode of confessing the sins of another: "The woman you put here with me—she gave me some fruit from the tree, and I ate it" (Gen. 3:12 NIV).

The pastoral care of the penitent includes training the penitent to draw his life from God's merciful and gracious words of absolution. Absolution is God's verdict. In this word, he declares sinners righteous and gives life to the dead. I think it was Gerhard Forde who described absolution as the verdict of the last day spoken ahead of time. In the face of Satan's hellish accusations and his demonic invitation to doubt, the pastor teaches the penitent to cling to that word of absolution when confronted by the father of lies.

The pastor will also help his people understand what absolution does and does not accomplish. Absolution is that word of the crucified and living Lord in the mouth of his pastors that "is just as valid and certain, even in heaven, as if Christ our dear Lord dealt with us himself." Because it is the word of the Lord, it is truth. Heaven and earth may pass away, but this word from the mouth of the One who is the Way, the Truth, and the Life endures forever.

Absolution delivers an eschatological reality. It is not a quick fix for psychological disorders or difficulties. It does not follow that one will "feel better" after confession and absolution. The opposite may be true. The penitent may still need psychological counseling from those whose calling it is to provide this service in the kingdom of the left hand. The pastor will want to shepherd the penitent in such a way as to guard against false expectations regarding the effects of absolution so that he or she learns to hold fast to this word even under the crosses and afflictions which still must be borne in this life.

In the Large Catechism, Luther writes:

> Further, we believe that in this Christian church we have the forgiveness of sins, which is granted through the holy sacraments and absolution as well as through all the comforting words of the entire Gospel. Toward forgiveness is directed everything that is to be preached concerning the sacraments and, in short, the entire Gospel and all the duties of Christianity. Forgiveness is needed constantly, for although God's grace has been won by Christ, and holiness has been wrought by the Holy Spirit through God's Word in the unity of

the Christian church, yet because we are encumbered with our flesh we are never without sin.

Therefore everything in the Christian church is so ordered that we may daily obtain full forgiveness of sins through the Word and through signs appointed to comfort and revive our consciences as long as we live. (LC II, 54–55; Tappert, 417–418)

Do we really believe these words of the Large Catechism? Or do we, in fact, believe that everything in the Christian church is so ordered that other goals—numerical growth, healthy families, self-esteem, deepened spirituality, or whatever—may be achieved? How pastors and congregations view confession and absolution will, in large part, reveal what they understand not only about the church but also about the very heart of the gospel—the forgiveness of sins.

Notes

1 Carl Braaten, *Justification: The Article by Which the Church Stands or Falls* (Minneapolis: Fortress Press), 155.

2 E. Brooks Holifield. *A History of Pastoral Care in America: From Salvation to Self-Realization* (Nashville: Abingdon, 1983), 248.

3 Braaten, 158–159.

4 Paul Pruyser, *The Minister as Diagnostician* (Philadelphia: Westminster Press, 1976), 10.

5 William Willimon, *Worship as Pastoral Care* (Nashville: Abingdon Press, 1979), 39.

6 Ibid., 35.

7 Thomas Oden, *Agenda for Theology: Recovering Christian Roots* (New York: Harper and Row, 1979), 165.

8 David Wells, *No Place for Truth, or Whatever Happened to Evangelical Theology?* (Grand Rapids: Eerdmans, 1993), 11.

9 Wells, 246.

10 See Marsha Witten, *All Is Forgiven: The Secular Message in American Protestantism* (Princeton: Princeton University Press, 1993).

11 See the excellent treatment given by Gerhard Forde, *On Being a Theologian of the Cross: Reflections on Luther's Heidelberg Disputation, 1518* (Grand Rapids: Eerdmans, 1997).

12 Peter Bender, *Lutheran Catechesis* (Sussex, WI: Concordia Catechetical Academy, 1999), 217–220.

49

Law and Gospel in Confession and Absolution

8th International Luther Symposium

CONCORDIA SEMINARIO,

Sao Leopoldo, Brazil

4 July 2019

Writing in 1528, Martin Luther states: "I have a high regard for private confession, for here God's word and absolution are spoken privately and individually to each believer for the forgiveness of his sins, and as often as he desires it he may have recourse to it for this forgiveness, and also for comfort, counsel, and guidance. Thus it is a precious, useful thing for souls, as long as no one is driven to it with laws and commandments but sinners are left free to make use of it, each according to his own need" ("Confession Concerning Christ's Supper" AE 37:368). Two years later, Melanchthon echoes Luther in the *Apology*: "For we also retain confession especially on account of absolution which is the Word of God that the power of the keys proclaims to individuals by divine authority. Therefore it would be unconscionable to remove private absolution from the church. Moreover, those who despise private absolution know neither the forgiveness of sins nor the power of the keys" (AP XII:99–101, K-W, 204).

By the eve of the Reformation, the practice of private confession as it had developed out of Celtic monastic practice had acquired a central place in Roman Catholic piety even though its theological significance was not always clear. Every Christian who had reached the age of discretion to avail themselves of confession at least annually. Luther's own experiences as a penitent are well known as are the difficulties he encountered over the reliance on indulgences as he took his turn hearing the confessions of the town folk in Wittenberg. Others have significantly covered the historical aspect[1]; this paper will specifically address the practice of confession and absolution theologically in light of the distinction of God's law from His Gospel.

Luther and his 16th-century colleagues realized that without confession and absolution, sinners will attempt in one way or another to deal with their own sins, making matters worse as they end up in either arrogance or despair for the default mode of human existence is self-justification. We are apt at confessing the sins of others only to make ourselves look less culpable. We seek justification. Indeed, we crave it.

Justification is both a problem and a solution. Oswald Bayer has described human existence as forensically structured[2]. That is to say, that life demands justification. Listen to the way people respond when confronted with a failure. It is the language of self-defense, rationalization, or blaming. No human being wants to be wrong. Or listen to the eulogies delivered at the memorial rites for unbelievers. They are, more often than not, attempts to vocalize why the deceased person's life was worthwhile. They seek to justify his or her existence. If one is not justified by faith in Christ, one will seek justification elsewhere in attitude or action.

To confess your sin is to cease the futile attempt to self-justify. Rather it is to join with David in saying to God: "Against you, you only, have I sinned and done what is evil in your sight, so that you may be justified in your words and blameless in your judgment" (Psalm 51:4). In confession, the sinner acknowledges that God is right. It is to agree with God's verdict: Guilty.

But to speak of guilt requires some clarification today for another word has come to attach itself to guilt. So we speak of guilt feelings. Guilt is seen as the subjective reaction of the doer to the deed, i.e., how I feel about what I have done.[3] But this is not the case with the Scripture's use of the word guilt. In the Bible guilt has not so much to do with emotions as it does with what happens in a court-room when a judge declares the defendant "guilty." The criminal may or may not have reactions of remorse, regret, or shame. It doesn't matter. The verdict of the judge establishes the reality. God's word of law unerring establishes His judgment. There is no appeal.

To deny the verdict means that the truth is not in us says the Apostle John (see I John 1:8). But denial can never bring release. Only God's absolution can release from the accusation of the law and unlock the sinner from his sins. Lutheran theology is nothing if it is not real-istic![4] Like the Scriptures, Lutheran theology does not start with notions about human freedom and the potential (great or small) that human beings have. Theologies that start with assumptions about human freedom end up in bondage.[5] Lutheran theology begins with man's terrible bondage in sin and ends up with the glorious liberty of the Gospel. The bondage to sin is not a slight defect that can be cor-rected by appropriate self-discipline. Neither is it a sickness that can be cured by the appropriation of the medication of regular doses of God's grace. Sin is enmity with the Creator that carries with it God's verdict of guilt and a divinely-imposed death sentence. To be a sin-ner is to be held captive in death and condemnation. The distance between God and humanity is not the gap between infinity and the finite but between a Holy God who is judge and man who is the guilty defendant. Stanzas 2 and 3 of Luther's hymn, "Dear Christians, One and All Rejoice" captures the fatal predicament:

Fast bound in Satan's chains I lay;
Death brooded darkly o'er me.
Sin was my torment night and day;
In sin my mother bore me.
But daily deeper still I fell;
My life became a living hell,
So firmly sin possessed me.
My own good works all came to naught,
No grace or merit gaining;
Free will against God's judgment fought,
Dead to all good remaining.
My fears increased till sheer despair
Left only death to be my share;
The pangs of hell I suffered. (LSB, 556:2–3)

Confession is the acknowledgment of this reality. So in the rite of individual confession and absolution based on Luther's order, we pray: "I, a poor sinner, plead guilty before God of all my sins. I have lived as if God did not matter and as if I mattered most . . ." (LSB, 292). The sin is named not in an effort to "get it off my chest" but to acknowledge it before the Lord to whom no secrets are hid. Where sin is not confessed, it remains festering and corrosive, addicting the sinner to yet another go at self-justification. Confession admits defeat and so leaves the penitent open for a word that declares righteousness, a verdict which justifies. That word is called absolution. It is absolution alone, says Gerhard Forde, that is the answer to absolute claim of God who is inescapably present to the sinner.[6]

The focus in confession and absolution is not on the confession per se, but on the absolution.[7] Disconnected from the absolution, confession turns into just another effort to save ourselves. Then the old Adam begins to reckon that he is right with God because his confession was so completely sincere or deeply heartfelt. Or that he has been so pious and courageous to make individual confession a part of his regular spiritual discipline. In the medieval church, the requirement of no less than an annual trip to the confessional booth and the enumeration of specific sins had transformed confession into a spiritual torture chamber rather than an occasion for broken bones to be made glad in the Word from the Lord: "I forgive you all your sins." As Oswald Bayer has demonstrated, the absolution is no mere sign pointing to a forgiveness located elsewhere, but rather the word actually carries and delivers the forgiveness of sins:

> That the verbal sign itself is the matter itself, that presents not an absent but rather a present matter, that was Luther's great hermeneutical discovery, his reformatory discovery in the strict sense of the word. He made this discovery first of all in his investigation of the sacrament of penance (1518). That the sign itself is already the matter and event means in view of absolution that the sentence 'I absolve you of your sins' is not merely a declaratory judgment of what already is, thus presupposing an inner, proper absolution. The word of absolution is rather a verbal act, which creates a relationship—between God in whose name it is spoken, and the person to whom it is spoken.[8]

Confession and absolution are an exercise in the ministry of the law and the Gospel. Through the law, people are brought to know their sins and are crushed with the recognition of their condemning consequences *coram Deo*. The heart broken by the law can only acknowledge that God's verdict is on target. The knowledge of sin, says Luther in his 1532 lectures on Psalm 51, "means to feel and experience the intolerable burden of the wrath of God" (AE 12:310). Such a heart has no sure place to turn for peace and healing other than the promises of God, that a broken and contrite heart He will not despise (Psalm 51:17).

It is at this point that Luther filters the old practice of private confession through the sieve of the Gospel so that it could be reclaimed for the sake of terrified consciences. Thus Luther develops five major points in his "A Brief Exhortation to Confession" included in the *Large Catechism*:

> First, confession should be voluntary and free of papal tyranny. "No one needs to drive you to confession by commanding it" (LC-Confession 20, K-W, 478). Those who do not come to confession and absolution out of a sense of their own need can hardly be cajoled by legalistic demands to make a salutary use of this practice. Those who do not come willingly had best stay away: "Hereby we completely abolish the pope's tyranny, commandments, and coercion, for we have no need of them. For as I have said, we teach this: Let those who do not go to confession willingly and for the sake of the absolution just forget about it" (LC-Confession 21, K-W, 478). Luther's encouragement is evangelical. Disciples are urged to make us of confession for the sake of the great treasure that is individually and personally bestowed in the absolution. Our beggarly neediness not an ecclesiastical requirement should incite us to avail ourselves of confession: "Their own consciences would persuade Christians and make them so anxious that they would rejoice and act like poor, miserable beggars who hear that a rich gift of money or clothes is being given out at a certain place; they would hardly need a bailiff to drive or beat them but would run there as fast as they could so as not to miss the gift" (LC-Confession 23–24, K-W, 478–479).
>
> Second, the practice of confession ought to be free of the unreasonable and tortuous demand that the penitent be able to enumerate his sins. We are absolved for the sake of Christ's merit and on the

basis of His divine promise not on the completeness or comprehensiveness of our own confession. Luther realized that the canonical requirement to enumerate all one's sins led only to a burdened and even more deeply troubled conscience. "We are released from the torture of enumerating all sins in detail" (LC-Confession 4, K-W, 476). It is enough to name the sins we know.

Third, people should be taught how to use confession evangelically for the comfort of terrified consciences. Confession is not a good work that we perform but the occasion to hear Christ's words of pardon and learn how to apply them to my conscience disrupted by guilt and trembling in shame. The goal of confession is not an increase of virtue but of faith in the divine promise.

Fourth, Christian liberty ought not be used as an excuse for setting private confession aside. Luther complained that some had learned the art of Christian liberty too well: "Unfortunately, people have learned it only too well; they do whatever they please and take advantage of their freedom, acting as if they should not or need not go to confession anymore" (LC-Confession 5, K-W, 476). Christian freedom is not freedom from the Gospel and Luther sees the Absolution is purest Gospel. Refusal of the Gospel leaves one not in freedom but bondage.

Fifth, private confession stands with other forms of confession in the church. Luther does not separate private or individual confession from other forms of confession. We confess our sins daily in the Lord's Prayer: "Indeed, the entire Lord's Prayer is nothing else than such a confession. For what is our prayer but a confession that we neither have nor do what we ought and a plea for a joyful conscience?" (LC-Confession 9, K-W, 477). We confess our sins publically to our neighbors and before God. But in the Large Catechism, Luther is particularly focused on private confession which comes into play "when some particular issue weighs on us or attacks us, eating away at us until we have no peace nor find ourselves sufficiently strong in faith" (LC-Confession 13, K-W, 477). For it is here, that God has placed His words in a human mouth so that I may hear and know that my sins are forgiven before God in heaven.

These pastoral themes are reflected in Luther's short order of confession included in the *Small Catechism*. The insertion of a short order of confession between Holy Baptism and the Sacrament of the Altar was intended by Luther to catechize people in the evangelical use of confession and absolution. "Luther's discussion of confession, along with the shape of his liturgical rite, shows how he redefines its essence and practice so that it ceases to be a burden and instead becomes an instrument by which the Gospel is conveyed personally to an individual."[9] The insertion of a short order of confession between Holy Baptism and the Sacrament of the Altar is indicative of Luther's intention: "Individual confession and absolution is properly placed between Baptism and the Lord's Supper. It marks the point where the *significatio* of Baptism is made specific, the daily drowning of the old man when the guilt is disclosed in the presence of a Christian brother, as well as the daily breaking forth of the new man, empowered by the divine absolution; it is what prepares us for the Lord's Supper."[10] Anchored in the final section of Baptism, "What does such baptizing with water indicate?" Luther's treatment demonstrates that to confess one's sins is to return to Baptism in the confidence of God's promise to forgive. "The eschatological baptismal path for a Christian, to which confession and absolution returns us again and again, is and remains encompassed within and protected by God's faithfulness to His gracious promises."[11]

In this new version of an ancient rite, the pastor is not there as an ecclesiastical detective to flush out hidden transgressions or an inspector who must assure that standards of quality control are indiscriminately applied to penitential acts.[12] Neither is the pastor a therapist trafficking in slogans of affirmation, a ministry of presence (whatever that frightening term might mean!), or a coach to get you enabled for a sanctified life. No, the pastor is here as the ear and the voice of the Good Shepherd. His words of forgiveness are not his own, but the Lord who has sent him (see John 20:21–23). These words of Jesus authorize the pastor to speak Christ's own forgiveness in His name and in His stead. Thus Karl-Hermann Kandler writes, "This authorization fundamentally distinguishes confession and absolution from all other forms of therapy; they can surely uncover guilt and failure, but they cannot forgive."[13]

The ear of the pastor becomes the grave that forever conceals the corpse of sin. It is buried there, never to be disinterred. In fact, the pastor's ordination vow puts him under orders never to divulge the sins confessed to him. Never means never. Pastors learn to practice God's own forgetfulness of sins (see Psalm 103:9–14). Sins confessed to the pastor are sealed away in silence.

But the pastor's lips are not sealed. He has a verdict to announce on the basis of the death of the Righteous One for the unrighteous. Your sin is not loaded on your own shoulders. It is carried by the Lamb of God who takes away the sin of the world. He takes it to Calvary. There it was answered for in His own blood. His verdict is the absolution: "I forgive you all your sins in the name of the Father and the Son and the Holy Spirit." That is justification in faith in action. "Therefore, since we have been justified by faith, we have peace with God through our Lord Jesus Christ" (Romans 5:1). In the words of Kandler: "Confession and absolution are thus lived justification."[14]

In the Catechism's brief order for confession and absolution, Luther notes that the pastor will know of additional passages of Scripture to comfort and guide the penitent. Significantly, this comes after the absolution has been spoken, demonstrating that Christ's forgiveness is now the source of the new life. On the strength of the absolution, the pastor is able now to counsel the penitent with God's Word so as to guard the conscience and equip the penitent to fight against entanglement in temptation and further enslavement to sin.

The basis for the practice of individual confession and absolution is found in the Office of the Keys. The language of the Office of the Keys is taken from Matthew 16:13–19, where Jesus bestows "the keys of the kingdom" and Matthew 18:18, where He speaks of binding and loosing sins on earth which are at the same time bound and loosed in heaven. The Catechism echoes these pericopes in explaining the power of the keys but cites John 20:22–23 as the dominical basis for the forgiving and retaining of sins. This is a power that Christ gives to the whole church, but it is publicly exercised by His called servants as they "deal with us by His divine command." This divine forgiveness is not locked away in the secrecy of the heavenly chambers, and it is not to be sought for there. Rather God locates this celestial gift here on earth. In his sermon on John 20:19–31 from April 23, 1536, Luther puts these words in the mouth of Christ:

[But Christ says:] 'Do not gape toward heaven when you want remission of sins. Rather, you have it here below. If [you have] a pastor, or a neighbor in the case of need, there is no need to seek the Absolution from above, because this Absolution spoken on earth is Mine. Why? Because I have so instituted it, and My resurrection will effect it. Therefore, no one will accuse you, neither death nor the devil nor I Myself, when you have received this Absolution since it is God's own,' etc. It is true that God alone forgives sins, [but] how will I get to heaven? There is no need. Go to the pastor; in the case of need, tell your neighbor to recite the Absolution in the name of Jesus Christ. Then you have the Word; when they do it, Christ has done it. (AE 69:416)

The absolution, because it is Christ's word, is sure and certain.

It is only in the surety of sins forgiven that we can call God our Father with boldness and confidence.[15] Confession of sins speaks the truth about who we are and what we have done. The silence is broken, and the heart is laid bare before the omniscient Lord. Confession, as Luther envisioned, it does not leave the sinner with his sins to deal with them the best he or she can. Nor is the sinner left with the cruel and ultimately blasphemous advice of pop psychology, "you must learn to forgive yourself." Self-forgiveness is an exercise that embodies either despair or presumption as it causes the sinner to pretend that he or she is, in fact, God. God alone has the power to forgive sins. This He has done by His own suffering and death for the sins of the world. The forgiveness accomplished at Calvary, announced at Easter, is now contained in the words spoken by the Lord's servant, "your sins are forgiven you." It is that Word which opens the heart and unlocks the lips for prayer, praise, and thanksgiving, as Luther demonstrates in the final stanza of his hymnic paraphrase of Psalm 130:

Though great our sins, yet greater still
Is God's abundant favor;
His hand of mercy never will
Abandon us, nor waver.
Our shepherd good and true is He;
Who will at last His Israel free
From all their sin and sorrow. (LSB, 607:5)

Notes

1 For historical background, I would particularly recommend the work of Ronald K. Riggers, "Penance and Indulgences" in *Martin Luther in Context* ed. David M. Whitford (Cambridge: Cambridge University Press, 2018), 85–91; "Luther's Reformation of Private Confession" *Lutheran Quarterly* (Autumn 2005), 312–331; *The Reformation of the Keys: Confession, Conscience, and Authority in Sixteenth Century Germany* (Cambridge, MA.: Harvard University Press, 2004); "Penance, Confession, Forgiveness, and Reconciliation" in *The Oxford Encyclopedia of Martin Luther* (Vol. III) ed Derek R. Nelson and Paul R. Hinlicky (Oxford: Oxford University Press, 2017), 63–74; "Confession (Private) and the Confessional" in *Dictionary of Luther and the Lutheran Traditions* ed. Timothy J. Wengert (Grand Rapids: Baker Academic, 2017), 157–159; "Private Confession and the German Reformation" in *Repentance in Christian Theology*, ed. Mark J. Boda and Gordon T. Smith (Collegeville: Liturgical Press, 2006), 189–207. Also helpful is Berndt Hamm, "The Ninety-Five Theses: A Reformation Text in the Context of Luther's Early Theology of Repentance" in *The Early Luther: Stages in a Reformation Reorientation* trans. Martin J. Lohrmann (Grand Rapids: Eerdmans, 2014), 85–109.

2 See Oswald Bayer, *Living by Faith: Justification and Sanctification*, trans. G. Bromiley (Grand Rapids: Eerdmans Publishing Company, 2003), 1–9.

3 On this point see the discussion of Werner Elert, *The Christian Ethos*, trans. Carl Schindler (Philadelphia: Fortress Press, 1957), 163–173. Elert traces the subjective understanding of guilt to F. Schleiermacher.

4 Here note the German New Testament exegete, Udo Schnelle's comment on Pauline anthropology: "his view of human beings is not merely pessimistic, but realistic" in *Theology of the New Testament* translated by M. Eugene Boring (Grand Rapids: Baker Academic Press, 2009), 319.

5 See Gerhard Forde, *The Captivation of the Will* (Grand Rapids: Eerdmans Publishing Company, 2005), 21.

6 Gerhard Forde, "Absolution: Systematic Considerations" in *The Preached God: Proclamation in Word and Sacrament*, edited by Mark C. Mattes and Steven Paulson (Grand Rapids: Eerdmans Publishing Company, 2007), 153.

7 Here note again the Apology to the Augsburg Confession: "For we also retain confession especially on account of the absolution, which is the Word of God that the power of the keys proclaim to individuals by divine authority. Therefore it would be unconscionable to remove private absolution from the church. Moreover, those who despise private absolution know neither the forgiveness of sins nor the power of the keys" (AP XII:99–101, K-W, 204).

8 Oswald Bayer, "Martin Luther" in *The Reformation Theologians* edited by Carter Lindberg (Blackwell, 2002), 54. Also note Löhe: "God's Word does not teeter-totter; what He uttered here on earth is true for the Last Day; His

absolution, which is a whispered breath here; will be a mighty absolution there, against which the gates of hell shall not prevail" cited in Albrecht Peters, *Commentary on Luther's Catechisms: Confession and Absolution*, trans. Thomas Trapp (St. Louis: Concordia Publishing House, 2013), 43.

9 Charles Arand, *That I May Be His Own: An Overview of Luther's Catechisms* (St. Louis: Concordia Publishing House, 2000), 169.

10 Peters V, 29.

11 Peters V, 74.

12 Here see Holsten Fagerberg: "Since in confession the pastor appears not as judge but God's voice of forgiveness, he need not investigate the sinner. Absolution covers all sins unconditionally, even those not acknowledged in confession"—*A New Look at the Lutheran Confessions 1529–1537*, trans. Gene J. Lund (Saint Louis: Concordia Publishing House, 1972), 223–224. Also see the Apology: "For Christ gave the command to remit sins; ministers administer this command. They do not have a command to investigate secrets. This can be understood from the fact that they remit sins without restriction, sins that not even we ourselves, to whom they are remitted, remember" (AP XII:105, K-W, 204).

13 Karl Hermann-Kandler, "Luther and Lutherans on Confession, 'the Forgotten Sacrament'" *Lutheran Quarterly* 31 (2017), 50–63.

14 Kandler, "Luther and the Lutherans on Confession, 'the Forgotten Sacrament,'" 53.

15 Here note the words of Werner Klän: ". . . forgiveness is the epitome of the gospel. It is a complete gift, the conferring of wholeness that is lacking in our existence. It is an equalization of a deficit that makes our life incomplete in the eyes of God when compared to the measure of his own completeness, with which we ought to comply. In the end, it is all about escape from eternal death, which threatens us as a consequence of God's justified wrath"—"The 'Third Sacrament:' Confession and Repentance in the Confessions of the Lutheran Church" *Logia* (Holy Trinity, 2011), 9.

50

Confession and Absolution

PREVIOUSLY PUBLISHED IN THE SPRING 2016 ISSUE OF LUTHERAN QUARTERLY, PP. 28-42

> For we also retain confession, especially on account of absolution, which is the Word of God that the power of the keys proclaims to individuals by divine authority. Therefore it would be unconscionable to remove private absolution from the church. Moreover, those who despise private absolution know neither the forgiveness of sins nor the power of the keys.[1]

Nowhere do systematic theology, and pastoral theology so unmistakably intersect as in confession and absolution. In the act of confession, sin is not theoretically defined but named *coram deo*, and in the absolution, there is no speculative inquiry into the nature of the forgiveness of sins. Instead, forgiveness is delivered in a powerful word granted by the authority of the crucified and risen Christ. This is no mere discussion *about* Christ and his reconciling work. Rather, it is the preaching of the healing Christ into the ears of those broken by sin. Systematically, as Gerhard Forde puts it, "The only solution to the problem of the absolute is actual absolution."[2]

It is the absolution that is the compass for Lutheran theology. Martin Luther radically reoriented a long tradition that gave theological priority to the act of confession. For the reformer, confession embraces the recognition and naming of sins and the word of God's forgiveness for the sake of Christ, the absolution. In contrast to the

Roman Catholic practice,[3] Luther shifted the emphasis from the act of confession to the speaking of the word of divine forgiveness. As Werner Klän observes, "Luther's concept of confession and repentance is marked by a dual structure consisting of human and divine actions, wherein the divine action carries the whole weight."[4]

Confession and Absolution and the Distinction of the Law from the Gospel

The human action of confession was confined to the recognition and naming of sins, which were known and felt in the conscience while acknowledging the totality of one's sinfulness. Luther was adamant that troubled Christians not be burdened with the Roman demand for the enumeration of every sin. Such an unachievable rubric would press broken sinners deeper into uncertainty and despair and subvert the evangelical comfort of the absolution. "Up to now, as we all know from experience, there has been no law quite so oppressive as that which forced everyone to make confession on the pain of the gravest moral sin. Moreover, it so greatly burdened and tortured consciences with the enumeration of all kinds of sin that no one was able to confess purely enough."[5] Luther's pastoral concern is echoed in Articles XI and XXV of the *Augsburg Confession*, which call for the retention of private absolution without the necessary enumeration of every sin; both Articles XI and XXV cite Psalm 19:12 as the biblical basis for the Reformation practice.

Confession and absolution are an exercise in the ministry of the law and the Gospel. Through the law, people are brought to know their sins before God and so are crushed with the recognition of their condemning consequences. The heart broken by the law can only acknowledge that God's verdict is true. This knowledge of sin, Luther says in his lectures on Psalm 51 (1532), "means to feel and to experience the intolerable burden of the wrath of God."[6] Such a heart has nowhere to turn except the promise of God: "a broken and contrite heart, O God, you will not despise" (Psalm 51:17). To this broken heart, incapable of mending itself, the absolution is spoken as the purest and most concentrated form of the Gospel: "I forgive you your sins."

Confession makes of us beggars before God. The divine wisdom of the Gospel is that God is merciful to sinners for the sake of

Christ Jesus. To confess one's sins is to make supplication to God for mercy. To pray for mercy as David does in Psalm 51 is not to trust in oneself or works. Luther says, "God does not want the prayer of a sinner who does not feel his sins, because he neither understands nor wants what he is praying for."[7] Such praying, Luther contends, is to be compared to a beggar who cries out for alms and, when offered money, begins to brag of his riches.

> Thus mercy is our whole life even until death; yet Christians yield obedience to the Law, but imperfect obedience because of the sin dwelling in us. For this reason let us learn to extend the word "Have mercy" not only to our actual sins but to all the blessings of God as well: that we are righteous by the merit of another; that we have God as our Father; that God the Father loves sinners who feel their sins—in short, that all our life is by mercy because all our life is sin and cannot be set against the judgment and wrath of God.[8]

David is like a beggar; he asks for forgiveness for no other reason than that he is a sinner.

To confess sin is to cease the futile attempt to self-justify. Indeed, it is to join with David in saying to God: "Against you, you only, have I sinned and done what is evil in your sight, so that you may be justified in your words and blameless in your judgment" (Psalm 51:4). In confession, the sinner acknowledges that God is right. It is to agree with God's verdict: guilty. "When sins are thus revealed by the Word, two different kinds of men manifest themselves. One kind justifies God and, by a humble confession, agrees to His denunciation of sin; the other kind condemns God and calls Him a liar when He denounces sin."[9] Confession of sin is the opposite of self-justification; it is the justification of God.

The Theological Location of Confession and Absolution

It is this theology of confession and absolution which undergirds Luther's pastoral practice embodied in the *Small Catechism*. The insertion of a short order of confession between Holy Baptism and the Sacrament of the Altar was intended by Luther to catechize people in the evangelical use of confession and absolution. "Individual confession and absolution is properly placed between Baptism and the Lord's Supper. It marks the point where the *signifactio* of Baptism is made specific, the daily drowning of the old man when the guilt is disclosed in the presence of a Christian brother, as well as the daily breaking forth of the new man, empowered by the divine absolution; it is what prepares us for the Lord's Supper."[10] Anchored in the final section on Baptism ("What does such baptizing with water indicate?"), Luther's treatment demonstrates that to confess one's sins is to return to Baptism in the confidence of God's promise to forgive. "The eschatological baptismal path for a Christian, to which confession and absolution returns us again and again, is and remains encompassed within and protected by God's faithfulness to His gracious promises."[11]

The original form of the Catechism did not contain material on confession or the Office of the Keys. The brief order for confession was added in June 1529. The questions were added to the brief order in 1531. The Office of the Keys was derived from the work of Andreas Osiander (1498–1552) and included in editions of the Catechism already in Luther's lifetime.[12]

Confession of sins before God, from whom no secrets are hid, is inclusive as "we should plead guilty of all sins even as we do in the Lord's Prayer." This acknowledgment of sin recognizes its totality and admits no righteousness before God. But before the pastor, Luther asserts, "we should confess only those sins we know and feel in our hearts." These sins are brought to light in the self-examination, which takes stock of one's life as it is evaluated from the perspective of the intersection of God's law (Ten Commandments) and one's "place in life," that is, one's calling.[13] Confession is not a meritorious act which becomes the cause of forgiveness. Rather, "the purpose of confession is to disclose sin in order that it may be forgiven, not to glorify our contrition."[14]

Luther saw confession in light of the words of Psalm 32:3, "For when I kept silent, my bones wasted away through my groaning all day long." The disclosure of sin brings it to light, thus depriving its cancerous capacity to gnaw away at the life of the believer and hold him or her within its lethal grasp. "Bringing it out into the open deprives sin of its power."[15] Left unconfessed, sin festers, leading to denial and suppression. This dynamic is broken as sin is laid out before the confessor, where it can be directly addressed by God's absolution. Confession without absolution would be devoid of Christ and end in either pride or despair, both of which are damning.

Therefore Luther moves quickly from the act of confession to the absolution, the word of forgiveness on the lips of the pastor, which is God's own word. Luther's aim is that the penitent would know and trust the evangelical word of absolution. At this stage in the Catechism, Luther has little to say about confession, simply "that we are to confess our sins." Instead, he weighs in on the absolution, what it is, and how we are to receive it. If the law brings about despair, then the Gospel spoken in the absolution delivers comfort, which, as Berndt Hamm points out, is for Luther, a "comforted despair."[16]

Where the accent is on the act of confession, questions are immediately introduced. Was it comprehensive enough to name all sins? Was it sincerely made? Was it motivated out of a pure love of God? And as a result, the conscience is left unprotected from the monster of uncertainty.[17] One can then never have the assurance that he or she is indeed forgiven by God.[18] For Luther, the only certainty is in the word and work of God, which is going on in the words spoken by the pastor where "we receive absolution, that is, forgiveness from the pastor as from God Himself." Here God would graciously interfere with our doubting so that we firmly believe that by the absolution, we know "our sins are forgiven before God in heaven." It is in this sense that "private confession exists for the sake of the certainty of salvation."[19]

No Conditional Absolution

There is nothing conditional about the absolution; it is the trustworthy verdict of the Triune God spoken by the pastor to be received by faith. "There is no such thing as a hypothetical absolution."[20] As Oswald Bayer has demonstrated, the absolution is no mere sign pointing to a forgiveness located elsewhere, but rather the word actually carries and bestows the forgiveness of sins:

> That the verbal sign itself is the matter itself, that it presents not an absent but rather a present matter, that was Luther's great hermeneutical discovery, his reformatory discovery in the strict sense of the

word. He made this discovery first of all in his investigation of the
sacrament of penance (1518). That the sign itself is already the matter and event itself means in view of absolution that the sentence "I
absolve you of your sins" is not merely a declaratory judgment of what
already is, thus presupposing an inner, proper absolution. The word
of absolution is rather a verbal act, which creates a relationship—
between God in whose name it is spoken, and the person to whom it
is spoken.[21]

After the questions on confession, Luther inserts a brief order
so that Christians might actually make an evangelical use of confession. "Luther's discussion of confession, along with the shape of his
liturgical rite, shows how he redefines its essence and practice so that
it ceases to be a burden and instead becomes an instrument by which
the Gospel is conveyed personally to an individual."[22] Luther's rite
is simple and straightforward. It opens not with an invitation from
the pastor but with the plea of the penitent imploring the confessor
to hear his or her confession and "pronounce forgiveness in order to
fulfill God's will." Luther then provides what might be best described
as a template or model for the penitent to use in confessing his or her
sins. After the admission of guilt "before God of all sins," there is the
particular confession of sins according to one's specific station in life.
Luther pastorally notes that if a person does not find him or herself
burdened with particular sins, none should be invented, nor should
the penitent scrutinize the conscience in order to search them out,
going beyond what is revealed in the Decalogue. Neither should the
pastor attempt to work as a detective to ferret out offenses. A general
confession would be preferable to an invented one.

Immediately after the confession is spoken, the pastor blesses
the penitent: "God be merciful to you and strengthen your faith."
This is followed by the confessional question posed toward the absolution: "Do you believe that my forgiveness is God's forgiveness?"
and the anticipated response, "Yes, dear confessor." Then the pastor
speaks the absolution. Here the pastor "is not the judge of souls, but
the comforter of the conscience that God himself has stricken."[23] The
pastor does not hold the office of judge or executioner but is instead
called to be Christ's voice of reconciliation to bestow the Lord's own
verdict of mercy in the forgiveness of sins to those who repent. It is

not the job of the pastor to weigh sins or to distinguish what is sinful from what is not. The minister's ears are there to receive the confession. The pastor's mouth is there to pronounce Christ's forgiveness. "Not determining sins, but comforting the sinner is the real art and function of the confessor."[24]

Absolution as Pastoral Care

If the mouth of the pastor is there as the voice of Christ, then the pastor's ear is the grave in which sin is forever buried. The confessional seal is, therefore, a theological necessity. To break this seal is not only a matter of personal betrayal; it also calls into question the truthfulness of the absolution itself.[25] If God has removed the sin as far as the "the east is from the west" (Psalm 103:12), the minister who hears the confession is forbidden from exposing it to the world in any way.

The absolution then becomes the basis for pastoral counsel and admonition as Luther notes that the confessor will know additional texts from Holy Scripture to use in consoling those with burdened consciences who are distressed and sorrowful. Such counsel does not supplement the absolution as though the forgiving word of Christ needed an additive of amendment of life to make it complete. Instead, the absolution is the only sure foundation for genuine care of consciences. Werner Klän rightly says, "Therefore, forgiveness is the epitome of the gospel. It is a complete gift, the conferring of a wholeness that is lacking in our existence. It is an equalization of a deficit that makes our life incomplete in the eyes of God when compared to the measure of his own completeness, with which we ought to comply. In the end, it is all about escape from eternal death, which threatens us as a consequence of God's justified wrath."[26] The absolution received by faith alone, that is, in the reliance that Jesus' verdict of forgiveness is trustworthy and sufficient, is now the context in which ongoing pastoral care can flourish.[27] As Jonathan Trigg states, "Faith is not certain of itself but attends to God's command and promise, and ultimately to Christ himself."[28] The absolution gives faith its divine certainty.

The basis for the practice of individual confession and absolution is found in the Office of the Keys. The language of the Office of the Keys is taken from Matthew 16:13–19, where Jesus bestows "the keys of the kingdom" and Matthew 18:18, where he speaks of bind-ing and loosing sins on earth which are at the same time bound and loosed in heaven. The Catechism echoes these pericopes in explain-ing the power of the keys but cites John 20:22–23 as the domini-cal basis for the forgiving and retaining of sins. This is a power that Christ gives to the whole church, but it is publicly exercised by his called servants as they "deal with us by His divine command." This divine forgiveness is not locked away in the secrecy of the heav-enly chambers, and it is not to be sought there. Rather, God locates this celestial gift here on earth. In his sermon on John 20:19–31 from April 23, 1536, Luther puts these words in the mouth of Christ:

> [But Christ says:] "Do not gape toward heaven when you want remis-sion of sins. Rather, you have it here below. If [you have] a pastor, or a neighbor in the case of need, there is no need to seek the Absolution from above, because this Absolution is spoken on earth is Mine. Why? Because I have so instituted it, and My resurrection will effect it. Therefore, no one will accuse you, neither death or the devil nor I Myself, when you have received this Absolution, since it is God's own," etc. It is true that God alone forgives sins, [but] how will I get to heaven? There is no need. Go to the pastor; in the case of need, tell your neighbor to recite the Absolution in the name of Jesus Christ. Then you have the Word; when they do it, Christ has done it.[29]

The absolution is trustworthy and reliable because it is Christ's word and his word is sure and certain.

Absolution: The Consolation of Justification by Faith Alone

Luther certainly did not want to jettison the practice of individual confession but instead to filter it through the evangelical sieve of jus-tification by grace alone through faith alone so that, purified from its Roman abuses, it might be restored as a means of consolation for those who were terrified by their sin. In the *Smalcald Articles*, Luther reflects this consolatory orientation present in the Catechism: "Because absolution or the power of the keys is also a comfort and help against sin and a bad conscience and was instituted by Christ in the gospel, confession, or absolution, should by no means be allowed to fall into disuse in the church—especially for the sake of weak consciences and for the wild young people, so that they may be examined and instructed in Christian teaching."[30] Ronald Rittgers observes:

> Luther and his early followers loathed the late-medieval version of private confession. However, it is important that we understand the source of their animosity. Luther and his fellow reformers attacked confession not because they opposed the practice as such, but because they believed it had been corrupted. They saw in private confession—in the individual application of the Word to the believer—the most effective way of preaching the Gospel to troubled souls.[31]

This is demonstrated in Luther's "A Brief Exhortation to Confession," which he appended to the 1529 edition of the *Large Catechism*.

In this exhortation, reworked from a 1529 Palm Sunday sermon, Luther argues that confession should not be set aside in the name of Christian freedom. This would be an abuse of liberty that separates the Christian from the very word, which brings freedom from sin, namely, the absolution.[32] Instead, burdened consciences should not be tortured with the unreasonable demand to enumerate all their offenses, but name only those sins which they know and feel. Individual confession rightly takes its place alongside other forms of confession, such as is made when praying the Lord's Prayer, which Luther sees as a "public, daily, and necessary confession."[33] Luther is adamant in his refusal to make individual confession a legal requirement since this would make of the evangelical gift an occasion for coercion and hypocrisy. Instead, Luther urges that "we teach what a wonderful, precious, and comforting thing confession is, and we urge that such a precious blessing should not be despised, especially when we consider our great need."[34] Confession should not be a tool of torture but a means of relief for broken sinners.

In confession and absolution, justification by faith alone is set into action.[35] Justification is both a problem and solution. Oswald Bayer has described human existence as forensically structured.[36] That is to say, life demands justification. Listen to the way people respond when confronted with a failure. It is the language of self-defense, rationalization, or blaming. No human being wants to be wrong. Or listen to the eulogies delivered at the memorial rites for unbelievers. They are, more often than not, attempts to vocalize why the deceased person's life was worthwhile. They seek to justify his or her existence. If one is not justified by faith in Christ, one will seek justification elsewhere in attitude or action. Self-justification, as we have seen, is the confirmation of guilt.

But to speak of guilt requires some clarification today since another word has been attached to that of guilt: guilt *feelings*. Guilt is seen as the subjective reaction of the doer to the deed, that is, how I feel about what I have done.[37] But this is not the case with the Scripture's use of the word guilt. In the Bible, guilt has not so much to do with subjective emotions but instead with a more objective scenario: a courtroom when a judge declares the defendant "guilty." The criminal may or may not have reactions of remorse, regret, or shame. It does not matter. The verdict of the judge establishes the reality. God's word of law unerringly establishes His judgment. There is no appeal.

To deny the verdict means that the truth "is not in us," as the Apostle wrote in I John 1:8. But denial can never bring release. Only God's absolution can release sinners from the accusation of the law and liberate them from their sins. Lutheran theology is nothing if it is not realistic![38] Like the Scriptures, Lutheran theology does not start with notions about human freedom and the potential (great or small) that humans have. Theologies that start with assumptions about human freedom end up in bondage.[39] Lutheran theology begins with a person's bondage in sin and ends up with the glorious liberty of the Gospel. The bondage to sin is not a slight defect that can be corrected by appropriate self-discipline. Neither is it a sickness that can be cured by the appropriation of regular doses of the medication of God's grace. Sin is enmity with the Creator that carries with it God's verdict of guilt and a divinely-imposed death sentence. To be a sinner is to be held captive in death and condemnation. The distance between God and humanity is not the gap between infinity and the finite but between a Holy God who is judge and the human being who is the guilty defendant.

Confession is the acknowledgment of this reality. So in one contemporary Lutheran rite of individual confession and absolution, the penitent prays: "I, a poor sinner, plead guilty before God of all my sins. I have lived as if God did not matter, and as if I mattered most. . . ."[40]

Confession and Absolution: Therapeutic or Eschatological?

The sin is named not in an effort to "get it off my chest" but instead to acknowledge it before the Lord to whom no secrets are hid. Where sin is not confessed, it remains festering and corrosive, addicting the sinner to yet another go at self-justification. Confession admits defeat and so leaves the penitent open for a word that declares righteousness, a verdict which justifies. That word is called absolution. It is absolution alone, says Gerhard Forde, that is the answer to absolute claim of God who is inescapably present to the sinner.[41]

The focus in confession and absolution is not on the confession per se, but on the absolution. Disconnected from the absolution, confession turns into just another effort to save ourselves. Then the old Adam begins to reckon that he is right with God because his confession was so completely sincere or deeply heartfelt. Or the old Eve begins to boast that she has been so pious and courageous to make individual confession a part of her regular spiritual discipline. In the medieval church, the requirement of no less than an annual trip to the confessional booth and the enumeration of specific sins had transformed confession into a spiritual torture chamber rather than an occasion for broken bones to be made glad in the Word from the Lord: "I forgive you all your sins."

All this is to say that individual confession and absolution is much more than a therapeutic technique in a pastoral counselor's tool kit. Likewise, it is no exercise in self-forgiveness, for this would establish a sinner as his or her own god.[42] Rather, the absolution is to be understood eschatologically. To paraphrase Gerhard Forde's language, it is the verdict of the Last Day slipping out ahead of time. In the absolution, the voice of the law is silenced, and peace with God is given in this word of promise, which actually bestows what it declares. "For it is not the voice or word of the person speaking it, but it is the Word of God, who forgives sin. For it is spoken in God's stead and by God's command . . . It is also taught how God requires us to believe this absolution as much as if it were God's voicing resounding from heaven and that we should joyfully find comfort in the absolution, knowing that through such faith we obtain forgiveness of sin."[43]

Notes

1   *The Book of Concord: The Confessions of the Evangelical Lutheran Church*, trans. Robert Kolb and Timothy Wengert (Minneapolis: Fortress Press, 2000), 204. *Apology* XII: 99–101. All citations from *The Book of Concord* are taken from this version and are hereafter abbreviated as BC. The author wishes to thank Pastor Jacob Corzine for his helpful comments on an earlier draft of this essay.

2   Gerhard Forde, "Absolution: Systematic Considerations," in *The Preached God: Proclamation in Word and Sacrament*, ed. Mark C. Mattes and Steven D. Paulson (Grand Rapids: Eerdmans, 2007), 152. Original italics.

3   See David N. Power, "Sacrament and Order of Penance and Reconciliation" in *Systematic Theology: Roman Catholic Perspectives*, ed. Francis Schüssler Fiorenza and John P. Galvin (Minneapolis: Fortress Press, 2011), 543–558. Powers notes the complexity of the relationship between penance and sacramental absolution in medieval theology but concludes that, "The sequence of contrition, confession, absolution, and satisfaction was the one presumed in the decree on the sacrament promulgated by the Council of Trent" (553). Robert Jenson's treatment of "penance" under the locus of "The Return to Baptism" in *Christian Dogmatics* places more emphasis on the liturgical and ecumenical implications of penitential practices than on the evangelical consolation of the absolution. See *Christian Dogmatics* Vol. II, ed. Carl Braaten and Robert Jenson (Minneapolis: Fortress Press, 1984), 368–375.

4   Werner Klän, "The 'Third Sacrament' Confession and Repentance in the Lutheran Church," *Logia* XX: 3 (Holy Trinity 2011), 5. Also see Luther in the *Large Catechism*: "Note, then, as I have often said, that confession consists of two parts. The first is our work and act, when I lament my sin and desire comfort and restoration for my soul. The second is the work that God does, when he absolves me of my sins through the Word placed on the lips of another person. This is the surpassingly grand and noble thing that makes confession so wonderful and comforting." "A Brief Exhortation to Confession": 15, BC, 478.

5   Large Catechism, "A Brief Exhortation to Confession" 1, BC, 477.

6   LW 12:310.

7   LW 12:315.

8   LW 12:321.

9   LW 12:341.

10 Albrecht Peters, *Commentary on Luther's Catechisms: Confession and Christian Life*, trans. Thomas H. Trapp (Saint Louis: Concordia, 2013), 29.

11 Peters, *Confession and Christian Life*, 74.

12 Here see Robert Hinckley, "Andreas Osiander and the Fifth Chief Part," *Logia* X:4 (Reformation 2001), 37–42. Hinckley notes "Osiander's explanation of the office of the keys had great impact upon the catechisms of his time, and is responsible for establishing the long-standing tradition among Lutheran catechisms concerning the teaching. The addition of John 20 and Osiander's 'office of the keys' to confession and absolution created a fifth chief part of in the Small Catechism, so that the Sacrament of the Altar became the sixth" (38). For more on this history, see Ronald K. Ritggers, *The Reformation of the Keys: Confession, Conscience, and Authority in Sixteenth-Century Germany* (Cambridge: Harvard University Press, 2004).

13 Here note Peters: "Our confession before God is to be comprehensive and complete, but it is to concentrate on specific offenses when it is uttered before human beings. Luther brings this into awareness by linking the Old Testament Decalogue with the New Testament Household Responsibilities, which demarcate our 'estate,' our God-ordained standing within the coordinated system that exists among human beings." *Confession and Christian Life*, 9.

14 Herbert Girgensohn, *Teaching Luther's Catechism*, Vol. II, trans. John Doberstein (Philadelphia: Fortress Press, 1960), 77. Helpful here is "Preparation for Confession and Absolution According to the Ten Commandments" in *A Treasury of Daily Prayer* ed. Scot Kinnaman (Saint Louis: Concordia, 2008), 1460–1462.

15 Girgensohn, *Teaching Luther's Catechism*, Vol. II, 69. Also Wilfried Härle: "The spoken confession of sins (*confessio oris*) is the first decisive step towards stripping sin of its power. That this step should be possible—and not just an act of despairing self-condemnation–is only conceivable within the context of the possibility of forgiveness, or of a forgiveness that has already been experienced." *Outline of Christian Doctrine: An Evangelical Dogmatics*, trans. Ruth Yule and Nicholas Sagovsky (Grand Rapids: Eerdmans, 2015), 464.

16 Berndt Hamm, *The Early Luther: Stages in Reformation Reorientation*, trans. Martin J. Lohrmann (Grand Rapids: Eerdmans, 2014), 131.

17 Note Luther's comments in the Galatians lectures (1535): "For anyone who has doubts about the will of God toward him and who does not believe for a certainty that he is in a state of grace cannot believe that he has forgiveness of sins, that God cares about him, or that he can be saved." LW 26:377.

18 Such was the case, Peters argues, in the Roman Church: "The pressure that had been placed heretofore on the works of the penitent made divine forgiveness dependent upon our having arrived at a sufficient level of sorrow, pushing the anguished soul thereby either into doubt or deluding it into false confidence," Peters, *Confession and the Christian Life*, 11.

19 Girgensohn, *Teaching Luther's Catechism* Vol. II, 67. In *Worship as Repentance: Lutheran Liturgical Traditions and Catholic Consensus* (Grand Rapids: Eerdmans, 2012), Walter Sundberg's aim is to re-establish the place of confession in the Divine Service with a formula of absolution that embodies both the loosing and binding key. Unfortunately his solution renders the absolution conditional in such a way that the terrified conscience is not provided with the certainty which faith alone grasps. Gerhard Forde's essay, quoted above (see note 2, "Absolution: Systematic Considerations"), is critical of the liturgical shift from the forgiveness of sins to a celebration which is a confusion of law and gospel. But Forde's solution is not to make the absolution conditional which would undercut faith in the promise of Christ. Girgensohn observes that, "A conditional absolution sends a person into the hell of doubt and despair. This is actually to deliver him over to the mercy of the Adversary." Girgensohn, *Teaching Luther's Catechism*, Vol. II: 86.

20 Girgensohn, *Teaching Luther's Catechism*, Vol. II, 80.

21 Oswald Bayer, "Martin Luther" in *The Reformation Theologians* edited by Carter Lindberg (Oxford: Blackwell, 2002), 54. Also Wilhelm Löhe: "God's Word does not teeter-totter; what He uttered here on earth is true for the Last Day; His absolution, which is a whispered breath here; will be a mighty absolution there, against which the gates of hell shall not prevail." Cited in Peters, *Confession and Christian Life*, 43.

22 Charles Arand, *That I May be His Own: An Overview of Luther's Catechisms* (Saint Louis: Concordia Publishing House, 2000), 169.

23 Peters, *Confession and Christian Life*, 79. Note Luther's language in a house postil on John 20:19–31 from April 16, 1531: "For we should beware of mixing the two [governments] and tossing them together, as the pope and his bishops have done, who have used the spiritual government in such a way that they have become worldly lords, and emperors and kings have had to bow before them. This was not Christ's mandate to His disciples, and He did not send them forth for secular government. Rather he committed to them the preaching office, and with it government over sin, so the proper definition of the office of preaching is this: that one should preach the Gospel of Christ and forgive the sins of the crushed, fearful consciences, but retain those of the impenitent and secure, and bind them." LW 69:383.

24 Edmund Schlink, *The Theology of the Lutheran Confessions*, trans. Herbert J.A. Bouman and Paul F. Koehneke (Philadelphia: Fortress Press, 1961), 139.

25 For this reason the ordination vow in the *Lutheran Service Book Agenda* (LCMS) puts this obligation on the candidate: ". . . will you promise never to divulge sins confessed to you?" *Lutheran Service Book Agenda* (Saint Louis: Concordia Publishing House, 2006), 166. Here also see John T. Pless, "Theses on the Seal of Confession," *Logia* XX:3 (Holy Trinity 2011), 54–55 and "The Seal of Confession" in Girgensohn II:82–84 where he makes the point that

legal authority cannot override ecclesiastical authority: "Fundamentally, the whole relationship of the confessor and the member of the church should be hermetically sealed against any intervention on the part of the state. The very worst kind of intervention on the part of the state in the life of the church occurs when the state compels the revelation of secrets learned in confession or makes spies of its ministers" (84).

26 Klän, "The 'Third Sacrament': Confession and Repentance in the Confessions of the Lutheran Church," 9.

27 This was an insight accented by Wilhelm Löhe (1808–1872), who was a leading proponent of the restoration of private confession and absolution in his day. See Wilhelm Löhe, *The Pastor*, trans. Wolf Knappe and Charles Schaum (Saint Louis: Concordia, 2015), 309–320.

28 Jonathan Trigg, "Luther on Baptism and Penance" in *The Oxford Handbook of Martin Luther's Theology*, ed. Robert Kolb, Irene Dingel, and L'ubomír Batka (Oxford: Oxford University Press, 2014), 316.

29 LW 69:416.

30 SA III, 8: 1, BC, 321.

31 Ronald K. Rittgers, "Private Confession in the German Reformation" in *Repentance in Christian Theology*, ed. Mark J. Boda and Gordon T. Smith (Collegeville: Liturgical Press, 2006), 194–195.

32 Thus Peters writes: "Whoever was seeking to use their evangelical freedom as freedom *from* our existence under God's Gospel and commandment should be cast once again under the chastening rod of the Law, as well as under God's satanic jailer. By contrast, whoever allows himself to be encouraged and summoned is to experience in this specific activity the full extent of the Gospel, without being treated harshly"—Peters, *Confession and Christian Life*:7.

33 LC "A Brief Exhortation to Confession": 13, BC, 477.

34 LC "A Brief Exhortation to Confession": 28, BC, 479.

35 Here note Wilhelm Löhe: "Absolution is the revelation of the justification by God in heaven. When a sinner, full of sorrow and pain over his sins, full of hunger and thirst for peace of conscience, full of trust in the eternal intercessor Christ and his merits, turns to the heavenly Father to obtain forgiveness and eternal life to all believing sinners, the man's ledger is torn up, his guilt sunk into an ocean of grace, never to appear again, not even in the judgment. The man is pronounced loosed and free by him who is the judge of all the living and the dead, and the man will not be judged again; he passed from death to eternal life." "Justification and Absolution in Harmony," *Logia* XX:3 (Holy Trinity, 2011), 57.

36 See Oswald Bayer, *Living by Faith: Justification and Sanctification*, trans. G. Bromiley (Grand Rapids: Eerdmans, 2003), 1–9.

37 On this point see the discussion of Werner Elert, *The Christian Ethos*, trans. Carl Schindler (Philadelphia: Fortress, 1957), 163–173. Elert traces the subjective understanding of guilt to Friedrich Schleiermacher.

38   Here note the German New Testament exegete Udo Schnelle's comment on Pauline anthropology: "His view of human beings is not merely pessimistic, but realistic" in *Theology of the New Testament* translated by M. Eugene Boring (Grand Rapids: Baker Academic Press, 2009), 319.

39   Here see Gerhard Forde, *The Captivation of the Will* (Grand Rapids: Eerdmans, 2005), 21.

40   *Lutheran Service Book* (Saint Louis: Concordia, 2006), 292. This order for individual confession and absolution is based on the rite in the *Small Catechism*. It represents an effort in contemporary American Lutheranism to restore the practice liturgically.

41   Gerhard Forde, "Absolution: Systematic Considerations," 153, see note 2 above.

42   Härle unfortunately tilts in this direction when he states "the person making the confession can then do what is perhaps the most difficult thing, letting forgiveness take effect for him- or herself, and practicing forgiveness of self by ceasing to say 'I'll never forgive myself for that.'" *Outline of Christian Doctrine: An Evangelical Dogmatics*, 464. Rather, those who confess and receive absolution are to be taught to cling to Christ's own words in the face of memories scarred by sin consciences violated by guilt. For more on this, see John T. Pless, "Your Pastor is Not Your Therapist: Private Confession—The Ministry of Repentance and Faith" in *A Reader in Pastoral Theology*, ed. John T. Pless (Fort Wayne: Concordia Theological Seminary Press, 2001), 97–102.

43   AC XXV:3–4, BC, 72.

51

Wilhelm Löhe as Pastoral Theologian

The Discipline of the Shepherd

A LECTURE DELIVERED AT THE CONVOCATION MARKING
THE 200TH ANNIVERSARY OF LÖHE'S BIRTH HELD AT
CONCORDIA THEOLOGICAL SEMINARY, FORT WAYNE,
ON OCTOBER 10, 2008. PREVIOUSLY UNPUBLISHED.

Over twenty-five years ago, in what would prove to be a pivotal text in recovering pastoral theology as a genuinely churchly discipline rather than a clinical or managerial undertaking, Thomas Oden begins his *Pastoral Theology: Essentials of Ministry* with this definition of pastoral theology: "Because it is a pastoral discipline, pastoral theology seeks to join the theoretical with the practical. It is *theoretical* insofar as it seeks to develop a consistent theory of ministry, accountable to Scripture and tradition experientially sound and internally self-consistent. Yet, it is not merely a theoretical statement or objective description of what occurs in ministry. It is also a *practical* discipline, for it is concerned with implementing concrete pastoral tasks rather than merely defining them. Its proximate goal is an improved theory of ministry. Its longer-ranged goal is the improved practice of ministry."[1] Wilhelm Löhe's work certainly fits with Oden's description. In the midst of religious, philosophical, and political turbulence of nineteenth-century Germany, the Bavarian cleric sought to articulate what he thought to be an improved doctrine of the office that he believed to yet unfolding out of the New Testament. But Löhe's ultimate goal had to do with the practice of the care of souls.

From 1837 until his death in 1872, Löhe was pastor of the Nicolai church in Neuendettelsau. This formed the context of his thinking. David Ratke observes, "Löhe's entire thought and perspective and life revolved around the axis of the congregation. It is here that the apostolic Word comes to life; it is in the congregation that the church finds expression. Löhe did not emphasize praxis at the expense of dogma. To be sure, doctrine was the pillar of fire that guided the church during the days when everything seemed lost. But the impulse for Löhe's reflections was always the congregation and its life."[2] Löhe would forge his pastoral theology out of his own work as a preacher, liturgist and pastor. Shaped by his childhood experiences in the village church at Fürth, university studies at Erlangen and Berlin, and several congregational assignments prior to his coming to Neuendettelsau, Löhe was drawn to reflection on the church's confession and life, the character and work of the pastor.

Löhe was the product of a pious Christian home. While his father, a successful merchant, died at the age of fifty-two when Löhe was only eight years old, his mother would exert a strong influence on her son's religious development. Barbara Löhe's own spiritual life was shaped by Johann Arndt's *Garden of Paradise* and J.F. Starck's *Daily Handbook*. Later Löhe would reminisce on his mother's influence, saying, "When my father died she did what she thought was right. Her love for the ministry and the church led her though she was a widow, to let me choose such a life's calling. I owe her a thousand thanks. Who knows whether I would have become a Christian if I had not become a pastor."[3] Löhe also tells of how he would play church: "In our small yard there was a chopping block, I gathered the children of the rent people who lived in our house, put on a black apron to serve as a gown, stepped on to the chopping block, which served as a pulpit, preached, sang and prayed. Sometimes my mother would say to my father: 'a minister is lost in that boy if you don't let him study."[4] The piety of his parental home insulated young Löhe from the Rationalism, which would have been present to some degree in the village church and school. His confirmation day was particularly memorable. After completing his studies at the *Gymnasium* in nearby Nürnberg, where Löhe, under the influence of its rector Karl Louis Roth, would confirm his aspirations to become a pastor, he would enter the University of Erlangen in November of

1826. Roth would have a similar impact upon J.W. Hoefling, Adolph von Hareless, Christoph Luthardt, and J.C.K. von Hoffmann, all of whom studied at the *Gymnasium* and eventually would play prominent roles at Erlangen.

It is at Erlangen that Löhe would begin to develop a strong Lutheran consciousness, although his presence as a student there predates the Erlangen School, which would develop in the coming decade. It was the Reformed preacher and adjunct professor at Erlangen, Christian Krafft, who would awaken in Löhe as he would in von Hoffmann, von Harless, and others an appreciation for the confessional character of Lutheranism in contrast to most of the rest of the faculty who were still captivated by Rationalism. Inspired not so much by Krafft's intellect as by his spirit, Löhe was led to read the theologians of seventeenth-century Lutheran Orthodoxy, especially David Hollaz, the last great dogmatician of that era. Löhe would follow his mentor in supporting the Basel Mission Society. It was not until 1842 that Löhe ceased supporting this group and instead sought to promote a confessionally-defined approach to missions.

In the summer of 1828, Löhe went to study in Berlin, where both Hegel and Schleiermacher were lecturing. Löhe referred to his sojourn in Berlin as his "desert" and "Patmos." After attending a lecture by Hegel at Berlin, the young Löhe penned in his diary: "understood nothing, nothing to understand." He was impressed by Schleiermacher's sermonic abilities but not his theology. More positively, Löhe appreciated Ernst Wilhelm Hengstenberg, August J.W. Neander, Ludwig F.F. Theremin, and especially the practical theologian, Gerhard F.A. Strauß, whose example of an intense but churchly piety would leave its imprint on him. Löhe learned from Strauß to distinguish mysticism from pietism. In Strauß, Löhe found a teacher who awed him with a piety and romantic, spiritual language that would correspond to his own religious instincts. In a letter dated 15 June 1828, Löhe wrote to his friend, H.W.E. Reichold, back in Erlangen:

> Esteem high the evangelical simplicity! Give the small writings of Luther, as far as you can, to the members of the lower strata. So your circle will remain in blessing, and the charge of mysticism will pass by. Do not encourage to make private hours of edification. Friends

may pray together with friends, but everyone finds nourishment in our church because the gospel is preached purely. I also desire that the mission circle deal less with prayer and singing, which have their place in home worship, in the church and otherwise, where one is together with those who belong to him—and instead read missionary reports and historical writings. The Bible is to be read but without explanations. I shall defend all this when I come back. . . . Neither the lecture circle nor the missionary circle may be edification hours, but Christian conversation. Surely, this is edifying, too. You will agree with me when I come. The *Pastorale* of Strauß, that I want to read and maybe dictate to you completely, has taught me much about the right distinction between mysticism and pietism from what is evangelical.[5]

Both Berlin and Erlangen contributed to Löhe's shift from one who was a child of the Awakening to a self-consciously Lutheran identity. Yet the shift was not abrupt. On the day of his ordination on 25 July 1831, Löhe would write emphatically of his fidelity to the Lutheran Symbols. Three years later, in 1834, he would still feel free to preach in a Reformed pulpit. Lothar Vogel observes that it was only in 1834–1835 when the church conflicts in Silesia heightened that Löhe embraced the confessional understanding that would mark him a convinced Lutheran.[6]

In 1867 Gottfried Thomasius would write of his own movement from the Awakening to a more deeply Lutheran position through the embrace of the justification of the sinner by grace through faith:

Thus we were Lutherans before we even knew it; without reflecting upon the confessional idiosyncrasy of our Church, or upon the confessional differences which separate it from others, we were (Lutherans) in fact. We were not even thoroughly familiar with these differences. We read the symbolic books of the church as testimonies of sound doctrine . . . but their symbolical significance concerned us little. But as soon as we began to realize that we were standing squarely in the middle of Lutheranism . . . so we became Lutherans, freely, from within.[7]

Thomasius' testimony seems to fit Löhe as well. Like others who would be identified with the revival of confessional Lutheranism known as the Erlangen School, Löhe would read and be influenced by the writings of Johann Georg Hamann (1730–1788).

After his ordination in 1831, Löhe would serve in several pastoral posts before beginning his work at Neuendettelsau on 1 August 1837. For a short time, he would serve as a vicar to the aged pastor in his hometown of Fürth, Pastor Ebert. This ended unhappily with the older pastor exhibiting jealousy over his younger associate's popularity as a visitor of the sick and the elderly. Most significant was his service as a vicar from 20 October 1831 to 26 February 1834 in Kirchenlamniz. Here Löhe worked under Pastor Christian Sommer and was "confronted by a range of demands that, as he met them, shaped the basic lines of his future ministry."[8] It was here that Löhe developed as both a preacher and curate of souls. Yet it was his pastoral success that would generate conflict. A prominent judge in the congregation felt himself unduly attacked by Löhe's preaching. Charges were leveled against the young cleric accusing him of holding forbidden conventicles. Löhe was charged with fostering "a debauching and pernicious mysticism by which you allow actions which lead to a disruption of familial and social order, the creation of a detrimental religious separatism, and a transformation of active Christianity into a dead, powerless, and lifeless religion of feeling."[9] Löhe was forced to leave Kirchenlamnitz, relieved by the consistory of his position. This was Löhe's first experience with church politics; it would not be his last.

After a string of temporary positions in Nürnberg and surrounding villages, Löhe applied for and was called to the pastorate of the Nicolai church in Neuendettelsau. He married a former catechumen, Helene Andrae, six years to the day of his ordination, 25 July 1837. A week later, Löhe and his eighteen-year-old bride would move to Neuendettelsau, a village of about 500, where they would remain for the rest of their lives.

Six years later, Helene, only twenty-four years old, would die from complications with the birth of their fourth child. Within a year, this infant son would also perish. Löhe would never get over his wife's death, and it would leave its mark on his piety and his work. In the writings that come after his wife's death, Löhe expresses something of a heavenly homesickness, a yearning for the consummation of the Christian community in the New Jerusalem. This is especially evident in his *Three Books About the Church* published in 1845. The impact of Helene's death echoes throughout Löhe's life as he commemorated the anniversary of her death, November 24, yearly. In 1859, he includes a prayer for widowers in a prayer book that very much reflects his own loss:

> O living God and Comforter of those who mourn, I have lost my dearest treasure on earth in childbirth. You have torn a rib and a piece of my heart from me. It is, however, your good will, Lord my God. You gave her to me and let her be with me for a short time and now she has been taken out of this misery back to you, because she knew and called upon your Son. Comfort me, a sad, miserable widower and help carry this pain and raise my children and send a holy glimpse that I and my children can come together before you in a new joy and eternal love, which you plant in all marital love and can make all suffering eternal joy and goodwill. We praise you in eternity. Amen.[10]

The death of his wife was one of several deaths impressed in Löhe, a profound awareness of the shortness of this temporal life, stirring in him a sense of longing for the resurrection of the body and the communion of saints. He writes of his father's death:

> On the day my father died, October 28, 1816—a Monday—I was in school. Our old servant, Susanna, came and got me. As I entered the room, my family was lying on their knees, praying for cessation of the painful struggle. Two of my sisters stood drowned in grief at the head and foot end of the death bed, respectively. My oldest sister, Anna, the sickly one, sat beside the stove without tears but with deep sobbing. As I entered the room, my mother rising from her prayers, took me by the hand and led me to my father, lying in his death rattle, put my hand in his and had me among other things which I don't remember anymore, promise that I would never be a disgrace to my previous father in his grave. Barely had I finished my promise when my father stopped breathing, and I was an orphan.[11]

Seven of Löhe's twelve siblings died in infancy or childhood.

The vacuum created by the death of his wife was filled with even more intense devotion to pastoral work, theological writing, and the organization of missionary and works of mercy. Beyond the confines of his parish, his reputation as a preacher would grow, prompting some to call Löhe "the Chrysostom of his century." Löhe understood the Divine Service as the place where the Heavenly Bridegroom meets His Bride. He sought to recover the best liturgical practices of previous centuries so that the congregation need not be dressed in the threadbare worship forms of Pietism and Rationalism but in the splendor that befits the Bride of Christ. For Löhe, the center of the church was the liturgy of Word and Supper, and from this lively and life-giving center, every aspect of the church's life, including pastoral care radiated.

Kenneth Korby was of the opinion "that whoever wills to enter the thought of Wilhelm Löhe on the matter of the cure of souls must enter via his understanding of the church."[12] Noting that Löhe did not develop his views on the church systematically in the way of a classical dogmatics text, Korby echoed the observation of Walter Bouman that, "His (Löhe's) whole life and thought, his correspondence, his parish duties, his world-wide concerns revolved around the nature of the Church so that a biography of him can at the same time be an ecclesiology."[13]

Three strands of Löhe's ecclesiological thinking relative to pastoral care emerge. First, there is the oneness of the church. Drawing on the Epistle to the Ephesians and the creedal confession that "I believe in one holy Christian and apostolic Church," Löhe provides a corrective to the conceptuality of the church as "visible and invisible" inherited from Lutheran Orthodoxy and widely used in the nineteenth century.[14] Löhe did not abandon this distinction as can be seen, among other places, in his *Agende* of 1844 and his *Three Books About the Church*. In the foreword to the *Agende*, Löhe writes that the church is the "marvelous creation of her one and only Lord and Master, which has demonstrated and will demonstrate herself independent of everything except Word and Sacrament. In her totality the church is and remains invisible and appears visibly sometimes here, sometimes there, as her banners wave in the breeze sometimes here, sometimes there, and her marks appear in Word and Sacrament, sometimes here, sometimes there."[15]

In attempting to maintain the confession that the church is one and avoid positing two churches, one visible and the other invisible, Löhe seeks to speak of the church as simultaneously visible and invisible. This Löhe does by using the analogy of the human being who is both body and soul, one not existing without the other in this life and by making a distinction between those who are "called" as those embraced in the visible church and those who are "chosen" as members of the invisible church.[16] Korby acknowledges that Löhe's treatment of the visible/invisible distinction is not without difficulties from the multiple perspectives of missiology, systematics and pastoral care.[17] He identifies what he sees as problematic when one attempts to use the distinction:

> To be caught in the tug of war initiated by the use of the words 'visible' and 'invisible' is to be threatened always to flee into the invisible, thereby turning every day churchly life over to machinations, devices, techniques, and powers of all sorts. Or, to choose to concentrate on that reality that corresponds to 'visible' is to shift the understanding of the Word of God and faith so that the inner life of the church is drained off into the quagmires of experientialism and into the legalisms of righteousness by works or rituals. And yet, to hold to both terms 'visible' and 'invisible' is very nearly to be caught defenseless against the 'two church solution' that has so often threatened the church's unity and the Gospel.[18]

Yet, positively, Korby argues Löhe is able to escape turning the doctrine of the church into an abstraction by avoiding a shift from oral/auditory images to visual ones in his ecclesiology. The inner life of the church, which is hidden, is given outward expression in preaching, baptizing, absolving and distributing the Lord's Supper.

> The inner and outer life of the church is joined together in a unity not to be broken. Löhe writes in his *Three Books About the Church*: "The visible church is the 'tabernacle of God among men,' and outside of it there is no salvation. A man separates himself from God the Father if he separates himself from the church, his mother. . . . As a man stands in relation to the church, so he stands in relation to God."[19]

Second, the apostolic character of the church means that the church is not a static institution but a living organism. The church is both called and calling. By the apostolic Word, that is the living voice of preaching that is in conformity to the apostolic Scriptures, the church is called to life in Christ Jesus.[20] This is the calling to faith as faith comes from hearing the Gospel. The church that is apostolic is constituted in and by this faith-creating Word. At the same time, the church that is apostolic is a calling church, as this church confesses Christ before the world and, through the preaching of Christ, gathers people from every tribe and tongue into the holy community whose head and center is the Lamb of God.

Acts 2:42 ("And they devoted themselves to the apostles' teaching and the fellowship, to the breaking of bread and the prayers") is crucial in Löhe's thinking on the nature of the life of the apostolic congregation expressed in worship. Löhe's use of this pericope is another example of Löhe's avoidance of abstractions as he concretely describes the character of the liturgical congregation as praying, preaching, and celebrating the Lord's Supper.[21]

Gathered by the apostolic Word, the church is fed by the body and blood of the Lord in the holy supper. While the appearance of four items noted in Acts 2:42 might appear in varying degrees in different gatherings of the congregation for worship, all four come to culmination and union in the service of Holy Communion. "One element may appropriately be stressed over the others in any given gathering. But the great high point, the fountain of all other life and worship, is the union of the four elements. That union is the celebration of Holy Communion."[22]

The Sacrament of the Altar shaped Löhe's understanding of the church as a living organism. The church is known from the altar. And it is from the altar that mission is generated and to the altar that mission returns. The movement of mission is from and to the altar as the church lives as "an organism of rescuing love."

Contrary to interpretations of Löhe that would see in him a hierarchal clericalism that demeaned the life of the laity, *disenfranchising* them from the life of the church, there is in Löhe a unity between the holy office and the holy priesthood. Both are from the Lord. The office is established by Christ for the sake of the apostolic Word so that it might be heard, believed, and confessed in the places where the priestly people called by the Lord live and work.[23] In his own way, Löhe revitalizes a Lutheran doctrine of vocation that enlivens the laity to live out their callings in the world, especially in the

Christian home where the Word of Christ is to dwell richly. Thus the laity are not only the objects of spiritual care; they are engaged in this work in union with the pastor. Korby observes that Löhe's "*Haus-Schul-und Kirchenbuch* proved to be a coherent statement expressing the union of the home, the school, and the church in mutual care of souls, and included valuable guidance for laymen to engage directly in that caring work."[24]

Third, the Lutheran Church is a confessional communion. As an heir of the confessional reawakening of the nineteenth century, Löhe embraced the Lutheran Confessions as the clear exposition of the Holy Scriptures. This led him to reject the Prussian Union and all that it entailed. Löhe's confessionalism may be described as a "sacramental confessionalism" in that Löhe understood all of Lutheran doctrine drawn together in the sacrament of the altar. This sacramental confessionalism had both ecclesiological and pastoral consequences. Ecclesiastically it meant that for Löhe, there could be no intercommunion with those of another confession. Pastorally it meant that the Confessions are embraced to keep the Lutheran Church centered in the purity of evangelical proclamation and administration of the Lord's Supper. For Löhe, the Confessions prevented involvement in inter-confessional mission societies and the embrace of what he identified as "methodistic" tactics of evangelization and pastoral care.

For Löhe, the ecclesiological foundation of pastoral theology would shape the practice of the care of souls in several ways. First, the care of souls properly belongs to the church. Korby writes,

> The shape of Löhe's pastoral theology can be designated as a tri-polar field. The basic pole is the Word of God; the other two poles are the congregation and the pastor. As the Spirit leads the congregation, giving them pastors and teachers as gifts, the same spirit gives the *means* for the church's life and work. The wisdom and power of the pastoral office lie in the *use* of that Word. The object of pastoral care is the creation of new creatures. In *Seelsorge*, therefore, God's Word, not human skills, is the essence of persuasion, for the aim of the Spirit is to make a new and holy people, not merely to modify behavior with human persuasion. Care of souls is the cure of souls.[25]

Set within the church is the holy office. It is through this office that Christ serves His bride. Löhe understands the pastor to be in succession with the apostles not by attachment to place or continuity of persons but by means of a common doctrine. Ordination places a man in the office which Christ instituted. For Löhe, the ministry is derived from neither the congregation nor the episcopacy; it is established by the Risen Lord with the sending of the apostles.

Löhe sees that the office of the keys is given to the whole church, but only ministers are entrusted with the responsibility to exercise the keys in loosing and binding sin. Rudolf Keller has pointed to Löhe's reliance on Andreas Osiander and the Brandenburg-Nurnberg church order at this point.[26] The minister does not serve by his own personal or charismatic authority but by the mandate of Christ. Ordination, for Löhe, binds the minister to this mandate rather than the whims of the congregation. Löhe deals explicitly with the nature and authority of the office in his *Aphorisms* (1849 and 1851). In his *Der Evangelische Geistliche* (Two volumes; 1852–1858), he explores various facets of the pastor's life and work, both in terms of his character and the skills needed for shepherding and teaching.

Second, Löhe insists on the primacy of private confession and absolution in pastoral Löhe: "Private confession is the mother of all care of souls, and for it, there is no substitute."[27] An evangelical reclaiming of confession and absolution is anchored in the chief article, justification by faith alone. Absolution is the enactment of the justifying word of the Gospel. For Löhe the *beichtvater*, the father confessor is not a judge over the penitent but a servant or ambassador who is sent with the verdict of the judge: forgiveness to those broken by their sin.

Gerhard von Zezschwitz, a professor of practical theology at Erlangen, who had Löhe as his father confessor, said that only he who knows Löhe as a *Seelsorger* and father confessor really knows him fully.[28] Already in the pre-Neuendettelsau years, Löhe wrote on confession as more important for man's eternal welfare than sowing and harvesting is for his temporal wellbeing.[29] An 1835 draft of what would be published two years later as his *Communion Booklet* would speak of the blessing and power of private confession. In 1843, six years after Löhe's coming to Neuendettelsau, did private confession emerge as a regular practice in the congregation. Three years later, in 1846, we learn that Löhe absolved 153 communicants in a single day.[30] Wolfhart Schlichting indicates Löhe heard 2,250 individual confessions in 1858.[31]

Löhe believed that the practice of general confession should be retained for weighty pastoral reasons. Private confession is to be urged not as a replacement for the general confession but as a means that makes it possible for the penitent to name specific sins and the pastor to provide spiritual care—exploration, examination, and absolution— appropriate to the condition of the penitent. Löhe gives guidance as to how confession is to be made so that it avoids what he calls a shameless rambling on about sin and its effects or a confession of one's circumstances but a naming of the sin before God. While private confession gives the pastor opportunity to counsel the penitent in the avoidance of new sins, Löhe praises confession as God's own way of humbling and mortifying the old Adam. Only the one whose bones have been crushed by the law are in a position to hear the words of absolution that restore broken sinners to joy and gladness.

Third, tied to the restoration of confession and absolution is the necessity of discipline within the church. The word of blessing in the absolution directed toward sinners who repent has its antithesis in the word of curse in the binding key spoken to hardened sinners who will not repent. Korby writes, "Löhe saw private confession and absolution as only a half measure if there is not joined with it the power to refuse absolution or to deny the Lord's Supper. To use only one key means the loss of both. Löhe judged easy or cheap care of souls to be worthless. 'There is no such thing as care of souls without training or discipline.' If there is no practice of excommunication, absolution loses some of its significance."[32] For Löhe, discipline in the church is the work of rescue. It may be compared to the physician setting a broken bone, painful but necessary for the healing of the patient. The binding key is necessary so that finally, the loosing key can be employed to set the person brought to repentance free.

On more than one occasion, Löhe's insistence on church discipline would get him in trouble. For example, in 1860, he refused to officiate at a wedding of a member who had divorced his wife. The state, through the Bavarian church, insisted that Löhe perform the wedding or else he would be suspended from his pastorate. Löhe refused and was suspended for a time. This episode is illustrative of Löhe's ongoing worry that a territorial church made church discipline nearly impossible. It was a worry that more than once prompted him to seriously ponder leaving the territorial church for a free church.

Fourth, sermon, sacrament, and catechization form a necessary triad in the care of souls. In *Three Books About the Church*, Löhe characterized his own time as "a time of one-sided and experimentation."[33] Writing in a time of liturgical experimentation and exploration of new paradigms for mission and ministry, Korby noted the parallels between Löhe's time and the late twentieth century in regard to what he believed was detrimental to the genuine care of souls. The care of souls requires church. That is, the care of souls is dependent on a context formed by preaching, the Lord's Supper, and catechetical instruction.

Löhe was himself a gifted preacher who possessed an extraordinary power of speech, energy of expression, pictorial richness, and passion grounded in deep conviction.[34] His preaching followed the traditional lectionary. He suggests that the Lutheran preacher would not replace it with free texts or with continuous readings from Holy Scripture. Instead, Löhe writes that "a man who changes texts every year is no good as a preacher for the people, or we might say for the church."[35] For Löhe, the preacher grows deeper into the text as he expounds the same well-known pericopes year after year.

Löhe understands the preacher as an ambassador of divine reconciliation who speaks with sincerity and forthrightness as one who is sent. The preacher does not need to decorate his proclamation with literary artfulness. As in pastoral care so also preaching is not given to the "new measures" of the Methodists as he calls them but to a confident reliance on the biblical Word. Thus Löhe says that,

> A sincere preacher therefore will not intentionally withdraw himself nor make himself prominent, but he comes with the Word and the Word comes with him. He is a simple, faithful witness to the Word, and the Word witnesses to him—he and the Word appear as one. All his preaching is based on holy calm. Even when he condemns and the zeal of God's house consumes him, it is not the wrath of the warlike God which is kindled in him. It is not primarily he who speaks but the Lord who speaks in him and through him, and the way he performs his duty is worthy of the Lord. Always it is the measure of manliness and maturity which distinguishes the preacher of the church.[36]

Hugh Oliphant Old describes Löhe's preaching as "doxological" in that his sermons not only exhort congregants to adoration and worship but are in and of themselves hymns of praise as they draw the congregation into the angelic hymn.[37]

While his preaching was doxological, it could also be sharp and stern. Sins known to the public in Neuendettelsau, such as drunkenness and immorality, were named. On one occasion, Löhe preached a funeral sermon for a woman who had borne eight children with a man to whom she was never married. Löhe had cared for the woman on her death bed; she confessed her sin and received absolution and Holy Communion. Nevertheless, Löhe referred to her in the funeral sermon as "this poor whore" warning the congregation to avoid her sinful ways even as he rejoiced in her repentance.[38]

Preaching, for Löhe, does not aim to excite the emotions of the hearers but to implant in their inmost being the living and active Word, which grows he says like a mustard seed. Good preaching brings about patient perseverance with the Word and in the Word. Preaching requires of the preacher careful study, contemplation, and meditation so that the preacher might learn what Löhe identifies as "the great secret of preaching," namely that a preacher uses "what is familiar to create an entrance for the unfamiliar and to expound all the doctrines of the church on the basis of texts which are familiar to all."[39]

Löhe's preparation for preaching was disciplined study and prayer. He typically began each day, Monday through Saturday, at 5:00 am with study of the text.

"I must give birth to my sermons with pain . . . I groan, pray and am fearful till I step into the pulpit, and then God's grace is renewed."[40] Generally, his sermons were carefully written out word for word except for funeral sermons that were generally done in outline form. Hermann Bezzel, perhaps Löhe's most prominent successor would say, "Löhe's sermons are nothing less than a reflection of the thoughts of God."[41]

The sermon is linked to the sacrament. While Löhe writes of preaching that "among the means which the church uses for the salvation of souls, preaching occupies the first place,"[42] he sees the sermon as necessarily moving to the sacrament. As Thomas Schattauer observes, "For Löhe, the Lord's Supper provided a comprehensive interpretation of Christian existence."[43] This can be seen in an 1853 sermon on I Corinthians 5:6–8 where Löhe proclaims,

> For Christians, the whole time from the sacrifice at Golgotha until the return of the Lord is a true and unceasing Easter celebration, a time of the Paschal Lamb and the Lord's Supper, not only in a figurative and symbolic way but in a most perfect and holiest solemnity. New Testament congregations live from the preparation to the partaking of the Paschal Lamb, from partaking to preparation: between preparation and partaking time passes, until he comes. Ever a new they desire to partake of their eternal salvation in the Lamb of God who was slain and to be assured thereby full peace and joy in the Holy Spirit, full light and power for sanctification. There is no higher view of earthly life than this–and therefore no more perfect blossom of earthly life, no more time which deserves the name 'high-time' than the time when one comes to the holy Supper and partakes of the Paschal Lamb. To celebrate the Lord's Supper—indeed, that is the highest, most glorious work of a Christian congregation–or rather, not a work, but where it lays down every work, where it lives entirely by faith.[44]

The Lord's Supper, according to Löhe, the energies inherent in the body and blood of Christ, enliven faith and love in the Christian individually and the church corporeally. Eating the body of Christ and drinking his blood, the church is most profoundly the Body of Christ.

Löhe sees the Lord's Supper as the ultimate gift of Christ Jesus, for here, the Lamb of God imparts His body and blood for the forgiveness of sins. With this gift, the communicants are bound together with their Lord and one another. At the altar, doctrine and life converge in Löhe's thinking. Contradiction of Christ's words must be laid aside; therefore, there could be no altar fellowship with those who twist or deny the Lutheran teaching. But Löhe held that there was more to the sacrament than simply having a correct doctrinal definition. Later in his life, addressing a pastoral conference in 1865, he says,

> I am the same good Lutheran as earlier, but in a more profound way. Before, Lutheranism was for me little more than affirmation of the confessions from A-Z; now the whole of Lutheranism is for me hidden

in the sacrament of the altar, in which, as can be shown all the chief doctrines of Christianity, especially those of the Reformation, have their center and focus. The essential thing for me now is not so much the Lutheran doctrine of the Lord's Supper, but the sacramental life and experience of the blessing of the sacrament possible only through partaking of it abundantly. The words 'sacramental Lutheranism' signifies my advance.[45]

The benefits of the sacrament are to be preached. The Lord's Supper was honored by frequent, reverent, and salutary use in the congregation. Preparatory services on Friday and Saturday prior to communion Sundays aimed to assist Christians in a beneficial partaking of the sacred body and blood. Löhe also prepared a variety of devotional aids to help communicants examine themselves and meditate on the benefits of the sacrament. Löhe promoted a more frequent celebration of the sacrament in Neuendettelsau, moving beyond the traditional spring and fall communions with several services in the spring beginning with Palm Sunday and continuing through the Easter Season. In the autumn, there would be multiple services in October and November, although parishioners typically commune only once during each cycle. In the 1850s the pattern changed to the celebration of the Lord's Supper every three weeks and on major feast days. In the 1860s, Löhe established "small communion" services—abbreviated celebrations held early on the morning of those Sundays when there was no celebration of the sacrament in the main service.[46]

Catechization is necessary for a fruitful hearing of God's Word and a holy reception of the Lord's Supper. Löhe lauds Luther's Small Catechism as a confession of the Evangelical-Lutheran Church, asserting that "no catechism in the world, but this can be prayed."[47] He recognizes Luther's genius in crafting with such simplicity of style and yet richness of meaning. In *Three Books About the Church*, Löhe warns pastors against using the Catechism as a pretext for delivering dogmatic monologues and instead urges that the catechist stick to the words of the Catechism itself. He draws attention to Luther's own prefaces to the Small and Large Catechism as providing a simple and churchly method of teaching the faith. In this way, Löhe argues, "the Catechism should be engraved on the memory of the child for its entire life."[48] He suggested that catechization move from the text to an exposition of its meaning to the clarification of its content for doctrine and life.

Fifth, Löhe maintains the necessity of making a distinction between the "ordinary" and "extraordinary" forms of pastoral care.[49] The ordinary means for the care of souls are sermon, liturgy, and catechesis. The extraordinary means would be those pastoral activities that attend to specific needs and crises in the lives of believers. Here again, we see that the church is fundamental to pastoral care. Korby writes,

> So radical was this contextual setting to be understood that Löhe argued: if one does not anchor the extraordinary means in this general setting of the ordinary, he will make the grave error of turning the extraordinary into the ordinary. That is, the private care, the care of the individual, will become the ordinary means of the pastor's work and preaching, catechesis, and liturgy will become occasional, peripheral, and insignificant. The private care of the individual is extraordinary, by Löhe's description. But if it is to be fruitful and blessed work, it must be done with those on whom the ordinary means of the care of souls have done their work.[50]

Korby also points out that Löhe spotted a tendency to replace the ordinary with extraordinary:

> Such an inversion is what he (Löhe) called 'methodism' in pastoral care. Löhe called this a one-sidedness, growing out of the conviction that the Word of God would work effectively only if it were used in a certain way. By the attempt to achieve something special, something spectacular in this way, was like cutting with the handle of a knife. The feverish creation of new measures for pastoral care will, in the long run, produce just that, 'new measures.' It does not take too long before the effects once produced by the 'new measures' begin to wear off, for in becoming the ordinary means for the care of souls, the extraordinary means do not have the staying power that the ordinary means contain within themselves.[51]

Pastoral care for Löhe does not seek after the "new measures" with the multiplicity of techniques but the "old means" in their evangelical simplicity.

Sixth, intercessory prayer is a necessary component. "There is no care of souls without intercession and common prayer."[52] The hallowing Word of God anchors the prayers of Christians in the gracious will of the Father. The General Prayer in the Divine Service is the priestly voice of the church, making intercession for the world according to the apostolic mandate. Löhe sees that the Litany especially lends itself to intercession as it provides both structure and elasticity in bringing before God the needs of the sick and dying, the tempted and distressed, expectant mothers and widows; in short, it is expansive enough to incorporate all who need our prayers. Löhe composed *Seed Grains*, for example, to assist the laity in hallowing all of life by the Word of God and prayer. Löhe was known for his prayer book and devotional literature but also for his fervent prayers made at the bedside of the sick and the dying and in the presence of the tormented and spiritually distressed. Hans Schwarz observes the similarities between Löhe and his contemporary with whom he was acquainted, Johann Christoph Blumhardt (1805–1880) in this respect.[53]

When Löhe died in January of 1872, he left behind a legacy that would extend far beyond the little village of Neuendettelsau, the seat of his life's work. His contributions to missions and diaconal work remain and are rightly celebrated. His contributions to pastoral theology have often been eclipsed by approaches derived from psychological disciplines. In recent times–that is, within the last fifty years-the only pastoral theology in English, at least, that utilizes Löhe is the Barthian Eduard Thurneysen's *A Theology of Pastoral Care*[54]. We would do well to listen again to the wisdom of Löhe's pastoral theology, to critically engage his thought toward a renewed understanding and practice of the care of souls in our spiritually needy world.

Notes

1 Thomas Oden, *Pastoral Theology: Essentials of Ministry* (New York: Harper and Row, 1983), x–xi.

2 David C. Ratke, *Confession and Mission, Word and Sacrament: The Ecclesial Theology of Wilhelm Löhe* (St. Louis: Concordia Publishing House, 2001), 55.

3 Wilhelm Löhe, *Three Books About the Church*, trans. James Schaaf (Philadelphia: Fortress Press, 1969), 3.

4 Hans Schwarz, *Theology in a Global Context: The Last Two Hundred Years* (Grand Rapids: Eerdmans, 2005), 92–93.

5 Wilhelm Löhe, *Gesammelte Werke* (GW), ed. Klaus Ganzert (Neuendettelsau: Freimund, 1951–1986), I:270.

6 Lothar Vogel, "Awakening and Confessionalism: Wilhelm Löhe's Theological Teachers" (unpublished lecture given at the meeting of the International Löhe Society in Neuendettelsau on 26 July 2008), 6.

7 Quoted by Hermann Sasse, "The Results of the Lutheran Awakening of the 19th Century–Part II" *Theological Quarterly* (October 1951), 244.

8 Kennth F. Korby, *Theology of Pastoral Care in Wilhelm Löhe with Special Attention to the Function of the Liturgy and the Laity* (Fort Wayne: Concordia Theological Seminary Printshop, n.d.), 91.

9 Quoted by Schaaf in *Three Books About the Church*, 9–10.

10 Quoted by Ratke, 35.

11 Quoted by Theodor Schober, *Wilhem Löhe: Witness of the Living Lutheran Church*, trans. Sister Bertha Mueller (n.p., n.d), 5.

12 Korby, *Theology as Pastoral Care in Wilhelm Löhe*, 307.

13 Ibid., 148.

14 See Heinrich Schmid, *Doctrinal Theology of the Evangelical Lutheran Church* trans. Charles A. Hay and Henry E. Jacobs (Minneapolis: Augsburg, 1961), 582–599 and Holsten Fagerberg, *Bekenntnis, Kirche, und Amt in der deutschen konfessionalellen Theologie des Jahrhunderts* (Uppsala: Almqvist & Wiksells Boktryckeri, 1952), 127–131.

15 Cited in Korby, *Theology of Pastoral Care in Wilhelm Loehe*, 178.

16 See Wilhelm Löhe, *Three Books about the Church* trans. James Schaaf (Philadelphia: Fortress, 1969), 87–89.

17 Korby, *Theology of Pastoral Care in Wilhelm Loehe*, 180–181.

18 Ibid., 182–183.

19 *Three Books About the Church*, 90.

20 Korby expresses the connection between the apostolic Word and mission: "As the mission is the church of God in motion, so the energy of that motion is the Word of God, the apostolic Word. That Word alone is the energy; that Word alone is the uniting center. It is not the constitutional order of the church, not a lord, not a bishop that is the uniting power in the center of the church, but this apostolic Word, the Scripture. Apostolic is the principle name for the church, for these clear Scriptures are not only the uniting word, but that clear Word that is always at the center and the church is never without 'its glorious center.' Löhe equates the apostolic Word and the Scriptures. However, at the same time he continues to keep alive the quality of the Word as spoke, as oral"—*Theology of Pastoral Care in Wilhelm Loehe*, 177.

21 Ibid., 170. Also see Kenneth Korby, "Wilhelm Loehe and Liturgical Renewal" in *The Lutheran Historical Conference: Essays and Reports 1972* (St. Louis: Lutheran Historical Conference, 1974), where Korby traces how Löhe develops the use of Acts 2:42 in his *Laienagende* of 1852 (71).

22 Korby, *Theology of Pastoral Care in Wilhelm Loehe*, 170.

23 See Kenneth Korby, "The Pastoral Office and the Priesthood of Believers" in *Lord Jesus Christ, Will You Not Stay: Essays in Honor of Ronald Feuerhahn on the Occasion of His Sixty-fifth Birthday* edited by J. Bart Day et al (Houston: The Feuerhahn Festschrift Committee, 2002), 333–371.

24 *Theology of Pastoral Care*, 173.

25 Kenneth Korby, "Loehe's *Seelsorge* for his Fellow Lutherans in America" *Concordia Historical Institute Quarterly* 45 (November 1972), 235.

26 Rudolf Keller, "Reformatorische Wurzekn der Amtslehre von Wilhelm Löhe" in *Unter einem Christus sein und straiten: Festschrift zum 70. Geburtstag von Friedrich Wilhelm Hopf, D.D.* eds. Jobst Schöne and Volker Stolle (Erlangen: Verlag der Evangelisch-Lutherischen Mission, 1980), 118.

27 GW IV:83.

28 Martin Wittenberg, "Wilhelm Löhe and Confession: A Contribution to the History of *Seelsorge* and the Office of the Ministry," in *And Let Every Tongue Confess: Essays in Honor of Norman Nagel on the Occasion of His Sixty-fifth Birthday* eds. Gerald Krispin and Jon Vieker (Dearborn, Michigan: Nagel Festschrift Committee, 1990), 119; also see Stephen van der Hoek, "The Unique Contribution of Wilhelm Löhe to the Renewal of the Practice of Private Confession" *Lutheran Theological Journal* (August 2008), 100–108.

29 Ibid., 120.

30 Ibid., 122.

31 Wolfhart Schlichting, "Löhe" in *Theologische Realenzyklopädie* Band 21 ed. Gerhard Müller (Berlin: Walter de Gruyter, 1991), 411.

32 Korby, *Theology of Pastoral Care in Wilhelm Loehe*, 189.

33 Löhe, *Three Books About the Church*, 173.

34 See Erika Gieger, *Wilhelm Löhe 1808–1872: Leben-Werk-Wirkung* (Neuendettelsau: Freimund-Verlag, 2003), 29. The standard work on Löhe's preaching remains Hans Kreßel, *Wilhelm Löhe als Prediger* (Gütersloh: C. Bertelsmann Verlag, 1929).

35 Wilhelm Löhe, *Three Book About the Church*, 169.

36 Ibid., 168.

37 Hughes Oliphant Old, *The Reading and Preaching of the Scriptures in the Worship of the Christian Church*. Volume 6: The Modern Age (Grand Rapids: Eerdmans, 2007), 122–123.

38 Johannes Deinzer, *Wilhelm Löhe's Leben* Band 2 (Nurenberg: Gütersloh, 1872–1892), 188.

39 Wilhelm Löhe, *Three Books About the Church*, 169.

40 Schober, *Wilhelm Loehe*, 85.

41 Ibid., 87.

42 Wilhelm Löhe, *Three Books About the Church*, 167.

43 Thomas Schattauer, "The Reconstruction of Rite: The Liturgical Legacy of Wilhelm Löhe" in *Rule of Faith, Rule of Prayer: Essays in Honor of Aidan Kavanagh* eds. Nathan Mitchell and John Baldovin (Collegeville, Minnesota: The Liturgical Press, 1996), 251.

44 GW 5/2: 673.

45 Quoted in Thomas Schattauer, "Sunday Worship at Neuendettelsau Under Wilhelm Löhe" *Worship* (July 1985), 371–372.

46 See Schattauer, "Sunday Worship at Neuendettelsau Under Wilhelm Löhe," 370–384. Also see Hans Kreßel, *Wilhelm Löhe als Liturg und Liturgiker* (Neuendettelsau: Freimund-Verlag, 1952), 114–164.

47 Wilhelm Löhe, *Three Books About the Church*, 171.

48 GW VII/2:590.

49 Wilhelm Löhe, *Three Books About the Church*, 245; also see Kenneth Korby, "Loehe's *Seelsorge* for his Fellow Lutherans in America," 227–246.

50 Ibid., 246.

51 Ibid., 247.

52 GW VII/2:590.

53 Hans Schwarz, "Wilhelm Loehe in the Context of the Nineteenth Century" *Currents in Theology and Mission* (April 2006), 94.

54 Eduard Thurneysen, *A Theology of Pastoral Care*, trans. Jack A. Worthington and Thomas Wieser (Richmond: John Knox Press, 1962). In addition to the previously cited works of Kenneth F. Korby there is Hans Kreße's important study, *Wilhelm Löhe als Katechet und als Seelsorger* (Neuendettelsau: Freimund-Verlag, 1955) and Armin Wenz, "Ministry and Pastoral Theology of Löhe and Vilmar" *Logia* (Holy Trinity 2007), 15–24.

CONFESSING THE FAITH

THESE LECTURES WERE GIVEN AT A THEOLOGICAL
CONFERENCE SPONSORED BY THE OFFICE OF
INTERNATIONAL MISSION (LCMS) IN WITTENBERG,
GERMANY ON MAY 13-15, 2020

52

Damnamus

A Confessional Necessity—
Insights from Hermann Sasse

It is the aim of these two lectures to examine how Hermann Sasse understood both the confessional and ecumenical necessity of not only confessing the truth of the Gospel but also speaking an anathema, a *damnamus* against any teaching, movement, or church practice that would deny or diminish that truth. In the language of the Formula of Concord, thesis demands antithesis. The flip side of every "we believe, teach, and confess is a strong we reject and condemn."[1]

To understand how Sasse does this, we need to pay some attention to his own biography.[2] Who was Hermann Sasse (1895–1976)? He was born into a middle-class family in Thuringia and would enter the University of Berlin, where he studied with some of the most prestigious theologians of the early twentieth century, including Adolph von Harnack, Adolph Deissmann, Julius Kaftan, Reinhold Seeberg, and Karl Holl. His university studies were interrupted by World War I as he enlisted as an officer in the Germany army, where he would see action in one of the most bloody battles: the battle of Passchendaele. Out of his infantry regiment of 150 men, only six survived.

Like many of his contemporaries, the war would be the crucible that would test and ultimately crush the convictions of classical liberalism, which were meditated to him by his Berlin teachers. The devastation and suffering that Sasse witnessed as a soldier convinced him of the futility of liberalism's optimistic view of the human capacity for ethical progress. Years after the war, he would write, "You can perhaps live on (Harnack's theology) in happy times, but you can't die with, and so the liberal theology and optimistic view of man died in the catastrophe of the First War."[3]

After the war, Sasse would complete his doctoral studies and serve as a pastor in Berlin. In the 1925–26 academic year, Sasse would pursue a year of post-doctoral studies at Hartford Seminary in the United States. This year was significant for two reasons. First, it would give Sasse intimate knowledge of church life, including that of the various Lutheran bodies in the United States. Second, Sasse himself states that it was during this year that he became a confessional Lutheran through his reading of Wilhelm Löhe's *Three Books About the Church.*[4]

Sasse's knowledge of the American religious scene in these years is reflected in his first book published in 1927 under the title, *American Christianity and the Church.* This monograph contains Sasse's observations on the place of "undogmatic Christianity" in American life. The young German theologian describes the pragmatism of the American church when he writes, "It is a church which has renounced the idea that it is possible to possess the truth and the requirements necessitated by that truth for carrying out its work."[5]

In contrast to mainline American Protestantism in 1927, Sasse held out hope for Lutherans in America. Largely spared the skirmishes of the so-called Modernist/Fundamentalist debate over the Bible, the works-righteousness of the Social Gospel Movement, and the suspicion that creeds and liturgy were detrimental to growth and unity, Lutherans were not institutionally united, and they were something of wallflowers in the American religious garden. Sasse wrote,

> And the Lutherans are not united, leading an isolated life, having little influence on the intellectual life of the nation. But they are living and growing churches. If the movement toward unity (the first great consequence of which was the formation of the United Lutheran Church in America in 1918) continues and leads to the unification of all Lutherans it will be one of the most significant churches in America. The life of these churches dispels the notion that Lutheranism's doctrine of justification necessarily leads to quietism. There is in America perhaps no more active a church than the Missouri Synod, which is the most dogmatically rigorous Lutheran Church in the country.

The history of the organization of this church demonstrates that Lutheranism can exist in forms other than a state church or dependent upon the state (as we hear happily repeated time and time again in Europe). Lutheranism is never more vibrant than where it is free from guardianship by a secular authority.[6]

Sasse would remain conversant with American Lutheran leaders and theologians for the remainder of his life. He was particularly interested in the Missouri Synod, for he saw in it the last large confessional Lutheran church body that stood against the forces of theological liberalism and unionism. Shifts in the Missouri Synod led Sasse to wonder if the Synod had buried its legacy and instead embraced a future more attune to the predominant ecumenical trends of the mid-twentieth century.

It was the nineteenth-century Bavarian pastor, Wilhelm Löhe, that Sasse would identify with most closely. He was impressed by Löhe's understanding of the church as apostolic, catholic, and confessional. Löhe's description of mission as the one church of God in motion would leave its imprint on Sasse. While he was not uncritical of Löhe, Sasse appreciated his courage in both confession and mission.[7]

It might be said that Sasse was both an ecumenical confessionalist and a confessional ecumenist. His passion for the truth of the apostolic Gospel and his love of the church catholic compelled him to be both. This commitment is seen early in Sasse's career and remains a continuing thread for the rest of his life. It is in the context of confessing that *damnamus* must also be made.

In 1927, Sasse would become involved with the Conference on Faith and Order. He was a member of the German delegation at Lausanne in 1927 and was the editor of their report made on that gathering. He attended ecumenical meetings in an official capacity until travel restrictions placed on him by the Nazi government prevented him from doing so in 1935, even though the next year (1936), he would travel illegally to Great Britain for a meeting with the Archbishop of York. Nonetheless, his ecumenical contacts ranged both broad and deep, including Bishop George Bell in England, Cardinal Bea in the Vatican, and Reformed theologians in Australia. Staunchly and unapologetically Lutheran, Sasse was no sectarian.

Sasse was one of the first theologians to speak out against Adolph Hitler and National Socialism. The Reformed church historian, Arthur Cochrane, who was no admirer of Sasse, admits: "It is to the lasting credit of Prof. Hermann Sasse, of the University of Erlangen, that he was the first to declare that because of this one plank [anti-Semitic] in the Party's program the Church could in no way approve of Nazism. It had to be categorically repudiated. The fact that Sasse eventually broke with the Confessing Church in the interest of a narrow Lutheran confessionalism, and thereby greatly weakened the Church's opposition to National Socialism, must not obscure the prophetic role he played at the outset."[8]

He collaborated with Georg Merz, Wilhelm Vischer, Friedrich von Bodelschwingh, and Dietrich Bonhoeffer to produce the Bethel Confession in 1933, but in 1934, he refused to endorse the Barmen Declaration which he considered to embody a unionistic confusion of law and gospel. After the war, in 1948, he would leave the Bavarian territorial church protesting its participation in the EiKD, which he could see as nothing less than a continuation of the nineteenth century Prussian Union complete with its failure to confess the bodily presence of Christ in the Sacrament. In 1949, Sasse would immigrate to Australia, where he would take a position on the faculty of Immanuel Seminary in Adelaide. It was from Australia that Sasse would write over 60 "letters to Lutheran pastors," which would be mimeographed and sent to Lutheran pastors and theologians all over the world. It was in these letters that Sasse sought to encourage and edify his brothers while at the same time commenting on ecclesiastical and ecumenical happenings, teaching, and contending for the Lutheran confession. Sasse would continue this activity after his retirement, up to the time of his death in August 1976.

There is much that we could examine in Sasse regarding the function of the *damnamus* as a confessional necessity. In our time together this hour, I will focus on two of his writings, "The Confession of the Church" and "Concerning the Nature of Confession."

In an essay from 1930, "The Confession of the Church," celebrating the 400th anniversary of the Augsburg Confession, Sasse notes the aversion to dogma and the compelling attraction of an undogmatic Christianity in the modern world. His words are prescient of contemporary experience as well: "There is scarcely any conviction today so widely dispersed as that which maintains that if Christianity is to have any future at all, it must be a religion of the love of God and people, an *undogmatic Christianity* of sentiment and deed."[9] It is against this backdrop that Sasse provides a definition of confession and its counterpart in the condemnation of false teaching.

Sasse notes the threefold sense of confession. It is the confession of sin, of the faith, and of the praise of God. These three types of confessing interpenetrate each other; they are inseparably together. Confession of sin entails acknowledgment of the truth of God's Word and gives glory to Him. The confession of faith is the praise of the Triune God who reconciles sinners to Himself. Doxological confession acknowledges the Lord for who He is and what He does. Drawing on Ethelbert Stauffer's *New Testament Theology*, Martin Franzmann suggests that the way of Christ is soteriological, doxological, and antagonistic.[10] The same might be also said of confession. It is acknowledgment of the saving work of the Triune God, it renders all glory to Him, and it is antagonistic of both the old Adam (confession of sins) and of every teaching that would contradict God's work for us.

While recognizing that confession is both personal and corporate, it is both "I believe" and "we believe." There is an interplay between the baptismal confessing of the believing Christian and the great "we confess" of the whole church. They are not set in position to one another in the way of modern individualism. Sasse takes up the nature of churchly confession evoked by God's revelation. This is demonstrated in Peter's confession of Christ in Matthew 16:16. This confession, according to Sasse, is not the product of Peter's cognitive rationality, nor is it a stimulation of his pious sentiment; it is faith answering historical revelation. Peter's confession of Christ is the nucleus of every genuine Christian creed.

Sasse observes that the apostolic confession that Jesus is the *Kyrios* (I Cor. 12:3) is possible only by the Spirit and that the church has never forgotten this linkage "between confession and possession of the Spirit."[11] It is a confession made both before God and the world. It is also a confession that distinguishes the church from every other religion, whether it be the synagogue or the variegated cults of the world. Thus the confession establishes boundaries and speaks a definite "No" to all that stands against the truth of God's revelation in Christ. Sasse puts it like this: "The *Kyrios* confession set the boundaries for the church over against the pagan religions, the mystery religions with their 'many lords' (I Cor. 8:5), and the Caesar cult, in which Caesar was honored as lord and god. Indeed, these strange religions had no opposition to the designation of Jesus as *Kyrios*. They were very tolerant. All paganism is tolerant. But for the Christians, there was only one who was the Lord!"[12] The confession is the boundary between that which is church and that which is not church.

Because this is the case, the confession is the line of demarcation between truth and error, between true doctrine and false doctrine. Sasse draws upon the introduction to the Formula of Concord to make the case: "Immediately after the time of the apostles—in fact, while they were still alive—false teachers and heretics invaded the church. Against them the early church prepared *symbola*, that is, short, explicit confessions, which were regarded as unanimous, universal, Christian creed and confession of the orthodox and true church of Christ, namely the Apostles' Creed, the Nicene Creed, and the Athanasian Creed. We pledge ourselves to these and thereby reject all heresies and teachings that have been introduced in the church contrary to them" (FC-Introduction 3, K-W, 486). Thus confession establishes the limits of truth and error. Sasse then concludes, "If the *improbant* ['they (our churches) reject'] and the *damnant* ['they condemn'] (by which is designated the impossibility of church fellowship), which sound so harsh to modern ears are silenced, the Augustana ceases to be confession."[13] For Sasse, this is especially significant for if the church fails to deny false teaching, it, in fact, denies Christ and the confessing church becomes the denying church.

Sasse answers those who claim that it is an act of arrogance and *hubris* that would make human formulations of doctrine such as we have in the Confessions absolute. Confession is rather made in the humility of faith, which submits to God's revelation and will not stand as judge over it. Sect and heresy lack this humility, for they assert themselves over God's Word.

Finally, in this essay, Sasse recognizes that the church remains the church militant on this side of the Last Day:

And just as the struggle between truth and error rings through all of Holy Scripture, so also it runs through the history of the church, and the church would cease to be the church of Christ, messenger of the redeeming truth of the revelation of God to people if it were to cease to fight this battle. Here lies the greatest and most difficult task of the formation of confession. Here is shown whether or not Christianity still knows what the confession of the church means. The manner in which an age approaches this task shows what of courage and strength of faith, and what humility and love are alive in Christianity. Here is shown whether the church knows of the reality of the Holy Spirit.[14]

Eighteen years later, in 1948, Sasse revisits the topic of confession and condemnation in one of his letters to Lutheran pastors entitled "Concerning the Nature of Confession." In this letter, Sasse sharpens and expands many of the points made in the earlier essay. Here he points out that confessions have a double function. They both gather and separate. With their "liturgical we," those who with one mind, heart, and mouth acknowledge Christ and His words are bound together. At the same time, those who share in this confession are separated from those who confess a contrary doctrine. In first-century Christianity, Sasse observes that it was the apostle of love, John, who used the confession that Jesus had come in the flesh to deny those who held to a gnostic interpretation of Christ a place in the church (see I John). This is so for "the gathering of the true Church and the elimination of heresy, that was the objective of all the great doctrinal pronouncements of the ancient Church as well as the Reformation."[15]

Condemnation is the flipside of confession for, as Sasse states, "in this world of sin, truth and error are not easy to distinguish, the difficulty increasing in the same degree as it is a higher truth that is at stake."[16] In this fallen world, the father of lies mishandles and falsifies the Word of God, undermining genuine faith and deceiving fallible human beings. Thus Sasse reminds his readers that the constant prayer of the church is "Lord, keep us steadfast in Your Word." Misleading and deceptive uses of the Holy Scripture must be named and rejected precisely for the sake of the truth of the one Gospel that is alone salvific.

Both confession and condemnation are made in light of the eschatological horizon. Once again, he cites the Formula of Concord that "we are also willing, by God's grace, to appear with intrepid hearts before the judgment seat of Jesus Christ, and give an account of it [FC SD Conclusion 40]."[17] Neither the confession of the truth or the rejection of error can be taken lightly. Both have eternal consequences.

It is this eschatological perspective that also leads Sasse to identify a crucial distinction between the Lutheran and Reformed conceptualities of confession. Lutherans understand every confession to be catholic and eschatological. The Reformed see confession making as local and provisional.[18] Sasse argues that Lutherans understand their Confessions to be catholic and eschatological because they are in agreement with the unchanging Word of God. The Reformed see their confessions as subordinate to Scripture; Lutherans hold that the Confessions are normed by the prophetic and apostolic Word and are, therefore, subscribed to because (*quia*) they are in agreement with Holy Scripture.[19] This also means that the condemnations are not provisional but stand as long as the error persists.

The heresies condemned in the ecumenical creeds repeat themselves. "It [the Lutheran church] knows all heresies are recurrent."[20] Article I of the Augsburg Confession repeats the condemnation of the ancient heresies such as the Manicheans and Arians. Because these heresies do not fade away to become only historical artifacts but reemerge in new dress, Sasse argues that the church is required to be vigilant and discerning as they continue to be accommodated in modern Protestantism even in the Lutheran territorial churches of German. Only a false and lethal security would lead Christians to abandon the condemnation of false teaching. Again Sasse sees false teaching as the work of the "father of lies" who does not cease or abdicate his diabolical work of contradicting the truth of the Gospel.

It is boldness and certainty, not arrogance, that sustains the Lutheran Church in confessing the truth of God's Word and rejecting error. There are two aspects that undergird this stance for Sasse. First, there is the recognition that our confession not only unites us with each other but with the saints who have gone before us:

> Thus the Confession not only unites the present generation but also the orthodox Church of all times. Not only are we united in the

fellowship of the Church in the consensus of the true faith with those who are living today but also with those who before us have confessed the true faith and those who will do so after us, with all believers from the beginning of the Church until the Last Day, from the confessors of the *ecclesia militans* on earth to those who in heaven are glorifying Christ in a confession that has now become purely a praising of God. That is the profound meaning of the Lutheran Confession.[21]

Only in heaven will the anathema cease, for, in the new creation, the former things of deception and error will be no more. The author of all heresy, the devil, will be forever excommunicated and have no access to the church triumphant. Then and only then will confession be purely doxological without the *damnamus*.

Second, the boldness and confidence that we are given comes from the knowledge that to make confession and condemn error is to be located between death and life. This was the attitude of Luther when in 1528 in his "Great Confession," he stated, "Upon this I intend to stand until death, so that in this faith I may with the help of God, depart from this world and come before the judgment seat of our Lord Jesus Christ."[22] Here Sasse notes we are not merely standing in an earthly court but before the celestial Judge: "A confessor is constantly standing at the boundary between time and eternity, between eternal life and eternal death. The confessors of the ancient Church knew this well. And they knew something else. As a confession of faith reaches from time to eternity, so the confession of faith made here on earth finds its continuation in heaven."[23] Both confessions and denials made on earth echo in heaven and have eternal consequences. There can be no indifference to the Truth.

Thus Sasse believed it necessary to reject the Barmen Declaration of 1934.[24] To be sure, he shared most profoundly the antagonism of the Confessing Church to the Nazi party, but he would not allow the political moment to elevate the act of confessing over the content of the confession itself. Five years after Barmen in 1937, Sasse reflects his frustration that those assembled at Barmen "were not concerned with doctrines but with posing a political will upon the church."[25] Lacking a unity in doctrine, they only seek some other unity. "But wherever this unity of the church has been lost, something else must be available to hold a churchly organization together."[26] Sasse observes a parallel in this regard between the decree of Frederick Wilhelm III in 1817 and the Synod at Barmen in 1937. In another essay from the same year, "The Barmen Declaration—An Ecumenical Confession?" Sasse's language is strong and uncompromising as he declares that, "Irresponsible fanatics [*Schwarmgeister*], however, have since proclaimed this declaration a confession, bind Lutheran and Reformed churches—yeas as a word given by the Holy Spirit, which must be respected as God's word."[27] By insisting that Barmen was not only a "declaration" but a "confession," its disciples were imposing it on the church, forcing it on Lutherans without regard for the fact that it intentionally avoids the doctrinal differences between Lutheran and Reformed churches.

Sasse recognized that the implications of confession and condemnation were many, and they were concrete for the Lutheran church of his day. Already in 1934, he wrote, "The Evangelical Lutheran Church is a church which has been sentenced to death by the world."[28] The death sentence had been pronounced by Rome at the Council of Trent. In different forms, it came through in the theology of Rationalism and Pietism. Sasse was acutely aware of how this "death sentence" was articulated by those who bore the name Lutheran but lacked the ability to make the confessions in the *Book of Concord* their own and who would gladly give up the legacy of their fathers to achieve ecumenical goals. He lamented with Löhe, a vision of the funeral of the Lutheran Church presided over by Lutheran pastors. For Sasse, a confessional church must be a confessing church.[29] It is not enough to merely recognize the Confessions as "historical witnesses;" they must actually be confessed both in their positive affirmations and in their condemnation of error. Or, as Sasse puts it in his essay, "Selective Fellowship" written in 1957: "But a confession cannot remain a real confession if it is only inherited. It must be confessed."[30]

For Sasse, the condemnations made in the Lutheran Confessions are true and necessary because the Holy Scriptures are true. Sasse recognized that the spirit of F. Schleiermacher's famous statement, "The person who possesses a holy scripture does not have religion, but rather it is the one who has no need of such writing, yet certainly would like to make such a thing"[31] is incarnate in much of modern Christianity as can be seen in theological relativism and ecclesiastical pluralism. Where the Scriptures can no longer be acknowledged as the Word of the Triune God, confession can be no more than an individual opinion or a school of thought. In this setting, any condemnation of false doctrine is viewed as ecumenically impolite and a sign of narrow, confessional rigidity. Yet, where the "No" of the *damnamus* cannot be solemnly spoken, the joyful "Yes" to Christ and His saving Gospel is muted and finally evaporates into silence. We conclude with a return to the beginning, the confession that Jesus is the *Kyrios* necessitates rejection of all that contradicts Him and His words that every thought might be held captive to Him. Sasse recognized this and was not ashamed to speak the *damnamus* so that Christ alone by be confessed as the Lord that He is.

Notes

1 Here see the classic work by Hans-Werner Gienschen, *We Condemn: How Luther and the Luther and 16ᵗʰ Century Lutheranism Condemned False Doctrine*, trans. Herbert J.A. Bouman (St. Louis: Concordia Publishing House, 1967). For a more recent example of maintaining the necessity of the condemnations, see the statement by the Faculty of Theology at Göttingen, *Outmoded Condemnations?* Trans. Oliver K. Olson and Franz Posset (Fort Wayne: Luther Academy, 1992).

2 For a fuller treatment, See John T. Pless, "Hermann Sasse 1895–1976" in *Twentieth-Century Lutheran Theologians*, ed. Mark C. Mattes (Göttingen: Vandenhoeck & Ruprecht, 2013), 155–177.

3 Hermann Sasse, "The Impact of Bultmannism on American Lutheranism" *Lutheran Synod Quarterly* (June 1965), 5.

4 For more on Sasse's use of Löhe, see John T. Pless, "Hermann Sasse's Reception of the Loehe Legacy" in *Die einigende Mitte: Theologie in konfessioneller und ökumenischer Verantwortung*, edited by Christoph Barnbrock and Gilberto da Silva (Göttingen: Ruprecht Edition, 2018), 334–342.

5 Hermann Sasse, "American Christianity and the Church," in *The Lonely Way, Vol. I: 1927–1939* edited Matthew C. Harrison (Saint Louis: Concordia Publishing House, 2002), 47.

6 H. Sasse, "American Christianity and the Church," 55.

7 For more on Sasse's critical appreciation of Löhe's work, see John T. Pless, "Hermann Sasse's Reception of the Loehe Legacy" in *"Die einigende Mitte" Theologie in konfessioneller und ökumenischer Vertantwortung: Festschrift für Werner Klän*, Hrsg. Christoph Barnbrock and Gilberto da Silva (Göttingen: Edition Ruprecht, 2018), 334–342.

8　Arthur Cochrane, *The Church's Confession Under Hitler* (Philadelphia: Westminster Press, 1962), 36.

9　Sasse, "The Confession of the Church," *The Lonely Way*, Vol. I, 101.

10　Martin Franzmann, "Three Aspects of the Way of Christ: An Approach to the Fellowship Problem," *Concordia Theological Monthly* (October 1952), 706.

11　Sasse, "The Confession of the Church," 111.

12　Ibid., 112. Also see where Sasse argues that the Formula of Concord is a confirmation of the Augsburg Confession: "But now its particular character, as had already been set forth in the Augsburg Confession, was sharply delineated. Thenceforth it was part of the nature of the Evangelical Lutheran Church, as a confessional church to draw a clear ecclesiastical line separating it, not only from Rome and from the Enthusiasts, but from the Reformed Churches of the Calvinistic order."—*Here We Stand*, trans. Theodore Tappert (Adelaide: Lutheran Publishing House, 1979), 113.

13　"The Confession of the Church," 113.

14　Ibid., 113.

15　Sasse, "Concerning the Nature of Confession in the Church" in *Letters to Lutheran Pastors*, Vol. I, 27.

16　Ibid., 27.

17　Ibid., 32.

18　Here see Jan Rohls, *Reformed Confessions: Theology from Zurich to Barmen*, trans. John Hoffmeyer (Louisville: Westminster/John Knox Press, 1998) as Rohls demonstrates that it is characteristic of Reformed confessions to be viewed as limited to specific critical occasions and open to revision. He cites Karl Barth, "A Reformed Creed is a statement, spontaneously and publicly formulated by a Christian community within a geographically limited area, which, until further action, defines its character to outsiders; and which, until further action, gives guidance for its own doctrine and life; it is a formulation of the insight given to the whole Christian Church by the revelation of God in Jesus Christ, which is witnessed to by the Holy Scriptures alone" (297).

19　"Here lies the basic reason why the Lutheran Church pledges its ministers upon the confession *because* [*quia*] 'it has been taken from God's Word and is founded firmly and well therein' (FC SC Comprehensive Summary III) and not only *insofar as* [*quatenus*] they agree with Scripture as is customary in the Reformed churches. This *quia* presupposes a firm faith in the Holy Scripture and its perspicuity"—Sasse, "Concerning the Nature of Confession in the Church," 31. For more on the *quia/quantenus*, see the exchange between a Pastor Höppl and Sasse from 1938, "*Quatenus* or *Quia*" in *The Lonely Way*, Vol. 1, 455–466.

20　Sasse, "Concerning the Nature of Confession in the Church," 31.

21　Ibid., 32.

22 Ibid., 32. Cited from AE 37:360.

23 Ibid., 33.

24 For more on the Barmen Declaration, see Rohls, 293–302. And overtly sympathetic reading of the Barmen Declaration can be found in Arthur C. Cochrane, *The Church's Confession Under Hitler* (Philadelphia: Westminister Press, 1962)

25 Sasse, "Confession and Confessing: Lessons from Five Years of the Church Struggle" *The Lonely Way*, Vol. I, 341.

26 Ibid., 341.

27 Hermann Sasse, "The Barmen Declaration?—An Ecumenical Confession" in *The Lonely Way*, Vol. I, 347–348. Also see, *Here We Stand*, 174–178. Here Sasse critiques the Barmen Declaration in light of the theology of its primary drafter, Karl Barth.

28 Hermann Sasse, *Here We Stand*, trans. Theodore Tappert (Adelaide: Lutheran Publishing House, 1979), 187.

29 Sasse uses is this language in a letter from 1949, "On the Problem of the Union of Lutheran Churches" where he states: "The history of American Lutheranism has a third thing to teach us about the question of what the Church of the Augsburg Confession really is: as a *confessional* church it must necessarily be a *confessing church*"—*Letters to Lutheran Pastors*, Vol. I, 172. Also see Sasse's observation in the 1951 letter, "Worldwide Lutheranism in the Way to Hanover": "In the sense of this 'Yes' confession is the distinguishing feature of the Lutheran Church. In it, the deepest life of our church comes to be expressed, just as the life and essence of other churches finds expression in liturgy, in ecclesiology, and in discipline"— *Letters to Lutheran Pastors*, Vol. I, 407.

30 Sasse, "Selective Fellowship," *The Lonely Way*, Vol. II, 252.

31 Cited by Sasse, "End of the Confessional Era?" *Letters to Lutheran Pastors*, Vol. III, 435.

53

Damnamus

An Ecumenical Necessity—
Insights from Hermann Sasse

We have said that Sasse was both an ecumenical confessionalist and a confessional ecumenist.[1] His passion for the truth of the apostolic Gospel and his love of the church catholic compelled him to be both. What did this mean for the way in which Sasse saw the *damnamus* as an ecumenical necessity? We first turn to Sasse's confession of the unity of the church, and its correlate his condemnation of false constructions of unity. Then we will examine two of Sasse's essays on mission where this comes to practical expression.

For Sasse, the unity of the one church of Jesus Christ is not an afterthought. Recognizing the truth of the one church from Ephesians 4 confessed in the Nicene Creed, the unity of the church is an article of faith. The church's unity is hidden; it is an article of faith not sight. The oneness of the church is not a goal to be achieved by ecumenical goodwill and careful negotiation. Writing in 1959, Sasse comments, "This oneness, this true unity, is a reality which is not made by man. Nor can it be destroyed by men. What can happen is that we as individuals or church bodies or congregations (Revelation 2–3) lose the true faith and apostatize from the true church and its 'oneness.' Every Christian is a potential traitor (Matt. 26:22), denier (Matt. 26:34), or apostate, as every church body is in danger of becoming heretical."[2] The oneness of the church is fundamental in Sasse's thinking, for it is the one body of the one

Christ. It is a unity to be guarded and preserved and for Sasse, as for Luther, only God is capable of that task:

> Lord, keep us steadfast in Your Word;
> Curb those who would by craft or sword
> Would wrest the kingdom from Your Son
> And bring to naught all He has done. (LSB 655:1)

Luther's hymn speaks of preservation in the truth. Writing in *Here We Stand*, Sasse asserts, "It is the plain teaching of the New Testament that the true unity of the church is *unity in the truth*. And it is the painful experience of church history, particularly during the last century, that whenever attempts have been made to unite churches without inquiring about pure doctrine—that is, without establishing what truth is, and what error [is], in Christianity— unity has not been achieved; and, what is worse, the divisions have been magnified."[3] Recalling Article VII of the Augsburg Confession, Sasse accents the fact that while it is enough (*satis est*) for the true unity of the church that the Gospel be preached purely and the sacraments administered according to the divine word, it is also necessary. Sasse's reading of Article VII is not minimalistic. Article VII requires the rejection of error and condemnation of all that pollutes the purity of the Gospel and deprives the sacraments of their God-given promises. Writing in a 1937 essay, Sasse draws out the implication of confession for the unity of the church: "We neither can nor shall ever recognize as church a church whose unity does not consist in the united teaching of the pure Gospel, a church in which various conflicting confessions are recognized as equally valid, a church in which pure doctrine and false teaching have the same right to exist."[4]

Jesus' High Priestly Prayer of John 17 contains petitions that bring truth and unity inseparably together as Sasse observes, "Nothing less will be needed for it to be clearly understood why the one petition in the high priestly prayer, 'That they may all be one,' is inseparably connected with the other, 'Sanctify them in your truth!' There must be an awakening which arouses a hunger for pure doctrine."[5]

Unity in the truth entails the recognition and rejection of the lie. In an essay written just prior to WWII in 1938, Sasse penned

these words: "Where man can no longer bear the truth, he cannot live without the lie."[6] In this wonderfully lucid little booklet, Sasse goes on to contrast the truth with the lie. He notes that from the beginning the lie and the truth have done battle within the church. So it was in the days of the apostles as Paul said to the congregation at Corinth: "For there must be factions among you in order that those who are genuine among you may be recognized" (I Cor. 11:19). The lie, Sasse said, takes on various forms. There is the **pious lie**, that hypocrisy with which man lies to himself, to others, and even to God. The pious lie easily becomes the **edifying lie**. This is the lie that takes comfort in untruth. Sasse sees an example of the edifying lie embraced by medieval Christians when they trusted in the power of the saints, relying on the excess of their merit to further them in the struggle toward righteousness. The edifying lie was the lie unmasked and expelled by the Reformation. Then there is the **dogmatic lie**; the assertion that we have come to greater doctrinal maturity and old teachings are to be changed for a more contemporary, relevant theology. Finally, there is, Sasse warned, the **institutional lie** when the churches embody the lie in their own life, instituting false teaching as normative. Without the truth, it is impossible to recognize the lie. Contemporary Protestantism is a "religion of perpetual uncertainty, doubt, and secret unbelief"[7] and hence is incapable of making assertions of truth or refutation of falsehood. Such a spirit, Sasse sees prefigured in Erasmus: "He [Luther] saw behind Erasmus' concept of an undogmatic Christianity the coming neo-paganism of the modern world."[8]

There are any number of issues where we might observe how Sasse handles the confession of the truth and the condemnation of error. Certainly, this figures prominently in his work on the Lord's Supper. Sasse wrote on the Lord's Supper more than other single topic, including his *magnum opus, This is My Body: Luther's Contention for the Real Presence in the Sacrament of the Altar*, first published in 1959. Confession of the presence of Jesus' true body and blood in the Sacrament necessitates a rejection of every teaching that would make this gift ambiguous or uncertain. For Sasse, the question of the church's unity and unity in the Sacrament are inseparable, as Werner Klän has demonstrated.[9] For Sasse, the Lord's Supper is no ancillary practice but the gift of the Lord at the very center of the church's life.

So he writes in the preface to a collection of essays on the Sacrament in 1941, "Where the Table of the Lord is deserted, where the Lord's Supper is longer known or celebrated, there the church dies, irretrievably lost."[10] The struggle over the Lord's Supper was not a mere battle over differing theological interpretations but went to the heart of the Gospel itself. It is for this reason that the Formula of Concord condemned contrary opinions with the strongest language, as Sasse shows in his 1941 essay, "The Formula of Concord's Decision About the Lord's Supper." Lutherans, Sasse contended, have an ecumenical responsibility to do what the authors of the Formula of Concord did. First, to test the doctrine by Scripture. Then he says, "The second thing to be done is the joyful proclamation of the truth given us to confess and proclaim. That [truth] is no longer the Lord's gift if we attempt to keep it only as ours; it is for all Christians, and this the more urgently so they are drawn in our day to an earnest probing of the Lord's Supper."[11] The condemnations of the Formula of Concord cannot be bypassed or set aside without diminishing the confession that Christ gives to you communicants His true body and blood to eat and to drink in the Sacrament.

The *damnamus* is also there in his encounter with Karl Barth on infant Baptism and Helmut Thielicke on the ordination of women to the pastoral office. It is there in his writings specific ecumenical organizations such as the Lutheran World Federation. But for our purposes today, I would like to focus on two essays that Sasse did on the church's mission for these two essays demonstrate how Sasse treated the *damnamus* as an ecumenical necessity.

The first essay, written in 1946, "The Question of the Church's Unity on the Mission Field" addresses a practical challenge that would naturally arise in the years immediately after WWII as western churches were able to either resume or initiate mission endeavors in Asia and Africa. In this piece, Sasse observes that given the multiplicity of denominations involved in evangelistic work in places where the Gospel had not been previously preached.

In this essay, Sasse notes that the contemporary question of the unity of the church arose from the mission field. The World Missionary Conference of Edinburgh in 1910 was the birthplace of the modern ecumenical movement. At Edinburgh, the issue of unity was not theoretical but pragmatically driven by the desire

to effectively evangelize the world in the twentieth century. John Mott (1865–1955), an American Methodist layman, spearheaded the conference, optimistically declaring, "It is our hope that before we close our eyes in death, all people on earth will have had the opportunity to know and await the living Lord Christ."[12] The Edinburgh Conference was more at home in the optimism of the nineteenth century rather than the disappointment that would come with the twentieth century. The missional optimism of Edinburgh would fade with two world wars and the rise of secularistic nihilism.

But for Sasse, there is a deeper issue: "How can Christian mission call the peoples of the world to the *one* truth of the *one* Gospel if its bearers themselves are not united on what the Gospel actually is?"[13] Sasse argues that the message of the Gospel has definite and identifiable content; it is the word of the cross. It is not a denominational message but the apostolic kerygma of Jesus Christ, the incarnate God and Lord, put to death and raised to life for the justification of sinners. This Gospel is not simply a message about Christ repeating the history of His life, death, and resurrection. It is the proclamation of His saving work always predicated for sinners, and it is delivered in the oral word of preaching and in Baptism and the Sacrament of the Altar instituted by the Lord Himself. It is not to be confused with a philosophy of life, a system of morality, or mystical experience. The Gospel is the word of the cross, the message of God's reconciliation of humanity with Himself, not the recipe of humanity to reconcile itself with God.

In contrast to the activism that prompted those inspired by Edinburgh, Sasse does not seek the unity of the church as a goal to be pursued for the sake of mission. Rather, the unity of the church is a given to be confessed: "Genuine faith in the *una sancta* as an indestructible, divinely established reality in the world can guard us all, Christians of churches young and old, from doubting the church of God. For the present state of Christianity will plunge anyone into despair who only sees the outer state and knows nothing of the hidden glory of the *regnum Christi* ('kingdom of Christ'), which stands behind it."[14] It is not that we see one, holy, Christian and apostolic church but that we believe in this church hidden under suffering, weakness, and the shame of external divisions.

The Christian stance is not despair but faithfulness and patience in the face of outward fissures in Christendom. The unity of the church is constituted in Christ alone. Where this is forgotten, Sasse observes, a lethal synergism sets in that would attempt to create some other unity than that described in Article VII of the Augsburg Confession, as that established by the pure preaching of the Gospel and the administration of the sacraments according to the divine word. This was the error, says Sasse, of Pietism expressed in the slogan, "Doctrine divides, service unites."[15] Such error was to be repudiated precisely to guard and maintain the unity of Christ's body.

Erudite church historian that he is, Sasse reminds his readers that if the ancient church would have neglected doctrine, Christianity would have come to an end. The Marcionites, Valentinians, Montanists, Nestorians, and Arians were not simply alternative versions of a single Christian reality. Had these heretical distortions of the Gospel been recognized as legitimate and reconcilable narratives of Jesus Christ, the church would no longer exist, and her mission ruined. "Just as a man whose kidneys no longer eliminate poisons which have accumulated in the body will die, so the church will die which no longer eliminates heresy."[16] Sasse's essay anticipated what would come to be known as the ecumenical paradigm of "reconciled diversity" and talk of "post-denominational Christianity." Yet he understands that both miss the point of the necessity of confession. Where there is a confessional vacuum, it will be filled by an eclectic mixture of truth with error. The outcome, Sasse predicts, will be a reversion to paganism: "And so today, too, wherever the church no longer is able to separate from heresy, it will fall back into paganism and be destroyed."[17]

Sasse does not end this article on a negative note of pessimism or despair for the Lord is exceedingly rich in mercy and preserves His Word in this dying world. Sasse takes His readers back to Jesus' high priestly prayer, which is a missionary prayer:

> These young Christians also read the apostolic warning against heresy. And there are many gripping testimonies to the fact that they have begun to understand why the high priestly prayer of the Lord, both the petition for the preservation of unity and the petition for the preservation of truth belong inseparably together. 'That they may

be one' (John 17:21) is merely the opposite side of 'Sanctify them in
your truth; your Word is truth' (John 17:17). It is Jesus Christ himself
and no one else who tells us that the question of the *one* church is the
question of the *true* church.[18]

When the truth of the Gospel is lost, unity is splintered by schism
and sectarianism. Truth and unity are coherent, and finally, they will
stand or fall together.

A second major essay from Sasse's pen would come in 1954
under the title, "The Lutheran Church and World Mission." Written
roughly five years after his arrival in Australia, Sasse is aware of the
challenges to the church's mission in India and Asia.[19] He recognizes
that many questioned whether there should be a Lutheran Church in
southeast Asia, referring to the particular circumstances of the Batak
Church, which had been accepted into membership in the Lutheran
World Federation even though it did not subscribe to either the Small
Catechism or the Augsburg Confession. He notes that some equate
the importing of Lutheran teaching to Asia as a kind of confessional
colonialism. Sasse observes that the question is pressed on us both
by Christians and non-Christians, why should there be a Lutheran
Church on the mission field?

Sasse answers this question by returning to the dominical words
that institute the preaching of the Gospel and the right administration of the sacraments. God has provided for these that human
beings might come to justifying faith to echo the language of Article
V of the Augsburg Confession. He is critical of Karl Hartenstein[20] and
others whom he believes ground mission in human energies rather
than the means of grace which are the marks of the church: "So the
world's mission churches are in danger of becoming churches without sacraments, at least without the real Sacrament, which is means
of grace and not a harmless sign which one can, if needed, even omit.
The LWF, with its mission department, can't help either. For the
Sacraments, without which Luther couldn't even imagine a church,
don't interest it very much, as both its words and deeds show."[21]

A product of the Rhenish Mission Society, the Batak Church
could not distinguish between the Lutheran and the Reformed doctrines of the Lord's Supper. Sasse recognized this as unionism incapable of making a clear confession. Without confession, mission is

made sterile no matter how impressive it may seem outwardly. In a similar vein, Sasse worries that the church in India is in danger of losing the Lutheran doctrine of Sacrament. Such a loss, he opines, would be particularly disastrous there and would deprive Indian Christians of teaching of "the real incarnation and the real presence as concrete forgiveness"[22] throwing them back on spiritualistic interpretations carried over from Hinduism.

Lutheran missions are such not simply in name but by actual confession. There is an urgency to Sasse's appeal that Lutherans not bury the treasure of the confession but proclaim it with boldness and confidence:

> As at home, so today also in the mission field, the Lutheran pastor stands before the difficult, and yet so thankful job of speaking the Gospel so clearly, as clearly as the catechism and the Augsburg Confession so. The Confession must become alive [in] us again, and we want to begin with ourselves. For basically, contemporary humanity of all races has had enough of nonbinding chatter. Communism would never have achieved such victories if it hadn't satisfied the hunger for dogma which the churches weren't able to satisfy anymore. But why have we kept from people the true dogma of the pure Gospel? May God strengthen us all for the battle for the true confession, and help us, in the power of Christ's love, to call back to the Gospel's truth a Christendom which is sinking into relativism.[23]

Lutheran mission will lead to Lutheran churches not merely in denominational affiliation but in doctrine and practice. This theme would be ably carried forward by Sasse's student and associate, Friedrich Wilhelm Hopf (1910–1982), director of the Bleckmar Mission from 1950 to 1978. In an essay entitled, "The Lutheran Church Plants Lutheran Mission," Hopf largely encapsulates the major themes of his mentor's thinking on mission, concluding,

> To stewards of the older and younger Lutheran churches, being trustworthy and faithful belongs to their ecumenical responsibility to the whole Christian church on earth. Woe to every Lutheran church who so misunderstands her confessional bond, as is she should introvertedly eke out her own meager existence in seclusion, protect her

stock, and leave parts of Christianity polluted or ruled by false doctrine to their own resources. If Lutheran mission should and must lead to Lutheran church, then this in no way means the isolation of a young Lutheran church that is just emerging. It means, rather, the responsibility of the mission to preserve the unity with all rightly believing Lutheran churches on earth, but just as much its responsibility to the testimony to the biblical truth of salvation and its consequences beyond all borders and boundaries of painful divisions in the church.[24]

For Hopf as for Sasse, the question of mission always stands or falls with the doctrine of the church and particularly the confessional unity of the church in the marks of the church.

For Sasse, doctrine and mission could never be played off one against the other. The whole of Sasse's theology runs through the assertion of Article VII of the *Augustana* that it is sufficient but also necessary for the true unity of the church that the Gospel preached purely and the sacraments be administered evangelically. It is this treasure that has been entrusted to the Lutheran church. Faithfulness in mission entails faithfulness to the means of grace from which the church has her life and growth. Sasse's sharp and often unwelcome critique of moves within global Christianity in general and Lutheranism[25] in particular were necessary that the one saving Gospel of Jesus Christ not be buried away under the rubble of ecclesiastical proposals that ignore the need for doctrinal truth in mission. In this sense, Hermann Sasse remains a prophetic figure for confessional Lutherans in our own day, calling us to embrace mission with boldness and confidence that the Word of the Lord might have free course in a dark and dying world.

Notes

1 Here see Ronald Feuerhahn, "Hermann Sasse: Theologian of the Church" in *Hermann Sasse: A Man for Our Times* ed. John R. Stephenson and Thomas M. Winger (Saint Louis: Concordia Publishing House, 1998), 11–36.

2 Hermann Sasse, "The Crisis of Lutheranism" in *The Lonely Way*, Vol. I (Saint Louis, Concordia Publishing House, 2001), 284. Also note his 1951 essay, "Worldwide Lutheranism on the Way to Hanover" where Sasse writes against those who accuse confessional Lutheranism of an "intellectual *Donatism*":

"There is no worse misunderstanding of the concern for the church's confession than this. The Lutheran Church knows of no ecclesiastical idea which we humans have to attempt to bring about. The church is no ideal, but rather a reality. The *una sancta* is a reality in every moment of church history. It is a great reality, which remains our comfort, even then, and especially then, when it appears 'as if there were no church,' and 'as if it were entirely wrecked' (Ap VII–VIII 9 [Tappert, 168–169])."—*Letters to Lutheran Pastors*, Vol. I, 417.

3 Hermann Sasse, *Here We Stand*, trans. Theodore Tappert (Adelaide: Lutheran Publishing House, 1979), 186.

4 Hermann Sasse, "The Confessions and the Unity of the Church" in *The Lonely Way*, Vol. I. ed. Matthew C. Harrison (Saint Louis: Concordia Publishing House, 2001), 356.

5 Ibid., 363.

6 Hermann Sasse, *Union and Confession*, trans. Matthew C. Harrison (Saint Louis: The Office of the President, The Lutheran Church-Missouri Synod, 1997), 1.

7 Hermann Sasse, "Did God Really Say?" in *The Lonely Way*, Vol. II, 322.

8 Hermann Sasse, "Erasmus, Luther, and Modern Christendom" *The Lonely Way*, Vol. II, 381.

9 See Werner Klän, "Eucharist and Eschatology: Marginal Comments Concerning the Inherent Coherence of the Theology of Hermann Sasse" in *Lord Jesus Christ, Will You Not Stay: Essays in Honor of Ronald Feuerhahn on the Occasion of his Sixty-fifth Birthday*, ed. J. Bart Day et al (Houston: Feuerhahn Festschrift Committee, 2002), 153–165. Also see John Stephenson, "Holy Supper, Holy Church" in *Hermann Sasse: A Man for Our Times?*, 224–239.

10 Hermann Sasse, "Preface to *Vom Sakrament Des Altars*" in *The Lonely Way*, Vol II, ed. Matthew C. Harrison (Saint Louis: Concordia Publishing House, 2002), 12.

11 Sasse, "Preface to *Vom Sakrament Des Altars*," 16.

12 Cited by Henning Wroegemann, *Intercultural Theology*, Vol. II: Theologies of Mission, trans. Karl E Böhmer (Downers Grove: Intervarsity Press, 2018). Sasse makes reference to Mott and this citation in numerous of his essays on unity and ecumenism. See, for example, "Thoughts About an Ecumenical Anniversary" in *Letters to Lutheran Pastors*, Vol. III, ed. Matthew C. Harrison (St. Louis: Concordia Publishing House, 2015), 225–246. For other assessments of the Edinburgh Conference and its impact on mission down to the present day, see *Walking Humbly with the Lord: Church and Mission Engaging Plurality* ed. Viggo Mortensen and Andreas Østerlund Nielsen (Grand Rapids, Eerdmans, 2010). This volume was published in commemoration of the centennial of Edinburgh and as such provides helpful historical background and critical analysis and reflection on the significance of the Conference.

13   Sasse, "The Question of the Church's Unity on the Mission Field," *Lonely Way*, Vol II: 1941–1976, 183.

14   Ibid., 186.

15   Ibid., 188.

16   Ibid., 190.

17   Ibid., 191. Here one may also see Sasse's essay from 1960 "On the Doctrine of the Holy Spirit" in *Letters to Lutheran Pastors*, Vol. III: 1957–1969, 200–222. Here Sasse notes the theological "enthusiasm" seeks to find God where He has not promised to be present and how this is manifest in those who look for outward success in numbers of converts or the size of ecumenical gatherings. Instead Sasse reminds his readers that discernment is a gift of the Spirit as by the Word, He enables churches to distinguish between truth and error.

18   Ibid., 191.

19   For example, see Hermann Sasse, "Die Kirche in Asien" in *In stau confessionis III*, Hrsg. Werner Klän und Roland Ziegler (Göttingen: Edition Ruprecht, 2011), 215–225.

20   Hartenstein was instrumental in the development of the *missio Dei*. See John G. Flett, *The Witness of God: The Trinity, Missio Dei, Karl Barth, and the Nature of Christian Community* (Grand Rapids: Eerdmans, 2010), 124–162.

21   Sasse, "The Lutheran Church and World Mission," 321.

22   Ibid., 327. Sasse was a keen observer of ecumenical developments in India. See, for example, his "Some Remarks on the Statement on the Lord's Supper Agreed Upon Between the Church of South India and the Federation of the Evangelical Lutheran Churches of India" (1956) in *Scripture and the Church: Selected Essays of Hermann Sasse*, edited Jeffrey J. Kloha and Ronald R. Feuerhahn (Saint Louis: Concordia Seminary Press, 1995), 260–270 and especially his 1962 piece, "The Union of South India as a Question for the Lutheran Church" in *Letters to Lutheran Pastors*, Vol. III: 1957–1969, 321–339.

23   Ibid., 333.

24   Wilhelm Friedrich Hopf, "The Lutheran Church Plants Lutheran Missions," trans. Rachel Mumme with Matthew C. Harrison, *Journal of Lutheran Mission* (April 2015), 28.

25   See for example the 1956 essay, "The Confessional Problem in Today's World Lutheranism" in *Letters to Lutheran Pastors, Vol. II: 1951–1956* edited Matthew C. Harrison (Saint Louis: Concordia Publishing House, 2014), 475–501, and Martin Kretzmann's critical response, "Letter to the Editor" in *The Lutheran Layman* (August 1, 1957), 7ff.

54

Damnamus

A Catechetical Necessity

It is often observed that the Small Catechism is remarkable for its lack of polemics.[1] It might be more accurate to say that Luther is only covertly polemical in the Small Catechism. His polemic in the SC is subversive, under the table. While it is true that he is not aggressively or openly attacking opponents, the Reformation controversies—both with Rome and the Sacramentarians—are lurking in the background and are addressed in the SC.

A surface reading of Luther's SC would seem to indicate that it completely lacks a polemical edge. There are no explicit condemnations of the false beliefs of Luther's opponents. Completely pastoral in tone, the rhetoric of the SC is marked by evangelical warmth and an appeal to trust in the sure and certain promises of God. Reformation scholars often find it rather remarkable that the SC is so pastoral and devoid of polemics as Luther himself was more often than not given to sharp (and some would say crude) statements in condemnation of the Pope, the Sacramentarians, and the Jews.[2]

The SC, by way of contrast, seems to work with a principle articulated by Luther that one cannot be too gentle with simple sheep or too harsh with the wolves. The SC was written for children and simple Christians. The SC would do this subtly, and we might even say an understated manner while the LC would be more direct and pointed. It is only in the Preface to the SC that Luther engages in an open and unabashed condemnation: "O you bishops! How are you going to answer to Christ, now that you have so shamefully neglected the people and have not exercised your office for even a single second? May you escape punishment for this! You forbid the cup [to the laity] in the Lord's Supper and insist on the observance of your human laws while never even bothering to ask whether the people know the Lord's Prayer, the Creed, the Ten Commandments, or a single section of God's Word. Shame on you forever!" (SC Preface 4–5, K-W, 348).[3]

In the Preface, Luther shames those who do not want to learn these core elements of the Christian faith, asserting that they should not be admitted to the Sacrament of the Altar, as baptismal sponsors, nor allowed to enjoy any aspect of Christian freedom. Instead, he says they "should simply be sent back home to the pope and his officials and, along with them, to the devil himself" (SC Preface 11, K-W, 348–349). Yet none of this strong and condemnatory rhetoric makes it into the body of the SC itself. Even in the LC, Luther's language would be measured, and opponents were not identified by name. In the LC, the polemics serve a pastoral aim.

Luther's pastoral aim was to strengthen the believer's life of faith and love. The SC originated in Luther's aim to reform preaching and the care of souls. Here it is helpful to take a look at the impulses which prompted Luther to prepare the SC not just as a book but "training in a certain body of knowledge."[4]

Martin Luther's Catechisms, both the Small and the Large, were born in the pulpit. Heinrich Bornkamm describes the birth: "The Large Catechism is one of Luther's greatest artistic achievements. From this initial work, a second sprang forth, The Small Catechism. While the mastery of the larger work lies in the wealth and liveliness of its articulating the faith, the beauty of the smaller work lies in the precision with which it made matters of faith luminous and memorable. Without the preparatory condensation of the catechetical sermons into The Large Catechism, there would have been no crystallization of the entire substance into The Small Catechism."[5] Not only were the catechisms derived from preaching, they would serve the hearers in providing a hermeneutical framework to understand the sermon. That is, they would assist hearers in identifying true evangelical proclamation based on the Holy Scriptures from counterfeit doctrines.

As early as July 1516, Luther preached on the Catechism. By 1522, the practice had been established in Wittenberg of preaching on the Catechism four times per year. Luther's Holy Week sermons of 1529 reflect much of the material used in his treatment of Confession and the Lord's Supper in the Large Catechism.

Luther's provided documents were designed to replace the "confessional manuals" of the medieval church. Included in this category would be such pieces as *Instructions on Confessions,* 1518 (WA 1:257–265); *A Short Explanation of the Ten Commandments, Their Fulfillment and Transgressions,* 1518 (WA 1:247–256); *The Sacrament of Penance,* 1519 (AE 35:3–22); *A Discussion on How Confession Should be Made,* 1519 (AE 39:27–47); *A Short Form of the Ten Commandments, A Short Form of the Faith, A Short Form of the Our Father,* 1520 (WA 7:204–214). Composed for lay use, these tracts were aimed at assisting evangelical Christians in making a salutary confession of their sins in repentance wrought by the law and then in laying hold of the promise by faith in the words of the absolution. These early pastoral texts would be building blocks as Luther moved to provide a concise form of Christian teaching geared toward repentance, faith and holy living.

Luther's devotional literature was also a source of influence in his preparation of the Catechisms. In particular, here we might note *Personal Prayer Book,* 1522, and *A Booklet for the Laity and Children,* 1525. Several of Luther's "Catechism Hymns" actually pre-date the publication of the Catechisms: "Here is the Tenfold Sure Command" (1524), "We All Believe in One True God" (1524); "From Depths of Woe I Cry to You" (1523); "O Lord, We Praise Thee" (1524). From both a literary and theological perspective, it may be observed that concepts expressed in these hymns will find their way into the Small Catechism.

Luther's own catechisms may be seen as a response to three events: (a) The request of Pastor Nicholas Hausmann for a catechism to use in the instruction of the "common folk" in 1524; (b) controversy between Agricola and Melanchthon on the place of the law in the Christian life; (c) a remedy to the maladies diagnosed in the Visitations of 1528. The impact of the Saxon Visitations is seen in Luther's preface to the Small Catechism:

"The deplorable, wretched deprivation that I recently encountered while I was a visitor has constrained and compelled me to prepare this catechism, or Christian instruction, in such a brief, plain, and simple version. Dear God, what misery I beheld! The ordinary person, especially in the villages, knows absolutely nothing about the Christian faith, and unfortunately many pastors are completely unskilled and incompetent teachers. Yet supposedly they all bear the name Christian, are baptized, and receive the holy sacrament, even though they do not know the Lord's Prayer, the Creed, or the Ten Commandments! As a result they live like simple cattle or irrational pigs and, despite the fact that the Gospel has returned, have mastered the fine art of misusing their freedom." (SC Preface 1–3, K-W, 347–348)

Albrecht Peters' description of Luther's fourfold direction in his work in formulating the catechism is helpful in understanding both the design of the SC and the Reformer's intentions for its usage in the evangelical congregations.

1. As a summary and digest of the Bible, the catechism strives to comprehend its central content, summarizing and laying out in simple terms the biblical witness of the revelation of God the Father through Jesus Christ, the Son, in the Holy Spirit as decisive for salvation.

2. The catechism enunciates the spiritual core of Scripture not as the insights of a spiritually gifted individual but by means of texts that have prevailed in Christendom and within the context of the history of interpretation of these decisive texts. This is how the reformer circumspectly makes his confession a part of the witness of the Western Church.

3. The catechism looks at the concrete daily life of the simple Christian taking both calling and estate into consideration and understands them as the place in life God gave us in the coordinate system of natural/creaturely, societal/social, as well as historical/cultural, relations. In this way the catechism teaches and exercises Christians in faith and love. The catechism desires to instruct for this

    purpose, not only as a doctrinal, confessional book but also a book of prayer and comfort.

4. The catechism moves Scripture, the confession of the Church, and our daily life into the light of the last day. The catechism should be viewed in light of the beginning of Luther's Invocavit Sermons of 1522 that "the summons of death comes to us all, and no one can die for another. Every one must fight his own battle with death by himself, alone. . . . Therefore, every one must for himself must know and be armed with the chief things that concern a Christian."[6]

We may note that Peter's four dimensions do not explicitly include anything of a polemical nature, although a condemnation of the contrary position is implicit in the positive statement. The implicit *damnamus* in the SC might be best understood in light of Luther's understanding of the life of faith as a life lived under constant threat and attack.

Oswald Bayer has contrasted Luther's approach to theology with that of Anselm as it was configured in the medieval tradition. For Anselm, theology was faith seeking understanding. For Luther, it was faith enduring attack.[7] It is in this light that we see Luther's intention in preparing the Catechisms and urging their use by disciples of Jesus Christ, ordinary Christians. In the words of Albrecht Peters: "Studying and praying the catechism takes place on the battlefield between God and anti-god; there is no neutrality here."[8]

This can be seen explicitly in Luther's Preface to the Large Catechism. Repeatedly Luther urges Christians not to take the catechism for granted or to believe that they have attained a sufficient knowledge of the faith. Not the least of Luther's concerns is that Christians are imperiled by the assaults of the devil, the world, and the sinful flesh and cannot withstand these attacks without God's Word: "Nothing is so powerfully effective against the devil, the world, the flesh, and all evil thoughts as to occupy one's self with God's Word, to speak about it and meditate upon it in the way that Psalm 1[:2] calls those blessed who 'meditate on God's law day and night.' Without doubt you will offer up no more powerful incense or savor against the devil than to occupy yourself with God's commandments and words and to speak, sing, or think about them" (LC-Preface 10, K-W, 381). If the fact the devil who constantly ambushes Christians with his "daily and incessant attacks" (LC-Preface 13, K-W, 381–382) is not enough to drive Christians to use the catechism, Luther says that we have God's command:

> If this were not enough to admonish us to read the catechism daily, God's command should suffice to compel us. For God solemnly enjoins us in Deuteronomy 6[:7–8] that we should meditate on his precepts while sitting, walking, standing, lying down, and rising, and should keep them as an ever-present emblem before our eyes and on our hands. God certainly does not require and command this without reason. He knows our danger and needs; he knows the constant and furious attacks and assaults of the devil. Therefore, he wishes to warn, equip, and protect us against them with good 'armor' against their 'flaming arrows,' and with a good antidote against the evil infection and poison. Oh, what mad, senseless fools we are! We must ever live and dwell in the midst of such mighty enemies like the devils, and yet we would despise our weapons and armor, too lazy to examine them or give them a thought! (LC-Preface 14, K-W, 382)

Preachers are warned not to become so vain as to imagine that they have mastered the catechism and already know all that they need to know. Luther urges preachers to study and meditate on the catechism so that they, in turn, are able to teach it to those committed to their care. Thus Luther returns to the neediness of common believers: "Let all Christians drill themselves in the catechism daily, and constantly put it into practice, guarding themselves with the greatest care and diligence against the poisonous infection or such security or arrogance. Let them constantly read and teach, learn and meditate and ponder. Let them never stop until they have proved by experience and are certain that they have taught the devil to death and have become more learned than God himself and all his saints" (LC-Preface 19, K-W, 382–383). The catechism is the weaponry for spiritual warfare as disciples need to be trained in the use of the Word of God and prayer in the battle against the pressures of the world, the gravitational pull of fallen human nature, and the crafty tactics of the evil one designed to draw us away the only true God and place trust instead in ourselves or some created thing.

One aspect of satanic attack are false teachers who would undermine the certainty of simple Christians with deceptive doctrine. As Hans-Werner Gensichen puts it, "From the Word he [Luther] drew for himself and for all Christians the obligation to ward off false teaching by means of the condemnatory verdict."[9] Luther's implicit condemnation of such teachers is there in the SC, but it is made explicit in the LC. We will examine three examples of how the implicit condemnation of false teachers and errant doctrines are made explicit in LC by examining his treatment of the First Commandment, Baptism, and the Sacrament of the Altar.

The succinct definition of the First Commandment in the SC that "we should fear, love, and trust in God above all things" is unpacked in the LC as Luther broadens the definition of God to include anything that the human heart looks to for every good and ultimately retreats to for security in life and death. Luther identifies mammon or wealth as an obvious candidate for "this desire for wealth clings and sticks to our nature all the way to the grave" (LC I:9, K–W, 387). But Luther quickly turns to the overtly religious forms of idolatry.

Such idolatry he sees as embodied in the papacy. He leads off with the practice of praying to the saints as a noteworthy example of sin against the First Commandment:

> Again, look at what we used to do in our blindness under the papacy. Anyone who had a toothache fasted and called on St. Apollonia; those who worried about their house burning down appealed to St. Laurence as their patron; if they were afraid of the plague, they made a vow to St. Sebastian or Roch. There were countless other such abominations, and everyone selected his own saint and worshiped and invoked his help in time of need. In this category also belong those who go so far as to make a pact with the devil so that he may give them plenty of money, help them in love affairs, protect their cattle, recover lost property, etc., as magicians and sorcerers so. All of them place their heart and trust elsewhere than in the true God, from whom they neither expect nor seek any good thing. (LC I:11–12, K–W, 387)

The First Commandment, as Luther understands it is broad and far-reaching. By its very nature, it is polemical, that is, is damning

and dismantling every rival deity that the human heart might conceive as a substitute for the living God. Saints are no substitutes for
Christ. Luther sees the invocation of the saints as a symptom of false
worship which comes naturally to fallen man as "there has never
been a nation so wicked that it did not establish and maintain some
sort of worship. All people have set up their own god, to whom they
looked for blessings, help and comfort" (LC I:17, K-W, 388). Luther
condemns the worship of the saints as an equivalent to the pagans
who put their trust in powers of nature embodied under the names
of Mercury, Venus, and the like. All forms of false worship are condemned because they do not expect good things from God or trust
in Him to help. If faith is praised, unbelief must be deconstructed
and condemned.

It is under the rubric of the First Commandment in the LC
that Luther engages the Roman Mass, which he calls "the greatest
idolatry that we have practiced up until now, and is still rampant in
the world" (LC I:22, K-W, 388). From the perspective of the First
Commandment, Luther sees the Mass as a fundamental form of
idolatry. He continues, "All the religious orders are founded upon it.
It involves only that the conscience that seeks help, comfort, and salvation in its own works and presumes to wrest heaven from God. It
keeps track of how often it has made endowments, fasted, celebrated
Mass, etc. It relies on such things and boasts of them, unwilling to
receive anything as a gift of God, but desiring to earn everything
by itself or to merit everything by works of supererogation, just as
if God were in our service and debt and we were his liege lords"
(LC I:22, K-W, 388–389).

It is here that we see that the doctrine of justification is necessarily a polemical teaching, going on the attack against everything
and anyone that does not seek good and every blessing from Christ
alone.[10] The commandment to fear, love, and trust in God above all
things is a condemnation of fear, love, and trust in humanly invented
works that are thought to secure God's favor. The condemnation
stands for the sake of the Gospel.

A second example of catechetical condemnation is to be found
in the LC's treatment of Baptism. In the LC, Luther is especially keen
to emphasize that Baptism is not the work of man but of God. He
complains about those who view Baptism with the eyes of human

reason, failing to recognize the treasure God has hidden there under the simplicity of ordinary water. The nature and dignity of Baptism is to be found in the Word of God connected to and combined with the water. He writes, "Here again you see how baptism is to be regarded as precious and important, for in it we obtain such an inexpressible treasure. This indicates that it cannot be simple, ordinary water, for ordinary water could not have such an effect" (LC IV:26, K-W, 459). The Word of God joined to the water overthrows human wisdom, making of Baptism a washing of regeneration. All of the themes Luther had articulated in the SC are present in the LC. What is unique to the LC is Luther's polemic against the "new spirits" who reject the Baptism of infants.

These "new spirits" first surfaced with the arrival of the so-called Zwickau prophets in Wittenberg late in 1521. They stirred confusion and doubt regarding the externality of God's dealing with sinners in the sacraments, splitting off the Spirit from the Word.

Luther's condemnation of the Anabaptists in the LC is best understood against the backdrop of his treatise from the previous year, "Concerning Rebaptism," written in reaction to the Anabaptist leader, Balthasar Hubmaier (ca.1480–1528),[11] who had spread rumors Luther agreed with him in rejecting infant Baptism. The major points made in this tract are repeated in the LC. Luther argues that the Baptism of infants is pleasing to God as "God has sanctified many who have been thus baptized and has given them his Holy Spirit" (LC IV:49, K-W, 462). Baptism is not founded on faith, rather faith receives what God promises in Baptism. Even though Luther asserts that infants can and do have faith, he does not build his argument on their faith but on the command and promise of God.

God's command and promise render invalid the objections of the sectarians whom he calls "presumptuous and stupid spirits" (LC IV:58, K-W, 464). Surely Baptism may be and is abused. But such abuse does not detract from its salutary use. It is on account of the "great and excellent" treasure that God gives in Baptism, namely through it He snatches us from the jaws of the devil and makes us Christ's beloved possession that Luther engages in a sharp condemnation of the Anabaptist position which he had already identified in "Concerning Rebaptism" as a making of God's work uncertain. In this treatise, he stated that "whoever permits himself to be rebaptized rejects his former faith and righteousness, and is guilty of sin and condemnation" (AE 40:249). Luther can use strong language in addressing the Anabaptists for their errant teaching, for he sees in Baptism, "full and complete justification" (AE 36:57) as he puts it in "The Babylonian Captivity of the Church."

Third, Luther takes up the condemnation of those who reduce the Sacrament of the Altar to only bread and wine. In the 1520s, we observe Luther fighting a battle for the Sacrament of the Altar on two fronts. His earlier works on the Lord's Supper were directed against the withholding of the cup from the laity, the teaching of transubstantiation, and especially the notion of the Mass as a sacrifice. The battle turns toward the Sacramentarians who denied the presence of Christ's body and blood in the middle and late 1520s. Having revisited his critique of the Mass as sacrifice under his treatment of the First Commandment in the LC, Luther now directs his attention to spiritualistic understandings of the Lord Supper. These debates, Charles Arand, says are reflected in the SC: "In four brief questions, Luther provides a single, yet full summary of these debates. Questions 1 and 3 appear to have in view the Sacramentarians. Questions 2 and 4 appear to be aimed more at the Roman Catholic church inasmuch as these questions deal with benefits of the Lord's Supper and the worthiness of those who receive it."[12]

The treatment of the Sacrament of the Altar in the LC is, in large part, a distillation of Luther's writings on the Lord's Supper in the middle and late 1520s especially the key treatises: "The Sacrament of the Body and Blood of Christ—Against the Fanatics" (1526), "That the Words of Christ, 'This is My Body,' etc. Still Stand Firm Against the Fanatics" (1527), and "Confession Concerning Christ's Supper" (1528).

He sees Ulrich Zwingli and his co-religionists as denying the clear words that Jesus used in instituting the Supper. The words which give us Christ's body and blood strengthen the conscience (LC V:12, K-W, 468). Where these words are set aside, Christians are robbed of the very comfort Christ has put in His Supper; His body and blood given and shed for our forgiveness. While the Reformer's treatment of the Lord's Supper in the LC is profoundly pastoral, focusing on the essence of the Sacrament and its power and benefits, this pastoral aim necessitates a renunciation of those whom he calls "clever spirits" who "comfort themselves with their own great learning and wisdom" as they "rant and rave" as to how bread and wine can forgive sins and strengthen faith (LC V:28, K-W, 469). He sees these opponents as tearing the treasure of Christ from the Sacrament, evacuating it of Christ's body and blood and robbing Christians of the Gospel itself as faith is deprived of the very gifts Christ here bestows. Albrecht Peters summarizes Luther's fundamental stance: "I have to separate myself from a faith community and the preacher who is responsible for them if they are not willing to permit what Christ instituted to have its proper place. . . . Christ binds Himself, as He binds us, to what He has instituted, as a warning to the complacent and as a comfort to those who struggle in temptation."[13]

What then do we learn from Luther's catechetical condemnations? We may summarize our findings in two points. First, Luther uses these condemnations, for he sees errors which dethrone the Gospel itself. Every departure from the pattern of sound words given by the Triune God in and through the Holy Scriptures leads to anthropocentric speculation where human reason is exalted as judge over the truthfulness of Christ. Doctrine belongs to Christ not man. When His doctrine is set aside or diminished, Christ is made unsure and uncertain. Hermann Sasse captures the essence of Luther's stance: "The assurance with which Luther confesses his faith is not the false *securitias* which he criticizes again and again, but rather the *certitudo*, the genuine certitude of faith, based on the Word of God."[14] This certainty emboldens Luther to condemn all that obscures the glory and merits of Christ alone. Luther esteems the glory of God, not of men. Earlier, he has written to his friend Georg Spalatan in 1522: "Isn't it more salutary to fight ungodliness, even if it offends many people, than to flatter men in order to preserve peace and quietness?" (AE 48:384).

Second, he sees condemnations necessary to guard and protect the consciences of simple believers so that their faith is in Christ alone. It is Luther's love for the sheep whose consciences are under attack and imperiled by false teachers who would mislead and deceive them into false belief and despair that compels him to invoke these catechetical condemnations. Luther's catechetical polemics have a deeply pastoral aim.

Notes

1 See, for example, the comment of Eero Huovinen, "The *Small Catechism* does not include any direct polemic"—Eero Huovinen, "A Common Teacher, *Doctor Communis*? The Ecumenical Significance of Martin Luther" in *Encounters with Luther: New Directions for Critical Studies*, ed. Kirsi I. Stjerna and Brooks Schramm (Louisville: Westminster/John Knox, 2016), 8.

2 For helpful overviews of Luther's polemics, see Thomas Kaufmann, "Polemicist, Luther as" in *The Oxford Encyclopedia of Martin Luther*: Vol. 3, edited by Derek R. Nelson and Paul R. Hinlicky (Oxford: Oxford University Press, 2017), 110–127; Anna Vind, "Luther's Thought Assumed Form in Polemics" in *The Oxford Handbook of Martin Luther's Theology*, edited by Robert Kolb et al (Oxford: Oxford University Press, 2014), 471–480; Hans Wiersma, "Luther's Treatises and Polemics" in *Martin Luther in Context*, ed. David M. Whitford (Cambridge: Cambridge University Press, 2018), 317–325.

3 For more on Luther's evangelical intentions for the Small Catechism, see John T. Pless, "Catechetical Discipleship" in *Handing Over the Goods: Essays in Honor of James Arne Nestingen* ed. Steven Paulson and Scott Keith (Irvine, 1517 Publishing, 2018), 103–116.

4 Friedrich Mildenberger, *Theology of the Lutheran Confessions*, trans. Erwin Lueker (Philadelphia: Fortress Press, 1986), 140.

5 Heinrich Bornkamm, *Luther in Mid-Career: 1521–1530*, trans. E. Theodore Bachmann (Minneapolis: Fortress Press, 1983), 601.

6 Albrecht Peters, *Commentary on Luther's Catechisms: Ten Commandments*, trans. Holger Sonntag (Saint Louis: Concordia Publishing House, 2009), 20.

7 Oswald Bayer, *Theology the Lutheran Way*, trans. Jeffery Silcock and Mark Mattes (Grannd Rapids: Eerdmans Publishing Company, 2007), 210–2013.

8 Peters, *Commentary on Luther's Catechisms: Ten Commandments*, 31.

9 Hans-Werner Gensichen, *We Condemn: How Luther and 16th Century Lutheranism Condemned False Doctrine*, trans. Herbert J.A. Bouman (Saint Louis: Concordia Publishing House, 1967), 67.

10 On the polemical nature of the doctrine of justification, see Steven D. Paulson, *Lutheran Theology* (New York: T & T Clark International, 2011), 1–5 and "The Augustianian Imperfection: Faith, Christ, Imputation and its Role in the Ecumenical Discussion of Justification" in *The Gospel of Justification in Christ: Where Does the Church Stand Today?* edited by Wayne C. Stumme (Grand Rapids: Eerdmans, 2006), 104–124.

11 For more on Hubmaier, see Robert Kolb, *Luther's Wittenberg World: The Reformer's Family, Friends, Followers, and Foes* (Minneapolis: Fortress Press, 2018), 293.

12 Charles Arand, *That I May Be His Own: An Overview of Luther's Catechisms* (Saint Louis: Concordia Publishing House, 2000), 171.

13 Albrecht Peters, *Commentary on Luther's Catechisms: Baptism and Lord's Supper*, trans. Thomas H. Trapp (Saint Louis: Concordia Publishing House, 2012), 168.

14 Hermann Sasse, *This is My Body: Luther's Contention for the Real Presence in the Sacrament of the Altar* (Adelaide: Lutheran Publishing House, 1977), 152.

LITURGY AND PREACHING

55

Can We Participate Liturgically

PREVIOUSLY PUBLISHED IN THE
EASTERTIDE 2010 ISSUE OF *LOGIA*, PP. 39–47

The assigned topic is a big one.[1] Do we start with atonement or liturgy? Atonement is something of an embarrassment to many in the theological guild these days. The scandal of the cross remains a stumbling block. God must be defended against charges of divine child abuse. Others claim that the cross-centered "Lutheran" Paul is a distorted reading of the New Testament; the ecumenical moment would be better served by alternate readings that would lessen the radical law-gospel distinction in Paul and replace the justification of the ungodly with alternate themes such as new creation and participation in Christ.[2] The claim made by Luther and the Confessions that the death of Christ is God's definitive act in history done for the forgiveness of sins—a claim that is both inclusive and exclusive—has not gone unchallenged even by Lutherans.[3] Where the atonement is reduced to a metaphor, the Lord's Supper cannot but shift into the Christian's Supper. Without the cross, the sacrament becomes dislocated, interpreted as a remembrance or representation of Christ's sacrifice on Calvary now accessed by ritual activity in the liturgical assembly.

In a paper entitled "The Gift We Cannot Give Ourselves: The Eucharist in the Geology of Pope Benedict XVI," James Massa, the Executive Director of the Secretariat for Ecumenical and Inter-Religious Affairs of the United States Conference of Catholic Bishops, argues that the current pope provides both an appreciative and critical assessment of Luther's sacramental theology that opens to move beyond the impasse created by Trent and the early Lutheran theologians. Massa writes, "From Ratzinger's standpoint, not everything Luther was opposing in the Roman Catholic theological arguments of the period can be defended. Yet the core Roman Catholic position on the unity of the Eucharist and the cross was something that the great German Reformer was unable to affirm on account of his view of history."[4] Massa then goes on to make the case that Benedict's "assimilative" understanding of *Eucharistic sacrifice*, aided by historical-critical research, has given us "a deeper understanding of what commemoration means in the biblical context."[5] Indeed, Wolflrart Pannenberg, in a recent article in *Pro Ecclesia*, maintains,

> The Eucharist is to be celebrated as a remembrance of the unique sacrifice of Christ on the cross, and, through that remembering, the celebrants allow themselves to be drawn into Christ's giving of his life. This new interpretation of the sacrificial character of the Eucharist, as well as agreement concerning the meaning transubstantiation, however, needs to be given expression in a joint declaration analogous to the one on justification (1999). That said, the basic lines of an understanding on these topics have already been won in ecumenical discussion.[6]

In order to test these assertions, we need to examine trajectories within recent scholarship on the Lord's Supper.

It is instructive to note how so much of contemporary scholarship is reluctant to begin with the *verba testamenti*. Joachim Jeremias, whose *Eucharistic Words of Jesus* would have a profound effect on twentieth-century New Testament scholarship, exemplifies this trend:

> The wrong way to develop an understanding of the Last Supper is to begin from the words of institution, because in this way the so-called "founding meal" is isolated. Indeed, it ought really to be said that this isolation of the Last Supper through the centuries has made it very difficult to recognize its . . . significance. In reality, the "founding meal" is only one link in a long chain of meals which Jesus shared with his followers and which they continued after Easter. These gatherings

at table, which provoked such scandal because Jesus excluded no one from them, even open sinners, and thus expressed the heart of his message, were types of the feast to come in the time of salvation. . . . The Last Supper has its historical roots in this chain of gatherings.[7]

Jeremias makes the move from Jesus' meals with those deemed outcasts and unrighteous to the Lord's Supper. He sees a continuum between these meals and the sacrament. The contrast between the meals where Jesus sits at table with sinners and the Easter Supper is overlooked by Jeremias. In the Last Supper, Jesus gathers only the twelve. It is not an open meal, but a supper with those called to the life of discipleship; they had followed Jesus throughout his public ministry. It is no ordinary meal that Jesus partakes of with his followers, but the last supper where he institutes the sacrament of the New Testament—the meal of his body and blood.

The particularity of this supper sets it apart from all previous meals. On the eve of his crucifixion, Jesus says of the bread, "This is my body," and of the cup, "This is my blood." No mere cipher for the gift of himself or his acceptance of the unrighteous, these words speak of his impending sacrifice. They declare the fruits of his sacrifice: body and blood, given and shed for you.

The words of Christ's new testament, like the cross itself, are an offense. They may not be reduced to vague assertions of presence, encounter, or mystery, as does Eduard Schweitzer, who writes: "The real presence of Christ in the Lord's Supper is exactly the same as his presence in the world—nothing more, nothing less. It is an event, not an object; an encounter, not a phenomenon of nature; it is Christ's encounter with his church, not the distribution of a substance."[8] Rather, the words of Christ, observed Werner Elert, are "extraordinary . . . without analogy of any kind."[9]

Historical-critical approaches to Holy Scripture created skepticism as to the reliability of the synoptic and Pauline accounts of the sacrament's institution.[10] If uncertainty exists as to the accuracy of the institution narratives, the practice of the Lord's Supper is linked either to the meals of the historical Jesus or the meals of the early church, thought of as experiences with the Risen Christ.[11] Moving beyond Hans Lietzmann's thesis that the Lord's Supper was derived from two sources, Gordon Lathrop proposes,

The growing awareness of the gift of Jesus, this finding of the center of the concentric circles of eucharistic meaning, yielded Eucharist in the churches. The Eucharist did not have two sources, an *agape* and a cross-cult meal. It had many sources—and yet, a single source—the gift and presence of Jesus Christ juxtaposed to that meal practice. Its origin was in a breaking of Hellenistic meal meanings to the purpose of the gospel, a breaking already found in the meal practices of Jesus and received and understood and believed in the texts of Paul, Mark and John.[12]

Closely linked to the language of encounter is the piety of human activity. Behind the Second Vatican Council's notion of "liturgy as the work of the people" is an understanding of liturgy that is rooted in ritual performance, reenactment or cultic activity. The key figure here is Dom Gregory Dix, whose book *The Shape of the Liturgy* would exert wide influence in the liturgical reforms that swept across Christendom in the wake of Vatican II. Dix asserts that early Eucharistic liturgies exhibit a fourfold pattern: (1) taking of bread and wine, (2) giving of thanks over bread and wine, (3) breaking of bread, (4) eating and drinking.[13]

For Dix and his disciples, the celebration of the sacrament is seen as adhering to the pattern of Jesus in the upper room. It is a sort of liturgical application of WWJD—what would Jesus do? Jesus took bread, gave thanks, broke it, and gave it to his disciples to eat. Similarly, he took wine, gave thanks, and gave it to his disciples to drink. Thus the sacrament is primarily a cultic mimesis of Jesus' last supper. So a Eucharistic Prayer is mandated on the grounds that Jesus gave thanks. Representative of this position is Robert Jenson, who writes:

> This rite is a sacrifice of thanksgiving, made with words embodied as the bread and cup. It must be the initial rule of teaching about the Eucharist: when the prescribed action is not carried out, there is nothing for the promise to be about. When thanksgiving is not offered to the Father for his saving acts, and therein specifically for Jesus, or when thanksgiving is not embodied in the ritual presenting and sharing of bread and cup, nothing happens about which "this is my body and blood" could be true.[14]

Here the accent is not on the promise and gift of Christ's body and blood but on ritual action. The liturgy becomes dramatic reenactment. The similarities with Zwingli are apparent. Performance of the sacrament memorializes Jesus and spurs faith to the knowledge of his atonement. But where are the fruits of the atonement located? Not in body and blood given under bread and wine but in communal memory.

Hailed by many as an ecumenical breakthrough, the new liturgical theology did not deal with the question of what is received in the sacrament as consensus was seen instead in a common ritual pattern. Hermann Sasse saw this consensus as a compromise that spelled death to the Lutheran doctrine of the Lord's Supper. His writings on the sacrament, beginning in the 1930s and continuing until near the end of his life in 1976, sought to defend the Lutheran doctrine and deepen in congregations an appreciation for a practice consistent with this confession.[15] His writings on the Sacrament of the Altar are in so many ways prophetic of our current circumstances. Sasse saw a genuine Lutheran confession of the sacrament jeopardized by both nonsacramental, unionizing Protestantism and a Romanizing liturgical movement. Both are unacceptable alternatives as each surrenders the evangelical character of the Lord's Supper. This happens as Lutherans set aside the confession that the word of Christ himself gives us his very body and blood to eat and drink in order to accommodate the Reformed. Reformed tendencies are not to be countered by becoming more Roman. Sasse was critical of the liturgical movement for adopting Roman liturgical practices without giving consideration to how these practices embody an alien doctrine that would transform the testament of Christ into a sacrifice. For Sasse, the answer to those Lutherans who sought their identity with the Reformed as well as those who saw themselves as drawing their theological identity from Rome was to be found in Article VII of the Formula of Concord.

It was from the Formula that Sasse would argue that the difference between the Lutherans and the Reformed on the doctrine of the Lord's Supper is as lively today as it was in the sixteenth century. It is not merely a debate over the how of Christ's presence but rather what is present. No Christian believes in a real absence. That was not the issue at the time of the Reformation, nor is it the issue now.

Thus communion announcements that ask that those who come to the altar "believe in the real presence of Christ in the sacrament" are meaningless. As Albert Collver has demonstrated, the language of the real presence is not yet a confession of Christ's body and blood.[16]

Michael Welker, a Reformed systematician teaching at the University of Heidelberg, seeks to articulate an ecumenical answer to that question building on earlier documents such as the Arnoldshain Theses (1957) and the Leuenberg Agreement (1973). Welker's work is instructive at a number of levels—not the least of which is the terminology that he uses in describing the action and gift of the sacrament. His book unfolds around three major themes:

1. In Holy Communion, human beings thank God and symbolically celebrate a community meal in a jeopardized world;
2. In Holy Communion, the presence of Jesus Christ is celebrated;
3. Holy Communion is the feast of the church of all times and regions of the world, the celebration of peace and of the new creation, and the joyful glorification of the Triune God.

The action in Holy Communion is anthropological, that is, it is the human action of ritual celebration according to Welker. "The recognition that in Holy Communion a gathered community celebrates a symbolic community meal is indispensable—and, as we will see, has major consequences."[17] This meal has symbolic function. Here Welker is consistent with the Arnoldshain Theses as this document defines the sacrament: "The Supper is an act of worship of the community gathered in Jesus' name."[18] This act is constituted as "with prayer, praise, and thanksgiving, bread and wine are taken, the Lord's words of institution are spoken, and bread and wine are given to the congregation to eat and to drink."[19]

Welker observes that the term Eucharist has found wide acceptance among both Roman Catholics and Protestants as it takes the focus away from the elements to the communal action of the assembly.[20] It is an ecumenically friendly term that is attractive both to Rome and the Reformed. Alasdair I.C. Heron comments:

Very early in the ancient church, "Eucharist" became the established name for the sacrament, as recorded around the middle of the second century by Justin Martyr and perhaps even earlier. It has remained in use ever since in both the Eastern, Greek Church and the Latin, Western Church; and appropriately so, for this is the *great act of thanksgiving* at the very heart of Christian worship. Calvin himself spoke of "the kind of sacrifice which we have called Eucharistic" (that is, the sacrifice of thanksgiving), and insisted "this kind of sacrifice is indispensable in the Lord's Supper." It is no very great jump from Calvin to restore the word itself as an alternative to "Supper"; and by doing so we make available to ourselves the most universally used and understood name for the sacrament, one which is free from narrower denominational or confessional associations, and which has for that reason been increasingly employed in modern ecumenical dialogue.[21]

Alongside the activity of thanksgiving, the Supper functions as a sign of mutual acceptance. Welker writes:

> Yet along with thanksgiving, there is a second center: the communal taking, breaking, and distributing of the bread, and the corresponding symbolic action with the cup and the wine. The action in connection with the bread and wine expresses human beings' welcome and acceptance of each other.[22]

This theme then translates into a completely open altar. The Apostle's words in I Corinthians 11 are taken to mean:

> The community, the church of Christ, must attend to the right celebration of the Supper. Each person must judge himself or herself. But no one has the power and the authorization to exclude a particular person or a particular group of persons from participation in the Supper! On the contrary, Paul's reproach to the Corinthians applies precisely to a celebration of the Supper which is misused to exercise moral control and for some persons to dominate others.[23]

A second major theme developed by Welker is the presence of Christ in the sacrament as he asserts: "In Holy Communion the risen and exalted Christ is present! With him, the reconciliation of human beings with God is present, and the reconciliation of humans among themselves becomes effective."[24] Foundational to Welker's argument is the Emmaus road account of Luke 24:30–35, not the institution narratives of the synoptic gospels or I Corinthians. The sacrament has to do with Christ's self-giving. Body and blood indicate that which is perceived externally: "In the Supper, Jesus identifies his externally perceivable, earthly vitality and his most concrete, internal vital power with the bread and the wine: I am giving you that which I live here on earth!"[25]

Drawing on the formulation of the Fourth Confessing Synod of the Evangelical Church of the Old Prussian Union in Halle in 1937, Welker observes that an understanding of "personal presence" moves beyond the impasse created by "real presence" and "spiritual presence."[26] Yet, Welker confesses that "personal presence" is inadequate to the task of articulating how Christ is present in the sacrament. Instead, Welker suggests a reworked doctrine of the "real presence" that moves away from a focus on the elements and is directed toward the reality that the hold is himself both giver and gift in the sacrament. The sacrament embraces praise of God, communal eating and drinking, and the celebration of reconciliation between God and humanity and among human beings. Welker says: "In this process, the whole Christ is present: the pre-Easter Jesus whom we remember, the Crucified One whom we proclaim, the Risen One to whom we bear witness, and the Human One whom we expect and await. In the celebration of the supper, the gathered community is permeated and surrounded by Christ, by the entire richness of his life. The notion of Christ's 'real presence' is better suited than that of Christ's personal presence to provide a framework for the difficult task of understanding this complex of relations."[27]

A third feature of the sacrament, according to Welker, is its eschatological, universal, and doxological character. This leads Welker to conclude, "Participation in the Supper cannot and must not be refused to any baptized person. Neither an absence of bodily or mental health, nor deficient education, development or morality can be a reason for excluding persons from the celebration of Holy Communion."[28] The universality of the Supper is grounded in the "priesthood of all believers" for Welker.[29] At this sacrament, all the baptized are given access to the presence of the risen Christ and raised up to glorify him as members of a new creation. In this way, the Supper anticipates the feast yet to come while giving God's children a vivifying, sensorial access to the present Christ.

The sacrament is seen as a Trinitarian event. Noting this theme in such ecumenical documents as the Lutheran-Roman Catholic *The Eucharist* and the so-called Lima document. *Baptism, Eucharist, and Ministry,* Welker observes the Trinitarian structure of the liturgy as thanksgiving to the Father, remembrance (*anamnesis*) of the Son, and invocation (*epiklesis*) of the Holy Spirit as narrating God's presence in the sacrament. "God's vitality and love can be recognized in the Trinity's work of creating, delivering, and raising up creatures. In the celebration of the Supper, we encounter the rich work of the triune God woven together in a way that can be cogently and clearly narrated and understood. In the poverty of a symbolic meal, God grants the divine glory to human beings."[30]

I have used Michael Welker's book as a compendium of contemporary thought on the doctrine and practice of the Lord's Supper. His work demonstrates something of a convergence in ecumenical thinking about the Lord's Supper and its relationship to the sacrificial work of Christ. Contemporary Roman Catholic theologies of the Mass do not appear to be that far removed from current Reformed articulations of the Lord's Supper, at least in the use of anamnesis as the participation in the sacrifice of Christ. But does this convergence—as widespread and inclusive as it appears to be—do justice to the Evangelical Lutheran claims of the gift-character of the Lord's Supper or, more specifically, of the Sacrament as the Lord's giving of his body and blood for sinners to eat and to drink and not a representation of the sacrifice of Christ? Is it true, as Massa asserts, that contemporary historical-critical scholarship has opened to us as a deeper, more sophisticated understanding of anamnesis that leads us beyond sixteenth-century controversies?[31] Was Luther wrong with his dogged insistence that in the Lord's Supper, sacrifice and sacrament, testament, and prayer be kept distinct, distinct as heaven and earth? Or to use the words of J. Michael Reu's essay of an earlier generation, "Can We Still Hold to the Lutheran Doctrine of the Lord's Supper?"

As our necessarily brief and selective overview of recent theological and liturgical scholarship on the Lord's Supper has pointed out, there does seem to be an echoing of several key themes: remembrance, representation, and the simultaneity of sacrament and sacrifice. It is impressive that these themes are often articulated in similar ways by voices from a variety of theological and liturgical traditions. Yet I would contend none of them finally come to the heart of what it is that God is doing in the Lord's Supper.

Massa's (and behind him, Benedict's) claim that Luther's view of history rendered him incapable of seeing the unity of the cross and the sacrament must be evaluated in light of what Luther actually said in his 1525 treatise, *Against the Heavenly Prophets in Matters of Images and Sacraments*:

> We treat the forgiveness of sins in two ways. First, how it is achieved or won. Second, how it is distributed and given to us. Christ has achieved it on the cross, it is true. But he has not distributed or given it on the cross. He has not won it in the supper or sacrament. There he has distributed and given it through the Word, as also in the gospel, where it is preached. He has won it once for all on the cross. But the distribution takes place continuously, before and after, from the beginning to the end of the world. . . . If I now seek the forgiveness of sins, I do not run to the cross, for I will not find it given there. Nor must I hold to the suffering of Christ, as Dr. Karlstadt trifles, in knowledge or remembrance, for I will not find it there either. But I will find in the sacrament or gospel, the word which distributes, presents, offers, and gives to me that forgiveness of sins which was won on the cross. (AE 40: 213–14)

Here the Reformer holds cross and sacrament together while distinguishing between them as between acquisition and bestowal. On the cross, Christ Jesus purchased and won redemption in the shedding of his blood. The sacrament does not make us contemporary with Good Friday nor Calvary contemporary with us. Rather the forgiveness of sins accomplished by the Lamb of God on the cross is now delivered to us in the gift of Christ's body and blood in the sacrament. This gift is "for you." Oswald Bayer has observed that,

> Luther does not concentrate on the threefold repetition of the two phrases "given for you" and "shed for the forgiveness of sins" just

by chance. God's turning toward the sinner, the promise that creates faith, empowered by the death and resurrection of Jesus Christ, cannot be summarized more succinctly and specifically than by using these words. This must be stated clearly as a critique of depersonalizing speech about the "bread of life" or the diminution of the Lord's Supper to become a generic lovefest. The Lord's Supper is not some diffuse celebration of life but is defined in a precise way in its essence by means of connection with the Word of Christ that has effective power and faith.[32]

There is in Luther a simplicity that does not need the framework of Neo-Platonic theologies of earthly and heavenly realities or anthropological theories of festivity to understand what is going on in the Supper. For Luther as for Paul, the Lord's Supper is the proclamation of the death of Christ in that in the sacrament, Christ himself gives the fruits of his sacrifice, his body and his blood, for us to eat and to drink for the forgiveness of sins. The very forgiveness of sins acquired by the Lord in his death on the cross is now declared and bestowed as gift "for you."

This is no narrowing of the sacrament contrary to the claims of Brilioth, Pannenberg, and others; it rather gets to the heart of what the Lord's Supper is. Simply put, it is Christ's testament.[33] Drawing on Hebrews 9:16–17, Luther finds the conceptuality of testament to be comprehensive of the evangelical message. Writing in 1520 in *A Treatise on the New Testament, That is, the Holy Mass*, Luther says, "For if God is to make a testament, as he promises, then he must die; and if he is to die, then he must be a man. And so that little word 'testament' is a short summary of all God's wonders and grace, fulfilled in Christ" (AE 35: 84; also see AE 36: 38). In the making of the new testament, God suffers death in his Son. The new testament is made not with the blood of a Passover lamb, but God himself. It is blood shed not for deliverance from Egypt, but for the forgiveness of sins. Thus it brings to an end the old; the Lord's Supper is not the new Passover but the new testament.[34] This is lost in Massa's assertion, "The Passover is the form in which the essential eucharistic reality—Christ's involvement of us in his self-offering—is imparted to the believing community."[35] The Christian's involvement in the self-offering of Christ is not the same as Christ imparting the benefits of his once and for all death to the believer.

The movement is not from humanity to God, but from God to humanity. In *The Babylonian Captivity of the Church*, also from 1520, Luther notes, "Whatever can be said about the forgiveness of sins and the mercy of God in the broadest and richest sense is all briefly comprehended in the word of this testament" (AE 36: 56). Then he goes on to argue that it is precisely the promissory, testamentary character of the Lord's Supper that necessitates a distinction between sacrifice and sacrament:

> Therefore these two things—mass and prayer, sacrament and work, testament and sacrifice—must not be confused; for the one comes from God to us through the ministration of the priest and demands our faith, the other proceeds from our faith to God through the priest and demands his hearing. The former descends, the latter ascends. (AE 36: 56)

Christ crucified is not a work we offer to God. The language of representation so noticeable in contemporary liturgical theologies is no great advance over the earlier claims of Trent, for it still leaves the traffic moving in the wrong direction, from earth to heaven. The initially promising title of Father Massa's article, "The Gift We Cannot Give Ourselves: The Eucharist in the Theology of Pope Benedict XVI," finally disappoints as the author concludes,

> At the end of the day, it must be said that Christians have nothing to give to God except Christ, and all that Christ enables us to do once we are united to him in faith and worship. The Eucharist can become the gift of the church only because it is Christ who associates himself with us as members of his ecclesial body.[36]

Rather than Christ given by the Father to sinners, Christ becomes the gift offered by the faithful to the Father. The church's mystical participation as the body of Christ in the life of the Head, not Christ's gift of the forgiveness of sins, becomes the defining center of the sacrament. Luther's accent on Christ as gift (*donum, sacramentum*) is displaced by themes of union and participation. Now the worshiper is no longer characterized by receptivity but by ritual and ethical activity in a covenantal community whose head is Christ.

Massa's appropriation of Benedict's Eucharistic theology does not move beyond Odo Casel's classic statement:

> Both of these sacrifices flow together; they are fundamentally one; the Church, as the woman of the new paradise and the bride of Christ, acts and offers in his strength. Christ living in time made his sacrifice alone on the cross; Christ raised up by the Spirit makes the sacrifice together with his church which he has purified with the blood from his own side and thus won her for himself. It is not as if the Lord, now in the *pneuma*, were making a new sacrifice with the Church: through the one sacrifice he has reached the term of offering, and reigns now forever at the Father's right hand; he himself the glorified sacrificial gift. The church, not yet brought to her completion, is drawn into this sacrifice of his; as he sacrificed for her, she now takes an active part in his sacrifice, makes it her own, and is raised thereby with him from the world to God, and glorified. Thus Christ becomes the Saviour of the body, and the head of the Church: God has given Christ to the ecclesia as the head which towers over all, given him her who is his body.[37]

The concept of the Lord's Supper as a representation of Christ's sacrifice has been borrowed by some Lutheran theologians—most notably, perhaps, Peter Brunner, whose magisterial *Worship in the Name of Jesus* would exercise deep influence in contemporary American Lutheranism. Brunner writes, "Thus in the act of Holy Communion, bracketed with its proclamation, the historical salvation-event concentrated in Jesus' cross is indeed present for us with its redemptive gift through 'effective representation.'"[38] More recently, Risto Saarinen, in attempting to articulate a theology of gift and giving responsive to both ecumenical concerns and philosophical or anthropological theories of the reciprocity of giving, has argued:

> The Mass does not add anything to the value of Christ's unique and complete sacrifice. In this sense the two are completely different. But there is also a moment of identity which can be described in temporal terms, as memory, or in iconic terms, as representation. The eucharistic sacrifice in some way represents the sacrifice of Christ and is done in remembrance of Christ's passion. Memory and representation thus

connect the eucharistic sacrifice to Christ's work of satisfaction on the cross.[39]

The mingling of the once-and-for-all sacrifice of Christ and the ongoing sacrifices of the Christian individually and corporately is to confuse law and gospel, sanctification, and justification. When the two sacrifices flow together, the certainty that Christ Jesus intends for broken sinners in the gift of his body and blood is lost as they are thrown back to their own pious activity and thus endangered by either presumption or despair.

There is yet another dimension of contemporary liturgical theology that needs to be addressed in relation to the question of liturgical participation in the atonement. It has to do with the place of the blood of Christ. The theologies that we have examined have all engaged the language of the body of Christ (both as church and in the sacrament), but what about the blood of Christ, which the New Testament explicitly links with the forgiveness of sins (see, for example, Mt. 26:28; Rom. 5:9; Eph. 1:7; Col. 1:4; Heb. 9:14–25; 1 Pt. 1:2, 19; 1 Jn. 1:7; Rev. 1:5, 5:9; and so forth)?[40] Why is it that these writers give only minimal, if any, attention to the words regarding the blood, the cup of the new testament in the instituting words of the sacrament? Perhaps it is easier to speak of a mystical body than mystical blood. Christ's words concerning his blood given in the cup of the New Testament link atonement and Lord's Supper not in the sense of a mystical reenactment or representation of the cross event but as Jesus' death yields the forgiveness of sins. Christ's blood shed on the cross now cleanses from sin and gives peace with God. The blood of Christ in the sacrament keeps the Lord's Supper from evaporating into a Platonic sphere that would reduce the atonement to a mere metaphor and make of the cross a metaphysical cipher for some higher but hidden reality.

The position that I am attempting to articulate in this article is not ecumenically convenient; it is a minority stance to be sure. The majority position fits well with the classically Reformed statement of the Heidelberg Catechism's Question and Answer 75:

> How are you reminded and assured in the holy supper that you participate in the one sacrifice of Christ on the cross and all his benefits?

In this way: Christ has commanded me and all believers to eat of this broken bread, and to drink of this cup in remembrance of him. He has thereby promised that his body was offered and broken on the cross for me, and his blood was shed for me, as surely as I see with my eyes that the bread of the Lord was broken for me, and that the cup is shared with me. Also, he has promised that he himself as certainly feeds and nourishes my soul to everlasting life with his crucified body and shed blood as I receive from the hand of the minister and actually taste the bread and the cup of the Lord which are given to me as sure signs of the body and blood of Christ.[41]

Given all of their diversity, there appears to be a point of convergence in current ecumenical thinking that is coherent with Heidelberg but not with Wittenberg. Liturgical forms should not simply be evaluated by standards of ecumenicity or antiquity, but by faithfulness to the gospel of God's grace in Christ, Jesus given to sinners to be received by faith alone. For Lutherans, this is the critical liturgical criterion.

Here the work of Oswald Bayer in his recently translated book *Theology the Lutheran Way* is particularly helpful. In a discussion of the divine service as the context for theology, Bayer observes,

Divine service (*Gottesdienst*) is first and last God's service to us, the sacrifice he made for us in Christ, which he distributes to us in the particular divine service: "Take and eat! I am here for you!" (compare I Cor 11:24 with Gen 2:16). We misunderstand this divine service, which is meant to delight us, if we want to give as a work what we are meant to take as a gift. Here we "are not offering a good work, we are not actively receiving the Lord's Supper," as if our actions could bring about the self-realization of the church. Rather, we receive through the "priest," as the servant of the divine word, "the promise and the sign, and we receive the Lord's Supper passively." The sacramental gift-giving word is not a prayer; and the gifts we receive are not to be offered to God as a sacrifice. The Lord's Supper is not a "sacrifice that we offer to God." Rather, God in his gracious condescension and self-surrender gives himself to us in this meal. We are the recipients; we simply receive his sacrifice.[42]

It is this insight that contemporary Lutherans need to reclaim and let shape our liturgical theology and practice.

Notes

1 This article was originally presented at the Theology of Christian Worship Conference held at Luther Seminary, Saint Paul, Minnesota, 22–23 June 2008.

2 See, for example, advocates of the so-called New Perspective, especially N.T. Wright, *The Climax of the Covenant: Christ and the Law in Pauline Theology* (Minneapolis: Fortress Press, 1991). By way of response, see Stephen Westerholm, *Perspectives Old and New on Paul: The "Lutheran" Paul and His Critics* (Grand Rapids: Eerdmans, 2004).

3 See, for example, David Brondos, *Paul on the Cross: Reconstructing the Apostle's story of Redemption* (Minneapolis: Fortress Press, 2006).

4 James Massa, "The Gift We Cannot Give Ourselves," *Concordia Theological Quarterly 72* (2008): 167.

5 *Ibid.*, 174.

6 Wolfhart Pannenberg, "Ecumenical Tasks ill Relationship to the Roman Catholic Church," *Pro Ecclesia 15* (2006): 171.

7 Joachim Jeremias, *New Testament Theology*, vol. 1, *The Proclamation of Jesus*, trans. John Bowen (London: SCM Press, 1971), 289–90. For challenges to Jeremias, see j. Michael Reu, "Can We Still Hold to the Lutheran Doctrine of the Lord's Supper," in *Two Treatises on the Means of Grace* (Minneapolis: Augsburg Publishing House, 1952), 1–38; a n d Hermann Sasse, "The Lord's Supper in the New Testament," in *We Confess the Sacraments*, trans. Norman E. Nagel (St. Louis: Concordia Publishing House, 1985), 49–97.

8 Eduard Schweitzer, *The Lord's Supper According to the New Testament*, trans. James M. Davis (Philadelphia: Fortress Press, 1967), 37–38.

9 Werner Elert, *The Structure of Lutheranism*, trans. Walter A. Hansen (St. Louis: Concordia Publishing House, 1962), 303.

10 For example, Willi Marxsen writes: "It is extremely difficult to refer the contents of the Pauline formula back to Jesus; and in the face of all that we can ascertain about the preaching and activity of Jesus, it is still less likely to assume the institution of a cult by Jesus. Thus the supposition that Jesus instituted the Lord's Supper on the eve of his death poses so many difficulties that the careful historian must put more than just a question mark here" (Willi Marxsen, "The Lord's Supper as a Christological Problem," in *The Beginnings of Christology*, trans. Paul Achtemeyer [Philadelphia: Fortress Press, 1969], 112); also Wolfhart Pannenberg, *Systematic Theology*, trans. G. w. Bromiley (Grand Rapids, MI: Eerdmans, 1993), 3:283–84.

11 See Oscar Cullmann, *Early Christian Worship*, trails. A. Steward Todd and James B. Torrance (Philadelphia: Westminster Press, 1978); and *Essays on the Lord's Supper*, trans. j. G. Davies (Atlanta: John Knox Press, 1958).

12 Gordon Lathrop, *Holy People: A Liturgical Ecclesiology* (Minneapolis: Fortress Press, 1999), 193.

13 Gregory Dix, *The shape of the Liturgy* (New York: Seabury Press, 1982), 48. Dix's influence in the Lutheran Church—Missouri Synod [LCMS] can be seen in the 1969 Worship Supplement in "The Holy Eucharist II," with its four actions of taking, blessing, breaking, and sharing (*Worship Supplement* [St. Louis: Concordia Publishing House, 1969], 6 0-6 2). See Oliver Olson's examination of the *fractio panis* uncritically adopted by Lutheran liturgies of this period (Oliver Olson, "The Liturgy and the Concomitant Aspects of the Lord's Supper," in *Lord Jesus Christ, Will You Not Stay: Essays in Honor of Ronald Feuerhahn on the Occasion of His Sixty-fifth Birthday*, ed. J. Bart Day and others [St. Louis: Concordia Publishing House, 2002], 121–29).

14 Robert W. Jenson, *Systematic Theology* (Oxford: Oxford University Press, 1999), 2:216. Contra this position see Oliver Olson, *Reclaiming the Lutheran Liturgical Heritage* (Minneapolis: Reclaim Resources, 2007), 65–86.; and Dorothea Wendebourg, "Nocheinmal 'Den falschen Weg Romszu Ende gegangen?'" *Zeitschrift zur Theologie und Kirche 99* (2002), 400–441. Wolfgang Sim on attempts to counter Wendebourg's presentation of the testamentary/ promissory character of the Sacrament of the Altar by noting the positive place of thanksgiving in the Luther texts cited by Wendebourg. He does so by rejecting Luther's distinction of "word and response" as a scheme of "non-communicative poverty." See Wolfgang Sim on, "Worship and the Eucharist in Luther Studies" *Dialog 47* (2008), 143–56. Luther certainly recognizes the place of thanksgiving as the confession of Christ's work and gifts, but thanksgiving is not at the heart of the sacrament; rather it flows from the gifts received. Hence, Luther's insistence on the distinction between Christ's testament and the prayers and praises of the believing congregation. Prayer and praise have their place but they are not the gift. Here see Bryan Spinks, *Luther's Liturgical Criteria and His Reform of the Canon of the Mass* (Braincote Notts.: Grove Books, 1982).

15 See especially the essays in *We Confess the Sacraments* and *The Lonely Way: Selected Essays and Letters*, volumes 1–2, trans. Matthew C. Harrison (St. Louis: Concordia Publishing House, 2001 and 2002). Also see John T. Pless, "Hermann Sasse and the Liturgical Movement," *Logia 7*, no. 2 (Eastertide 1998), 47–51.

16 See Albert B. Collver III, *"Real Presence": A Confession of the Lord's Supper* (Ph.D. diss., Concordia Seminary, St. Louis, 2001).

17 Michael Welker, *What Happens in Holy Communion?* trans. John F. Hoffmeyer (Grand Rapids: William B. Eerdmans, 2000), 29.

18 *Ibid.*, 36.

19 *Ibid.*

20 *Ibid.*, 57–58.

21 Alasdair I.C. Heron, *Table and Tradition: Toward an Ecumenical Understanding of the Eucharist* (Philadelphia: Westminster Press, 1984), xiii.

Lowell Green observes that the term "eucharist" is used only twice in the Lutheran Confessions. See L. Green "The Holy Supper," in *A Contemporary Look at the Formula of Concord*, ed. Robert Preus and Wilbert Rosin (St. Louis: Concordia Publishing House, 1977), 207. On the other hand, the Tetrapolitan Confession of 1530 uses Eucharist to identify the chapter on the Lord's Supper. See *Reformed Confessions of the Sixteenth Century*, ed. Arthur C. Cochrane (Philadelphia: Westminster Press, 1966), 75. Zwingli's preference for "eucharist" is noted by Geoffrey Bromiley. See G. Bromiley, "Lord's Supper," in The Westminster Handbook of Reformed Theology, ed. Donald K. McKim (Louisville: Westminster John Knox, 2001), 142. My colleague, Professor Naomichi Masaki, pointed me to this line by Feodor Kliefoth: "The Lord's Supper is held to in terms of what the congregation does in it, namely, remembering and showing forth the death of Jesus, thanksgiving, and so forth. Therefore they (the Reformed) prefer to call the Lord's Supper by the name Eucharist" (T. Kliefoth, *Die ursprüngliche Gottesdienstordnung in den deutschen Kirchen lutherischen Bekenntnisses: ihre Destruktion und Reformation* [Rostock and Schwerin: Stiller, 1847], 27). For a Lutheran analysis of the use of the term "eucharist" for the sacrament, see Gerhard Forde, "What's in a Name? Eucharist or Lord's Supper?" *Logia 2*, no. 2 (Eastertide 1993), 48. Forde comments, "An age which has already reduced God pretty much to a meaningless cipher, a sentimentality characterized as 'love in general,' cannot afford to lose sight of the fact that this sacrament is the Lord's Supper not ours. He gives it. He is the gift. We are indeed to give thanks for this unspeakable gift. But the thanksgiving must be quite distinct; it must not displace the gift itself, when the Lord's Supper becomes the Eucharist everything is run together and confused and the sheer gift of the gospel is obscured, if not lost" (48). For Sasse's critique of the terminology of "eucharist," see Hermann Sasse, "Consecration and Real Presence," in *Scripture and in the Church: Selected Essays of Hermann Sasse*, ed. Ronald Feuerhahn and Jeffry Kloha (St. Louis: Concordia Seminary Press, 1995), 300–303. The liturgy contains a "eucharistic prayer." It is Luther's post-communion collect of 1526 that gives thanks for the salutary gift of Jesus' body and blood and implores God that this gift would strengthen the communicants in faith toward him and fervent love toward one another. Eucharist happens in the world as those who have received Christ's body and blood now give themselves to the neighbor in love. For more on this point see Paul Rorem, "Augustine and Luther For and Against Contemporary 'Spirituality,'" Currents in Theology and Mission 30 (2003), 102–3. Also see John T. Pless, "Taking the Divine Service into the Week," *Christ's Gifts in Liturgy: The Theology and Music of the Divine Service*, ed. Daniel Zager (Fort Wayne: CTS Press, 2002), 71–82. Welker notes that the term "eucharist" is more friendly to feminist theologians who find the language of the "Lord's" Supper offensive (Welker, *What Happens*, 3). Also see Andrea Bieler and Luise Schottroff, *The Eucharist: Bodies, Bread, and Resurrection* (Minneapolis: Fortress Press, 2007), who suggest a liturgy that echoes "God's heartbeat" and a "woman's labor" in giving birth (112).

22 Welker, *What Happens*, 67.

23 *Ibid.*, 71. Contrast Werner Elert, *Eucharist and Church Fellowship in the First Four Centuries*, trans. Norman E. Nagel (St. Louis: Concordia Publishing House, 1966).

24 *Ibid.*, 87.

25 *Ibid.*, 89. Rather than speaking of the gift of Christ's body and blood, there is the language of the self-giving of Christ in the sacrament. See, for example, James F. white, *Sacraments as God's Self-Giving* (Nashville: Abingdon Press, 1983), 52–69.

26 *Ibid.*, 92.

27 *Ibid.*, 100. Note the similarity to Yngve Brilioth's argument that the sacrament is a multidimensional reality of thanksgiving, communion, commemoration, eucharistic sacrifice, and mystery. See Yngve Brilioth, *Eucharistic Faith and Practice: Evangelical and Catholic*, trans. A.G. Hebert (London: Society for the Promotion of Christian Knowledge, 1930), 288. Also see G. Bromiley, "Lord's Supper," in *The Westminster Handbook to Reformed Theology*, 142–46.

28 *Ibid.*, 146.

29 *Ibid.*, 147.

30 Ibid., 176. Ernst Volk suggests that such Trinitarian richness is obtained at the expense of evangelical clarity. See Ernst Volk, "Evangelical Accents in Understanding the Lord's Supper," *Lutheran Quarterly 1* (1987), 185–204.

31 So also Robert W. Jenson writes: "The specific sacramental relation of the eucharistic sacrifice of Christ to the sacrifice on Calvary is anamnesis, 'the making effective in the present of an event of the past.' Catholic-Reformation consensus is achieved when it is understood on both sides that Trent's word 'representation' need not mean 'doing again' but as a translation of the biblical anamnesis must mean 'presenting again.' Recovery of a biblical and patristic understanding has made it 'possible . . . to state faith's conviction (both) of the uniqueness and perfection of Jesus Christ's offering on the cross and the breadth of its anamnesis in the church's celebration of the Eucharist. . . . We may simply summarize and appropriate the results of the Catholic-Protestant dialogue devoted specifically to this matter. Jesus on the Cross gave himself to the Father for us and gave himself to us in obedience to the Father; just this is his sacrifice. Thus what he gives us is communion: with him and so with the Father and so with one another. Conversely, what we materially share in this communion is Jesus himself, and specifically his sacrificial self-giving. And insofar as this sacrifice is anamnetically present, so that it is the bread and cup of the Eucharist by which he now gives himself, the eucharistic event is determined by these relations" (Robert W. Jenson, *Systematic Theology, vol. 2, The Works of God* [Oxford: Oxford University Press, 1999], 266–67). One may also

note the similarity with Wolfhart Pannenberg on this score. See W. Pannenberg, *Systematic Theology*, 3:305–11. Pannenberg's influence should not be underestimated here. See his *Christian spirituality* (Philadelphia: Westminster, 1998) as well as the articulate refutation by Steven D. Paulson, "What is Essential in Lutheran Worship?" *Word & World 26* (2006): 149–61.

32 Oswald Bayer, *Martin Luther's Theology: A Contemporary Interpretation*, trans, Thomas Trapp (Grand Rapids: Eerdmans, 2008), 271–72.

33 See Gerhard Forde, "The Lord's Supper as the Testament of Jesus," in *The Preached God: Proclamation in Word and Sacrament*, ed. Mark C. Mattes and Steven D. Paulson (Grand Rapids: Eerdmans, 2007), 146–51; and Reinhard Schwarz, "The Last Supper: the Testament of Jesus," *Lutheran Quarterly 9* (1995): 391–403.

34 See Hebrews 8:13. On this point also see Mark Throntveit, "The Lord's Supper as New Testament, Not New Passover," *Lutheran Quarterly 11* (1997): 271–89.

35 Massa, "The Gift," 171.

36 *Ibid.*, 175.

37 Odo Casel, *The Mystery of Christian Worship* (London: Darton, Longman & Todd, 1962), 13. Compare to Arthur Carl Piepkorn: "Yet the good that we do, even though we do it in Christ, *we* do. It is our sacrifice of praise and thanksgiving, our oblation of service, our offering of faith. But because the impulse and the power come from Christ, because he works both the will and the deed within us, it is still Christ who is the ultimate Priest, the One who is really offering the sacrifice of perfect obedience in deed and in suffering to his heavenly Father. To deny this or to minimize this, is to deny the biblical doctrine the Head and the Body, of the Bride and the Bridegroom" (Arthur Carl Piepkorn, "Sacrament, Stewardship and Sacrifice," in *The Church: Selected Writings of Arthur Carl Piepkorn*, ed. Michael Plekon and William Wiecher [Delhi, New York: ALPB Books, 1993], 212). More recently John Milbank, a key thinker in so-called Radical Orthodoxy, makes a similar connection: "The fully efficacious character of Christ's death must mean that in his death this continuously renewed mode of life is already present, such that this death occurs already within the context of the Church, which is both the transmission of the signs of atonement, and the repetition of an atoning practice (as spelt out by Paul and the Epistle to the Hebrews). One can add that the Eucharist is both these aspects at once" (John Milbank, *The Word Made Strange: Theology, Language, Culture* [Malden, MA: Blackwell Publishers, 1997], 161). Already in 1941, Hermann Sasse critiqued the notion of L.A. Winterswyl, who made the case that the union of Christ with his body makes it possible to speak of a heavenly offering made present in the eucharistic anamnesis. See Sasse, "The Lord's Supper in the Catholic Mass," in *The Lonely Way*, 2: 28–30.

38   Peter Brunner, *Worship in the Name of Jesus*, trans. Martin H. Bertram (St. Louis: Concordia Publishing House, 1968), 170. Oliver Olson has pointed out Brunner's indebtedness to Casel. See Oliver Olson, "Liturgy as Action," *Dialog 14* (1975): 108–13; and "Contemporary Trends in Liturgy Viewed from the Perspective of Classical Lutheran Theology," *Lutheran Quarterly 26* (1974): 110–57. Pannenberg draws extensively from Brunner in that the anamnesis "was deeply rooted already in Jewish tradition, particularly in connection with remembrance of Passover. From that point of view it is not a great step to the view of Christian worship, especially baptism and the Eucharist, that Casel shows extensively to be that of the fathers, namely, that we have in it a presentation and representation of the paschal mystery of the death and resurrection of Jesus" (Systematic Theology, 3:306).

39   Risto Saarinen, *God and the Gift: An Ecumenical Theology* (Collegeville, M N: Liturgical Press, 2005), 83.

40   Here see the helpful section on the "Ritual Use and Abuse of Blood" in John Kleinig, *Leviticus, Concordia Commentary* (St. Louis: Concordia Publishing House, 2003), 354–72.

41   *Confessions and Catechisms of the Reformation*, ed. Mark A. Noll (Grand Rapids: Baker Book House, 1991), 151.

42   Oswald Bayer, *Theology the Lutheran Way*, trans. Jeffrey Silcock and Mark Mattes (Grand Rapids: Eerdmans, 2007), 90.

56

Learning to Preach in Advent and Christmas from Luther

PREVIOUSLY PUBLISHED IN OCTOBER 1998 ISSUE OF
CONCORDIA THEOLOGICAL QUARTERLY, PP. 269-286

"For whatever reason, in the ineffable wisdom of God, the speech of Martin Luther rang clear where others merely mumbled."[1] The clarity of Luther's voice is surely apparent in his Advent and Christmas preaching—the Lord's Palm Sunday entry into Jerusalem, the preaching of John the Baptist, the annunciation, and the nativity. Showing remarkable theological insight and pastoral warmth, Luther crafts vivid and graphic pictures of the meanness and misery of the biblical stories of the Lord's birth. All the great themes of Luther's theology—incarnation, justification, the "happy exchange," sacraments, the theology of the cross—are present in these sermons. Advent and Christmas evoke the best in Luther's preaching as he proclaims Bethlehem's crib in light of the cross. Ulrich Asendorf rightly notes that "Luther's Advent sermons are a microcosm of his spiritual world."[2]

Luther's preaching in Advent and Christmas is extensive. No less than 110 of Luther's Christmas sermons have been preserved. Roughly half of these sermons are based on Luke 2:1–20, although he clearly delighted in preaching the prologue of the Fourth Gospel. Reading Luther's Advent and Christmas sermons confirms the observation of Johann Gerhard that Luther's preaching was "heroic disorder."[3] This paper does not aim to systematize Luther's preaching (that would be an impossible task), but to lift up several central themes in his Advent and Christmas preaching that can help shape, inform, and enliven our preaching in this segment of the Church Year. To that end we will look primarily to Luther's church postils of 1521 and his house postils of 1532–1534.[4]

Some of Luther's most potent Advent preaching is based on Matthew 21:1–9, the gospel for the first Sunday in Advent. Luther's preaching of the Palm Sunday account focuses on the character of the "Beggar-King," as Luther calls Jesus, and the nature of our reception of Him. Luther glories in the lowliness of the Beggar-King, noting in a 1533 sermon:

> Christ comes riding along like a beggar on a borrowed donkey without saddle or other trappings, necessitating that the disciples place their cloaks and garments on the donkey in a makeshift arrangement for the poor king. Accordingly in no way could the Jews excuse themselves. The prophecy had been so perfectly clear: when Christ would ride into Jerusalem, he would not do so as some earthly monarch with armor, spear, sword, and weaponry, all of which betoken bloodshed, severity, and force; but as the Evangelist says, meekly, or in the words of the prophet, poor and lowly. It is as though the prophet wanted to forewarn everyone to take good note of the donkey and realize that the one riding it is the Messiah indeed. So be aware and don't be gawking for a golden throne, velvet garments and pieces of gold, or impressive mounted retinue. For Christ will come in lowliness, meekness, and sorrowful of heart, for all to see, riding on a donkey. That would be the extent of the pomp and splendor he would display with his entry into Jerusalem.[5]

Yet hidden in the weakness of the Beggar-King is God's own power to rescue sinners. Here Luther's theology of the cross leaves its imprint on his preaching as he vividly describes the outcome of the Lord's coming in our flesh: "This King is and shall be called sin's devourer and death's strangler, who extirpates sin and knocks death's teeth out; he disembowels the devil and rescues those who believe on him from sin and death, conducting them to be among the angels where eternal life and blessedness are."[6] In his coming to die for the sins of the world, Jesus "is life personified," says Luther, "and he comes to give you life."[7] The fact that Christ comes not on a proud steed with pomp and power, but on a donkey demonstrates that He is coming not to make war against sinners but to save them. "He indicates by this that he comes not to frighten man, nor to drive him or crush him, but to help him and carry his burden for him."[8] Christ comes as gift and blessing.

Luther's Advent preaching is, therefore, a call to faith. Luther warns his hearers not to be like the Jews who rejected their Messiah, failing to discern that He would not be like a secular lord. Instead Luther points to the humility of the Lord Christ as a very sign that He is the Savior promised by the prophets, saying to the congregation: "Don't gawk with your eyes but let your ears give insight to your eyes."[9]

In his preaching on the first Sunday in Advent, Luther does not weary of emphasizing that we do not come to the King, but that the King comes to us. In a 1521 sermon Luther drives home this point saying:

> This is what is meant by "Thy king cometh." You do not seek him, but he seeks you. You do not find him, he finds you. For preachers come from him, not from you; their sermons come from him, not from you; your faith comes from him, not from you; and where he does not come, you remain outside; and where there is no Gospel there is no God, but only sin and damnation, free will may do, suffer, work, and live as it may and can. Therefore you should not ask, where to begin to be godly; there is no beginning, except where the king enters and is proclaimed.[10]

It should come as no surprise, then, that Luther directs his hearers to the preached word and the sacraments as the concrete places where the King makes His entry.[11] Even as Christ humbled Himself in His incarnation, so He stoops to us in the lowliness of the preaching, baptism, and the Sacrament of the Altar. According to Luther, the lowliness of the means that the Lord uses to distribute the gifts of salvation parallels the humility of His coming in the flesh. In both cases, faith clings to what is heard, not to what is seen.

> If we don't want to understand this with our ears, but accept only that which our eyes see and our hands touch, we will miss our King and

be lost. There's a big difference between this King and other kings. With the latter everything is outward pomp, great and gallant appearance, magnificent air. But not so with Christ. His mission and work is to help against sin and death, to justify and bring to life. He has placed his help in baptism and the sacrament, and incorporated it in the Word and preaching. To our eyes baptism appears to be nothing more than ordinary water, and the Sacrament of Christ's body and blood simple bread and wine, like other bread and wine, and the sermon, hot air from a man's mouth. But we must not trust what our eyes see, but listen to what this King is teaching us in his Word and Sacrament, namely, I poured out my blood to save you from your sins, to rescue you from death and bring you to heaven; to that end I have given you baptism as a gift for the forgiveness of sins, and preach to you unceasingly by word of mouth concerning this treasure, sealing it to you with the Sacrament of my body and blood, so that you need never doubt. True, it seems little and insignificant, that by the washing of water, the Word, and the Sacrament this should all be effected. But don't let your eyes deceive you. At that time, it seemed like a small and insignificant thing for him to come riding on a borrowed donkey and later be crucified, in order to take away sin, death, and hell. No one could tell this by his appearance, but the prophet foretold it, and his work later fulfilled it. Therefore we must simply grasp it with our ears and believe it with our hearts, for our eyes are blind.[12]

Luther located the rejection of Jesus by the Jews in "their carnally minded thinking," which did not recognize the eternal God clothed in human flesh. As Luther preaches the offense of Advent, he identifies the same "carnally minded thinking" as the cause for continued contempt of Christ as He comes in word and sacrament.

But the rejection of Christ does not happen only with the Jews, but also among us, for the high and mighty scorn us because of our gospel and sacraments. What folly, they say, that I should let myself be baptized with water poured on my head, supposedly to be saved thereby; or that some poor parish preacher, barely able to put a coat on his back, should pronounce forgiveness and absolve me from my sins; or that receiving bread and wine in the Sacrament I should be saved. On that basis they despise a Christ-preacher. For it goes with the territory to be despised by reason of Christ's poverty. As a result, when a man becomes a preacher he is more despised than some lowly knave of no reputation. There is no station in life quite as scorned and humble as that of a preacher. That happens not because of us or the preacher, but because Christ is despised on all sides in the world. No wonder that the aristocrats and plutocrats say, Why should we believe some tramp-like, beggarly cleric? Why doesn't our Lord God send us a fine pulpit-prince to preach to us? Him we would believe. However, just as Christ's preachers are despised, so people despise his baptism and the Sacrament of the Altar. Virtually no peasant retains respect for them, let alone burghers and nobles. Under the papacy people mocked at indulgences and pilgrimages, and yet they were highly regarded. Now, however, the prevailing word is, Huh, if all you can do is preach about Christ and faith, I'm fed up with that already, I've heard it all many times before.[13]

In the traditional lectionary, the Second Sunday in Advent sounds an eschatological note based on Luke 21:25–36. Luther contrasted the previous Sunday's focus on the coming of Christ to suffer with the apocalyptic message of the Gospel for the Second Sunday in Advent:

Last Sunday you heard about his riding into Jerusalem on a donkey, minus all pretentious show. He had no place to call his own, not even a foot of space; and besides, he later was crucified. He is facing a poor, miserable future, not as a master but as a servant, whose desire was to serve in such a way as to die for us. To sum up, during his first advent he rendered the greatest service which no angel, no creature was able to render, and prepared a kingdom for his believers and elect, but when the number of elect is complete, he will return not as a servant but as a master, in order to free us from earth, maggoty mire, death, and decay.[14]

Compared with much of the eschatological preaching of the late Middle Ages, Luther's preaching seems mild.[15] While Luther's preaching for the Second Sunday in Advent is replete with warnings regarding the quickness of the Lord's return to judgement and the need for constant watchfulness lest that Day overtake people unprepared, he strives to have his hearers "discern Judgement Day correctly, to know what he (Christ) means for us and why we hope and await his return."[16] After describing how the pope preaches a Christ who is a stern judge with whom we must be reconciled by our works, Luther goes on to preach the comfort which is to be found in Christ's final advent:

> ... in this Gospel he teaches us differently, namely, that he will come not to judge and damn us but to redeem and save us, and to fulfill all for which we have petitioned him, and to bring us his kingdom. To the ungodly and the unbelievers he will come as judge and punish them as his enemies and the Christians' foes, who have afflicted Christians with all kinds of misery. But to the believers and Christians he will come as a redeemer.[17]

In a similar fashion, Luther chides the fanatics for robbing Christians of the comfort of the Lord's return.

> The godless fanatical preachers are to be censured who in their sermons deprive people of these words of Christ and faith in them, who desire to make people devout by terrifying them and who teach them to prepare for the last day by relying on their good works as satisfaction for their sins. Here despair, fear, and terror must remain and grow and with it hatred, aversion, and abhorrence for the coming of the Lord, and enmity against God be established in the heart; for they picture Christ as nothing but a stern judge whose wrath must be appeased by works, and they never present him as the Redeemer, as he calls and offers himself, of whom we are to expect that out of pure grace he will redeem us from sin and evil.[18]

While Luther expresses his personal opinion that the end times are near, he does not engage in detailed speculation regarding the parousia.[19] Instead, Luther's preaching on this theme is "an eschatology of faith," to use the words of T.F. Torrance, as Luther urges his hearers to find joy in the glad announcement that "your redemption draweth nigh."[20]

The traditional Gospel pericopes for the Third and Fourth Sundays in Advent tell of John the Baptist. Luther develops two major themes in his preaching on Matthew 11:2–10 and John 1:19–28—the offense of Christ and the function of John the Baptist as God's finger. In his sermons for the Third Sunday in Advent, Luther underscores our Lord's words to the disciples of John, "And blessed is the one who is not offended by me" (Matthew 11:6). Here Luther notes that the Jews are offended by the Christ who establishes His kingdom among the poor, the lame, and the blind. John the Baptist points to a Savior who offends the spiritual instincts of the self-righteous. "The world is offended that Christ is so miserable and poor."[21]

Originally, God sent John the Baptist to the Jews. Thus Luther says in a sermon on Matthew 11:2–10, that Jesus did not preach this sermon for the sake of John the Baptist. "Rather he preached this sermon for the sake of the Jews that they might recognize John the Baptist and understand his mission."[22] Now John the Baptist preaches to us for "to the Jews he (Christ) came in the flesh; to us he comes in the Word."[23] It is the mission of John the Baptist that Luther takes up in his sermons for the Fourth Sunday in Advent. Here Luther holds up John the Baptist as finger of God. "Let us look to the mouth and finger of John with which he bears witness and points, so that we do not close our eyes and lose our Lord and Savior, Jesus Christ; for to the present day John still very diligently, faithfully, and richly points and directs us here, in order that we may be saved."[24] According to Luther, John is the great preacher of the law, but he is an even greater preacher of the gospel. Luther calls John "an image, and a type, and also a pioneer, the first of all preachers of the Gospel," because he points to the Lamb of God who takes away the sin of the world.[25]

John's proclamation of the Lamb of God prepares the way for the preaching of Christmas. Thomas Wabel has characterized Luther's Christmas sermons as reflecting "the simplicity of Scripture."[26] At the beginning of a 1522 Christmas sermon on Luke 2:1–14, Luther suggests that "this Gospel is so clear that it requires very little explanation, but it should be well considered and taken deeply to the heart."[27] For the most part, Luther follows his own rule; he simply narrates the events of the nativity. Luther's Christmas preaching is marked by a simplicity that assists the hearer in pondering the profound things that are taking place as God's Son is born.

Luther sees the incarnation of Jesus in light of His atonement, His birth in light of His death. We have already noted how Luther's theology of the cross left its imprint on the Advent sermons; this is true to an even greater degree with the Christmas sermons, as Herman Sasse appropriately notes:

Obviously the "theology of the cross" does not mean that for a theologian the church year shrinks together into nothing but Good Friday. Rather it means that Christmas, Easter, and Pentecost cannot be understood without Good Friday. Next to Irenaeus and Athanasius, Luther was the greatest theologian of the incarnation. He was this because in the background of the manger he saw the cross. His understanding of the Easter victory was equal to that of any theologian of the Eastern Church. He understood it because he understood the victory of the Crucified One.[28]

Luther saw Bethlehem through the lens of Calvary. Luther's theology of the cross, formulated in the Heidelberg Theses of 1518, is given expression in his commentary on the Magnificat three years later. There Luther speaks of God's work in Mary as a work that "is done in the depths," a work that cannot be perceived by carnal eyes. He writes: "Even now and to the end of the world, all His works are such that out of that which is nothing, worthless, despised, wretched, and dead, he makes that which is something, precious, honorable, blessed, and living."[29] Mary, no more than "a simple maiden, tending the cattle and doing the housework," hardly esteemed in the eyes of the world is chosen and exalted by the Most High God to be the mother of the Savior. "Thus God's work and His eyes are in the depths, but man's only in the height."[30] The "foolishness of God" (I Corinthians 1:25) is not confined to Calvary, but embraces the incarnation as well.

Luther sees God operating "in the depths" at Bethlehem. Drawing attention to the ordinariness of the circumstances surrounding the Lord's birth—the poverty of Mary and Joseph, the arduous journey from Nazareth to Bethlehem, and the birth in the stable—Luther concludes:

Nobody notices or understands what God performs in the stable. Thus God indicates that he pays no attention at all to what the world is or has or can do, and on the other hand the world proves that it knows nothing at all of, and pays no attention to what God is or has or does. Behold, this is the first symbol wherewith Christ puts to shame the world and indicates that all of its doing, knowledge, and being are contemptible to us, that the greatest wisdom is in reality foolishness, that its best performance is wrongdoing, and that the greatest good is evil.[31]

In obscure Bethlehem, God demonstrates His goodness "by stepping down so deep into flesh and blood."[32]

Luther's Christmas preaching hangs on to the flesh and blood of God in the manger. Sentimental reflections on the "little baby Jesus" are not present in his preaching. Rather Luther leads his hearers to the crib that now holds the enfleshed God. In a 1534 sermon, Luther exults in the fact that God did not become an angel but a man:

> The angels are much more glorious creatures by nature than we human beings. But God did not consider that; he is not an angel, nor did he become an angel. The angels, moreover, are blameless and holy. But he sets the course, chooses the lowly, poor human nature, lost in sin and subject under the devil's rule and power of death, plagued and troubled through and through by the devil and his ceaseless pressure. That meant sinking to the lowest depths.[33]

In "sinking to the lowest depths" God raises our humanity above and beyond the angels; He exalts our flesh to the right hand of God. "That is why we can boast that God has become our brother."[34]

As Luther preaches the Lukan birth narrative, he approaches Christmas from the perspective of Mary, the angels, and the shepherds. Luther emphasizes the naturalness of our Lord's birth in a sermon for Christmas Eve in 1522:

> There are some who express opinions concerning how this birth took place, claiming Mary was delivered of her child while she was praying, in great joy, before she was aware of it, without any pains. I do not condemn these devotional considerations—perhaps they were devised for the benefit of simple-minded folk—but we must stay with the Gospel text which says "born of the Virgin Mary." There is no deception here, but, as the words indicate, it was a real birth The birth happened to her exactly as to other women, consciously with her mind functioning normally and with the other parts of her body helping along, as is proper at the time of birth, in order that she should be his natural mother and he her natural normal son. For this reason her body did not abandon its natural functions which belong to childbirth, except that she gave birth without sin, without shame, without pain, and without injury, just as she had conceived without sin. The curse of Eve, which reads: "In pain you shall bear your

children" (Genesis 3:16) did not apply to her. In other respects things happened to her exactly as they happen to any woman giving birth.[35]

From the body of the Virgin, the Son of God takes on our flesh and blood and so is born to be our Redeemer. Luther's Christology controls his view of Mary, leading him to acknowledge her as the Mother of God.

Luther esteems Mary as the mother of the incarnate Savior and he honors her as the model of faith for all believers. It is from Mary that we learn to meditate rightly on the Lord's birth. In an illustration which he attributes to St. Bernard, Luther declares:

> There are three miracles here (in the incarnation): that God and man should be joined in this Child; that a mother should remain a virgin; that Mary should have such faith as to believe that this mystery would be accomplished in her. The last is not the least of the three. The Virgin birth is a mere trifle for God; that God should become a man is a greater miracle; but the most amazing of all is that this maiden should credit the announcement that she, rather than some other virgin, had been chosen to be the mother of God . . . Had she not believed, she could not have conceived. She held fast to the word of the angel because she had become a new creature. Even so must we be transformed and renewed in heart from day to day. This is the word of the prophet: "Unto us a child is born, unto us a son is given" (Isa. 9:6). This is the hardest point, not so much to believe that he is the son of the Virgin and God Himself, as to believe that this Son of God is ours.[36]

As Mary heard the heavenly words of the angel, believed those words, and so conceived and carried the Son of God in her womb, so we hear the words of God and by those words faith is conceived. In fact, Luther says "He is more mine than Mary's."[37]

The first Christmas sermon was preached by angels to a congregation of shepherds. In a 1532 sermon on the Lukan pericope, Luther points out that "this Gospel has two parts. The first has to do with the account itself and its meaning for us today. The second part is the message of the angels telling of its fruit and power, and how we are to profit from it."[38] It is not enough that Christ is born. Without the proclamation of His birth, we would left without its blessing; the newborn Savior would still be the "hidden God."[39] God not preached remains hidden and inaccessible, that is, we are left under the terror of His silence. In the same sermon, Luther asserts that "Christ might have been born a hundred times over, but it would all have been in vain if it had not been preached and revealed to us." Through the gift of preaching, the angel brings joy to the shepherds by proclaiming, "For unto you is born this day in the city of David a Savior, who is Christ the Lord" (Luke 2:11). This angelic message, says Luther, is a short sermon but one which "compresses the entire Holy Scripture in one bundle."[40]

In a 1533 sermon Luther dwells on the doxological character of the angelic anthem. "It could justly be called the true SANCTUS, in letters of gold, even as the message might rightly be called the angel's sermon, because it was an angel, not a human being, that delivered it. So this song is properly the angels' hymn, because a heavenly host sang it, not human beings."[41] In their hymn, angels tutor human beings in the true worship of God, a worship that is grounded in the flesh of Jesus. Luther understands the true worship of God in light of the First Commandment.[42] As Luther knows of no God apart from the one who sleeps in Mary's lap and hangs dead on the cross, his understanding of worship is normed by the First Commandment and given incarnational content with the flesh of Jesus. Thus Luther preaches on the Gloria:

> Accordingly this angel anthem proclaims that whatever is outside of or apart from Christ stands condemned before God as blasphemy, idolatry, and abomination. God can only be honored in and through this child who is Christ the Lord. Apart from him no person can find and worship God, but grossly offends and dishonors him. That means that everything across the world that is called worship and service of God must end. Truly holy and God-pleasing offerings, genuine service of God, will bear Christ's name or is in Christ; otherwise it is no divine service. God has channeled his worship in this child, and where he is not worshiped in this way, true worship is not present.[43]

The angels deliver their sermon to the shepherds, held captive by sin, death, and the devil. Because "this hymn did not originate on

earth but was brought down from heaven to the earth by the angels"
it gives joy and courage to the shepherds.[44] As good preachers, the
angels direct the shepherds to the place where Christ is—to the manger in Bethlehem. "If these shepherds had not believed the angel,
they would not have gone to Bethlehem nor would they have done
any of the things which are related of them in the Gospel."[45] From
the shepherds we learn "that the preaching and singing of the angels
were not in vain."[46]

For Luther, the revelation of the glory of God in the birth of
His Son to the shepherds is consistent with the way in which God
uses what the world holds to be weak and foolish to make His
mercy manifest. Like Mary, the shepherds are models of faith, which
lives from the word. Luther also sees in the shepherds a model for
Christian vocation.

> Here is another excellent and helpful lesson, namely, that after the
> shepherds have been enlightened and have come to a true knowl-
> edge of Christ, they do not run out into the desert—which is what
> the crazy monks and nuns in the cloisters did! No the shepherds
> continue in their vocation, and in the process they also serve their
> fellow men. For true faith does not create people who abandon
> their secular vocation and begin a totally different kind of living, a
> way of life which the totally irrational monks considered essential
> to being saved, even though it was only an externally different way
> of existence.[47]

Although most of Luther's preaching was based on the Lukan
account of the nativity, he demonstrates a fondness for John's Gospel
and his preaching of the Christmas story often echoes John 1:1–14.[48]
Luther asserts that this pericope "is the most important of all the
Gospels of the church year, and yet it is not, as some think, obscure
or difficult. For upon it is clearly founded the important article of
faith concerning the divinity of Christ."[49] In a sermon on John's prologue, Luther says, "John begins his Gospel in such an exalted tone
and continues in the same vein so that in almost every single letter
he preaches the deity of Christ, which is done by no other evangelist."[50] Luther loves John's Gospel because the evangelist makes it
clear that "whoever has touched Christ's skin has actually touched

God."[51] The Christian's comfort is only to be found in the Word made flesh. A Christmas sermon from 1527 makes this point in a most striking way:

> He has power to cast us into hell and yet he took soul and body like ours. . . . If he were against us he would not have clothed himself in our flesh. . . . Here God is not to be feared but loved, and that love brings the joy of which the angel speaks. . . . Satan, on the other hand, brings home to me the Majesty and my sin, and terrifies me so that I despair. . . . But the angel does not declare that he is in heaven. . . . 'You shall find . . .' He points out that he has come to us in our flesh and blood . . . Our joy is not that we ascend and put on his nature as is the case when the Mass is made a boastful decking of ourselves in divinity. Do not be driven to distraction, but remain down here and listen, 'Unto you a Saviour.' He does not come with horses but in a stable. . . . Reason and will would ascend and seek above, but if you will have joy, bend yourself down to this place. There you will find that boy given for you who is your Creator lying in a manger. I will stay with that boy as he sucks, is washed, and dies. . . . There is no joy but in this boy. Take him away and you face the Majesty which terrifies. . . . I know of no God but this one in the manger . . . Do not let yourself be turned away from this humanity. . . . What wonderful words (Col 2:9)! . . . If you separate them, the joy is gone. O Thou boy, lying in the manger, thou art truly God who hast created me, and thou wilt not be wrathful with me because thou comest to me in this loving way—more loving cannot be imagined.[52]

In Luther's preaching Christology and soteriology are never separated. Or as Ulrich Asendorf notes: "Christ shares all He is and has with those who belong to Him. In this way Christological facts are directly transformed soteriologically."[53]

Luther's Advent and Christmas preaching, like all good preaching, is finally doxological. In many respects his ballad-like "From Heaven Above to Earth I Come" is a summation of Luther's Christmas preaching.[54]

In his book *Against the Protestant Gnostics*, Philip Lee suggests that if contemporary Protestantism is to be delivered from its enslavement to gnostic captivity, preaching that is faithful to the biblical narrative, Christological in content, and liturgical in shape will need to be restored to the church's pulpits.[55] The gnostic forces of our age threaten the church nowhere as much as they do in December as the clear preaching of repentance in Advent is often muted by the sentimentalism encouraged by the hungry consumerism of our culture and Christmas is transformed into a festival of moralisms. Preaching cannot but benefit greatly from that preacher of Wittenberg who always proclaimed that we have God in the flesh for our forgiveness, life, and salvation.[56]

Notes

1 Mark Noll, "The Lutheran Difference," *First Things* (February 1992): 31.

2 Ulrich Asendorf, "Luther's Sermons on Advent as a Summary of His Theology," in *A Lively Legacy: Essays in Honor of Robert Preus*, edited by Kurt Marquart, John Stephenson, and Bjarne W. Teigen (Fort Wayne: Concordia Theological Seminary, 1985), 13.

3 Fred Meuser, *Luther the Preacher* (Minneapolis: Augsburg Publishing House, 1983), 57. On Luther's preaching, also see Ulrich Asendorf, *Die Theologie Martin Luther nach Seinen Predigten* (Goettingen: Vandenhoeck & Ruprecht, 1988); Martin Brecht, *Martin Luther: Shaping and Defining the Reformation 1521–1532*, translated by James Schaaf (Minneapolis: Fortress Press, 1990), 284–288; Richard Lischer, "Luther and Contemporary Preaching: Narrative and Anthropology," *Scottish Journal of Theology* (1983): 487–504.

4 *Sermons of Martin Luther*, volume 1, edited by John Nicholas Lenker (Grand Rapids: Baker Book House, 1983). All citations from this volume will be noted as Lenker; *The House Postils*, volume 1, edited by Eugene Klug (Grand Rapids: Baker Book House, 1996). All citations from this volume will be noted as Klug.

5 Klug, 26.

6 Klug, 27.

7 Klug, 18.

8 Lenker, 19.

9 Klug, 27.

10 Lenker, 27.

11 Luther accents the preached word. Note his comment in his 1521 sermon on the First Sunday in Advent: "This agrees with the word 'Bethphage,' which means, as some say, mouth-house, for St. Paul says in Romans 1, 2, that the Gospel was promised afore in the Holy Scriptures, but it was not preached orally and publicly until Christ came and sent out his apostles. Therefore the church is a mouth-house, not a pen-house, for since Christ's advent that Gospel is preached orally which before was hidden in written books" (Lenker, 44).

12 Klug, 28.

13 Klug, 35.

14 Klug, 38.

15 John Dolan describes such preaching at the threshold of the Reformation: "Preachers were preoccupied with the theme of sin and the grim face of death waiting for the moment of merited punishment. There was an emphasis on the horrors of hell and the suffering of the damned. Their sermons were filled with descriptions of burning trees on which hung the souls of those who did not attend church services, vultures gnawing at men's vitals, venomous serpents stinging the unholy, boiling lakes, frozen fens, heated ovens and vile dungeons . . . Everywhere the emphasis was on the negative side of man's salvation, his sins and punishment" (*History of the Reformation* [New York: The New American Library, 1965], 186, cited in Stanley Schneider, "Luther, Preaching, and the Reformation," *Interpreting Luther's Legacy*, edited by Fred Meuser and Stanley Schneider [Minneapolis: Augsburg Publishing House, 1969], 124).

16 Klug, 51.

17 Klug, 51.

18 Lenker, 78.

19 For example, in a 1521 Advent sermon Luther states: "I do not wish to force any one to believe as I do; neither will I permit anyone to deny me the right to believe that the last day is near at hand. These words and signs of Christ compel me to believe that such is the case" (Lenker, 62). For a treatment of Luther's apocalyptic views, see Mark Edwards, *Luther's Last Battles* (Ithaca: Cornell University Press, 1983), 97–114.

20 T.F. Torrance, "The Eschatology of Faith: Martin Luther," in *Luther: Theologian for Catholics and Protestants*, 145–213, edited by George Yule (Edinburgh: T & T Clark, 1986).

21 Klug, 66.

22 Klug, 69.

23 Klug, 95.

24 Klug, 91.

25 Lenker, 130.

26 Thomas Wabel, "The Simplicity of Scripture in Luther's Christmas Sermons," *Lutheran Quarterly* (Autumn 1995): 241.

27 Lenker, 137.

28 Hermann Sasse, *We Confess Jesus Christ*, translated by Norman Nagel (St. Louis: Concordia Publishing House, 1984), 39. For the influence of the theology of the cross on Luther's preaching, see John T. Pless, "Martin Luther: Preacher of the Cross," *Concordia Theological Quarterly* (April-July 1987): 83–101.

29 *Luther's Works* (American Edition) 21:299. The text of the Heidleberg Theses may be found in *LW* 31:35–70.

30 *LW* 21:301, 302.

31 *LW* 52:9–10.

32 *LW* 52:12.

33 Klug, 113.

34 Klug, 133.

35 *LW* 52:11–12.

36 Roland Bainton, *The Martin Luther Christmas Book* (Philadelphia: Fortress Press, 1967), 22–23.

37 *LW* 51:215.

38 Klug, 100.

39 One may see Chapter 4, "The Preached God," in Gerhard Forde, Theology is for Proclamation, 87–133 (Minneapolis: Fortress Press, 1990).

40 Klug, 109, 119.

41 Note the implications here for liturgical preaching. The Divine Service is founded on the twin pillars of word and sacrament. As Christ comes to us in His word, the congregation welcomes Him with the angelic hymn that announces the incarnation. As the same Lord comes to us in His body and blood, the congregation anticipates this gift with the angelic hymn (the Sanctus) that proclaims His presence. Note the way in which the Gloria and the Sanctus are parallel in the liturgical structure of the Divine Service.

42 One may see Vilmos Vatja, *Luther on Worship*, translated by Ulrich Leupold (Philadelphia: Muhlenberg Press, 1958), 3–63.

43 Klug, 122–123.

44 Klug, 143.

45 *LW* 52:32.

46 Klug, 144.

47 Klug, 148. In Luther's homiletical treatment of the shepherds, we are given an excellent window into his doctrine of vocation—a doctrine that contemporary Lutheranism desperately needs to recover in light of the "neo-monasticism" of contemporary American Evangelicalism. One may see Harold Senkbeil, *Sanctification: Christ in Action* (Milwaukee: Northwestern Publishing House, 1989), 12–15. In his treatise of 1520, "On the Freedom of a Christian," Luther writes (*LW* 31:371): "We conclude, therefore, that a Christian lives not in himself, but in Christ and in the neighbor. Otherwise he is not a Christian. He lives in Christ through faith, in his neighbor through love. By faith he is caught up beyond himself into God. By love he descends beneath himself into his neighbor." This is expressed liturgically in the Post-Communion Collect: "We give thanks to you, almighty God, that you have refreshed us through this salutary gift, and we implore you that of your mercy you would strengthen us through the same in faith toward you and in fervent love toward one another . . ." Homiletically, Luther gives expression to this in his Christmas sermons. For example in a 1521 Christmas sermon Luther says

(Lenker, 146): "These are the two things in which a Christian is to exercise himself, the one that he draws Christ into himself, and that by faith he makes him his own, appropriates to himself the treasures of Christ and confidently builds upon them; the other that he condescends to his neighbor and lets him share in that which he has received, even as he shares in the treasures of Christ." Contra Richard Caemmerer's distinction of "faith-goal sermons" from "life-goal sermons" (*Preaching for the Church* [St. Louis: Concordia Publishing House, 1959], 179–190), Luther preaches faith which is active in love.

48 On Luther and the Fourth Gospel see Victor Pfitzner, "Luther as Interpreter of John's Gospel," *Lutheran Theological Journal* (August 1984): 65–73; Carl Stange, "The Johannine Character of Luther's Doctrine," *Lutheran World Review* (October 1949): 65–77.

49 Lenker, 173.

50 *LW* 52:53.

51 Ian Siggins, *Martin Luther's Doctrine of Christ* (New Haven: Yale University Press, 1970), 232. In addition to Siggins' outstanding treatment of Luther's incarnational Christology, one may see Marc Lienhard, *Luther: Witness to Jesus Christ* (Minneapolis: Augsburg Publishing House, 1982), 153–194; Norman Nagel, "Martinus: 'Heresy, Doctor Luther, Heresy!' The Person and Work of Christ," in *Seven-Headed Luther*, edited by Peter Newman Brooks (New York: Oxford University Press, 1983), 25–49; and Franz Posset, *Luther's Catholic Christology* (Milwaukee: Northwestern Publishing House, 1988).

52 Quoted in Nagel, 48.

53 Asendorf, 2.

54 *TLH* 85; *LW* 37/38.

55 Philip J. Lee, *Against the Protestant Gnostics* (New York: Oxford University Press, 1987), 218–225. One may also see Maxwell Johnson, "Let's Keep Advent Right Where It Is," *Lutheran Forum* (November 1994): 45–47.

56 Recommended for the pastor's own devotional reading and spiritual formation in preparation for Advent-Christmas preaching (and liturgical preaching in general) are *Day By Day We Magnify Thee: Daily Readings for the Church Year From the Writings of Martin Luther*, edited and translated by M. Steiner and P. Scott (Minneapolis: Fortress Press, 1982); *Luther's Family Devotions*, edited by Georg Link and translated by Joel Baseley (Dearborn: Mark V Publications, 1996).

57

Divine Service

Delivering Forgiveness of Sins

PREVIOUSLY PUBLISHED IN THE REFORMATION 1996 ISSUE OF LOGIA, PP. 25-29

The debate over the use or non-use of traditional Lutheran liturgical forms has emerged as a hot topic in the life of American Lutheranism. In the Summer 1994 issue of *dialog*, Ted Peters characterized it as "worship wars." For some, no doubt, what I have to say will create more heat. My intention, however, is not to enflame the debate but to shed light. I shall attempt to speak as forthrightly as possible, not to offend, but to set the issue before us with clarity.

Contra David Luecke, the current controversy is not a matter of "style" versus "substance." It is clear from the apostolic church as well as from the Evangelical-Lutheran Reformation that the substance of the gospel shapes and defines the style of that gospel's delivery. Further, I believe it is spiritually dangerous to equate liturgy with adiaphora. Liturgy will always confess or deny the gospel, and the gospel is never an adiaphoron. This brings me to the major thesis of this essay: The crisis over the liturgy is a result of confusion over the forgiveness of sins. As such, it is a doctrinal issue and, therefore, ultimately church-divisive.

Liturgy is Divine Service

The "high church/low church" labels may have their usefulness within Anglicanism, where churchmen are identified as "high and

crazy, broad and hazy, or low and lazy." These titles are inadequate for
the Church of the Augsburg Confession, however. Liturgical renewal
movements in the early part of this century (such as the Society of
St. James and the old *Una Sancta* magazine) may bear part of the
blame for our present predicament, as some of their champions
tended toward a liturgical romanticism that was long on aesthetics
and short on doctrine. Thirty-five years ago, Hermann Sasse opined
"that the great tragedy of the Liturgical Movement was its inability
to face doctrinal issues."[1] For Lutherans, liturgy is not a matter of
aesthetic sensitivities or antiquarian preferences, but of doctrine,
of confession.

Article VII of the Augsburg Confession "defines the church
liturgically," to borrow a phrase from the Australian Lutheran theologian John Kleinig. Article VII confesses that "it is sufficient for the
true unity of the Christian church that the Gospel be preached in
conformity with a pure understanding of it and that the sacraments
be administered in accordance with the divine Word" (AC VII, 2;
Tappert, 32). Notice that the Augustana does not define the church
on the basis of the mere presence of word and sacrament, but by the
fact that the gospel is purely preached and the sacraments are rightly
administered in accordance with the divine word. Preaching of the
word and administration of the sacraments require liturgy. Word
and sacrament are not static commodities, but means through which
the Lord himself is working to constitute and sustain his church. To
be sure, Angustana VII holds that the true unity of the church is not
grounded in the uniformity of ceremonies instituted by men, but
these humanly devised ceremonies are not the liturgy.

The liturgy is *Gottesdienst*,[2] divine service, the Lord's service to
us through the proclamation of his word and the giving out of his
body and blood. In the theology of the Lutheran Confessions, God
is the subject, not the object of liturgical action. The trajectory is
from the Lord to his church and then from the church to her Lord.
In Luke 22:27, just after he had established the Supper of his body
and blood, the Lord says, "I am among you as the one who serves."
This verse embodies the Lutheran understanding of the liturgy; it
is the service that Jesus renders to his church, given by grace and
received through faith. Rome had reversed the flow with the insistence that the Mass is essentially a sacrifice that the church offers to

God. Reformed Protestants likewise define worship as human activity, namely, the church's obedient ascription of praise to the majesty of a sovereign God.

Gordon Lathrop[3] and the framers of "The Graceful Use of the Means of Grace: Theses on Worship and Worship Practices"[4] are representative of a stream in contemporary American Lutheranism that sees liturgy as ritual re-enactment. Here we have shades of ancient mystery religions. In the Winter 1996 issue of *dialog*, Roy Harrisville, in his typically humorous manner, pokes fun at such ritual performance, calling it "liturgical hocus pocus" and "cult magic."[5]

For confessional Lutherans, liturgy is not about human activity, but about the real presence of the Lord who stoops down to put his words into our ears and his body and blood into our mouths. Liturgy, as it is divine service, delivers the forgiveness of sins. The liturgy does not exist to provide edifying entertainment, motivation for sanctified living, or therapy for psychological distresses, but the forgiveness of sins. In his treatise "Against the Heavenly Prophets," Luther writes:

> If I now seek the forgiveness of sins, I do not run to the cross, for I will not find it given there. Nor must I hold to the suffering of Christ as Dr. Karlstadt trifles, in knowledge or remembrance, for I will not find it there either. But I will find in the sacrament or the gospel the word which distributes, presents, offers, and gives to me that forgiveness which was won on the cross. (AE 40: 214)

In the liturgy God himself is present to forgive sins. The real presence of Christ, the forgiver of sins, in his words and with his body and blood has shaped the *cultus*, the liturgical forms of confessional Lutheranism.

Confusion About Forgiveness

At the present time, Lutherans are being invited to trade off a liturgical form shaped by the real presence of Christ the Forgiver for another form. The form that we are invited to make our own has its roots in American Evangelicalism. The forgiveness of sins has no real presence within the theology of Evangelicalism. At best, troubled sinners are pointed back to Calvary. The problem is, as Luther has reminded us, that forgiveness was achieved at Calvary but not delivered there. Calvary is back there in time almost two thousand years ago. At its worst, Evangelicalism turns the troubled sinner inward to his own conscience. This is a gross mishandling of law and gospel, as Dr. Walther reminds us in Thesis IX of his *Proper Distinction between Law and Gospel*:

> The Word of God is not rightly divided when sinners who have been struck down and terrified by the Law are directed, not to the Word and the Sacraments, but to their own prayers and wrestlings with God in order that they may win their way into a state of grace; in other words, when they are told to keep on praying and struggling until they feel that God has received them into grace.[6]

This subjectivism is embodied in the hymnody and liturgical practices of Evangelicalism. The *cultus* of Evangelicalism exchanges the absolution for assurances of grace, the gospel as the efficacious Word of salvation for a gospel that invites and requires a human decision, and the supper of the Lord's body and blood for a symbolic recollection of the upper room. Where is the forgiveness of sins?

As I stated earlier, the crisis over the liturgy stems from confusion regarding the forgiveness of sins. Evidence for this assertion can be seen in a new book by Timothy Wright, one of the pastors at the ELCA's Community Church of Joy in Phoenix. In his book *A Community of Joy: How to Create Contemporary Worship*,[7] Wright attempts to answer the question "How can we use worship to attract and hold irreligious people?" Wright finds the structures of Lutheran liturgy to be a roadblock in the evangelistic task. At the very least, Wright urges Lutherans to "warm up the liturgy" with a visitor-friendly campus, name tags, careful directions, and a corps of well-trained greeters and ushers. But more is needed. The confession of sins will have to go. Wright says:

> Some congregations begin the worship service with a time of confession and forgiveness. Long time churchgoers may appreciate opening with this important liturgical rite, but starting the service with confession and forgiveness says to the guests: "You are sinners!" For

years some people have stayed away from church, fearing such condemnation. Finally, having the courage to come, they hear from the
start how bad they are—that they cannot worship until they confess
their failures and shortcomings.[8]

We are told to "watch out for religious phrases in hymns." All
this talk about "cherubim and seraphim bowing down before him"
and "a bulwark never failing" will only confuse visitors. Preachers
are instructed to remember "in preparing a message, the question
is not, 'What shall I preach about?' but 'To whom shall I preach?'"
Therefore preachers get this advice from Wright: "The how-to section of a bookstore provides a great resource for relevant sermon
ideas. The psychological and self-help sections prove especially helpful. Written to meet the needs of people (and to make money), the
authors focus on sure-fire concerns." When it comes to the sacrament of the altar, Wright has this to say on closed communion: "This
policy will not work in a visitor-oriented service. 'Excluding' guests
will turn them off. It destroys the welcoming environment that the
church tried to create."[9] Again, my question: Where is the forgiveness of sins?

Wright would have us abandon Lutheran liturgy for the sake
of "cross-culturalism." He is, in effect, inviting us to abandon the
means-of-grace-centered culture of Lutheranism for the increasingly
pragmatic culture of American Evangelicalism.[10] This is an invitation
that we must decline for the sake of the gospel.

The American Context

What is to be done? First, let us recognize that the ecclesial-religious
culture of North America is Evangelicalism. This culture has its roots
first in Puritanism, which is basically Calvinistic, and secondarily in
the great revival movements of the late eighteenth and early nineteenth centuries. The ethos of American Evangelicalism is at home
in North America. As Nathan Hatch has pointed out in his book *The
Democratization of American Christianity*,[11] the Jeffersonian ideas of
individual freedom and equality are congenial to Evangelicalism's
emphasis on conversion as a personal decision and the church as
a spiritual democracy. Evangelicalism's stress on the autonomy of

the believer and the immediacy of spiritual experience apart from sacramental means has shaped a religious culture that accents individual faith over churchly life and tends to characterize baptism, absolution, and the Lord's Supper as externals at the periphery of the Christian life, at best. Subjectivity, coupled with a suspicion of the intellect, has produced a religious culture that elevates heart over head, emotion over intellect. Lutherans can no more compromise with this culture than Luther could strike an agreement with Zwingli or than the confessional Lutherans of the nineteenth century could join the Prussian Union. Evangelicalism is of a different spirit.

In a culture that has been so deeply influenced by Evangelicalism, it is imperative that we emphasize our Lutheran distinctiveness. As the Formula of Concord confesses:

> We believe, teach, and confess that in a time of confession, as when the enemies of the Word of God desire to suppress the pure doctrine of the holy Gospel, the entire community of God, yes, every individual Christian, and especially the ministers of the Word as leaders of the community of God, are obligated to confess openly, not only by words but also through deeds and actions, the true doctrine and all that pertains to it, according to the Word of God. In such a case we should not yield to adversaries even in matters of indifference, nor should we tolerate the imposition of such ceremonies on us by adversaries in order to undermine the genuine worship of God and to introduce and confirm their idolatry by force or chicanery. (FC SD, X10; Tappert, 612)

At the time of the Formula, the challenge was an attempt to impose Roman ceremonies on Lutherans in order to give the impression of unity. Today the challenge is from the other side of the fence as some Lutherans give the impression that there are no substantial differences between themselves and American Evangelicals.

Actually, this is not a new challenge to the Missouri Synod. The so-called American Lutheranism championed by Samuel Simon Schmucker in the last century caused C.F.W. Walther to write:

> We refuse to be guided by those who are offended by our church customs. We adhere to them all the more firmly when someone wants

to cause us to have a guilty conscience on account of them. . . . It is truly distressing that many of our follow Christians find the differences between Lutheranism and papism in outward things. It is a pity and dreadful cowardice when one sacrifices the good ancient church customs to please the deluded American sects, lest they accuse us of being papistic! Indeed! Am I to be afraid of a Methodist, who perverts the saving Word, or be ashamed in the matter of my good cause, and not rather rejoice that the sects can tell by our ceremonies that I do not belong to them? . . . With this we are not insisting that there be uniformity of perception or feeling or of taste among all believing Christians—neither dare anyone demand that all should be minded in this as he is. Nevertheless it remains true that the Lutheran liturgy distinguishes Lutheran worship from the worship of other churches to such an extent that the houses of worship of the latter look like lecture halls in which hearers are merely addressed or instructed, while our churches are in truth houses of prayer in which Christians serve the great God publicly before the world.[12]

Thus it is for good reason that the Constitution of the Lutheran Church—Missouri Synod follows Walther in making a condition for membership in the synod the "exclusive use of doctrinally pure agenda, hymnbooks, and catechisms in church and school."[13]

The Lutheran Cure

There are several implications for congregational life and pastoral practice. Rejection of the "alternative worship movement" is not an affirmation that all is well in congregations that stick to the hymnal. Kenneth Korby has commented that there are three kinds of churches: (1) churches with the liturgy, (2) churches without the liturgy, and (3) liturgical churches. There are congregations that never depart from page 5 or 15 in *TLH* or page 158 in *LW*; they have the liturgy, although they really don't know why. Then there are congregations that have abandoned the liturgy altogether. Genuinely liturgical churches, however, are at home in the liturgy; it is the source and center of their life.

I have no doubt that one of the reasons "alternate worship forms" have been so eagerly embraced by many in the Missouri Synod is that the liturgy was never taught, and the richness of our hymnbooks was left largely untapped. It is not the liturgy that is the problem, but the way it has been misused. In his chapter "Liturgical Renewal in the Parish" in *Lutheran Worship: History and Practice*, Arthur Just writes:

> A chapter on liturgical renewal suggests that the liturgy is in need of renewal. . . . Perhaps what is wrong is not the liturgy but those who use the liturgy. The targets of liturgical renewal are the clergy and the congregation.[14]

Congregations should expect the seminaries of the synod to provide pastors who are fully at home in the liturgy. At the present time, our seminaries require only one course in liturgy. This is hardly sufficient in preparing pastors who must be equipped to understand the theology of the divine service and plan and lead liturgy accordingly. A basic course in the theology of the liturgy should be foundational for at least two other required courses in the mechanics of the divine service: (1) the rubrics and the actual conduct of the service, and (2) liturgy as it relates to pastoral care, namely, the occasional services. A strengthened curriculum in liturgical theology needs to be set in the context of a vibrant liturgical life on campus. The chapel should model the absolute best of our heritage.

If we get the forgiveness of sins right, we will get the liturgy right. Luther writes in the Large Catechism:

> We believe that in this Christian church we have the forgiveness of sins, which is granted through the holy sacraments and . . . in short, the entire Gospel and all the duties of Christianity. . . . Therefore everything in the Christian church is so ordered that we may daily obtain full forgiveness of sins through the Word and through signs appointed to comfort and revive our consciences as long as we live. (LC, II, 54–55; Tappert, 417–418)

For Luther and the confessions, the church is constituted in the liturgy—that is, she receives her life from Christ in his words and gifts, which deliver the forgiveness of sins. No wonder, then, that our confessions place sermon and sacrament at the center, insisting that our churches have not abolished the Mass but celebrate it every Sunday and on other festivals (AP XXIV).

Our concern for the liturgy is not fueled by a traditionalism that is intent on merely preserving the past. It is a concern that the forgiveness won by our Lord in his suffering and death be proclaimed and distributed in their truth and purify for the salvation of sinners. Liturgical texts and practices are to be evaluated from this perspective.

Our historic, Lutheran, liturgical orders are Christ-centered as opposed to man-centered; they reflect the theology of the cross rather than the theology of glory; they center on special revelation not natural revelation; they tie us to the means of grace; they appeal to faith instead of emotions; and they anchor us not in myth but in the incarnation.

Two comments on the importance of teaching are in order. Let the pastor begin by teaching the board of elders or church council. Why not build in forty-five minutes to an hour of study time to each meeting of the board of elders? Over the period of a year, the pastor could work through the basics of our doctrine and practice of liturgy on the basis of the Scriptures and the confessions.[15] Any liturgical changes that are to be made in the worship life of the congregation must be undergirded with substantial teaching.

The teaching of the liturgy is a key component in the catechesis of new members. I have argued elsewhere that catechesis is the lively link between evangelism and liturgy.[16] The liturgy is not readily understandable or accessible to the unbeliever. Through catechesis the unbeliever is transported from the culture of this world to the culture of God's colony on earth, the holy church.[17] The culture of God's colony has its own language, the language of faith. The language of faith is the language of the liturgy. Drawing on Neil Postman's analysis of entertainment, Cornelius Plantinga Jr. of Calvin Seminary, Grand Rapids, describes what happens when Christians forget this basic fact and fashion services in the mode of entertainment:

> Naturally, services of this kind give an impression of a religion somewhat different from historic Christianity. One could imagine a visitor walking away from such a service and saying to himself: 'I had it all wrong. I had thought Christianity included a shadow side—confession, self-denial, rebuke of sin, concern with heresy, willingness to lose one's life for the sake of Jesus Christ. Not so, apparently.'

The Christian religion isn't about lament or repentance or humbling oneself before God to receive God's favor. It's got nothing to do with doctrines and the struggle to preserve the truth. It's not about the hard, disciplined work of mortifying our sinful self and learning to make God's purposes our own. It's not about the inevitable failures in this project and the persistent grace of Jesus Christ that comes so that we might begin again. Not at all! I had it all wrong! The Christian faith is mainly about celebration and fun and personal growth and five ways to boost my self-esteem. And especially, it's about entertainment.[18]

The language of the liturgy, the language of faith, aims not for entertainment but edification. Catechesis teaches the convert this language. Three books are essential to this catechesis: the Holy Scriptures, the Small Catechism, and the hymnal. The doctrine that is drawn from the Scriptures is confessed in the catechism and expressed doxologically in the liturgy and hymns.

Conclusion

Remember the story of the golden calf in Exodus 32? The children of Israel, fresh out of Egypt, are encamped in the Sinai wilderness. They do not know what has become of Moses. The people go to Aaron with the request for "new gods." Aaron is responsive to their "felt needs" and fashions for them a golden calf, a "worship form" that was culturally relevant to their Canaanite context. This was entertainment evangelism at its best, as we read that "the people sat down to eat and drink and rose up to play" (Ex. 32:6). Even though Aaron called it "a feast to the Lord" (Ex. 32:5), God called it idolatry. The apostle Paul writes: "Now all these things happened to them as examples, and they were written for our admonition, upon whom the ends of the ages have come. . . . Therefore, my beloved, flee from idolatry" (I Cor. 10:11, 14 NKJV).

The opposite of idolatry is faith in Jesus Christ. Indeed, faith is the highest worship of God, as the confessions so often remind us. No forgiveness of sins, no faith. The liturgy delivers us from self-chosen forms of worship, drawing us out of idolatry to repentance and faith. The introduction to *Lutheran Worship* gets it right:

Saying back to him what he has said to us, we repeat what is most true and sure. Most true and sure is his name, which he put upon us with the water of our Baptism. We are his. This we acknowledge at the beginning of the Divine Service. Where his name is, there is he. Before him we acknowledge that we are sinners, and we plead for forgiveness. His forgiveness is given us, and we, freed and forgiven, acclaim him as our great and gracious God as we apply to ourselves the words he has used to make himself known to us.[19]

Notes

1 Hermann Sasse, "The Liturgical Movement: Reformation or Revolution?," *Una Sancta* 17 (St. Luke the Evangelist 1960): 18.

2 For a fine exposition of *Gottesdienst* see Norman Nagel, "Whose Liturgy Is It?," *Logia* 2 (Eastertide 1993): 4–8. Also see *Lutheran Worship: History and Practice*, ed. Fred Precht (St. Louis: Concordia Publishing House, 1993), 44–57.

3 See Gordon W. Lathrup, *Holy Things* (Minneapolis: Fortress Press, 1995).

4 See *Lutheran Forum* 29 (August 1995): 18–24.

5 Roy Harrisville, "On Liturgical Hocus Pocus," *dialog* 55 (Spring 1996):150.

6 C.F.W. Walther, *The Proper Distinction Between Law and Gospel*, trans. W.H.T. Dau (St. Louis: Concordia Publishing House, 1928), 2. Also see Robert Schaibley, "A Lutheran Strategy for Urban Ministry: Evangelism and the Means of Grace," *Logia* 3 (Holy Trinity 1994): 6–13.

7 Timothy Wright, *A Community of Joy: How to Create Contemporary Worship* (Nashville: Abingdon Press, 1994), 24.

8 Ibid., 42.

9 Ibid., 46, 86, 102, 122.

10 See the following critiques written from within Evangelicalism: Os Guinness, *Dining with the Devil: The Megachurch Movement Flirts with Modernity* (Grand Rapids: Baker Book House, 1995); Douglas Webster, *Selling Jesus: What's Wrong with Marketing the Church* (Downers Grove, IL: Inter-Varsity Press, 1992); Michael Scott Horton, *Made in America: The Shaping of American Evangelicalism* (Grand Rapids: Baker Book House, 1991); David Wells, *No Place for Truth: Or Whatever Happened to Evangelical Theology?* (Grand Rapids: Eerdmans, 1993); and David Wells, *God in the Wasteland: The Reality of Truth in a World of Fading Dreams* (Grand Rapids: William B. Eerdmans, 1994).

11 Nathan Hatch, *The Democratization of American Christianity* (New Haven: Yale University Press, 1989).

12   C.F.W. Walther, *Essays for the Church* (St. Louis: Concordia Publishing House, 1992), 1: 194.

13   *Handbook of the Lutheran Church–Missouri Synod* (St. Louis: The Lutheran Church–Missouri Synod, 1992), 11.

14   Arthur Just, "Liturgical Renewal in the Parish," in *Lutheran Worship: History and Practice*, 21.

15   Additional resources for the teaching of the liturgy include Lutheran Worship: History and Practice; Roger D. Pittelko, *Worship and Liturgy, Touchpoint Bible Study* (St. Louis: CPH, 1995); Harold L. Senkbeil, *Dying to Live: The Power of Forgiveness* (St. Louis: CPH, 1994); Harold L. Senkbeil, *Sanctification: Christ in Action—Evangelical challenge and Lutheran Response* (Milwaukee: Northwestern Publishing House, 1989); John T. Pless, *Real Life Worship Reader* (Minneapolis: University Lutheran chapel, 1994).

16   See my GEM module entitled *Catechesis: The Lively Link between Evangelism and Worship*.

17   I would argue, along with David Wells, that much of Evangelical worship is reflective of "the world's view." Lutheran worship is reflective of "the Christian view." Also see Gene Edward Veith, *Postmodern Times* (Wheaton, IL: Crossway Books, 1994); Philip J. Lee, *Against the Protestant Gnostics* (New York: Oxford University Press, 1987); Dean O. Wenthe, "Entrance Into The Biblical World View: The First and Crucial Cross-Cultural Move," *Logia* 4 (Easter 1995):19–23.

18   Cornelius Plantinga Jr., Not the Way It's Supposed to Be: A Breviary of Sin (Grand Rapids: William B. Eerdmans, 1995), 193.

19   *Lutheran Worship* (St. Louis: Concordia Publishing House, 1982), 6.

VOCATION AND CATECHESIS

58

Vocation

Fruit of the Liturgy

PREVIOUSLY PUBLISHED IN THE
TRINITY 2002 ISSUE OF LOGIA, PP. 3-8

The supper is ended.
Oh, now be extended
The fruits of this service
In all who believe. (LW 247)

Omer Westendorf's popular hymn accents the linkage between the Lord's Supper and our life in the world. The words of the hymn are echoed in the Introduction to *Lutheran Worship* where we are told: "Our Lord gives us his body to eat and his blood to drink. Finally his blessing moves us into our calling, where his gifts have their fruition."[1] Indeed, this is "the liturgy after the liturgy,"[2] to use the helpful phrase that Carter Lindberg borrowed from the eastern tradition.

With the advent of *Lutheran Worship* in 1982, we have rediscovered something of the richness of the evangelical Lutheran understanding of *Gottesdienst*, Divine Service. The liturgy is not about our cultic activity; it is about God giving his gifts in sermon and sacrament to the people that he has gathered together in his name. Oswald Bayer notes, "Worship is first and last God's service to us, his sacrifice which took place for us, which he bestows in specific worship—'Take and eat! I am here for you' (cf. I Cor. 11:24 with

Gen. 2:16). This feature of worship is lost if we want to do as a work what we may receive as a gift."[3] Here Bayer reflects Article IV of the Apology as it confesses, "Faith is that worship which receives the benefits that God offers; the righteousness of the law is that worship which offers to God our own merits. God wants to be honored by faith so that we receive from him those things that he promises and offers" (AP IV, 49; Kolb-Wengert, 128). In Lutheran liturgical theology God is the subject rather than the object. Christ is the donor and benefactor. He gives his gifts to be received by faith alone.

Rome had reversed the flow, making the Supper into a sacrifice to be offered, a work to be performed, rather than a gift to be received. Lutheran theology distinguishes between God's *beneficium* and man's *sacrificium*. To confuse the two is to muddle law and gospel. This is at the heart of the critique of the Roman Mass in the Augsburg Confession and the Apology. Luther and the Confessions understood liturgy not as the work of the priest or the people, but the very work of God himself as he comes to serve his church with the gifts of redemption won on the cross and now distributed in word and sacrament.

Salvation's accomplishment on Calvary and its delivery at font, pulpit, and altar are the work of God. This Luther confesses in the Large Catechism:

> Neither you nor I could ever know anything about Christ, or believe in him and receive him as Lord, unless these were first offered to us and bestowed on our hearts through the preaching of the gospel by the Holy Spirit. The work is finished and completed; Christ has acquired and won the treasure for us by his sufferings, death, and resurrection, etc. But if the work remained hidden so that no one knew of it, it would have all been in vain, all lost. In order that this treasure might not be buried but be put to use and enjoyed, God has caused the Word to be published and proclaimed, in which he has given the Holy Spirit to offer and apply to us this treasure, this redemption. (LC II, 38; Kolb-Wengert, 436)

All of this is *beneficium*, gift. Faith clings to the gift, drawing its life from the bounty of God's mercy and grace in Jesus Christ. He is the servant, the liturgist in the Divine Service.

Sacrificium, on the other hand, is the work of man. Luther rejected the Roman understanding of the mass as sacrifice because it was built on a presumption that God could be placated by man's efforts. This Luther deemed to be idolatrous. In the Large Catechism he wrote:

> This is the greatest idolatry that we have practiced up to now, and it is still rampant in the world. All the religious orders are founded upon it. It involves only that conscience that seeks help, comfort, and salvation in its own works and presumes to wrest heaven from God. It keeps track of how often it has made endowments, fasted, celebrated Mass, etc. It relies on such things and boasts of them, unwilling to receive anything as a gift of God, but desiring to earn everything by itself or merit everything by works of supererogation, just as if God were in our service or debt and we were his liege lords. (LC I, 22, Kolb-Wengert, 388)

It was this conviction that compelled Luther to reform the canon of the mass so that God's speaking and giving were clearly distinct from the church's praying.

Luther has not been without his critics. Yngve Brilioth judged Luther to be one-sided in his focus on the gift of the forgiveness of sins, while ignoring or downplaying such themes as thanksgiving, communion, commemoration, eucharistic sacrifice, and mystery.[4] More recently, Eugene Brand opined that Luther's liturgical surgery left the patient disfigured.[5] It took an Anglican scholar, Bryan Spinks,[6] to save Luther from the Lutherans as he demonstrated that Luther's revisions were a thoughtful unfolding of the liturgical implications of the doctrine of justification.

The faithful come to church not to give, but to receive. Luther gives doxological expression to this in stanza 4 of his catechetical hymn "Here is the Tenfold Sure Command" (LW #331):

> And put aside the work you do,
> So God may work in you.
> Have mercy, Lord!

Vilmos Vatja explains:

> In no sense is this worship a preparatory stage which faith could ultimately leave behind. Rather faith might be defined as the passive cult

(*cultus passivus*) because in this life it will always depend on the worship by which God imparts himself—a gift granted to the believing congregation.

This is confirmed in Luther's explanation of the Third Commandment. To him sabbath rest means more than a pause from work. It should be an opportunity for God to do his work on man. God wants to distract man from his daily toil and so open him to God's gifts. To observe sabbath is not a good work which man could offer to God. On the contrary, it means pausing from all our works and letting God do his work in us and for us.

Thus Luther's picture of the sabbath is marked by the passivity of man and the activity of God. And it applies not only to certain holy days on the calendar, but to the Christian life in its entirety, testifying to man's existence as a creature of God who waits by faith for the life to come. Through God's activity in Christ, man is drawn into the death and resurrection of the Redeemer and is so recreated a new man in Christ. The Third Commandment lays on us no obligations for specific works of any kind (not even spiritual or cultic works), but rather directs us to the work of God. And we do not come into contact with the latter except in the service, where Christ meets us in the means of grace.[7]

Lutherans are rightly uncomfortable with the slogan made popular after the Second Vatican Council that liturgy is the "work of the people." Liturgy does not consist in our action, but the work of God, who stoops down to give us gifts that we cannot obtain for ourselves. Does the passivity of the Lutheran definition leave no room for worship? Does not the Small Catechism bid us to "thank, praise, serve, and obey" God? If God serves us sacramentally, do we not also serve him sacrificially?

To address these questions, we turn to the post-communion collect that Luther included in his 1526 *Deutsche Messe*: "We give thanks to you, almighty God, that you have refreshed us through this salutary gift, and we implore you that of your mercy you would strengthen us through the same in faith toward you and in fervent love toward one another; through Jesus Christ, your Son, our Lord, who lives and reigns with you and the Holy Spirit, one God, now and forever."[8]

In this collect, Luther gives doxological expression to a theological proposition that he had made six years earlier in *The Freedom of the Christian*, where he argued "that a Christian lives not in himself, but in Christ and the neighbor . . . He lives in Christ through faith, and in his neighbor through love" (AE 31: 371). The existence of the old Adam is focused on self. The old Adam is curved in on himself, to use the imagery of Luther. This egocentric existence stands in contrast to the life of the new man in Christ. The new man lives outside of himself, for his calling is to faith in Christ and love for the neighbor. Thus Luther continues, "By faith he is caught up beyond himself into God. By love he descends beneath himself into his neighbor" (AE 31: 371). Faith is active in love and so takes on flesh and blood in service to the neighbor just as Christ became incarnate not to be served, but to give himself in service to the world.

The post-communion collect has a pivotal place in the liturgy. It is the hinge that connects God's service to us in the sacrament with our service to the neighbor in the world. This thought is also demonstrated in Luther's hymnody. In his hymn on the Lord's Supper, "Lord, We Praise You" (LW #238), Luther confesses the blessings bestowed by God in the body and blood of his Son in the first two stanzas. The final stanza is a prayer that the sacrament might be fruitful in the lives of those who have received the Lord's testament:

> May God bestow on us his grace and favor
> To please him with our behavior
> And live together here in love and union
> Nor repent this blest communion
> O Lord, have mercy!
> Let not your good spirit forsake us,
> But heavenly minded he make us.
> Give your Church, Lord to see
> Days of peace and unity,
> O Lord, have mercy!

Luther also translated and revised a fifteenth-century hymn generally attributed to John Hus, "Jesus Christ, Our Blessed Savior" (LW #236–237).[9] The ninth stanza of his hymn expresses the thought that the sacrament both nourishes faith and causes love to flourish:

Let this food your faith nourish
That by love its fruits may flourish
And your neighbor learn from you
How much God's wondrous love can do.

Luther's understanding of vocation is consistent with his litur-gical theology. God serves us sacramentally in the Divine Service as we receive his benefactions by faith, and we serve God sacrificially as we give ourselves to the neighbor in love. The *communio* of the sacrament exhibits both faith and love, according to Luther. "This fellowship is twofold: on the one hand we partake of Christ and all saints; on the other hand we permit all Christians to be partakers of us, in whatever way they are able," wrote Luther in 1519 (AE 35: 67). In his 1526 treatise *The Sacrament of the Body and Blood of Christ— Against the Fanatics*, Luther is more pointed:

> For it is necessary for each one to know that Christ has given his body, flesh, and blood on the cross to be our treasure and to help us receive the forgiveness of sins, that is, that we may be saved, redeemed from death and hell. That is the first principle of Christian doctrine. It is presented to us in the words, and his body and blood are given to us to be received corporeally as token and confirmation of this fact. To be sure, he did it only once, carrying it out and achieving it on the cross; but he causes it each day anew to be set before us, distributed and poured out through preaching, and he orders us to remember and never forget him. The second principle is love. . . . . *As he gives himself to us with his body and blood in order to redeem us from our misery, so ought we to give ourselves with might and main for our neighbor.* (AE 36:352, emphasis added)

For Luther, the distinction between faith and love is necessary both in liturgy and vocation. In the liturgy, faith receives the gifts of Christ. In vocation, love gives to the neighbor even as Christ has given himself to us. The distinction between faith and love lies behind the discussion of sacrifice in Article XXIV of the Apology. The Apology notes that there are two kinds of sacrifice. First of all, there is the atoning sacrifice, the sacrifice of propitiation whereby Christ made satisfaction for the sins of the world. This sacrifice has achieved rec-onciliation between God and humanity and so merits the forgiveness of sins. The other type of sacrifice is the eucharistic sacrifice. It does not merit forgiveness of sins, nor does it procure reconciliation with God, but is rather a sacrifice of thanksgiving. According to Article XXIV of the Apology, eucharistic sacrifices include:

> The preaching of the gospel, faith, prayer, thanksgiving, confession, the affliction of the saints, indeed all the good works of the saints. These sacrifices are not satisfactions for those who offer them, nor can they be applied to others so as to merit the forgiveness of sins or reconciliation for others *ex opere operato*. They are performed by those who are already reconciled. (Ap XXIV, 24; Kolb-Wengert, 262)

Luther and the early Lutherans did not do away with the category of sacrifice. Luther relocated sacrifice. He removed it from the altar and repositioned it in the world. Sacrifice was offered to God indirectly through service to the neighbor. This is "the liturgy after the liturgy." God's gifts given us sacramentally in the Divine Service now bear fruit sacrificially as we go back into the world to thank, praise, serve, and obey the God and Father of our Lord Jesus Christ. "The whole of a Christian's life is liturgical life,"[10] writes William Willimon.

This understanding of sacrifice reflects Romans 12, where Paul writes, "I beseech you therefore, brethren, by the mercies of God, that you present your bodies a living sacrifice, holy, acceptable to God, which is your reasonable service" (Rom. 12:1 NKJV). In the ancient world, everyone knew that a sacrifice was dead. The sacrificial victim was slaughtered. To the ears of those who first heard the apostle's letter, the term "living sacrifice" would have struck them as strange, as an oxymoron. Yet Paul is purposeful in his use of this imagery. The body of the Christian is rendered unto God as a living sacrifice, for the Christian has been joined to the death of Jesus in baptism. Plunged into Jesus' saving death in baptism, we now share in his resurrection from the grave (compare Rom. 6:11). Baptism is the foundation for the Christian life of sacrifice.

Vilmos Vatja writes:

> The Christian brings his sacrifice as he renders the obedience, offers the service, and provides the love which his work and calling require of

him. The old man dies as he spends himself for his fellowmen. But in his surrender of self, he is joined to Christ and obtains a new life. The work of the Christian in his calling becomes a function of his priesthood, his bodily sacrifice. His work in the calling is a work of faith, the worship of the kingdom of the world.[11]

The sacrifices offered by the royal priesthood are the "spiritual sacrifices" noted in I Peter 2:5 (NKJV), "You also, as living stones, are being built up a spiritual house, a holy priesthood, to offer up spiritual sacrifices acceptable to God through Jesus Christ." These spiritual sacrifices are what the Apology calls eucharistic sacrifices, and they embrace all that the believer does in love toward the neighbor flowing from faith in Christ.

Spiritual sacrifices are rendered in the bodily life of the believer as his life is a channel of God's love and care for the neighbor in need. These sacrifices do not merit salvation or make a person righteous, but rather express love for the neighbor. God is not in need of our good works, but the neighbor is in need of them. Freed from the notion that he must make himself good in order to earn eternal life, the Christian is directed toward the neighbor's well-being. In *The Freedom of the Christian* Luther wrote,

> Although the Christian is thus free from all works, he ought in this liberty to empty himself, take upon himself the form of a servant, be made in the likeness of men, be found in human form, and to serve, help and in every way deal with his neighbor as he sees that God through Christ has dealt and still deals with him. (AE 31: 366)

Here the Christian is the *larvae Dei*, the mask of God, by which God gives daily bread to the inhabitants of the world. In this sense, the Christian is a "little Christ" to his neighbor. In *The Freedom of a Christian* Luther said:

> Just as our neighbor is in need and lacks that in which we abound, so we were in need before God and lacked his mercy. Hence, as our heavenly Father has in Christ freely come to our aid, we also ought freely to help our neighbor through our body and its works, and each one become as it were a Christ to the other that we may be Christ to one another. (AE 31: 367–368)

Just as Christ sacrificed himself for us on the cross, we give ourselves sacrificially to the neighbor in love. This is expressed by Luther in the seventh of his Invocavit sermons, preached at Wittenberg on March 15, 1522:

> We shall now speak of the fruit of this sacrament, which is love; that is, that we should treat our neighbor as God has treated us. Now that we have received from God nothing but love and favor, for Christ has pledged and given us his righteousness and everything he has; he has poured out upon us all his treasures, which no man can measure and no angel can understand or fathom, for God is a glowing furnace of love, reaching even from the earth to the heavens. Love, I say, is a fruit of the sacrament. (AE 51: 95)

In his 1530 treatise *Admonition Concerning the Sacrament*, Luther makes a similar point:

> Where such faith is thus continually refreshed and renewed, there the heart is also at the same time refreshed anew in its love of the neighbor and is made strong and equipped to do all good works and to resist sin and all temptations of the devil. Since faith cannot be idle, it must demonstrate the fruits of love by doing good and avoiding evil. (AE 38:126)

Luther's teaching on the dual existence of the Christian in faith and love leads us to observe a connection with the teaching of the two governments or two kingdoms. Leif Grane points out that for Luther "the place where the two kingdoms are held together is the calling."[12] This calling is lived within the structures of creation. Luther identified these structures as the three "hierarchies" of "the ministry, marriage, and government." It is within these structures of congregation, political order, and family life (which for Luther included the economic realm) that one exercises "the liturgy after the liturgy." The Christian does not seek to escape or withdraw from the world as in monasticism, but rather he lives out his calling in the particular place where God has located him.

In the Table of Duties of the Small Catechism Luther identifies these duties as "holy orders," in an obvious play on words over against monastic teaching. Holy people do holy work. Sacrifice is relocated. No doubt, Ernst Kaesemann was influenced by the older liberalism that pitted "priestly religion" against "prophetic religion." Nevertheless, he does echo a Lutheran theme in his exposition of Romans 12 as he states, "Christian worship does not consist of what is practiced at sacred sites, at sacred times, and with sacred acts (Schlatter). It is the offering of bodily existence in the otherwise profane sphere."[13] In a less polemic tone, Carter Lindberg makes a similar point: "Daily work is a form of worship within the world (*weltlicher Gottesdienst*) through service to the neighbor."[14] The "thank, praise, serve, and obey" in the conclusion of the explanation of the First Article find their fulfillment in the entire Table of Duties.

Luther identifies this service to the neighbor as a genuine *Gottesdienst*. "Now there is no greater service of God than Christian love which helps and serves the needy, as Christ himself will judge and testify on the last day" (AE 45:172) said Luther in his 1523 writing *Ordinance of a Common Chest*.

The Christian then lives the life of worship in the realm of creation, in the terrain of God's left-hand regime. This is affirmed in Article XVI of the Augustana as the point is made that the gospel does not undercut secular government, marriage, or occupations within the world "but instead intends that a person keep all this as a true order of God and demonstrate in these walks of life Christian love and true good works according to each person's calling" (AC XVI, 5; Kolb-Wengert, 50). Contrary to Rome's teaching that holiness is to be found in religious pursuits and the Anabaptist contention that discipleship means disengagement from the world, the Augsburg Confession maintains that evangelical perfection is to be found in the fear of God and faith, not in the abandonment of earthly responsibilities.

To flee from the demands that come to us by way of these earthly responsibilities is to flee from the cross that God lays upon us in order to put to death the old man. It is one of the enduring strengths of Gustaf Wingren's classic study *Luther on Vocation* that he demonstrates that in the place of our calling, God destroys the self-confidence of the old Adam who seeks to justify his existence by his own works:

In one's vocation there is a cross—for prince, husband, father, daughter, for everyone—and on this cross the old human nature is to be crucified. Here the side of baptism, which is concerned with death, is fulfilled. Christ died on the cross, and one who is baptized unto death with Christ must be put to death by the cross. To understand what is meant by the cross of vocation, we need only remember that vocation is ordained by God to benefit, not him who fulfills the vocation, but the neighbor who, standing alongside, bears his own cross for the sake of others.[15]

The cross of vocation drives the baptized back to Christ as he enlivens us with his body and blood, thus renewing and strengthening them in faith and love. Einar Billing describes the Christian life going on between the two poles of the forgiveness of sins and our calling: "The forgiveness of sins continually restores us to our calling, and our calling . . . continually refers us to the forgiveness of sins."[16] Thus we see an ongoing rhythm between liturgy and vocation. Served with Christ's gifts in the liturgy, we are sent back into the world to live sacrificially as his royal priesthood. This is not a life that is lived by our own energies or resources but by the gospel of Jesus Christ alone. It is a life that is lived by the daily return to baptism in repentance and faith. It is a life sustained by Jesus' words and nourished with his body and blood. In a Maundy Thursday sermon (1529), Luther exhorted the congregation to use the sacrament as God's remedy against the world, the flesh, and the devil:

> For this reason, because Christ saw all this, he commanded us to pray and instituted the Sacrament for us to administer often, so that we are protected against the devil, the world, and the flesh. When the devil attacks, come for strength to that dear Word so that you may know Christ and long for the Sacrament! A soldier has his rations and must have food and drink and be strong. In the same way here: those who want to be Christian should not throw the Sacrament to the winds as if they did not need it.[17]

God's holy people live an embattled existence in their various callings in the world. They are ever in need of comfort and refreshment. Therefore the royal priesthood is constantly drawn back to the Divine Service to receive forgiveness of sins over and over again until the day when our baptism will be completed in the resurrection of the body and our earthly callings will be fulfilled in the eternal sabbath of the heavenly kingdom.

We conclude by asking the quintessential Lutheran question: "What does this mean" for faithful pastoral practice and the life of the church in our own day?

The evangelical understanding of the liturgy might help us recover the robust reality of the doctrine of vocation that has, in large part, been lost in contemporary American Lutheranism. Vocation has been collapsed into what Marc Kolden refers to as "occupation-alism."[18] Vocation is thought of only in terms of what a person does for a job. By way of contrast, Luther understood that the Christian is genuinely bi-vocational. He is called first through the gospel to faith in Jesus Christ and he is called to occupy a particular station or place in life. The second sense of this calling embraces all that the Christian does in service to the neighbor, not only in a particular occupation, but also as a member of the church, a citizen, a spouse, parent, or child, and as a worker. Here the Christian lives in love toward other human beings and is the instrument by which God does his work in the world.

Luther abhorred self-chosen works both in liturgy and daily life. In his exposition of the Sermon on the Mount, he wrote:

> Reason is the devil's bride, which plans some particular course because it does not know what may please God . . . The best and highest station in life is to love God and one's neighbor. Indeed, that station is filled by the ordinary manservant or maidservant who cleans the meanest pot.[19]

Medieval Roman Catholicism presupposed a dichotomy between life in the religious orders and life in ordinary callings. It was assumed that the monastic life guided by the evangelical counsels (namely, the Sermon on the Mount) provided a more certain path to salvation than secular life regulated by the Decalogue. American Evangelicalism has spawned what may be referred to as "neomonasticism." Like its medieval counterpart, neomonasticism gives the impression that religious work is more God-pleasing than other tasks and duties associated with life in the world. According to this mindset, the believer who makes an evangelism call, serves on a congregational committee, or reads a lesson in the church service is performing more spiritually significant work than the Christian mother who tends to her children or the Christian who works with integrity in a factory. For the believer, all work is holy because he or she is holy and righteous through faith in Christ.

Similar to neomonasticism is the neo-clericalism that lurks behind the slogan: "Everyone a minister." This phrase implies that work is worthwhile only insofar as it resembles the work done by pastors. Lay readers are called "Assisting Ministers," and the practice of the laity reading the lessons is advocated on the grounds that it will involve others in the church, as though the faithful reception of Christ's gifts were insufficient. It is no longer enough to think of your daily life and work as your vocation. Now it must be called your "ministry." When this happens "the vocation of the baptized is no longer the liturgy after the liturgy, but a substitute liturgy."[20] First things first. First God serves us with his gifts in word and sacrament. Then we serve God as we live in the freedom of the forgiveness of sins, attending to the neighbors that God has put into our world. It is the way of grace and works, faith and love, sacrament and sacrifice. The liturgy is the source of vocation as the gifts that God bestows now bear fruit in the callings of those who have been called out of darkness into light.

Notes

1 *Lutheran Worship* (St. Louis: Concordia Publishing House, 1982), 6.

2 Carter Lindberg, *Beyond Charity: Reformation Initiatives for the Poor* (Minneapolis: Fortress Press, 1993), 164.

3 Oswald Bayer, "Worship and Theology," in *Worship and Ethics: Lutherans and Anglicans in Dialogue* (New York: Walther de Gruyter, 1996), 154.

4 Yngve Brilioth, *Eucharistic Faith and Practice: Evangelical and Catholic*, trans. A.G. Herbert (London: SPCK, 1963), 94–152, 276–288.

5 Eugene Brand, "Luther's Liturgical Surgery," *Interpreting Luther's Legacy: Essays in Honor of Edward C. Fendt*, ed. Fred W. Meuser, and Stanley D. Schneider (Minneapolis: Augsburg Publishing House, 1969), 108–119.

6 Bryan Spinks, *Luther's Liturgical Criteria and His Reform of the Canon of the Mass* (Bramcote Notts: Grove Books, n.d.), 21–37.

7 Vilmos Vatja, *Luther on Worship*, trans. U.S. Lupold (Philadelphia: Muhlenberg Press, 1958), 130.

8 *Lutheran Worship*, 153. Also see AE 53:137–138 and *Works of Martin Luther* (Philadelphia: Muhlenberg Press, 1932), 6: 329–332 for material on the background and usage of this collect.

9 See Robin Leaver, "Luther's Catechism Hymns 7. Lord's Supper," *Lutheran Quarterly* (Autumn 1998): 303–312, for an argument that Luther, in fact, substantially rewrites this hymn so that it reflects more clearly his teaching that the body and blood of Christ are present and received in the sacrament. Leaver also notes the parallel between stanza 9 and the post-communion collect (309).

10 William Willimon, *The Service of God: How Worship and Ethics are Related* (Nashville: Abingdon Press, 1985), 18.

11 Vatja, 169.

12 Leif Grane, *The Augsburg Confession: A Commentary*, trans. John Rasmussen (Minneapolis: Augsburg Publishing House, 1987), 174.

13 Ernst Kaesemann, *Commentary on Romans* (Grand Rapids: Eerdmans, 1980), 329. Also note the comment of Paul Rorem in "The End of All Offertory Processions," *dialog* (Fall 1996), 249: "Forgiven and renewed, we offer ourselves once again to God, not in mystery and ritual at the altar but in the gritty realities of the poor and the mission fields of our neighborhoods and work places." Luther speaks in the same way when in a 1527 letter to John Hess he describes how Christians are to go to the aid of the sick: "I know for certain in that this work is pleasing to God and all angels when I do it in obedience to his will and as a divine service . . . Godliness is nothing but divine service, and divine service is service to one's neighbor" (cited from *Letters of spiritual Counsel*, ed. Theodore Tappert, [London: SCM Press, 1955], 238–239). Also note the remarks of Carl Wisloff: "We, not the Sacrament, are the sacrifice. But we live from the gifts of God's grace; that is, we are led through them from death to life. Sacrifice finds expression in just this. This event finds expression in worship through thanksgiving, praise, creed, and witness. But a true sacrifice is only this when it is consecrated through faith by daily walking in baptism, that is, walking in fear and faith, death and resurrection." Carl Wisloff, "Worship and Sacrifice," in *The Unity of the Church: A Symposium* ed. Vilmos Vatja (Rock Island, IL: Augustana Book Concern, 1957), 164–165.

14 Lindberg, 108.

15 Gustaf Wingren, *Luther on Vocation*, trans. Carl Rasmussen (Philadelphia: Muhlenberg Press, 1957), 29.

16 Einar Billing, *Our Calling*, trans. Conrad Bergendoff (Philadelphia: Fortress Press, 1964), 38.

17 Martin Luther, *The 1529 Holy Week and Easter Sermons of Dr. Martin Luther*, trans. Irving Sandberg (St. Louis: Concordia Publishing House, 1999), 78.

18 Marc Kolden, "Luther on Vocation," *Word and World* (Fall 1983): 385.

19 Wingren, 88.

20 Carter Lindberg, "The Ministry and Vocation of the Baptized," *Lutheran Quarterly* (Winter 1992), 396.

59

Holy Lord, Holy Gifts, Holy People

PREVIOUSLY PUBLISHED IN THE FALL 1999 ISSUE
OF LUTHERAN FORUM, PP. 12-15

Moses was in the wilderness watching over his father-in-law's sheep. There was nothing extraordinary about that. But as Moses tended to that ordinary task something extraordinary took place. Before his eyes, the angel of the Lord appeared to him in a flame of fire that burned from a bush without consuming the bush. Moses was caught off guard, taken by surprise. How could this bush burn without being reduced to ashes? He turns to gaze at this wondrous sight. Out of that flame the Lord speaks, calling Moses by name. God says to Moses, "Do not come near; put off your shoes from your feet, for the place on which you are standing is holy ground" (Exodus 3:5 RSV). Holy ground: it is God's ground; his space. Our "God is a consuming fire," says the book of Deuteronomy (4:24) and the Letter to the Hebrews (12:29). Yet the bush is not consumed. The fire is the manifestation of the Lord's presence, that is, of his holiness.

Thus we sing in the Gloria in Excelsis, "For thou only art holy." Likewise the Sanctus confesses the Holy God who comes to us in the Body and Blood of his Son to cleanse us from our sins: "Holy, holy, holy, Lord God of Sabaoth; heaven and earth are full of thy glory."

God reveals his holiness to Moses in the fire of the burning bush. This revelation gives us an insight into the nature of God's holiness. It is the nature of fire to be either beneficial or destructive. Take for example, that great mass of flame, the sun. The sun can scorch the earth, causing plants to wither and die. The sun can also radiate warmth causing plants to grow and be fruitful. It all depends on the position that one occupies in relation to the sun. So is it with God and his holiness. If one is positioned in unbelief and sin over against the holiness of God, his holiness is a fire that destroys. But if one stands before God on his own terms, that is, in faith, God's holiness is a flame that generates the warmth of mercy, bestowing light and life.

In his book, *The Trivialization of God: The Dangerous Illusion of a Manageable Deity*, Donald McCullough writes:

> God is not safe, but God is good, very good. For the dangerous otherness is a transcendent, loving commitment not to be separate—a threat to our egos that establishes our true selves, a danger that is our only safety. "Our God is a consuming fire" (Hebrews 12:29). As children we were told not to play with matches, and as adults we treat fire with caution. We must. Fire demands respect for its regal estate: it will not be touched, it will be approached with care, and it wields its scepter for ill or for good. With one spark it can condemn a forest to ashes and a home to memory as ghostly as the smoke rising from the charred remains of the family album. Or with a single flame it can crown a candle with power to warm a romance and set to dancing a fireplace blaze that defends against the cold. Fire is dangerous to be sure, but we cannot live without it; fire destroys but it also sustains life. (p. 68)

So also is the holiness of the God who is to be feared, loved, and trusted above all things.

Is Nothing Holy Any More?

For many the word "holy" is a red flag. They confuse holiness with morality or a strict and dour lifestyle like that espoused by the Pietists of the seventh century, or the Methodists of the eighteenth century, or the Pentecostal Holiness churches in our own day. Holiness is then seen as something we do or achieve, like those who claim not to have sinned in several years.

But I suspect there is another reason that we have trouble with the Biblical language of holiness. We have been influenced by a cultural secularism that maintains nothing is holy, that is, nothing really belongs to God. Not the unborn baby in its mother's womb who is granted life only if the mother so chooses. Marriage is being redefined so as to ignore the fact that God established it as a life-long union of fidelity between one man and one woman. Men and women are encouraged to view their bodies as toys rather than as temples of the Holy Spirit. And we have Dr. Kevorkian to take care of those toys once they break.

Now this is not detached from what we see happening in many churches. Churches were once built to reflect the fact that here we come into the presence of the Holy God. The chancel was lifted up giving prominence to the altar as the symbol of the Lord's presence. An altar rail drew a line between God and the world. The baptismal font was given a prominent place, often near the door of the church, reminding worshipers that we have access to God only through the cleansing waters of Holy Baptism. Stained glass windows illustrated the holy history of our salvation.

Nowadays church buildings are designed to look like secular auditoriums. It is no wonder that the things which transpire within these churches have little connection with heavenly realities. Ministers act as though they were talk show hosts, not stewards of the mysteries of God. Homemade liturgies tell us more about the creativity of those who devised them than the Holy Trinity. The practice of closed communion is dismissed as downright unfriendly as in some churches all are invited to belly up to the altar without regard to catechesis, confession, or pastoral care. Indeed we may ask, "Is nothing holy anymore?"

What has happened? David Wells, Professor of Systematic Theology at Gordon-Conwell Seminary, has authored three immensely insightful books on the Church and culture: *No Place for the Truth* (1993), *God in the Wasteland* (1994), and *Losing Our Virtue: Why the Church Must Recover Its Moral Vision* (1998). In these books he helps us understand the loss of the holy in contemporary American churches. In *God in the Wasteland*, Wells notes that holiness has become irrelevant in many of our churches:

> The Church has succumbed to the seductions of our therapeutic culture, and in that context it seems quite natural to favor the relational dimensions over the moral dimensions, mysticism over

cognitive conviction, self-fulfillment over personal surrender, self-image over character, pluralistic religious equality over the uniqueness of the Christian faith. When all is said and done, modernity dispatches the God who is outside, and all that remains is the God who is inside. (p. 136)

This culture then shapes the life of the Church. In *Losing Our Virtue*, Wells provides this analysis:

The wisdom common to many of our marketers is that, if it wants to attract customers, the Church should stick to a positive and uplifting message. It should avoid speaking of negative matters like sin. Not only so, but what has distinguished the Church in its appearance and functions should now be abandoned. In order to be attractive to people today, church buildings should not look that different from corporate headquarters, malls, or country clubs. Crosses and robes should go; dress should be casual; hymns should be contemporary and empty of the theological substance by which previous generations lived, because this is incomprehensible today; pews should be replaced by cinema-grade seats, organs by synthesizers and drums, solemnity by levity, reflection by humor, and sermons by light dialogues or catchy readings. The theory is that people will buy Christianity if they don't have to deal with what the Church has traditionally been. (p. 201)

Others, such as Walter Kallestad, urge the Church to "entertainment evangelism" as a primary means for reaching our secular world. The argument is made that gospel substance can be packaged in a style that has been shaped by the entertainment industry. We are told that the format of a television talk show is an appropriate style for Christian proclamation. Musical styles ranging from hard rock to country-western are encouraged as fitting vehicles for the songs of the faith. If you are a fan of the 50s you can go to a service and be treated to "I found my thrill on Calvary's Hill." Or if you prefer country-western you can opt for a service where you lift up your achy breaky heart to the Lord.

Entertainment is a poor substitute for reverence. Neil Postman worries over how the entertainment industry has influenced education, politics, and religion in North America. Cornelius Plantinga, Jr., draws on Postman's analysis and describes what happens when church services seek to entertain rather than lead worshipers to stand on the holy ground of God's saving presence:

> Naturally services of this kind give an impression of a religion somewhat different from historic Christianity. One could imagine a visitor walking away from such a service and saying to himself: 'I had it all wrong. I had thought Christianity included a shadow side—confession, self-denial, rebuke of sin, concern with heresy, willingness to lose one's life for the sake of Jesus Christ. Not so, apparently.' The Christian religion isn't about lament or repentance or humbling oneself before God to receive God's favor. It's not about the hard, disciplined work of mortifying our sinful self and learning to make God's purposes our own. It's not about the inevitable failures in this project and the persistent grace of Jesus Christ that comes so that we might begin again. Not at all! I had it all wrong! The Christian faith is mainly about celebration and fun and personal growth and five ways to boost my self-esteem. And especially, it's about entertainment. (p. 193)

A Holy God Calls for a Holy People

God is not present to entertain or amuse us but to save us. Our sin and God's holiness are a deadly combination. When God's holiness and human sin mix you have an explosion and it is not God who gets burned. Or does he? A Holy God whose passion it is to have a holy people stand in his presence for all eternity sent his Son into this world to take on all of our sin, all that makes us unholy, all that alienates us from his holy presence. As the sacrifices were consumed by fire in the Old Testament Temple, so the Lord Jesus Christ offers himself in our place. He is the Lamb of God; he becomes the holocaust—the whole burnt offering that takes away our sin. His holy blood shed on the cross of Calvary cleanses us from all sin and makes us a holy people, a "holy nation" as Peter calls us in his first Epistle (2:9). In his flesh, Jesus is the very Temple of God and those who are joined to him in Holy Baptism are made members of his royal priesthood, sanctified by his blood to offer spiritual sacrifices.

Holy people live holy lives. Luther's doctrine of vocation begs to be rediscovered in our church. Slogans such as "everyone a minister" have in fact promoted a kind of clericalism which, in effect, says to the laity that they are most worthwhile when they are doing ministerial things. The implicit message is that God is more pleased with the laity if they are making evangelism calls, teaching a Bible class, or reading the Scriptures in a church service than taking care of their children at home, or doing a good job at the office or on the farm.

Luther's doctrine of vocation rightly understood, however, is the setting and the context for both the doctrine of the royal priesthood and the doctrine of sanctification as can be seen in Luther's treatise, *The Freedom of the Christian*. Wilhelm Maurer called this writing "the most perfect expression of Luther's reformation understanding of the mystery of Christ" (Juengel, 20). Here Luther defends two propositions: "A Christian is a perfectly free lord of all, subject to none. A Christian is a perfectly dutiful servant of all, subject to all" (AE 31: 344). Faith lives in the freedom of Christ Jesus. Love lives a life of service to the neighbor.

In other words *vocatio* or the calling of the Christian faith is a double calling. First of all, it is the call to faith. It is the calling of the third article of the Apostles' Creed: "I believe that I cannot by own reason or strength believe in Jesus Christ, my Lord, or come to him, but the Holy Spirit has called me through the Gospel." It is also a calling to live the holy life of love within the created structures of this world. There is no better summary of this understanding than in the conclusion of Luther's *The Freedom of a Christian*:

> We conclude, therefore, that a Christian lives not in himself, but in Christ and in his neighbor. Otherwise he is not a Christian. He lives in Christ through faith, in his neighbor through love. By faith he is caught up beyond himself into God. By love he descends beneath himself into his neighbor. (AE 31: 371)

From the Altar Into the World

The holy gifts—the forgiveness of sins, life, and salvation—which we receive in the Divine Service hallow us for they are the fruits of

Christ's redeeming sacrifice. Here we see the heart of the Lutheran understanding of "liturgy." Liturgy is not our response to God, or the "work of the people" as the Second Vatican Council defined it. Liturgy is divine service, God's service, *Gottesdienst*. Faith receives all that Christ gives in and through his Word and Supper. The liturgy, in fact, draws us outside of ourselves to live in Christ by faith alone. That is why the Apology to the Augsburg Confession declares, "Faith is that worship which receives God's offered blessings; the righteousness of the law is that worship which offers God our own merits. It is by faith that God wants to be worshiped, namely, that we receive from him what he promises and offers" (IV.49). Faith receives the gifts which God bestows in the Divine Service.

Our vocation in the world is an extension of the Divine Service. The Lord's gifts bear fruit in lives lived in fervent love for the neighbor. So we sing in the hymn, "Sent Forth by God's Blessing": "The supper is ended. Oh, now be extended the fruits of this service in all who believe."

In the Divine Service we receive the fruits of Christ's propitiatory sacrifice (to use the language of the Apology, Article XXIV). That is, we receive the gospel Word that forgives our sin and we receive the Body and Blood of Christ given and shed for the sins of the world. We do not come to church to offer God a sacrifice but to receive the benefits of his Son's all-sufficient atonement. The sacrifices which we offer God are eucharistic sacrifices; that is, sacrifices of praise and thanksgiving. These take place primarily in the world and only secondarily in the church service.

Jobst Schöne writes,

The royal priesthood means to serve just as Christ served us. The royal priesthood serves through prayer, by comforting and encouraging, and by giving spiritual and material help to others. This service is rendered in the place and situation where the Lord has placed you as father or mother to your children, as husband and wife to each other, as members of the congregation mutually to each other, and so on. It is a service that continues after the Divine Service where we receive what Christ gives us—namely, the Gospel in all its forms—and we are to spread this Gospel in word and deed. This is not identical to what the minister in the Divine Service does when he handles the sacraments and preaches the Gospel. Rather the royal priesthood echoes it. The royal priesthood passes on to others what it has received in the Divine Service. (p. 16)

This understanding of vocation is grounded in the liturgy where our Holy God first serves us with his holy gifts. Here God bends down to us sinners to bestow on us the righteousness won for us by the obedient life and atoning blood of his Son. Salvation was accomplished on the cross but it is distributed to us in the preaching of the Holy Gospel, Holy Baptism, Holy Absolution, and the Holy Supper. It is only through these holy gifts which are received in faith that we have access to the holiness of God.

When we come to church we set foot on holy ground. Not in a magical sense, but because in this place the same God who appeared to Moses on Horeb in the burning bush comes to us in his Word and Supper and where he makes himself present. There is holy ground. We come with the prayer which the Holy Son of God has taught us to pray: "Hallowed be thy name," knowing that "God's name is holy in itself, but we pray in this petition that it may also be holy for us." And remembering that the Catechism goes on to say: "When the Word of God is taught clearly and purely and we, as children of God, lead holy lives in accordance with it. Help us to do this, dear Father in heaven! But whoever teaches and lives otherwise than the Word of God teaches, profanes the name of God among us. From this preserve us, Heavenly Father!"

Moses took off his shoes to stand in the presence of God. We do not take off our shoes, but we do lay aside our sin. Laying aside our sin, we come to the Holy Communion to receive the holy Body and Blood of the Lamb of God who makes us holy people. We are standing on holy ground in the company of angels, archangels, and the whole company of heaven. I conclude with a pastoral word from Hermann Sasse:

We can desire nothing more beautiful and greater for our parishioners than that they be present when the Holy Supper is celebrated according to the institution of Jesus Christ; when a believing congregation gathers around the altar to receive the true Body and Blood of our Lord. Only then will the Church, the Gospel, the Church of the pure doctrine remain among us, and only then. But the Church will then remain and the gates of hell shall not overcome her. And especially then, when a congregation is gathered around her altar in the deepest faith in the One who is her Lord and head—because he is her Redeemer—when she begins to sing the Kyrie and the Gloria and lifts up her heart to heaven, and with all angels and archangels and the entire hosts of the heavenly multitude she sings "Holy, holy, holy," then will the Church truly be a house of God, a place of the real presence of Christ in the midst of a boisterous and unholy world. And then the words will apply to her, "The Lord is in his holy temple. Let all the world be still before him." (Hab. 2:20)

Sources Cited

Book of Concord. Philadelphia: Muhlenberg Press, 1959.

Juengel, Eberhard. *The Freedom of a Christian: Luther's Significance for Contemporary Theology*. Minneapolis: Augsburg Fortress, 1988.

Luther's Works [LW]. Philadelphia: Muhlenberg Press, 1957.

McCullough, Donald. *The Trivialization of God: The Dangerous Illusion of a Manageable Deity*. Colorado Springs: Nav Press, 1995.

Plantinga, Cornelius, Jr. *Not the Way It's Supposed to Be: A Breviary of Sin*. Grand Rapids: Eerdmans, 1995.

Sasse, Hermann. *Lutherische Kirche*, Vol. 21, No. 5 (1939).

Schöne, Jobst. *The Christological Character of the Office of the Ministry and the Royal Priesthood*. Plymouth, MN: LOGIA Books, 1996.

Wells, David. *God in the Wasteland*. Grand Rapids: Eerdmans, 1994.

Losing Our Virtue: Why the Church Must Recover Its Moral Vision. Grand Rapids: Eerdmans, 1998.

DOCTRINE, LIFE, AND MISSION

60

Tracking the Trinity
in Contemporary Theology

PREVIOUSLY PUBLISHED IN THE APRIL 2005 ISSUE OF
CONCORDIA THEOLOGICAL QUARTERLY, PP. 99–118

"The dogma has more than once been thrown to the scrap heap, but has proved to be more lasting than many of the alternatives."[1] Or, at least, so thought Gerhard Sauter regarding the Trinity. Without doubt, the doctrine of the Trinity has emerged as a central issue in current theological inquiry. A quick perusal of theological journals published in the last twenty-five years yields dozens of articles on some aspect of trinitarian theology. Since 1982, *Word & World* has devoted two complete issues to the Trinity. This is not atypical when compared to other periodicals. A relatively new journal, *Pro Ecclesia*, founded by Carl Braaten and Robert Jenson, has become a primary outlet for trinitarian studies utilizing both patristic and ecumenical scholarship. A host of recent books have taken up one aspect or another of the doctrine of the Trinity. In March 2003, the teaching theologians of The Lutheran Church-Missouri Synod gathered in Dallas for a convocation that had as its theme "Confessing the Trinity Today." Not only systematic theology, but also biblical studies, liturgics, ethics, missiology, and pastoral theology have felt, in one way or another, the influence of contemporary trinitarian studies.

I. Bearings from Barth

Whence comes this resurgence of trinitarian theology, and where is it going? While the Reformation witnessed a rise of anti-trinitarian figures such as Faustus Socinus and Michael Servetus, the major attack on this doctrine would occur with the advent of a historical-critical approach to the New Testament in the eighteenth and nineteenth centuries. As the fourth Gospel was reckoned ahistorical (J.G. Herder, D.F. Strauss, and F.C. Baur), fundamental doubts regarding the biblical authenticity of the Trinity likewise began to surface.[2] The dogmatic response to the findings of these exegetes comes in Frederich Schleiermacher's relocation of the doctrine to the appendix of his systematic theology, *The Christian Faith*. Convinced that the doctrine was unnecessary for "Christian self-consciousness," Schleiermacher dismissed the ecclesiastical confession of the Trinity in favor of a God "unconditioned and absolutely simple."

> We have only to do with the God-consciousness given in our self-consciousness along with our consciousness of the world; hence we have no formula for the being of God in the world, and should have to borrow such a formula from speculation, and so prove ourselves disloyal to the character of the discipline with which we are working.[3]

At best, Schleiermacher could see the doctrine of the Trinity only in Sabellian-like terms, which hold the persons of the Godhead as operating in respect to various modes in the world. Schleiermacher's assessment of the doctrine of the Trinity would dominate the nineteenth century as it was congenial to the themes of divine simplicity and human morality.

Karl Barth's (1886–1968) articulation of the doctrine of the Trinity stands in sharp contrast to Schleiermacher's revisionism. Rescuing the Trinity from Schleiermacher's doctrinal attic, Barth sets the doctrine in the prolegomena of his dogmatics. Far from being a theological afterthought, the doctrine of the Trinity, according to Barth, has both a positive and critical function in Christian theology. The root of the Trinity for Barth is in the fact that God reveals himself as Lord. Thus Barth begins his dogmatic treatment of the Trinity by asserting: "God's Word is God Himself in His revelation. For God

reveals Himself as the Lord and according to the Scripture this signifies for the concept of revelation that God Himself in unimpaired
unity yet also in unimpaired distinction is Revealer, Revelation,
and Revealedness."[4] Positive assertions can be made only because
God has revealed himself as the triune Lord. This revelation, for
Barth, is God's own interpretation of himself. Critically, the trinitarian
doctrine serves to keep all language about God monotheistic. That is
to say, the doctrine of the Trinity prevents man from understanding
the being of God as a human construction, which is idolatry.

Barth reclaims and employs traditional trinitarian terminology.
God's being *ad extra* corresponds to his being *ad intra*. God does not
become an economy that is alien to his essence. Dogmatics, argues
Barth, must guard against both modalism and subordinationism. To
speak of three personalities in God "would be the worst and most
pointed expression of tritheism."[5]

Eberhard Jüngel, one of the most perceptive interpreters of
Barth, observes: "The Church Dogmatics is the ingenious and diligent attempt to think the proposition 'God corresponds to himself' through to the end."[6] Barth seeks to speak of God as he is in
himself. Therefore Barth does not begin with an abstract definition of the deity but with God's fundamental revelation of himself
in Christ. Consistent with Barth's rejection of any natural theology is
his dismissal of all moves to find analogies to the Trinity (vestigium
trinitatis) in nature, history, or psychology. Simply put, for Barth all
speaking about God must be trinitarian if it is to be Christian.

Nevertheless, old habits die slowly. It is not surprising that Barth's
reassertion of the Trinity was vigorously repudiated by the older liberalism, which, firmly entrenched in Harnack's opinion, maintained
that this doctrine represented the epitome of the Hellenization of
the primitive kerygma. Accusing Barth of resurrecting supernatu-
ral metaphysics and engaging in unwarranted speculation, Wilhem
Pauck impatiently dismissed Barth's trinitarian approach:

> As if it were really a matter of life and death, that as members of the
> church of the Twentieth Century—we should accept the dogma of
> the Trinity! Professional theologians may think that it is absolutely
> necessary for us to be concerned with theological thought-forms of
> the past, but—God be thanked!—the common Christian layman is

no professional theologian, and he may be a better Christian for that reason . . . What (the preacher) needs to know is who God is and how man can be put in right relation with him into the abundant, full, rich, meaningful life.[7]

The old liberalism represented by Pauck and the other heirs of Harnack was fading. Whatever else one may think of Karl Barth, it must be granted that he restored the topic of the Trinity to respectable theological discourse.

In the twentieth century, Karl Rahner (1904–1984) ranks second only to Karl Barth in the development of the new trinitarian theology. This Austrian-born Roman Catholic theologian attempted to connect the classical theology embodied in Augustine and Thomas Aquinas with the worldview created by the Enlightenment. Representative of the climate that was created by Vatican II, Rahner is perhaps best known for his definition of anonymous Christians. It is his trinitarian theology, however, that continues to engage current scholarship. Following in the path of Barth, Rahner also concludes that the word *person* is an unsatisfactory way of speaking of Father, Son, and Spirit as the term is freighted with individualistic definitions. Rahner, similar to Barth, argues that hypostasis be defined as "a distinct manner of subsisting."

Rahner observed: "Despite their orthodox confession of the Trinity, Christians are, in practical life, almost mere 'monotheists.' We must be willing to admit that, should the doctrine of the Trinity have to be dropped as false, the major part of religious literature could well remain virtually unchanged."[8] In an effort to bring clarity to the use of the traditional trinitarian categories, Rahner asserted what would come to be known as Rahner's Rule: "*The 'economic' Trinity is the 'immanent' Trinity and the 'immanent' Trinity is the 'economic' Trinity.*"[9] Trinitarian theology for the remainder of the twentieth century and into the twenty-first century is an engagement with or qualification of this axiom.

II. Teutonic Terrain

Barth and Rahner set the stage for what is to follow. The most prolific and perhaps best known theologian in the generation after Barth and

Rahner is Wolfhart Pannenberg (1928–). While indebted to Barth's articulation of the necessity of revelation for theology, Pannenberg distinguishes himself from Barth in that he locates revelation in God's acts within history. Thus, for Pannenberg, theology begins from below in the arena of history but can only be apprehended eschatologically from its fulfillment in the reign of the resurrected Jesus. It is from this perspective that Pannenberg develops his doctrine of the Trinity.

Asserting that "one can know the intertrinitarian distinctions and relations, the inner life of God, only through the revelation of the God, not through the different spheres of the operation of the one God in the world," Pannenberg grounds his discussion of the Trinity in Jesus' relationship to the Father and the Spirit.[10] Here Pannenberg recognizes his distance from Barth as he observes that Barth does not develop the doctrine of the Trinity from the data of historical revelation of the three persons but "from the formal concept of revelation as self-revelation."[11] Rather, Pannenberg engages the biblical narrative that testifies to Jesus disclosing his relationship to the Father while also distinguishing himself from the Father. More specifically, the Trinity can be known only through the events of the cross and resurrection. Revealing that a Hegelian imprint remains on his trinitarian doctrine, Pannenberg writes:

> Jesus is the Son of the eternal Father only in total to the will of the Father, a resignation which corresponded to the unconditionality of Jesus' historical sending and which, in view of the earthly wreck of that sending, had to become a complete abandonment of his self to the Father. Jesus' absolute practiced unity of will with the Father, as this was confirmed by God's raising him from the dead, is the medium of his unity of essence with the Father and the basis for all assertions about Jesus' divine sonship.[12]

Pannenberg speaks of the relationships within the Trinity as reciprocity, acknowledging that the traditional dogmatic language of *perichoresis* and circumincession point to this reality but "had only a limited impact because of the one-sided viewing of the intratrinitarian relations as relations of origin."[13] There is, according to Pannenberg, not only a relationship of origin (e.g., the Father begets the Son and sends the Spirit), but there also exists a relationship of giving within the Trinity (e.g., the Son glorifies the Father and is filled with the Spirit). While there is reciprocity between the persons of the Trinity, the relations between the persons are irreversible. The Father in every respect is God of himself.

> This view seems to rule out genuine mutuality in the relations of the trinitarian persons, since it has the order of origin running irreversibly from the Father to the Son and Spirit. Athanasius, however, argued forcibly against the Arians that the Father would not be the Father without the Son. Does that not mean that in some way the deity of the Father has to be dependent on the relation to the Son, although not in the same way as that of the Son is on the relation to the Father? The Father is not begotten of the Son or sent by him. These relations are irreversible. But in another way the relativity of fatherhood that finds expression in the designation 'Father' might well involve a dependence of the Father on the Son and thus be the basis of true reciprocity in the trinitarian relations.[14]

In contrast to theories of abstract transcendence of God or notions of divine unity that leave no space for plurality, Pannenberg asserts: "Christian trinitarian belief is concerned only with the concrete and intrinsically differentiated life of the divine unity. Thus the doctrine of the Trinity is in fact concrete monotheism."[15]

Jürgen Moltmann (1926–), a contemporary of Pannenberg, also had studied at Gottingen under Hans Joachim Iwand, and the two were colleagues for a time (1958–1961 at Wuppertal). Taking up the challenge of Schleiermacher that the doctrine of the Trinity is due for a complete overhaul, Moltmann sets about to achieve just this by finding "the relationship of God to God in the reality of the event of the cross."[16] In this sense, Moltmann and Pannenberg share a similar approach, although Moltmann's conclusions will prove to be far more radical than those of Pannenberg.

The death of Jesus, according to Moltmann, is a "trinitarian event" between God and God.

> In the cross, Father and Son are most deeply separated in forsakenness and at the same time are most inwardly one in their surrender. What

proceeds from this event between Father and Son is the Spirit which justifies the godless, fills the forsaken with love and even brings the dead alive, since even the fact that they are dead cannot exclude them from this event of the cross; the death in God also includes them.[17]

Moltmann admits his indebtedness to Hegel at this point.

For Moltmann, the theology of the cross is the hermeneutical key that provides access to the mystery of the Trinity.

> I myself have tried to think through the theology of the cross in trinitarian terms and to understand the doctrine of the Trinity in light of the theology of the cross. In order to grasp the death of the Son in its significance for God himself, I found myself bound to surrender the traditional distinction between the immanent and the economic Trinity, according to which the cross comes to stand only in the economy of salvation, but not within the immanent Trinity.[18]

According to Moltmann, God relates to the world in such a way as to determine its fate, however history also affects God. In this relationship the three persons of the Trinity relate reciprocally, both to each other and to the world. In the Trinity, "the three Persons are equal; they live and are manifested in one another and through one another."[19] God relates to the world as he acts within history, making his love operative in the suffering of the crucified Christ, an event seen as both temporal and eternal. In the cross, Moltmann argues, God's own being is an open fellowship of love. Thus, the trinitarian communion of the three persons of the Trinity is the source and model for genuine human community characterized by love and freedom, openness and acceptance rather than domination and exclusion.

> The history of salvation is the history of the eternally living, triune God who draws us into and includes us in his eternal triune life with all the fullness of its relationships. It is the love story of the God whose very life is the eternal process of engendering, responding and blissful love. God loves the world with the very same love which he is in himself. If, on the basis of salvation history and the experience of salvation, we have to recognize the unity of the triune God in

the perichoretic at-oneness of the Father, the Son and the Holy Spirit, then this does not correspond to the solitary human subject in his relationship to himself; nor does it correspond, either, to a human subject in his claim to lordship over the world. It only corresponds to a human fellowship of people without privileges and without subordinances. The perichoretic at-oneness of the triune God corresponds to the experience of the community of Christ, the community which the Spirit unites through respect, affection and love. The more open-mindedly people live with one another, for one another and in one another in the fellowship of the Spirit, the more they will become one with the Son and the Father, and one in the Son and the Father.[20]

I Corinthians 15:28 ("that God may be all in all") is a key text in Moltmann's discussion of the eschatology of the Trinity. "The cross does not bring an end to the trinitarian history in God between the Father and the Son in the Spirit as eschatological history, but rather opens it up."[21] Thus, for Moltmann, the triune identity is itself moving toward consummation; it is as becoming rather than a static being.[22] The consummation of the Trinity will be a consummation of love as the Son surrenders the kingdom to his Father, that "love may be all in all."[23] Moltmann's trinitarian eschatology is necessarily universalistic as the Trinity is open and inclusive.

Eberhard Jüngel (1933–) of Tübingen has distinguished himself as a foremost interpreter of Barth by recasting Barth's trinitarian theology in the setting of the hermeneutical approach of Ernst Fuchs (1903–). Like Moltmann, Jüngel sees the doctrine of the Trinity as christologically anchored in the event of the cross. The doctrine of the Trinity is inexplicable apart from the death and resurrection of Jesus. But what is revealed in the cross corresponds to the way God is within himself. There is relationality within God. God's involvement in history *ad extra* corresponds to the divine life *ad intra*.

God's self-relatedness thus springs from the becoming which God's being is. The becoming in which God's being is a becoming out of the word in which God says Yes to himself. But to God's affirmation of himself there corresponds the affirmation of the creature through God. In the affirmation of his creature, as this affirmation becomes event in the incarnation of God, God reiterates his self-relatedness in his relation to the creature, as revealer, as becoming revealed and being revealed. This christological relation to the creature is also a becoming in which God's being is. But in that God in Jesus Christ became man, he is as creature exposed to perishing. Is God's being in becoming, here a being unto death?[24]

Jüngel goes on to answer his own question citing the Easter hymn: "Were he not raised/Then the world would have perished; But since he is raised/Then praise we the Father of Jesus Christ/ Kyrie eleison!"[25] God remains true to himself as triune in the death of Jesus. In this way God's being for us in Christ expresses and is grounded in God's being for himself. This Jüngel sees, echoing Barth, as revelation—God's own interpretation of himself.[26] Thus he affirms the position of Rahner:

> Karl Rahner's thesis should be given unqualified agreement: '*The economic Trinity is the immanent Trinity and the immanent Trinity is the economic Trinity.*' This statement is correct because God himself takes place in Jesus' God-forsakenness and death (Mark 15:34–37). What the passion story narrates is the actual conceptualization of the doctrine of the Trinity.[27]

III. Liberated Trinity: South and North

Leonardo Boff (1938–) and Catherine Mowry LaCugna (1952–1997) stand as examples of contemporary theologians who espouse a social trinitarianism. Leonardo Boff is a Brazilian liberation theologian and author of the 1986 book, *Trinity and Society*. Fueled by Moltmann, Boff attempts to locate in the Trinity the basis for a liberated society. The divine unity that exists between the three persons of the Trinity is reflected in human beings living together in community. As God is a union of three uniques so the human society does not blot out individuality but maintains a unity of egalitarian persons who live in co-relatedness. The communal or social exposition of the Trinity is seen by Boff as a way to move beyond the categories of essence and substance, which he deems to be static. Boff's communal Trinity embraces both masculine and feminine dimensions in Father, Son, and Spirit. Boff anticipates the charge of tritheism and believes that he avoids it by means of his articulation of the perichoresis of the three persons.

The *vestigia trinitatis* so vehemently rejected by Barth comes back in full force in Boff:

> As there are traces of the Trinity in the whole cosmic order, so there are in human lives. Every human being is undoubtedly a mystery, with unfathomable depths not communicated to oneself or to others; this is the presence of the Father as deep, inner mystery in every human person. All men and women possess a dimension of truth, self-knowledge and self-revelation, the light and wisdom of their own mystery; this expresses the presence of the Son (Word and Wisdom) acting in them, developing the communication of their mystery. All human beings feel an urge to commune with others and be united in love; the Holy Spirit is present in this desire and in the joys of its fulfillment in this life. Mystery, truth and communion live together in each individual; they are interwoven realities that together make up the unity of life. They provide a reflection of trinitarian communion and are the ultimate foundation for humanity being the image and likeness of the Trinity.[28]

As Moltmann sought to bring history into the Trinity, so Boff seeks to bring creation into the life of the Trinity.

> [Creation] prolongs and reflects the outpouring of life and love that eternally constitute the being Father, Son, and Holy Spirit. To use anthropomorphic language: the Trinity does not wish to live alone in its splendid trinitarian communion; the three divine Persons do not love just one another, but seek companions in communion and love. Creation arose from this wish of the three divine Persons to meet others (created by them) so as to include them in their eternal communion. Creation is external to the Trinity only so as to be brought within it.[29]

Finally, Boff retreats to the language of mystery.

> What is manifested in our history is indeed God as God is, trinitarian. But the Trinity as absolute and sacramental mystery is much more than what is manifested. What the Trinity is in itself is beyond our reach, hidden in unfathomable mystery, mystery that will be partially revealed to us in the bliss of eternal life, but will always escape

us in full, since the Trinity is a mystery in itself and not only for human beings. So we have to say: the economic Trinity is the immanent Trinity, but not the whole immanent Trinity.[30]

A second exponent of social trinitarianism is Catherine LaCugna, who was teaching at Notre Dame at the time of her death from cancer in 1997. She is the author of *God For Us: The Trinity and the Christian Life* published in 1991. In this book, LaCugna seeks to show the practicality of the doctrine of the Trinity with its consequences for the Christian life. Like Boff, but with greater precision and more engagement of both classical and contemporary sources, LaCugna sees the Trinity in communal or relational categories. "Trinitarian theology could be described as par excellence a theology of relationship, which explores the mysteries of love, relationship, personhood and community within the framework of God's self-revelation in the person of Christ and the activity of the Spirit."[31]

The central thesis of LaCugna's book is that "soteriology and theology belong together because there is an essential unity between *oikonomia* and *theologia*."[32] Reviewing the history of the trinitarian doctrine, LaCugna concludes that, from the late fourth century on, theologians in both the East and West deviated from the earlier pattern of approaching the Godhead through the economy and instead explored questions of intratriniarian life such as the equality of the persons. This, she argues, led to "the defeat of the doctrine of the Trinity."[33] Thus she confirms Rahner's conviction that most Christians are, in practice, mere monotheists. LaCugna maintains further that insofar as contemporary theologians continue to focus on the immanent Trinity they reinforce the impression that the doctrine of the Trinity has limited soteriological significance as it is limited to God's internal life and has no connection with the Christian life in the world.

LaCugna devotes the remainder of her book developing the claim that, "The doctrine of the Trinity is not ultimately a teaching about 'God' but a teaching about *God's life with us and our life with each other*. It is the life of communion and indwelling, God in us, we in God, all of us in each other. This is the '*perichoresis*,' the mutual interdependence that Jesus speaks of in the Gospel of John."[34]

Drawing on the work of John Zizioulas, a contemporary Eastern Orthodox theologian, LaCugna seeks to develop a definition of person as relation in keeping with the Cappadocian pattern of speaking of the "unique hypostatic identity and distinction 'within' God without postulating a difference in substance between the divine persons."[35] Being constitutes personhood. "Being, existence, is thus the event of persons in communion."[36] LaCugna then goes on to describe *perichoresis* as a "divine dance."[37]

Ultimately the questions of trinitarian theology are not, for LaCugna, speculative but practical. Trinitarian salvation is *theosis* according to LaCugna. Thus the basic, practical question of trinitarian theology is: "How are we to live and relate to others so as to be most Godlike?"[38]

LaCugna holds that relational trinitarianism has great promise for feminist theology because it lifts up mutuality rather than patriarchy. "As a revised doctrine of the Trinity makes plain, subordinationism is not natural but decidedly unnatural because it violates *both* the nature of God and the nature of persons created in the image of God."[39] LaCugna argues that authentic trinitarian existence will always be liberationist in character as the economy of Jesus Christ has established a new household unbounded by patriarchal distinctions. She admits that the church lost this vision quite early as the household codes of the post-Pauline and pastoral letters of the New Testament represent an accommodation to non-trinitarian patterns.[40]

IV. Blazing New Trails: East and West

There are certainly others who ought to be mentioned to round out any survey of contemporary theologians who have engaged the doctrine of the Trinity. We have already noted the significance of John Zizioulas (1931–) in the work of Catherine LaCugna. Although suspect in some Orthodox circles, his work, *Being As Communion: Studies in Personhood and the Church*, probes the connection between ontology and the communion that transpires between the persons of the Trinity.[41] In conversation with the Cappadocian discourse on the Trinity, Zizioulas maintains that, "Being is simultaneously relational and hypostatic."[42] His work has also been a source of influence for Miroslav Volf (1956–), a student of Moltmann, especially in his efforts to develop a trinitarian ecclesiology in *After Our Likeness: The Church as the Image of the Trinity*.[43] The legacy of Karl Barth continues to find a lively voice in the work of Thomas Torrance (1913–).[44] Robert Jenson has emerged as perhaps the leading North American representative of contemporary trinitarian theology with his provocative assertion that the triune God is "one event with three identities" as an attempt to free the doctrine from a Hellenized abstraction.[45] In the tradition of George Lindbeck, Bruce Marshall (1955–) examines epistemic dimensions of the doctrine of the Trinity in *Trinity and Truth* published in 2000.[46] Colin Gunton (1941–2003) has produced several impressive contributions including *The Promise of Trinitarian Theology* (1991) and *The Triune Creator: A Historical and Systematic Study* (1998).[47] Shortly before his untimely death last year, his final work, *Act and Being: Towards a Theology of the Divine Attributes* was published.[48] In this book, Gunton engages in a critique of the separation of God's being from his actions in theologies that approach the attributes of God apart from his trinitarian being. Two recent books approach the doctrine of the Trinity through the practices of the church. Reinhard Hütter's *Suffering Divine Things: Theology as Church Practice* sees the work of the Trinity in the core practices or marks of the church, making the case that there can be no division between trinitarian dogma and the concrete practices that define and order the identity and character of the church.[49] Hütter, along with several other theologians, make this case explicit in a collection of essays edited by James Buckley and David Yeago entitled, *Knowing the Triune God: The Work of the Spirit in the Practices of the Church*.[50] Using Luther's hymn, "Dear Christians, One and All Rejoice," Oswald Bayer (1939–) teases out what he describes as a "poetological" doctrine of the Trinity asserting that this doctrine "considers nothing other than the *gospel*."[51]

V. Where Is This Highway Going?

It is difficult to summarize the vast and varied work in contemporary trinitarian theology. It would be even more difficult to attempt a meaningful assessment that avoids generalizations. Nevertheless, I will single out a few themes that deserve some reflection and critique.

Mark Twain once remarked that in the beginning God created man in his own image and ever since man has returned the compliment. It seems that this is what we see in the social trinitarians—Moltmann, Boff, and LaCugna. Moltmann's early work, *The Theology of Hope*, was his own attempt to provide a theological parallel to the Jewish Marxist Ernst Bloch's *Principle of Hope*, and Moltmann continues to work out the eschatological implications of this theme in his later works on the Trinity. Boff sees the Trinity as a model of liberation for the poor and the oppressed. LaCugna finds in social trinitarianism a resource for an egalitarian, non-patriarchal God and church. The Trinity is abstracted from creation and history, which is ironically the very error Moltmann claims to avoid.

Here we might inquire as to what this means for ethics. Paul Jersild, a recently retired professor from the Lutheran Theological Southern Seminary in Columbia, South Carolina, published a book in 2000 entitled *Spirit Ethics: Scripture and the Moral Life*. In this volume, Jerslid seeks to ground Christian ethics in the work of the Holy Spirit. While he does not cite Moltmann or LaCugna, his argument runs parallel to theirs in significant ways.

After a critique of the presumed authoritarianism of antiquated notions of reading the Scriptures, Jersild opts for a view of biblical authority that is open-ended. Thus a Spirit ethic, while recognizing the inspiration of the Scriptures, will nevertheless be an ethic of openness to the future. A broadened concept of inspiration will enable the church to engage the Bible in a meaningful conversation. This dialogical method of listening to Scripture encourages the "fruitful engagement of moral imagination" in an impossible way seeing Scripture as a source of moral absolutes.[52] "The notion of a deposit of eternal truths 'once for all delivered to the saints' is entirely inappropriate in regard to our moral tradition, for in this realm we are dealing with our response to the Gospel, not the Gospel itself."[53]

Rather than attempting to extract specific and concrete moral teachings from the New Testament, the church, Jersild opines, ought to concentrate on a cluster of images—love, freedom, and responsibility—that are at the heart of the New Testament's ethical vision. According to Jersild, a Spirit ethic will bear the marks of God's presence and display his empowering love. A Spirit ethic will listen to the Scriptures and "the contemporary experience of the church as it grapples with difficult moral issues."[54]

Having established the basis for his ethics, Jersild then turns to the current debate surrounding homosexuality. Worried that many Christians, under the influence of natural law thinking have adopted an "excessively physicalist approach to homosexuality," Jersild instead urges the church to revise its traditional stance on homosexuality in a way that exhibits acceptance and responsible freedom.[55]

Jersild has effectively collapsed the Trinity into the Spirit. His concern over an "excessively physicalist approach to homosexuality" evidences his lack of a trinitarian doctrine of creation. Christoph Schwöbel observed: "The search for relevance, so it appears, comes into conflict with fundamental dogmatic tenets of a Christian theology of creation. What seems to be needed is not an ethics of creation, but an *ethic of createdness* which is informed by *a theology of creation*."[56]

The ethic that Schwöbel calls for cannot be sustained by the trinitarian theology of LaCugna. LaCugna pits personhood against nature in such a way as to dismiss the significance of the createdness of male and female. She endorses the conclusion of Margaret Farley:

> If the ultimate normative model for relationship between persons is the very life of the Trinitarian God, then a strong eschatological ethic suggests itself as a context for Christian justice. That is to say, interpersonal communion characterized by equality, mutuality, and reciprocity may serve not only as a norm against which every pattern of relationship may be measured but as a goal to which every pattern of relationship is ordered.[57]

Here we must ask if equality, mutuality, and reciprocity are derived from the biblical doctrine of the Trinity or from our postmodern culture that is characterized by its drive toward autonomy. Creational distinctions are lost as the self-differentiation within the Trinity, which is exchanged for a communal theology that is but a murky reflection of our culture's gnostic spirituality. Any sexual activity that reflects equality, mutuality, and reciprocity is deemed to be iconic of the Creator.

> Sexuality can be a sacred means of becoming divinized by the Spirit of God instead of a tool to exercise control over others, or an aspect

of ourselves that is to be feared and avoided. Alienated or alienating expressions of sexuality, practices that are truly 'unnatural' in the sense of being contrary to personhood, contravene the very life of God. In contrast, fruitful, healthy, creative, integrated sexuality enables persons to live from and for others. Sexual practices and customs can be iconic of divine life, true images of the very nature of the triune God.[58]

What is unnatural in LaCugna's estimation is not that which is contrary to our being creatures of the triune God but rather contrary to our personhood. As defined by the categories of autonomy and capacity, personhood becomes ambiguous as we witness in Justice Harry Blackmun's declaration that "the word person as used in the 14th Amendment does not include the unborn."[59] The initial promise of LaCugna's book to offer a soteriological theology of the Trinity that has as its corollary in the life of the Christian in and with God is lost.

VI. Conclusion

There are many issues that this brief overview of contemporary trinitarian theology has addressed only minimally or not at all. The debate over the *filioque* will continue. The avoidance or the complete exclusion of the name of the Trinity in liturgical forms and hymns will be a most obvious feature distinguishing orthodoxy from the new unitarianism already evident in the mainline churches. On both scholarly and popular fronts, the likes of Marcus Borg offer up another Christ *sans* Trinity who is confessed not as the only-begotten Son of the Father but as a mistaken mystic.[60] In today's world, we are confronted anew with questions relative to the triune God versus the gods of the nations. The significance of these topics cannot be fully apprehended apart from a critical engagement of the theologians we have examined. This survey has attempted to identify some of the leading players in contemporary theological discussion of the Trinity and map out at least a few key features of their thinking. We have noted the twists and the turns, both the rediscovery of the church's confession of the triune God and not a few detours from the path of biblical orthodoxy. Thus, Uwe Siemon-Netto, a Lutheran lay theologian, offers this timely challenge:

. . . postmodernity's profusion of bogus and ever-changing 'truths' and 'values' can only be overcome by a renewal of trinitarian theology—not in the watered-down version of liberal theology: No cheap anthropocentric metaphors are in order here. Rather theologians must learn to speak about the triune God in a new language that resonates with the post-post-modern people who are attempting to come out of the spiritual bankruptcy into which the quest for autonomy has led them. This may well be one of the most important tasks for theologians in the almost 2000 years of church history. It is an urgent task. There is no time to lose.[61]

Notes

1 Gerhard Sauter, *Gateways to Dogmatics: Reasoning Theologically for the Life of the Church* (Grand Rapids: William B. Eerdmans Publishing Company, 2003), 39. Two significant books appeared after this paper was completed that should be noted. First, there is Stanley Grenz, *Rediscovering the Triune God: The Trinity in Contemporary Theology* (Minneapolis: Fortress Press, 2004). Grenz does an admirable job of surveying twentieth-century theologians who have worked on the doctrine of the Trinity. Also worthy of note are several essays (especially those by Jenson, Schwobel, Gregersen, and Saarinen) in *The Gift of Grace: The Future of Lutheran Theology*, ed. Niels Henrick Gregersen, et al. (Minneapolis: Fortress Press, 2005).

2 Overviews of the place of the doctrine of the Trinity in nineteenth-century theology can be found in E.J. Fortman, *The Triune God: A Historical Study of the Doctrine of the Trinity* (Grand Rapids: Baker Book House, 1982), 250–259; S.M. Powell, *The Trinity in German Thought* (Cambridge: Cambridge University Press, 2001), 104–141; and Claude Welch, *In This Name: The Doctrine of the Trinity in Contemporary Theology* (New York: Charles Scribner's Sons, 1952), 3–41.

3 Friederich Schleiermacher, *The Christian Faith*, tr. D.M. Baillie et al. (Edinburgh: T & T Clark, 1928), 748.

4 Karl Barth, *Church Dogmatics* I:I, tr. G.W. Bromiley (Edinburgh: T & T Clark, 1975), 295.

5 Welch, *In This Name*, 187.

6 Eberhard Jüngel, *The Doctrine of the Trinity: God's Being is in Becoming* (Grand Rapids: William B. Eerdmans Publishing Co., 1976), 24.

7 Wilhelm Pauck, *Karl Barth* (New York: Harper and Row, 1931), 189–190.

8 Karl Rahner, "The Trinity," in *A Map of Twentieth-Century Theology: Readings from Karl Barth to Radical Pluralism*, ed. Carl Braaten and Robert Jenson (Minneapolis: Fortress Press, 1995), 190.

9 Rahner, "The Trinity," 195; emphasis original. On the distinction between the economic and immanent Trinity in contemporary theology, see Fred Sanders, "Entangled in the Trinity: Economic and Immanent Trinity in Recent Theology" *Dialog* (Fall 2001): 175–182; Ted Peters, *God as Trinity* (Louisville: Westminster/John Knox Press, 1993), 20–24; and David Coffey, *Deus Trinitas: The Doctrine of the Triune God* (Oxford: Oxford University Press, 1999), 33–65.

10 Wolfhart Pannenberg, *Systematic Theology–Volume I*, tr. G.W. Bromiley (Grand Rapids: William B. Eerdmans Publishing Co., 1991), 273.

11 Pannenberg, *Systematic Theology–Volume I*, 296.

12 Quoted in Robert Jenson, "Jesus in the Trinity: Wolfhart Pannenberg's Christology and the Doctrine of the Trinity," in *The Theology of Wolfhart Pannenberg*, ed. Carl Braaten and Philip Clayton (Minneapolis: Augsburg Publishing House, 1988). Also see Panneberg, *Systematic Theology–Volume I*, 308–319 and "Problems of a Trinitarian Doctrine of God," *Dialog* 26 (Fall 1987): 250–257.

13 Pannenberg, *Systematic Theology–Volume I*, 319.

14 Pannenberg, *Systematic Theology–Volume I*, 311–312.

15 Pannenberg, *Systematic Theology–Volume I*, 335.

16 Jürgen Moltmann, *The Crucified God*, tr. R.A. Wilson and John Bowden (New York: Harper and Row, 1974), 239.

17 Moltman, *The Crucified God*, 244.

18 Jürgen Moltmann, *The Trinity and the Kingdom*, tr. Margaret Kohl (New York: Harper and Row, 1981), 160. Cf. John Thompson, *Modern Trinitarian Perspectives* (Oxford: Oxford University Press, 1994), 33–34.

19 Moltmann, *The Trinity and the Kingdom*, 176.

20 Moltmann, *The Trinity and the Kingdom*, 157–158. This point is further developed in Moltmann's *The Spirit of Life*, tr. Margaret Kohl (Minneapolis: Augsburg Fortress, 1992).

21 Moltmann, *The Crucified God*, 265. Moltmann finally abandons the "conceptual framework" of the immanent and economic Trinity and instead describes the Trinity according to four patterns: monarchical Trinity, historical Trinity, eucharistic Trinity, and the doxological Trinity. See *The Spirit of Life*, 290–306.

22 John Thompson writes that, in Moltmann's view, the Trinity "is an evolving event between three divine subjects and the world and that the triune God is not complete until the end. Therefore, he can speak of a trinitarian history of God. The difficulty with this view is that it ties God to his relationship to the world and makes the world a contributory factor to the ultimate nature of God. God is therefore not Father, Son, and Holy Spirit without this relationship and reciprocity between himself and the world;" Modern Trinitarian Perspectives, 51.

23 Moltmann, *The Crucified God*, 255.

24 Jüngel, *The Doctrine of the Trinity: God's Being is in Becoming*, 107; emphasis original.

25 Jüngel, *The Doctrine of the Trinity: God's Being is in Becoming*, 108.

26 Jüngel, *The Doctrine of the Trinity: God's Being is in Becoming*, 15–25; and *God as the Mystery of the World*, tr. Darrel Guder (Edinburgh: T & T Clark, 1983), 184–225.

27 Jüngel, *God as the Mystery of the World*, 369–370; emphasis original. Also see Jüngel's discussion of justification by faith as an "event in the being of the triune God" in *Justification: The Heart of the Christian Faith*, tr. Jefferey F. Cayzer (Edinburgh: T & T Clark, 2001), 82–85.

28 Leonardo Boff, *Trinity and Society*, tr. Paul Burns (Maryknoll, NY: Orbis Books, 1988), 223–224.

29 Boff, *Trinity and Society*, 221–222.

30 Boff, *Trinity and Society*, 215.

31 Catherine Mowry LaCugna, *God For Us: The Trinity and the Christian Life* (San Francisco: HarperCollins Publishers, 1991), 1; emphasis original. Also see Catherine Mowry LaCugna and Kilian McDonnell, "Returning from the Far Country: Theses for a Contemporary Trinitarian Theology," *Scottish Journal of Theology* 41 (1988): 191–215. For a positive assessment of LaCugna's work by a feminist theologian, see Mary Catherine Hilkert, "The Mystery of Persons in Communion: The Trinitarian Theology of Catherine Mowry LaCugna," *Word & World* (Summer 1998): 237–243.

32 LaCugna, *God For Us*, 13.

33 LaCugna, *God For Us*, 210.

34 LaCugna, *God For Us*, 228.

35 LaCugna, *God For Us*, 243.

36 LaCugna, *God For Us*, 249.

37 LaCugna, *God For Us*, 271. Here LaCugna draws on the work of Patricia Wilson-Kastner who argues that perichoresis is the glue that holds the three persons of the Trinity together in such a way as to establish an ethic that upholds three central values: inclusiveness, community, and freedom; see *Faith, Feminism, and the Christ* (Philadelphia: Fortress Press, 1983), 131–133. For further research, also see David S. Cunningham, *These Three Are One: The Practice of Trinitarian Theology* (Cambridge: Cambridge University Press, 1998). Cunningham proposes that the titles Source, Wellspring, and Living Water be substituted for the traditional Father, Son, and Holy Spirit. For a critique of feminist interpretations of the Trinity see Donald Bloesch, *The Battle for the Trinity: The Debate Over Inclusive God-Language* (Ann Arbor, MI: Servant Publications, 1985) and especially Alvin F. Kimel Jr., ed., *Speaking the Christian God: The Holy Trinity and the Challenge of Feminism* (Grand Rapids: William B. Eerdmans Publishing Co., 1992). This volume contains essays by Colin Gunton, Robert Jenson, Gerhard Forde, Thomas Torrance, Thomas

Hopko and others who make an incisive critique of feminist proposals on the basis of orthodox trinitarian theology.

38   LaCugna, *God For Us*, 249.

39   LaCugna, *God For Us*, 398, emphasis original.

40   LaCugna, *God For Us*, 392. LaCugna's argument that the household code in Ephesians represents a loss of trinitarian vision is curious in light of the fact that she begins her book by citing Ephesians 1:3–14 as testimony to the trinitarian shape of salvation history.

41   John D. Zizioulas, *Being as Communion: Studies in Personhood and the Church* (Crestwood, NY: St. Vladimir's Seminary Press, 1985).

42   John D. Zizioulas, "The Doctrine of the Holy Trinity: The Significance of the Cappadocian Contribution," in *Trinitarian Theology Today: Essays on Divine Being and Act*, ed. Christoph Schwöbel (Edinburgh: T & T Clark, 1995), 50.

43   Miroslav Volf, *After Our Likeness: The Church as the Image of the Trinity* (Grand Rapids: William B. Eerdmans Publishing Co., 1998).

44   See especially Thomas Torrance, *The Trinitarian Faith: The Evangelical Theology of the Ancient Catholic Church* (Edinburgh: T & T Clark, 1988).

45   Like Pannenberg, Jenson studied with the liturgical scholar Peter Brunner and the Lutheran Barthian, Edmund Schlink, at Heidelberg. Jenson's major works on trinitarian theology include *Triune Identity: God According to the Gospel* (Philadelphia: Fortress Press, 1982); *Systematic Theology–Volume I: The Triune God* (New York: Oxford University Press, 1999); and "Locus II: The Triune God" in *Christian Dogmatics–Volume I*, eds. Carl Braaten and Robert Jenson (Philadelphia: Fortress Press, 1984), 79–191. For a variety of engagements with Jenson's contributions, see *Trinity, Time, and the Church: A Response to the Theology of Robert Jenson*, ed. Colin Gunton (Grand Rapids: William B. Eerdmans Publishing Co., 2000).

46   Bruce Marshall, *Trinity and Truth* (Cambridge: Cambridge University Press, 2000).

47   Colin Gunton, *The Promise of Trinitarian Theology* (Edinburgh: T & T Clark, 1990); and *The Triune Creator: A Historical and Systematic Study* (Edinburgh: T & T Clark, 1998).

48   Colin Gunton, *Act and Being: Towards a Theology of Divine Attributes* (Grand Rapids: William B. Eerdmans Publishing Co., 2003).

49   Reinhard Hütter, *Suffering Divine Things: Theology as Church Practice* (Grand Rapids: William B. Eerdmans Publishing Co., 2000).

50   James Buckley and David Yeago eds., *Knowing the Triune God: The Work of the Spirit in the Practices of the Church* (Grand Rapids: William B. Eerdmans Publishing Co., 2001).

51   Oswald Bayer, "Poetological Doctrine of the Trinity" *Lutheran Quarterly* 15 (Spring 2001): 43–58; emphasis original. For further discussion, see also

"The Triune God" in *Living By Faith: Justification and Sanctification* (Grand Rapids: William B. Eerdmans Publishing Co., 2003), 52–57.

52 Paul Jersild, *Spirit Ethics: Scripture and the Moral Life* (Minneapolis: Fortress Press, 2000), 21.

53 Jersild, *Spirit Ethics*, 134.

54 Jersild, *Spirit Ethics*, 135.

55 Jersild, *Spirit Ethics*, 139.

56 Christoph Schwöbel, "God, Creation and the Christian Community: The Dogmatic Basis of a Christian Ethic of Createdness" in *The Doctrine of Creation: Essays in Dogmatics, History and Philosophy*, ed. Colin Gunton (Edinburgh: T & T Clark, 1997), 150; emphasis original. Also see Oswald Bayer, "Nature and Institution: Luther's Doctrine of the Three Orders," *Lutheran Quarterly* 12 (Summer 1998): 125–160.

57 LaCugna, *God For Us*, 282.

58 LaCugna, *God For Us*, 407. David Cunningham follows LaCugna in drawing out the implications for the acceptance of homosexual unions: "I have already suggested that the doctrine of the Trinity can help us to understand and evaluate the nature of the relationships among bodies, including relationships that involve sexual desire. The question which remains, is whether it necessarily limits those forms to opposite-sex relationships. And as far as I can see, there is nothing in trinitarian doctrine that has a word to say, in any *prima facie* sense, against monogamous gay or lesbian relationships. In such relationships, mutual participation is clearly possible, just as in opposite-sex relationships. The same-sex partner is still an 'other,' and fully capable of embodying the trinitarian view of particularity. The doctrine of the Trinity does not seem to address anatomical features of the desired body; God manifests yearning, desire, and love for the otherness of the other, but this otherness is not limited to-nor does it necessarily even involve-questions of sexual differentiation." *These Three Are One: The Practice of Trinitarian Theology* (Oxford: Blackwell Publishers, 1998), 300. Only a hermeneutic completely detached from the trinitarian narrative of the Scriptures could arrive at such a conclusion. Barth rightly points to the "structural differentiation" of man's duality as male and female; see *Church Dogmatics III:II*, 286.

59 John Breck, *The Sacred Gift of Life: Orthodox Christianity and Bioethics* (Crestwood, NY: St. Vladimir's Seminary Press, 1998), 146–147.

60 Marcus J. Borg, *Jesus: Uncovering the Life, Teachings, and Relevance of a Religious Revolutionary* (San Francisco: Harper San Francisco, 2006).

61 Uwe Siemon-Netto, *One Incarnate Truth: Christianity's Answer to Spiritual Chaos* (St. Louis: Concordia Publishing House, 2002), 157.

61

Hell

The Consummation of the Law

PREVIOUSLY PUBLISHED IN THE MAY/JUNE 2002 ISSUE
OF MODERN REFORMATION, PP. 36–37

Hell was a prominent theme in Jesus' preaching, but the same is not true in contemporary Christianity. The Revised Common Lectionary, used in many mainline churches has trimmed articles dealing with hell, condemnation, and wrath from its cycle of readings. The universalism that has come to characterize the popular piety of our nation was implicitly assumed in the "Prayer for America" interfaith service presided over by Oprah Winfrey in Yankee Stadium shortly after the tragedy of September 11. Incredibly, a district president from the conservative Lutheran Church-Missouri Synod took his place along-side religionists who deny Christ and who boldly proclaim that there is strength in such a union, as though the power of human love could remedy sin and death. Any mention of hell, beyond a purely met-aphorical reference to the September 11 tragedy, would have been seen as a breach of ecumenical sensitivity. So Christian clergy, by their participation and their silence, assented to the universalism of civil religion there presented.

Commenting on the theology reflected by the Second Vatican Council, Lutheran theologian Hermann Sasse once quipped that in post-Vatican II Rome, it is hard for even a self-respecting pagan to go to hell. Hell is not a popular topic in contemporary theological discourse.

German Lutheran systematician Gerhard Sauter's recent book, *What Dare We Hope?*, does not even include an entry for "hell" in its index. Among many it is believed that Christianity must be understood as inclusive; inclusive even of "anonymous Christians"—of those who are Christians even though they do not yet know it. And, some argue, the scope of God's mercy is so wide that the thought of hell must be dismissed altogether, replaced by universalism or reduced to a merciful annihilation of obdurate unbelievers.

Discomfort with notions of unquenchable fire and the undying worm are not confined to modern theology. The early Church father Origen's speculation of an *apokatastasis*—a divine restoration of all things that finally brings even the demons into the realm of God's kingdom—has in various ways plagued the Church throughout the ages. This fanciful eschatology was also asserted in Anabaptist theology in the sixteenth century. Against this biblically unwarranted hope, Article 17 of the Lutheran Augsburg Confession speaks:

> It is also taught that our Lord Jesus Christ will return on the Last Day to judge, to raise all the dead, to give eternal life and eternal joy to those who believe and are elect, but to condemn the ungodly and the devils to hell and eternal punishment. Rejected, therefore, are the Anabaptists who teach that the devils and condemned human beings will not suffer eternal torture and torment. Likewise rejected are some Jewish teachings, which have also appeared in the present, that before the resurrection of the dead saints and righteous people alone will possess a secular kingdom and will annihilate the ungodly.

At that time, Rome voiced no opposition to this article, as the Lutheran Book of *Concord's Apology* notes: "The opponents accept this article without qualification. In it we confess that Christ will appear at the consummation of the world and will raise up all the dead, giving eternal life and eternal joys to the godly but condemning the ungodly to endless torment with the dead." But five centuries after Augsburg there is no such unanimity among Lutherans or Roman Catholics; and there is a resurgence among some evangelicals of the belief that unbelievers will not suffer hell.

The challenges raised by those who either espouse universalism or advocate a doctrine of annihilation have been addressed by

Lutherans since the Reformation. Early in the twentieth century, the Lutheran dogmatician Franz Pieper summarized the position of Lutheran orthodoxy: "The claim that the punishments of hell are intended to be remedial or restorative is just as unscriptural as the claim that these punishments are a means of annihilation." Centuries before, Johann Quenstedt railed against the so-called "mercy theologians" (*misericordes theologi*) who denied Scripture's clear teaching by arguing that the doctrine of hell is unworthy of God. And while opinions have varied regarding the nature of hell—is the fire physical or hyper-physical?—Lutheranism's classical theologians agree that hell is both real and unending. As Pieper quotes Johann Gerhard, "It is wiser to be concerned about escaping this eternal fire by true repentance than to engage in unprofitable arguments as to the nature of the fire."

Lutheran theology understands hell as "the consummation of the law" in those who are finally impenitent, according to John Stephensen in *Confessional Lutheran Dogmatics: Escatology*.

Rejecting the doctrine of eternal damnation diminishes Christ's work. Unlike Reformed theology, Lutheran theology teaches universal atonement: Christ Jesus suffered and died for the sins of the whole world (Matt. 20:28; I Tim 2:6; I John 2:2). By the atoning death of his Son, God reconciled the world unto himself (II Cor. 5:18–21). To refuse the gift of the gospel of reconciliation is to be left only with the Law that accuses and finds its final consummation in a hell prepared for the devil and his angels (see Matt. 25:41). Indeed, hell is utterly inhuman. The finality of this banishment is aptly expressed by Werner Elert in *Last Things*, "But in the last Judgment even the most obstinate ear will be opened, not to give man a chance to reconsider his decision but to shut the door to that possibility forever."

Lutheran theology takes hell with utmost seriousness because it takes Christ's work utterly seriously. The Son of God came in the flesh as the friend of sinners, to seek and to save the lost. He did not come to boost self-esteem, to provide psychological wholeness, or to establish a new social order. He came to redeem sinners from God's wrath by his blood. This is confessed in the Explanation to the Second Article of the Apostles' Creed in Luther's *Small Catechism*: "He has redeemed me, a lost and condemned human being. He has purchased and won me from all sins, from death, and from the power of the devil, not with gold or silver but with his holy, precious blood and with his innocent suffering and death. He has done all this in order that I may belong to him, live under him in his kingdom, and serve him in eternal righteousness, innocence, and blessedness, just as he is risen from the dead and lives and rules eternally."

With this same confidence, the writers of the *Formula of Concord* found profound comfort in Christ's descent into hell, confessing that "we believe simply that the entire person, God and human being, descended to hell after his burial, conquered the devil, destroyed the power of hell, and took from the devil all his power . . . Thus, we retain the heart of this article and derive comfort from it, so that 'neither hell nor the devil can capture or harm us' and all who believe in Christ."

In this article, John T. Pless has cited Lutheran doctrinal standards which can be found in the *Lutheran Book of Concord*, translated by Robert Kolb and Timothy Wengert. His quotations of Pieper, Quenstedt, and Gerhard are all found in Pieper's *Christian Dogmatics* (St. Louis: Concordia Publishing House, 1950–1957).

62

The Use and Misuse of Luther in Contemporary Debates on Homosexuality

A Look at Two Theologians

PREVIOUSLY PUBLISHED IN THE PENTECOST 2005 ISSUE OF THE LUTHERAN FORUM, 50–57, THIS PAPER WAS ORIGINALLY PRESENTED AT THE AQUINAS-LUTHER CONFERENCE AT LENOIR RHYNE UNIVERSITY IN HICKORY, NC ON OCTOBER, 2004

Writing over forty years ago, the Lutheran systematician and ethicist Helmut Thielicke observed, "One cannot expect to find in the theological ethics of German-speaking Protestantism a clear, consistent attitude toward homosexuality simply because hitherto the writers on ethics have taken little or no notice of the mere fact itself and therefore a body of opinion—to say nothing of a unanimity of judgment—is almost nonexistent. The indexes of many well-known works on ethics do not contain the word at all" (p. 269). A survey of contemporary texts in ethics reveals that homosexuality has moved front and center even as a clear, consistent attitude toward homosexuality remains elusive.

How elusive this issue has been may be seen by contrasting the approaches of two living Lutheran theologians, Edward Schroeder and Gerhard Forde. I have chosen to examine the work of these two theologians as both appeal to a classical distinction in Lutheran theology, the distinction of the Law from the Gospel, yet come to radically different conclusions. Some have argued that it is this very distinction that has landed present-day Lutherans in a state of moral disarray.[1] I will suggest that it is not the Law/Gospel distinction that is at issue but a particular misuse of this dialectic. Through these two theologians, I will also assess how Luther is used and misused in the present debate.

Schroeder's Law/Promise Hermeneutic

Edward Schroeder was part of the post-World War II generation of theologians in the Lutheran Church-Missouri Synod who were influenced and formed by the theology emanating from Erlangen, especially that of Werner Elert and to a lesser degree Paul Althaus. Elert seemed especially attractive to many young Missourians of this period because his emphasis on law and Gospel resonated with that of the Missouri Synod's patriarch, C.F.W. Walther. Schroeder himself completed his doctorate, not with Elert who died in November of 1954, but with Helmut Thielicke at Hamburg. Returning to the United States, Schroeder took a position on the theology faculty at Valparaiso University and from there moved to Concordia Seminary in Saint Louis. In 1974 Schroeder was part of the faculty majority that left Concordia to form Concordia Seminary in Exile or Seminex, later called Christ Seminary. Writing from his home in Saint Louis, Schroeder publishes his Thursday Theology by e-mail each week. It is through this medium that Schroeder has set forth his approach to homosexuality.

For Schroeder, the questions of blessing same-sex unions and the ordination of homosexuals are answered in the affirmative on the basis of his application of a law/promise hermeneutic that he claims is derived from Luther. According to Schroeder's construal of this hermeneutic, Luther's approach to the Scripture is to see Christ at the heart and center of the Bible. The Scripture itself consists of two words from God, a word of law and a word of promise. Schroeder puts it like this: "Scripture's law serves as God's diagnostic agent-diagnosis of our malady, not prescription for our healing. God's Law is X-ray, not ethics. The healing for patients diagnosed by the Law is God's promise, the Christ-quotient of both OT and NT. The law's purpose

(Paul said it first—after he received his 'new' hermeneutics beginning at Damascus) is to 'push sinners to Christ'" (TT 159 [Jan. 28, 2001] 4). Once sinners are in Christ, they are no longer under the law but under grace. Thus Schroeder continues:

> Once Christ-connected they come into the force-field of his "new commandment," and it really is new, not refurbished "old" commandment, not "Moses rehabilitated." Christ supersedes Moses— not only for salvation, but also for ethics. In Paul's language the touchstone for this new commandment is the "mind of Christ" and being led by, walking by, his Holy Spirit. More than once Paul makes it "perfectly clear" that this is a new "law-free" way of life.

Schroeder then goes on to ask and answer the question of what we are to do with all the commands and imperatives in the Bible in light of this new way of life, free of the law. He concludes, "First of all, this new hermeneutic relativizes them."

Here Schroeder sees himself in company with Luther, especially Luther's treatise of 1525, *How Christians Should Regard Moses* (AE 35: 155–174), to which we shall return a bit later. Arguing that the Law applies only to the old creation while the promise constitutes life in the new creation, Schroeder asserts that human sexuality is clearly a component of the old creation, and hence is under the governance of the Law.

Surely there is much in Luther and the Lutheran confessional writings that seems to give credence to Schroeder's argument. In 1522, Luther wrote in his treatise *The Estate of Marriage* that marriage was a bodily and outward thing: "Know therefore that marriage is an outward, bodily thing, like any other worldly undertaking" (AE 45: 25). Thus Luther recognizes the place of civil authority in regulating matters of sexuality and marriage.[2]

Does Luther's assessment of marriage as an outward thing, an artifact of the old creation, make questions of sexual ethics a matter of relativity as Schroeder contends and therefore lead to a definition of marriage elastic enough to include same-sex unions? I think not. There are several difficulties with Schroeder's approach. The first has to do with his understanding of the place of creation in Luther's thinking.

In contrasting old creation with new creation, Schroeder is concerned to show that the law is operative in creation both to deliver
justice (recompense, as he puts it) and to preserve the fallen world
from plunging into total chaos. Of course, these are themes that are
readily found in Luther. But then Schroeder makes an interpretative
move that Luther does not make. While Luther surely sees that neither the laws of Moses nor civil laws that indeed vary from place to
place and one historical epoch to another work salvifically, he does
not view the law as being merely set aside by the Gospel. To use
the language of the Formula of Concord, "the distinction between
law and gospel is a particularly glorious light" (SD V.1), but it is not
a light that blinds us to the normative character of Holy Scripture.
To reduce the distinction to an ideology abstracted from the actual
content of the biblical texts blurs both God's judgment and his
grace. Schroeder's law/promise hermeneutic ends up with a divorce
between creation and redemption, a schism between faith and life
that is foreign to Luther.[3]

Luther understands creation as the arena for God's work.
Schroeder introduces a relativism and subjectivism to creation
that is not there in Luther, when he makes the claim that homosexuals are simply "wired differently" from heterosexuals (TT 34
[Jan. 28, 1999] 2). Luther in fact sees human identity as male
and female as a creational reality. Or to use the words of William
Lazareth, God's ordering of creation is heterosexual.[4] This fact can
be seen in Luther's exposition of the sixth commandment in the
Large Catechism, where he writes, "He has established it (marriage) before all others as the first of all institutions, and he created
man and woman differently (as is evident) not for indecency but
to be true to each other, to be fruitful, to beget children, and to
nurture and bring them up to the glory of God" (LC 1.207). This is
also expressed in a letter Luther wrote to Wolfgang Reissenbusch
in March 1527. After counseling Reissenbusch that he is free to
renounce his vow of celibacy without committing sin, Luther
observes, "Our bodies are in great part the flesh of women, for by
them we were conceived, developed, borne, suckled, and nourished. And it is quite impossible to keep entirely apart from them.
This is in accord with the Word of God. He has caused it to be so
and wishes it so" (*Luther: Letters* 273).

Earlier, in his *The Estate of Marriage* (1522), after noting God's design and purpose in creating humanity as male and female, Luther speaks of this ordinance or institution as "inflexible," beyond alteration (LW 45:18). What Luther sees as a given biological reality, Schroeder now moves into the realm of the subjective with an appeal to the explanation of the First Article of the Creed in the Small Catechism. Luther's doxological confession that "God has created me together with all that exists. God has given and still preserves my body and soul, eyes, ears, and all limbs and senses" is now used by Schroeder to make God the author of homosexuality. Schroeder writes,

> Luther doesn't mention sexuality in that gift-list, but today God puts it on the lists we have. If "hetero-" is one of the creator's ordainings, then wouldn't "homo-" also be on the gift-list for those so ordained? Isn't it "most certainly true" for both that they "thank, praise, serve and obey God" as the sexual persons they have been ordained to be? Both homosexuals and heterosexuals have a common calling to care for creation, carrying out the double agenda in God's secular world—the law of preservation and the law of recompense. If the gifts are different, the pattern of care will be different. What examples are already available within the ELCA of Christians—gay and straight—doing just that—preservation and recompense—with the sexual gift that God has ordained? Despite the current conflict, is it true about sexuality too that "what God ordains is always good?" (TT 51 [May 27, 1999] 3)

Luther's rejection of required clerical celibacy is seen by Schroeder as a precedent for relaxing requirements for individuals who understand themselves to be homosexual. Schroeder writes:

> For outsiders to "require" celibacy of them as a prerequisite for the validity of their Christ-confession is parallel to the Roman church's "requirement" of celibacy for the clergy. Concerning that requirement the Lutheran Reformers said: God created the sexual "pressure" that surfaces at puberty. To "require" celibacy of the clergy—or anybody—is blatantly contradicting God. For those whom God "wired differently" as a student once described himself—regardless of how that different wiring came to pass—requiring celibacy for him sounds

like the same thing to me. It is God, not the gay guy, who is being contradicted. (TT 159 [Jan. 28, 2001] 5)[5]

Here Schroeder reveals a basic premise that is not shared by
Luther, namely, that homosexuality is ordained by God. Luther does
not speak of a generic sexual drive or instinct but of the desire of
man for woman and woman for man: "This is the Word of God,
through whose power procreative seed is planted in man's body and
a natural, ardent desire for woman is kindled and kept alive. This
cannot be restrained either by vows or laws" (*Luther: Letters* 273).[6]
Luther seldom mentions homosexual behavior. But when he does,
his evaluation is always negative. For example, Luther identifies the
sin of Sodom with homosexuality. Commenting on Genesis 19:4f.,
he writes:

> I for my part do not enjoy dealing with this passage, because so far
> the ears of the Germans are innocent of and uncontaminated by this
> monstrous depravity; for even though disgrace, like other sins, has
> crept in through an ungodly soldier and a lewd merchant, still the
> rest of the people are unaware of what is being done in secret.
> The Carthusian monks deserve to be hated because they were the first
> to bring this terrible pollution into Germany from the monasteries of
> Italy. (AE 3: 251f.)

In the same section of the Genesis lectures, Luther refers to
"the heinous conduct of the people of Sodom" as "extraordinary,
inasmuch as they departed from the natural passion and longing
of the male for the female, which is implanted into nature by God,
and desired what is altogether contrary to nature. Whence comes
this perversity? Undoubtedly from Satan, who after people have
once turned away from the fear of God, so powerfully suppresses
nature that he blots out the natural desire and stirs up a desire that is
contrary to nature." (AE 3: 255)[7]

Luther's rejection of homosexual activity is not merely a matter
of aesthetic preference but rather a theological judgment rooted in
the reality of the way the wrath of God is revealed against all ungodliness that will not acknowledge God to be the Creator and Lord that
he is. For Luther homosexuality is a form of idolatry, of false worship,

as we see in his lectures on Romans.[8] In attributing homosexuality to the creative will of God for certain human beings, Schroeder strangely enough overlooks the teaching of his mentor Werner Elert, who maintained that creation places humanity in an ordered world of nomological existence.[9]

Schroeder's "Creator's Orders" vs. "Orders of Creation"

Schroeder sees his law/promise hermeneutic threatened by what he would term as a literalistic reading of the Bible and an appeal to the orders of creation or anything for that matter resembling natural law.[10] Especially troubling for Schroeder is any appeal to the orders of creation in defense of the traditional teaching that human existence is heterosexual by its very nature. Schroeder outlined his objections to both the terminology and content of the orders of creation in a March 1972 article published in the *Concordia Theological Monthly* under the title "The Orders of Creation—Some Reflections on the History and Place of the Term in Systematic Theology." In this article Schroeder makes the case for "Creator's order" rather than "orders of creation."[11] His aim is to avoid any hierarchical and static notion of the orders and to show rather that God has put a person on earth in particular place and time. He writes:

> The explanation of the First Article of the Creed in Luther's Small Catechism is a classic expression of such localized specific placement "ordained" or "given" a person by the Creator. Perhaps the word "*Ordnung*" would be better translated into English with the verbal form "ordain." This makes it easier to get to the present-tense character of the notion of the Creator's order, as well as the personal quality involved in one's understanding that God has put him on earth in a particular place, with particular parents, in a particular century, as a member of a particular race and community or a particular language group or national state, with a particular economic order, particular siblings, and so on. This is what God has ordained for him. (p. 172)

Schroeder's fundamental revision of the orders theology is essentially in place in the 1972 article. In his more recent missives, he brings his reading of the "Creator's order" to bear on sexual identity, concluding that the homosexual person is to understand him- or herself as created this way by God. Thus acceptance, not repentance; affirmation, not exhortations to self-denial are said to characterize the Church's ministry to men and women who find themselves created with sensual urgings for persons of the same gender.

While the nineteenth-century rendition of the orders of creation was certainly misused by some Lutheran theologians in their eager endorsement of National Socialism in Germany in the last century, Carl Braaten takes upon himself the task of rehabilitating this teaching. His article "God in Public Life: Rehabilitating the 'Orders of Creation'"[12] is most relevant to the current discussion, for Braaten has demonstrated that these orders are not as subjective and individualistic as Schroeder has suggested.

Braaten's work, along with that of the Tubingen theologian Oswald Bayer, offers theological resources that are a corrective to what actually turns out to be a "flight from creation"—to borrow the title of the book by Gustaf Wingren (Augsburg, 1971). Particularly helpful is Bayer's treatment of Luther's use of the three orders or three estates. Luther speaks of three basic structures that are essential to human life: church, government, and home. While "none of these orders is a means of salvation" (AE 37: 365)[13]—that is found in Jesus Christ alone—the believer is not taken out of these temporal orders but now lives within them by faith and love. Christian faith is not limited to one estate but thrives in all of them. As Bayer points out, Luther avoids a move that is made in nineteenth-century liberalism of pitting an "ethic of radical obedience" against an "ethic of the household code." Luther's theological achievement, according to Bayer, is "the indissoluble bonding of the ethics of the table of duties and the ethics of discipleship and having them guard one another."[14] The Christian lives under the First Commandment within the God-ordained estates. Love as the fulfillment of the Law does not explode the orders but is fulfilled within them.

These estates or orders are not personalized or individualized in the way that Schroeder argues. Rather, to use the language of Bayer, "element and institution" (p. 141) are bound together. God's Word of institution is definitive in both creation and the sacraments. Nature then is not defined by the Gnostic self but by God whose almighty Word brings creation out of nothingness. Thus there is no room for enthusiasm in either theology or ethics. The "element cannot become autonomous," in Bayer's words (p. 143).

Yet is this autonomy not exactly what has happened in Schroeder's appeal for a new ethic of homosexuality? The Word is stripped from the element, as it were. We see then an ethical enthusiasm in Schroeder and others who take this approach. Careful exegetical study of the Biblical texts, such as that done by Robert Gagnon,[15] is dismissed as legalistic Biblicism. Promise trumps the law, Spirit rules over the text, new creation triumphs over old creation, and we are left with some rather fanciful attempts to justify a radical departure from biblical teaching and historic Christian practice. The new obedience is emptied of content and so evaporates into the new disobedience.

Schroeder dismisses New Testament texts that condemn homosexual behavior with an appeal to Article XXVIII of the Augsburg Confession. He writes:

> But surely the rules laid down by the apostles in the NT are permanent aren't they? Not really, says Article 28. "Even the apostles ordained (sic!) many things that were changed by time, and they did not set them down as though they could not be changed" (Apology 28.16). Here's an example: "The apostles commanded that one should abstain from blood, etc. . . . Those who do not observe (this) commit no sin, for the apostles did not wish to burden consciences with such bondage but forbade such eating for a time to avoid offense. In connection with the (blood) decree one must consider what the perpetual aim of the Gospel is." (AC 28.65) (TT 51 [May 27, 1999] 4)

From this citation of the Augustana, Schroeder concludes that New Testament prohibitions against homosexual expression are time-bound, related perhaps to a linkage between homosexuality and idolatry in the ancient world.

Schroeder overlooks the fact that "the perpetual aim of the Gospel" is the forgiveness of sins, not the overthrow of natural orders. Article XVI of the Augsburg Confession declares, "the Gospel does not overthrow secular government, public order, and marriage, but instead intends that a person keep all this as a true order of God and demonstrate in these walks of life Christian love and true good works according to each person's calling" (XVI.5). Rather than rightly distinguishing Law from Gospel, Schroeder has done exactly what he accuses those who support the traditional Christian teaching on homosexuality of doing—he offers another gospel, a gospel unlike the Gospel confessed in Augsburg XVI, which seeks to overthrow the good orders created and instituted by God to preserve his world. Underneath Schroeder's deeply flawed law/promise hermeneutic lies an understanding of creation that is foreign to Luther and the Lutheran Confessions. Others have identified the Gnostic character in an approach that parades itself as relevant to current challenges for inclusiveness and tolerance.[16] Such a "search for relevance," writes Christoph Schwoebel, "comes into conflict with fundamental dogmatic tenets of a Christian theology of creation. What seems to be needed is not an ethics of creation, but an *ethic of createdness* which is informed by a *theology of creation*."[17] An ethic of createdness so prominent in Luther cannot be sustained by the shallow reductionism of Schroeder's approach.

Forde's Law/Gospel Dialectic

Gerhard Forde is the second contemporary Lutheran theologian that I wish to examine in this paper. Recently retired after a distinguished teaching and writing career at Luther Seminary in St. Paul, Forde is recognized as both a Luther scholar and systematician. A recent *Festschrift—By Faith Alone*—bears witness to his broad influence both in the Lutheran-Roman Catholic dialogue and in Reformation studies. Like Schroeder, Forde makes use of the law/gospel distinction. His first book, a reworked version of his doctoral dissertation at Harvard, is entitled *The Law-Gospel Debate* (Augsburg, 1969). Unlike Schroeder, Forde does not slip into antinomianism.

For Forde, Romans 10:4 is a crucial text in understanding the law/gospel dialectic: "For Christ is the end (*telos*) of the Law, that everyone who has faith may be justified." This leads Forde to inquire as to the nature of the Law, in terms of both content and function.[18] Forde faults those calling for a revision of the Church's moral teaching on homosexuality of missing a fundamental Lutheran insistence: the

Law always accuses. The accusation of the Law can only be answered in Christ, who was made sin for us. The Law offers no compassion. Therefore Forde begins his essay on "Law and Sexual Behavior" by reminding his readers that, "This is an essay about the function of the Law as it confronts sexual behavior. Therefore the first thing that needs saying is that this paper cannot be about compassion."

The Law, Forde argues, has two uses or functions.[19] In its civil or political use it regulates human behavior. Here the Law works horizontally to protect and preserve life. It curbs chaos and reins in outbursts of immorality that would destroy the fabric of human community. The Law in its second use unmasks sin *coram Deo* and reveals the wrath of God against every idol. Forde notes that the Law in its civil function does not have to do with a so-called "orientation," which he deems a rather "modern invention that seems particularly pernicious" (p. 4). Here the Law has to do with human actions, with behavior. Yet ultimately the Law accuses the sinner before God. But these two uses cannot be so easily segregated:

> The doctrine of the uses of the Law is simply an attempt analytically to discern what the Law actually does. Law does two things to us, come what may. It sets limits to sinful and destructive behavior, usually by some sort of persuasion or coercion—ultimately by death itself; and it accuses of sin. That is simply what it does. We have no choice in the matter. (p. 7)

Forde sees antinomianism, in whatever form it takes, as an attempt to find some end for the Law other than Christ crucified. So for example, in the current debate on homosexuality, he observes that there are those who attempt to change the content of the Law. He writes:

> . . . when we come up against laws that call our behavior into question we usually attempt by one means or another to erase, discredit, or change the laws. We become antinomians. If we don't like the law we seek to remove or abolish it by exegetical circumlocution, appeals to progress, to genetics, to the authority of ecclesiastical-task force pronouncements, or perhaps just to the assurance that "things have changed." (p. 5)[20]

510 PART III: THEOLOGICAL ESSAYS

510   PART III: THEOLOGICAL ESSAYS

But the Law will not disappear by exegetical attempts to expunge difficult texts from our hearing or by invocation of the latest scientific research to lessen the claim of Scripture; nor will it be housebroken in the name of compassion or tolerance. The Law cannot be so easily silenced. We cannot bring an end to the Law. Only Christ is the end of the Law for faith. Forde then proceeds to take up Paul's rhetorical question and answer in Romans 3:31: "'Do we then overthrow the Law by faith? By no means! On the contrary, we uphold the Law." Faith does not set the Law aside but rather lives with trust in Christ alone. Faith does not overthrow the Law but establishes it "in its rightful place" (p. 6).

The "rightful place" of the Law then continues as it orders human community and as it accuses people of sin, driving broken sinners to Christ alone. It is a pernicious misuse of the law/gospel distinction to legitimize homosexual unions or ordinations. Forde writes, "The idea that Law could be so altered in content that the civil use would be somehow milder or even contrary to the theological use is quite contrary to the doctrine. Law may indeed be applied variously according to the situation but the basic content remains the same" (p. 8). This point can be demonstrated from Luther's treatise *How Christian's Should Regard Moses*. In this writing Luther develops the distinction between the laws of Moses that pertain only to the political entity of Old Testament Israel (ceremonial and civic ordinances) and the commandments of God which are also inscribed in the heart. "Nature also has these laws" (AE 35: 168) says Luther and they are reflected in the Ten Commandments.

"It is not enough," says Luther, "simply to look and see whether this is God's Word, whether God has said it; rather we must look and see to whom it has been spoken, whether it fits us" (AE 35: 170). One may not simply place the Old Testament prohibition against the eating of pork alongside the sixth commandment. Forde's argument, consistent with Luther, is that the Law of God in creation itself orders human existence in the bipolarity of male and female. Creation itself is structured heterosexually. The nature of sexual intercourse as a one-flesh union of two who are other, who are biologically different demonstrates this structure. "The two become one flesh, a substantial unity in difference" (p. 10).[21] Civil law rightly has a stake in regulating and protecting marriage for the good of the human race.

The civic realm draws us into Luther's understanding of life in the world, of the "three orders or estates." This is the location of vocation or calling. Forde writes:

> If marriage is to be understood as entry into an estate under the civil use of the Law, then it should be the case that genital sexual activity involved must itself be seen in light one's vocation to serve God and the neighbor through a life of love in the world. "The heart of the matter rests with the claim that the sexual activity itself must be an essential aspect of the exercise and realization of [one's] vocational calling and have social as well as personal import" (James Hanigan). Same-gender sexual relations cannot fulfill this vocational calling. In the first place, the calling is that in sexual activity the "two shall become one flesh." This is not possible for persons of the same sex. The most obvious outcome and instance of the two becoming one flesh is in their children. Homosexual sexual intercourse obviously cannot do that. Furthermore, persons of the same gender cannot become one flesh in the sense of a shared life of love as unity in difference. They cannot become one out of two in the sexual act itself. At best the sexual activity of homosexuals can only imitate but not participate in what the act symbolizes. (p. 16)[22]

Forde concludes that it is impossible for the church to bless same-sex unions or authorize the ordination of practicing homosexuals without resorting to antinomianism, which finally undermines the Gospel itself.

Conclusion

I will conclude with several observations gleaned from examining these two approaches to the questions of the church's stance on homosexual practice. In the last century, the Swedish theologian Gustaf Wingren argued the necessity of the doctrine of creation for evangelical theology. Every other article of the faith will be deformed, he contended, if the doctrine of creation is mishandled.[23] In a recent article, Gilbert Meilaender has demonstrated the importance of honoring the bios in Lutheran bioethics.[24] The same must be asserted for a sexual ethic as well. Too often the biological reality of our being created male and female is dismissed in the current debates on homosexuality as long as the relationship is consensual, committed, and caring. Thus one Lutheran ethicist Paul Jersild in his *Spirit Ethics* (Fortress, 2000) is worried that some Christians have adopted an "excessively physicalist approach to homosexuality" (p. 139). Creation is seen as secondary if not irrelevant. But without creation there is no incarnation. Without creation, the new creation is reduced to a spiritualistic construct of our own imagination. Is not God "excessively physicalist" in Jesus? Do we not confess the resurrection of the body?

Being open to the guidance of the Spirit, reliance on experience and reason, dialogue with others becomes a cover for a new enthusiasm that seeks God apart from the Word. It is not given to us to speak as though God has not spoken. When the Bible is reduced to merely a conversation partner, we may be assured that the Scriptures will not have the final word. Homosexuality is a disordering of God's design as expressed in Genesis 1 and 2. Whatever else may be said about the causes of homosexuality, it cannot be attributed to God. From the standpoint of theological ethics it is irrelevant whether homosexuality is a result of a genetic disorder, environmental influences, or personal choice, as the Scriptures teach us that all of creation after the fall is subject to bondage, disorder, and death. Robert Jenson is on target here:

> We need not here resolve the question of whether there are such things as "sensual orientations" and if so how they are acquired. What must anyway be clear is that "homosexuality," if it exists and whatever it is, cannot be attributed to creation; those who practice forms of homoerotic sensuality and attribute this to "homosexuality" cannot refer to the characteristic as "the way God created me," if "create" has anything like its Biblical sense. No more in this context than in any other do we discover God's creative intent by examining the empirical situation; as we have seen, I may indeed have to blame God for the empirically present in me that contradicts his known intent, but this is an occasion for unbelief, not a believer's justification of the evil. (p. 93)[25]

Self-justification is ultimately the justification of the evil [in the self?]. The opposite of self-justification is repentance. Luther defines repentance in relationship to Baptism in both catechisms. In the Small Catechism:

> What then is the significance of such a baptism with water? It signifies that the old creature [the Old Adam] in us with all sins and evil desires is to be drowned and die through daily contrition and repentance, and on the other hand that a new person is to come forth and rise up to live before God in righteousness and purity forever. (IV.12)

And in the Large Catechism:

> Thus a Christian life is nothing else than a daily baptism, begun once and continued ever after. For we must keep at it without ceasing, always purging whatever pertains to the old Adam, so that whatever belongs to the new creature may come forth. What is the old creature? It is what is born in us from Adam, irascible, spiteful, envious, unchaste, greedy, lazy, proud—yes—and unbelieving; it is beset with all vices and by nature has nothing good in it. (IV.66)

Martha Ellen Stortz contributed an article, "Rethinking Christian Sexuality: Baptized into the Body of Christ" to the volume *Faithful Conversation: Christian Perspectives on Homosexuality* (Fortress, 2003). Stortz proposes a discussion of sexuality that begins with baptism, thus avoiding the reality of humanity created as male and female. Her conclusions are predictable. Baptismal identity supersedes the identity conferred in creation. The old Adam is not put to death but affirmed. Baptism, to paraphrase Bonhoeffer, then becomes the justification of the sin, not the sinner. What suffers finally is not just morality but the Gospel itself. We now find ourselves in a world, in which "everything is permitted and nothing is forgiven."[26]

Acceptance and accommodation are not substitutes for absolution. Any use of Luther that aims for anything less misses the mark.

Sources Cited

The Book of Concord. Ed. Robert Kolb & Timothy Wengert. Minneapolis: Fortress, 2000. Augsburg Confession [AC]; Large Catechism [LC]; Small Catechism [SC]; Solid Declaration [SD]

By Faith Alone: Essays on Justification in Honor of Gerhard O. Forde. Ed. Joseph Burgess & Marc Kolden. Grand Rapids, MI: Eerdmans, 2004.

Forde, Gerhard. "Law and Sexual Behavior" in *Lutheran Quarterly* IX (Spring 1995) 3–22.

Jenson, Robert. *Systematic Theology, Volume 2, The Works of God.* New York: Oxford University Press, 1999.

Luther: Letters of Spiritual Counsel. Ed. Theodore G. Tappert. Philadelphia: Westminster, 1955.

American Edition: Luther's Works [AE]. St. Louis: Concordia & Philadelphia: Fortress, v.d.

Confession Concerning Christ's Supper (1528), v. 37 (1961).

How Christians Should Regard Moses (1525), v. 35 (1960).

Lectures on Romans (1515–1516), v. 25 (1972).

On War Against the Turk (1529), v. 46 (1967).

Schroeder, Edward. *Thursday Theology* [TT] (www.crossings.org).

Thielicke, Helmut. *The Ethics of Sex.* Tr. John W. Doberstein. New York: Harper & Row, 1964.

Notes

1   See David Yeago, "Martin Luther on Grace, Law, and the Moral Life: Prolegomena to an Ecumenical Discussion of Veritatis Splendor" in *The Thomist* 62 (1998) 163–191.

2   Luther sees marriage as grounded in creation. It is not a sacrament that bestows forgiveness but there is no higher social calling where faith is exercised than that of the family. Marriage is the arena for demonstrating one's faith and love. In 1519 Luther still regarded marriage as a sacrament. The change is evident, however, in the *Babylonian Captivity* of 1520. In divesting marriage of its sacramental status, Luther actually elevated marriage as he made it equal or superior to celibacy. See Scott Hendrix, "Luther on Marriage" in *Lutheran Quarterly* XIV (Autumn 2000) 335–350; James Nestingen, "Luther on Marriage, Vocation, and the Cross" in *Word & World* XXIII (Winter 2003) 31–39; William Lazareth, Luther on the Christian Home (Philadelphia: Muhlenberg Press, 1960); and Carter Lindberg, "The Future of a Tradition: Luther and the Family," in *All Theology is Christology: Essays in Honor of David P. Scaer*, ed. Dean Wenthe et al. (Fort Wayne, IN: Concordia Theological Seminary Press, 2000), 133–151. For a picture of Luther's contribution to the place of marriage in Western culture, see John Witte, Jr., *From Sacrament to Contract: Marriage, Religion, and Law in the Western Tradition*

(Louisville, KY: Westminster/John Knox Press, 1997), 42–73. Lindberg aptly summarizes Luther's impact on marriage: "Luther's application of evangelical theology to marriage and family desacramentalized marriage; desacralized the clergy and resacralized the life of the laity; opposed the maze of canonical impediments to marriage; strove to unravel the skein of canon law, imperial law, and German customs; and joyfully affirmed God's good creation, including sexual relations" (133).

3 Contra this divorce, see Bemd Wannenwetsch, "Luther's Moral Theology" in *The Cambridge Companion to Martin Luther*, ed. D. McKim (Cambridge, UK: Cambridge University Press, 2003), 120–135; William Lazareth, *Christians in Society: Luther, the Bible and Social Ethics* (Minneapolis: Fortress, 2001); Reinhard Huetter, "The Twofold Center of Lutheran Ethics" in *The Promise of Lutheran Ethics*, ed. Karen Bloomquist & John Stumme (Minneapolis: Fortress, 1998) 31–54. Schroeder asserts that "Huetter's conclusion really is 'the end' of the promise of Lutheran ethics" in *Thursday Theology* 26 (Nov. 12, 1998) 1.

4 William Lazareth, "ELCA Lutherans and Luther on Heterosexual Marriage" in *Lutheran Quarterly* VIII (Spring 1994), 235–268. Lazareth writes, "Clearly, same-sex 'unions' do not qualify as marriages to be blessed for Christians who have been baptized as saints into the body of Christ. The Lutheran church should not condone the sinful acts (conduct) of an intrinsic disorder (orientation) in God's heterosexual ordering of creation" (236).

5 Similar arguments are advanced by Christian Batalden Scharen, *Married in the Sight of God* (Landham, MD: University of America Press, 2000), although he finally must admit that "an ethic for same-sex relationships goes nowhere with the 'letter' of Luther's views" (128). Likewise, Martha Ellen Stortz, "Rethinking Christian Sexuality: Baptized into the Body of Christ" in *Faithful Conversations: Christian Perspectives on Homosexuality*, ed. James M. Childs, Jr. (Minneapolis: Fortress, 2003) 64–66.

6 For similar statements in Luther see *Luther on Women: A Sourcebook*, ed. Susan C. Karant-Nunn & Merry E. Wiesner-Hanks (Cambridge, UK: University of Cambridge Press, 2003) 137–170.

7 Also note Luther's comment in *On War Against the Turk* (1529): "Both the pope and the Turk are so blind and senseless that they commit the dumb sins shamelessly, as an honorable and praiseworthy thing. Since they think so lightly of marriage, it serves them right that there are dog-marriages (and would to God that they were dog-marriages), indeed, also 'Italian marriages' and 'Florentine brides' among them; and they think these things good. I hear one horrible thing after another about what an open and glorious Sodom Turkey is, and everybody who has looked around a little in Rome or Italy knows very well how God revenges and punishes the forbidden marriage, so that Sodom and Gomorrah, which God overwhelmed in days of old with fire

and brimstone (Gen. 19: 24), must seem a mere jest and prelude compared with these abominations" (AE 46:198).

8 Luther links homosexual behavior with idolatry in his exposition of Romans 1:26. "*For this reason*, namely: idolatry, *God gave*, not only to the above-mentioned disgrace, *them*, some of them, *up to dishonorable passions*, to shameful feelings and desires, before God, although even they, like Sodom, called this sin . . . 27. *And the men likewise*, with an overpowering drive of lust, *gave up natural relations with women and were consumed with passion*, which overpowered the judgment of their reason, *for one another, men with men*, and thus they deal with each other in mutual disgrace, *committing shameless acts*, and consequently, *receiving the penalty*, punishment, *due for their error*, fitting and just for so great a sin, the sin of idolatry, *in their own persons*, according to the teaching and arrangement of God" (AE 25:12f.).

9 See Werner Elert, *The Christian Ethos*, tr. Carl J. Schneider (Philadelphia: Fortress, 1957). Elert writes, "Creation places man into the world, *nomos* binds him to the world. In the first place, nomological under law means only that we, like all other creatures, are subject to the orderly rule of God and that we do not live in a world of chaos and arbitrariness" (51).

10 For a more positive view of the place of "natural law" in Luther, see Carl Braaten, "Natural Law in Theology and Ethics" in *The Two Cities of God: The Church's Responsibility for the Earthly City*, ed. Carl Braaten & Robert Jenson (Grand Rapids, MI: Eerdmans, 1997) 42–58; and Antti Raunio, "Natural Law and Faith: The Forgotten Foundations of Ethics in Luther's Theology" in *Union with Christ: The New Finnish Interpretation of Luther* ed. Carl Braaten & Robert Jenson (Grand Rapids, MI: Eerdmans, 1998) 96–128; Also see Paul Althaus, *The Ethics of Martin Luther*, tr. Robert Schultz (Philadelphia: Fortress, 1972) 25–35; Heinrich Bomkamm, *Luther and the Old Testament*, tr. Eric & Ruth Gritsch (Philadelphia: Fortress, 1969) 124–149; F. Edward Cranz, *Luther's Thought on Justice, Law, and Society* (Mifflintown, PA: Sigler Press, 1998) 41–72; Wannenwetsch, *op. cit.* (n. 3 above), 123–126.

11 Edward Schroeder, "The Orders of Creation—Some Reflections on the History and Place of the Term in Systematic Theology" in *Concordia Theological Monthly* XLIII (Mar. 1972) 165–178. Schroeder attempts (unsuccessfully in my view) to pin "the orders of creation" on Calvinism. His target in this article is Fritz Zerbst, *The Office of Woman in the Church*, tr. A.G. Merkens (St. Louis: Concordia, 1955). Schroeder accuses Zerbst of being a "Calvinist" (170). The same label is used for Robert Gagnon. See *Thursday Theology* 323 (Aug. 19, 2004) 2–3. In fact it was Adolph von Harless (1806–1879), a confessional Lutheran theologian of Erlangen who popularized the term in his *Christliche Ethik* (Stuttgart, 1864) 477.

12 Carl Braaten, "God in Public Life: Rehabilitating the 'Orders of Creation'" in *First Things* (Dec. 1990) 32–38.

13 Luther treats the three estates or three orders in any number of places, most representative is the section in the 1528 *Confession Concerning Christ's Supper*—AE 37: 363ff.

14 Oswald Bayer, "Nature and Institution: Luther's Doctrine of the Three Orders" in *Lutheran Quarterly* XII (Summer 1998) 139. Other writings of Bayer relevant to this discussion are "I Believe That God Has Created Me with All That Exists: An Example of Catechetical-Systematics" in *Lutheran Quarterly* VIII (Summer 1994) 129–161; and "Luther's Ethics as Pastoral Care" in *Lutheran Quarterly* IV (Summer 1990) 125–142. Also see his book *Schopfung als Anrede* (Tubingen: J.C.B. Mohr, 1986).

15 Robert Gagnon, *The Bible and Homosexual Practice: Texts and Hermeneutics* (Nashville, TN: Abingdon Press, 2001). See Schroeder's polemical response to Gagnon in *Thursday Theology* 323 (Aug. 19, 2004) 1–4.

16 See for example Philip Lee, *Against the Protestant Gnostics* (New York: Oxford University Press, 1987) and David Yeago, "Gnosticism, Antinomianism, and Reformation Theology: Reflections on the Cost of a Construal" in *Pro Ecclesia* II (Winter 1993) 37–49. Also note B. Wannenwetsch's critique of the "docetic" turn taken by advocates of homosexual unions in Wannenwetsch, "Old Docetism—New Moralism? Questioning a New Direction in the Homosexuality Debate" in *Modern Theology* XVI (July 2000) 353–364.

17 Christoph Schwoebel, "God, Creation, and the Christian Community: The Dogmatic Basis of a Christian Ethic of Createdness" in *The Doctrine of Creation: Essays in Dogmatics, History, and Philosophy*, ed. Colin Gunton (Edinburgh, Scotland: T & T Clark, 1997) 150.

18 For a helpful overview of Forde's method, see James Nestingen, "Examining Sources: Influences on Gerhard Forde's Theology" in *By Faith Alone*, 10–21.

19 I will forgo the question of the Law's third use in this discussion of Forde. The issue of the third use of the Law in recent American Lutheranism is well treated by Scott Murray in *Law, Life, and the Living God: The Third Use of the Law in Modem American Lutheranism* (St. Louis: Concordia, 2002).

20 See also Forde's description of antinomianism as a "fake theology" in his article "Fake Theology: Reflections on Antinomianism Past and Present" *dialog* 22 (Fall 1983) 246–251; and in "The Normative Character of Scripture for Matters of Faith and Life: Human Sexuality in Light of Romans 1:16–32" *Word & World* XIV (Summer 1994) 305–314; also Gerhard Forde, *A More Radical Gospel: Essays on Eschatology, Authority, Atonement, and Ecumenism*, ed. Mark Mattes and Steven Paulson (Grand Rapids, MI: Eerdmans, 2004), 33–49, 137–155.

21 On this "unity in difference," note Gilbert Meilaender, *The Limits of Love* (University Park, PA: Pennsylvania State University Press, 1987) 129: "The mutuality for which we are destined is a loving union of those who are

other. And for creatures who are finite, historical, and earthly—for embodied human beings—that otherness has a biological grounding. Homosexual acts are forbidden precisely because lover and beloved are biologically, not sufficiently other. The relationship approaches too closely the forbidden love of self."

22 The fact that homosexual unions are nonproductive is not a biological irrelevancy ". . . in a world in which the languages of love and consent have gradually come to trump all other moral language, we do well to remind ourselves at the outset that marriage, the first of all institutions, is not simply about love in general. It is about the creation of man and woman as different yet made to be true to each other; it is about being fruitful, begetting and rearing children. This pours content and structure into our understanding of sexual love, and it takes seriously the body's character within nature and history"—Gilbert Meilaender, "The First of Institutions" in *Pro Ecclesia* VI (Fall 1997) 4465f.

23 Gustaf Wingren, *Creation and Law*, tr. Ross MacKenzie (Philadelphia: Muhlenberg Press, 1961) 25–26. Also James Nestingen, "Luther on Marriage, Vocation, and the Cross" in *Word & World* XXIII (Winter 2003), 31–39; and "The Lutheran Reformation and Homosexual Practice" in *Childs, op. cit.* (n. 5 above) 41–58.

24 Gilbert Meilaender, "Honoring the Bios in Lutheran Bioethics" in *dialog* 43 (Summer 2004) 118–124.

25 This remark stands in contrast not only to Schroeder but also Jersild who opines, "But for those who discover their homosexual orientation, the norm becomes homosexual behavior" (141).

26 Alan Jones quoted by Gerhard Forde, *On Being a Theologian of the Cross* (Grand Rapids, MI: Eerdmans Publishing Company, 1997), x.

63

The Evangelization of Missouri

Review of David Luecke, *Evangelical Style and Lutheran Substance* (Saint Louis: Concordia Publishing House, 1988) Paper. 160 pp.

PUBLISHED IN THE PENTECOST 1989 ISSUE
OF *LUTHERAN FORUM*, PP 30, 31

It is no secret that the Church Growth Movement has made an impact on the Lutheran Church-Missouri Synod. Approaches to evangelism and church planting based on "church growth principles" are widely used in the Synod. Fuller Seminary, perhaps the front-runner among theological schools committed to the transmission of church growth theory, attracts more Missouri pastors to its Doctor of Ministry program than does the combined programs at the Synod's two seminaries in St. Louis and Fort Wayne. Very little has been done, the recent Commission on Theology and Church Relations document, "Evangelism and Church Growth" (September 1987) notwithstanding, to attempt to provide a serious theological rationale for the involvement of confessional Lutherans in the Church Growth Movement. Perhaps the most substantial attempt to provide such a rationale comes from a Missouri Synod clergyman who serves on the faculty at Fuller. Unfortunately, Professor Luecke's proposals run counter to the very heart of the Lutheran Confessions.

This can be seen in the title of the book itself, as Luecke assumes that one may maintain a "Lutheran substance" while adopting an "Evangelical style" of church life and practice. Theology has its place in preserving "substance," although Luecke never tells his readers what that substance is. Instead, Luecke urges that a distinction be made between "substance" and "style":

> Draw a clear line between substance and style, between what a church cannot change and what it can. Confidence in theological substance can bring exciting freedom in styles of worship, Bible study, social service, and outreach. This allows the celebration of changed styles while preserving necessary substance. (p. 155)

Luecke works on the highly questionable assumption that the Lutheran Church-Missouri Synod enjoys a high degree of "theological confidence" as a result of its bout with the forces of higher criticism in the early part of the last decade. This theological confidence that is rooted in the authority of the Holy Scriptures puts Missouri in the position to learn from American Evangelicals, says Luecke.

> The style [Evangelical] is worth considering because of the theological substance described in the current meaning of the name 'Evangelical.' Above all else, it summarizes some basic, distinctive theological emphases. I believe conservative Lutherans are in sympathy with the most basic of those emphases. Lutheran theology need not be sacrificed to borrow from Evangelical style. When current Evangelical leaders look at American church bodies they usually consider The Lutheran Church-Missouri Synod to be in the same theological camp as they are. This is especially true after the doctrinal battles of the 1970s. (p. 50)

There are at least three areas in which conservative Lutherans may learn from their Evangelical neighbors, according to the Fuller professor. The first is worship. In Luecke's analysis of worship, he repeatedly refers to the congregation as an "audience." Those gathered for worship are thus viewed as consumers to be satisfied rather than the royal priesthood of believers gathered in the name of God to receive all that He promises to bestow in Word and Sacrament. Luecke's critique of Lutheran worship practices is flawed in its very foundation as he fails to see that Lutheran liturgical practice is not merely a matter of "style" but rather a confession of the work of the Triune God in Word and Sacrament. Since Luecke does not understand this fundamental assertion of the Confessions (see *AC* XXVIII:53–56; *AP* XV:38; *AP* XXIV; *FC-SD* X), he cannot help but see the historic liturgy of the church as detrimental to evangelism and church growth. One should not be surprised at Luecke's criticism of vestments, liturgical forms, and movements within the Service as "this style does not lend itself well to initiating fellowship" (p. 109).

By making a selective use of quotations from Luther's 1523 treatise, "Concerning the Ministry," Luecke builds his case for a completely functionalistic view of the ministry. Luecke, of course, must ignore statements by Luther (see, for example, Luther's "Infiltrating and Clandestine Preachers" *Luther's Works*, Volume 40, pp. 383–394) which show that Luther was no functionalist. Likewise Article XIV of the *Augustana* with its statement of the necessity of the rite vocatus is completely ignored. Luecke observes the "success" of the "ministry of the laity" in American Evangelical circles. As ministry is but a matter of style, Luecke sees no reason why Lutherans should not borrow from this style which seemingly works so well in contemporary American culture.

A third and in many ways perhaps the most troublesome of Luecke's proposals has to do with evangelism. As Luecke reads the situation, Lutherans,

> are weak on marketing, that is, marketing understood as listening to the needs and expectations of other people, who do have choices. More precisely, I think Lutherans shape and package their Gospel offering according to the felt needs of only a small segment of American society. That 'market' is now getting smaller. But there are millions more people who are looking for God's presence in their lives. Can Lutherans learn how to package their offering better? (p. 72)

Luecke answers with a resounding "yes" to his own question. He then goes on to suggest that Lutherans have a lot to learn from Evangelicals regarding evangelism.

Lutherans, we are told, need not be overly concerned that "decision theology" will "detract from the necessary understanding that an individual's justifying faith is ultimately an act of God, and not something a person can come to do on his or her own" (p. 83).

Really? Is it indeed the case, as Luecke argues, that "decision-oriented practitioners of evangelism are usually quite clear on *sola gratia* as they look for a response to God's promise" (p. 83)? This reviewer has yet to come across any evangelistic material produced by American Evangelicalism that is consistent with the scriptural understanding expressed in Luther's Explanation of the Third Article in the *Small Catechism*, let alone Article II of the *Formula of Concord*. Luecke's whole approach to the evangelistic task is based on the premise condemned in Article XIII of the *Apology*, namely, that human beings must in some fashion prepare for the coming of the Gospel if that Gospel is to have effect among its hearers. This is a far cry from the *ubi et quando visum est Deo* of *Augustana* V.

By his own admission, Luecke is attracted to Pietism. In fact, he sees several key themes in Pietism that are reflected in the Church Growth Movement. However, Luecke seems to be unaware of the critical ways in which Pietism deviated from confessional Lutheranism in doctrine, churchly understanding, and worship. Carter Lindberg in an article entitled "Pietism and the Church Growth Movement in a Confessional Lutheran Perspective" (*Concordia Theological Quarterly*-July/April 1988, pp. 129–147) convincingly demonstrates that the errors and excesses of Pietism are duplicated in the Church Growth Movement. It appears that Luecke is more at home with Schmucker than he is with Löehe or Walther.

Working out of this neo-pietistic orientation, Luecke fails to take seriously the fact that the Lutheran Church is the Church of Word and Sacrament. "To be 'born again' is to come under the influence of the Holy Spirit" (p. 66). For Luecke, the Real Presence is defined without reference to the Body and the Blood of Jesus which are actually distributed in the Sacrament of the Altar. Instead Luecke argues rather vaguely that the Real Presence "is a special presence which happens when the words of God's promise . . . are joined to the external elements" (p. 85). For Luecke, the Lutheran sacramental principle implies,

> that God can use human experience to convey the Word of His offer of forgiveness of sins, life and salvation . . . Feelings of joy, love, and togetherness can come from many sources. They can become shared signs of God's special life-renewing presence when they are

grounded in and attributed to the Word of His action in Christ that consecrates those experiences. (p. 85)

Luecke's argument brings to mind the words spoken by George Forrell some years ago, "When everything becomes sacramental nothing is a sacrament."

What, then, are we to make of *Evangelical Style and Lutheran Substance*? In a negative way, this book is an example of what happens when a wedge is driven between *doctrina* and *praxis*. We are left not merely with faulty and inadequate practice, but with distorted doctrine as well. Our doctrine shapes our practice but then, in turn, what we do shapes what we believe. Purity of doctrine cannot long survive when purity of preaching, liturgy, and churchly life is lacking. The content shapes the delivery. Is this not the point that the confessors made at Augsburg when they insisted "that the Gospel be preached in conformity with a pure understanding of it and the sacraments be administered in accordance with the divine Word" (*AC* V 11:2, Tappert, p. 32)?

The appearance of *Evangelical Style and Lutheran Substance* raises another question. What does this book indicate regarding the current state of affairs in the Lutheran Church-Missouri Synod? Just two years before the publication of *Evangelical Style and Lutheran Substance*, Concordia Publishing House released *We Confess the Church* by Hermann Sasse. The essays contained in *We Confess the Church* contradict Luecke at nearly every point. Which book most clearly reflects the mind of contemporary Missouri? Perhaps the appearance of *Evangelical Style and Lutheran Substance* is indicative of a certain "double-mindedness" in the Lutheran Church-Missouri Synod. There are plenty of impassioned cheers for "Scripture and the Confessions" but in the day-to-day life of the Synod the pragmatism of American Evangelicalism will get a crowd, so we are told. *Veni Creator Spiritus!*

Scriptural Index

Names Index

CPSIA information can be obtained
at www.ICGtesting.com
Printed in the USA
BVHW080859221221
624594BV00010B/835

9 781948 969611